# Trajectories of Conflict and Peace
## Jerusalem and Belfast Since 1994

*Creating peace for a city's intimate enemies is harder than making war.*

This book is about the trajectories of urban conflict and peace in the politically polarized cities of Jerusalem and Belfast since 1994 – how sometimes there has been hopeful change while at other times debilitating stasis and regression. Based on extensive research, fieldwork, and interviews, Scott Bollens shows how seeking peace in these cities is shaped by the interaction of city-based actors and national elites, and that it is not just a political process, but a social and spatial one that takes place problematically over an extended period. He intertwines academic precision with ethnography and personal narrative to illuminate the complex political and emotional kaleidoscopes of these polarized cities. With hostility and competition among groups defined by ethnic, religious, and nationalistic identity on the increase across the world, this timely investigation contributes to our understanding of today's fractured cities and nations.

*Scott A. Bollens* is Professor of Urban Planning and Public Policy and holds the Warmington Chair in Peace and International Cooperation at the University of California, Irvine, USA.

# *Planning, History and Environment Series*

**Editor:**
Ann Rudkin, Alexandrine Press, Marcham, Oxon, UK

**Editorial Board:**
Professor Arturo Almandoz, Universidad Simón Bolivar, Caracas, Venezuela and
  Pontificia Universidad Católica de Chile, Santiago, Chile
Professor Nezar AlSayyad, University of California, Berkeley, USA
Professor Scott A. Bollens, University of California, Irvine, USA
Professor Robert Bruegmann, University of Illinois at Chicago, USA
Professor Meredith Clausen, University of Washington, Seattle, USA
Professor Yasser Elsheshtawy, UAE University, Al Ain, UAE
Professor Robert Freestone, University of New South Wales, Sydney, Australia
Professor John R. Gold, Oxford Brookes University, Oxford, UK
Professor Michael Hebbert, University College London, UK

## *Selection of Published Titles*

*Planning Europe's Capital Cities: Aspects of nineteenth century development* by Thomas Hall
*Selling Places: The marketing and promotion of towns and cities, 1850–2000* by Stephen V. Ward
*The Australian Metropolis: A planning history* edited by Stephen Hamnett and Robert Freestone
*Utopian England: Community experiments 1900–1945* by Dennis Hardy
*Urban Planning in a Changing World: The twentieth century experience* edited by Robert Freestone
*Twentieth-Century Suburbs: A morphological approach* by J.W.R. Whitehand and C.M.H. Carr
*Council Housing and Culture: The history of a social experiment* by Alison Ravetz
*Planning Latin America's Capital Cities, 1850–1950* edited by Arturo Almandoz
*Exporting American Architecture, 1870–2000* by Jeffrey W. Cody
*The Making and Selling of Post-Mao Beijing* by Anne-Marie Broudehoux
*Planning Middle Eastern Cities: An urban kaleidoscope in a globalizing world* edited by Yasser Elsheshtawy
*Globalizing Taipei: The political economy of spatial development* edited by Reginald Yin-Wang Kwok
*New Urbanism and American Planning: The conflict of cultures* by Emily Talen
*Remaking Chinese Urban Form: Modernity, scarcity and space, 1949–2005* by Duanfang Lu
*Planning Twentieth Century Capital Cities* edited by David L.A. Gordon
*Planning the Megacity: Jakarta in the twentieth century* by Christopher Silver
*Designing Australia's Cities: Culture, commerce and the city beautiful, 1900–1930* by Robert Freestone
*Ordinary Places, Extraordinary Events: Citizenship, democracy and urban space in Latin America* edited by Clara Irazábal (paperback 2015)
*The Evolving Arab City: Tradition, modernity and urban development* edited by Yasser Elsheshtawy
*Stockholm: The making of a metropolis* by Thomas Hall
*Dubai: Behind an urban spectacle* by Yasser Elsheshtawy (paperback 2013)
*Capital Cities in the Aftermath of Empires: Planning in central and southeastern Europe* edited by Emily Gunzburger Makaš and Tanja Damljanović Conley (paperback 2015)
*Lessons in Post-War Reconstruction: Case studies from Lebanon in the aftermath of the 2006 war* edited by Howayda Al-Harithy
*Orienting Istanbul: Cultural capital of Europe?* edited by Deniz Göktürk, Levent Soysal and Ipek Türeli

*Olympic Cities: City agendas, planning and the world's games 1896–2016*, 2nd edition edited by John R. Gold and Margaret M. Gold
*The Making of Hong Kong: From vertical to volumetric* by Barrie Shelton, Justyna Karakiewicz and Thomas Kvan (paperback 2014)
*Urban Coding and Planning* edited by Stephen Marshall
*Planning Asian Cities: Risks and resilience* edited by Stephen Hamnett and Dean Forbes (paperback 2013)
*Staging the New Berlin: Place marketing and the politics of reinvention post-1989* by Claire Colomb
*City and Soul in Divided Societies* by Scott A. Bollens
*Learning from the Japanese City: Looking east in urban design*, 2nd edition by Barrie Shelton
*The Urban Wisdom of Jane Jacobs* edited by Sonia Hirt with Diane Zahm (paperback 2014)
*Of Planting and Planning: The making of British colonial cities*, 2nd edition by Robert Home
*Healthy City Planning: Global health equity from neighbourhood to nation* by Jason Corburn
*Good Cities, Better Lives: How Europe discovered the lost art of urbanism* by Peter Hall
*The Planning Imagination: Peter Hall and the study of urban and regional planning* edited by Mark Tewdwr-Jones, Nicholas Phelps and Robert Freestone
*Garden Cities of Tomorrow? A new future for cottage estates* by Martin Crookston (paperback 2016)
*Sociable Cities: The 21st-century reinvention of the Garden City* by Peter Hall and Colin Ward
*Modernization, Urbanization and Development in Latin America, 1900s–2000s* by Arturo Almandoz
*Planning the Great Metropolis: The 1929 Regional Plan of New York and Its Environs* by David A. Johnson (paperback 2015)
*Remaking the San Francisco–Oakland Bay Bridge: A case of shadowboxing with nature* by Karen Trapenberg Frick (paperback 2016)
*Great British Plans: Who made them and how they worked* by Ian Wray
*Homeland: Zionism as a housing regime, 1860–2011* by Yael Allweil
*Olympic Cities: City agendas, planning and the world's games 1896–2020*, 3rd edition edited by John R. Gold and Margaret M. Gold
*Globalizing Seoul: The city's cultural and urban change* by Jieheerah Yun
*Planning Metropolitan Australia* edited by Stephen Hammnet and Robert Freestone
*Trajectories of Conflict and Peace: Jerusalem and Belfast since 1994* by Scott A. Bollens

# Trajectories of Conflict and Peace
## Jerusalem and Belfast Since 1994

Scott A. Bollens

LONDON AND NEW YORK

First published 2018
by Routledge
2 Park Square, Milton Park, Abingdon, Oxfordshire OX14 4RN

and by Routledge
711 Third Avenue, New York, NY 10017

*Routledge is an imprint of the Taylor & Francis Group, an informa business*

© 2018 Scott A. Bollens

This book was commissioned and edited by Alexandrine Press, Marcham, Oxfordshire

The right of the author has been asserted in accordance with sections 77 and 78 of the Copyright, Designs and Patents Act 1988.

All rights reserved. No part of this book may be reprinted or reproduced or utilized in any form or by any electronic, mechanical or other means, now known or hereafter invented, including photocopying and recording, or in any information storage or retrieval system, without permission in writing from the publishers.

The publisher makes no representation, express or implied, with regard to the accuracy of the information contained in this book and cannot accept any legal responsibility or liability for any errors or omissions that may be made.

*Trademark notice:* Product or corporate names may be trademarks or registered trademarks, and are used only for identification and explanation without intent to infringe.

*British Library Cataloguing in Publication Data*
A catalogue record of this book is available from the British Library

*Library of Congress Cataloging in Publication Data*
A catalogue record has been requested for this book

Typeset in Aldine and Swiss by PNR Design, Didcot

ISBN: 978-1-138-08772-9 (hbk)
ISBN: 978-1-138-08780-4 (pbk)
ISBN: 978-1-315-11022-6 (ebk)

 Printed in the United Kingdom by Henry Ling Limited

# Contents

| | | |
|---|---|---|
| Preface | | vii |
| List of Illustrations | | ix |
| 1 | National and Urban Co-Production of Conflict and Peace | 1 |
| 2 | Jerusalem I: Urban Spatial Changes amid Political Impasse | 29 |
| 3 | Jerusalem II: Interlocking Trajectories of National Politics and Urban Dynamics | 87 |
| 4 | Jerusalem III: The Self-Perpetuating Cycle of Israeli Hegemonic Territoriality | 102 |
| 5 | Belfast I: Building Peace in a Post-Violent Conflict City | 128 |
| 6 | Belfast II: Peacebuilding as Process – Disrupted Trajectories and Urban Outcomes | 166 |
| 7 | Belfast III: The Competing Demands of Political Stability and Urban Peacebuilding | 183 |
| 8 | Conflict and Peace: Political and Spatial Trajectories | 204 |
| Interviews | | 226 |
| References | | 232 |
| Index | | 240 |

# Preface

Jerusalem and Belfast have been my constant companions since the early 1990s when the compelling nature of their historic and contemporary urban and political challenges redirected my entire research agenda as a young associate professor away from the study of urban and regional growth management in the United States. I have never looked back nor regretted this fundamental shift in my academic landscape. The study of these two cities and seven other politically contested cities in the world over the past three decades has fascinated and mesmerized me to this day. My allegiance to these cities is based on my being an urbanist who is interested in how the spatial and policy dynamics in cities influence, and are influenced by, broader nationalist politics. Much as these cities are captured by deeper nationalist politics, I have been held hostage, albeit a willing one, to the gripping political and urban narratives of these cities. These cities tell us much about who we are and what we aspire to; their seemingly extreme circumstances only make more visible urban characteristics that hundreds of more 'normal' cities throughout the world share. In a world with increasing religious and ethnic conflict and warfare, fragmentation of the common public interest, of Brexit and of Trump, and of rhetoric espousing nativism and walls, Jerusalem and Belfast confront scholars and city-builders with the existential challenge of whether we are hopeful or pessimistic about our ability to get along together across identity group boundaries. I am a realist who oscillates between feelings of scepticism and guarded hopefulness. While recognizing the insufferable hurt imposed upon individuals and families in these circumstances, I also have become intimately aware of the ability of the human spirit to sustain, even uplift, itself amid the hatreds and aggressions.

I wish to thank my host at Hebrew University, Professor Eran Razin, along with Gillad Rosen, Israel Kimhi, Shlomo Hasson, Daphna Oren, and Muhannad Bannoura. In Belfast, my host at Queen's University was Professor Frank Gaffikin, who provided support and insight. I also thank in Belfast Frederick Boal for his durable friendship, John Brewer, Stanley McDowell and the fellowship at Fitzroy Presbyterian Church. On a more personal level, Jonna Stopnik co-journeyed with me and 'Jinty Adie' shared her own spiritual trek. My children, Damon and Denali, grew up while I was exploring the world; I thank them for their interest and tolerance. The Sunrise group in Irvine and my friend David Schwarm have sustained my spirit through the years. I thank students in my International Divided Cities undergraduate class who catch on to my passion and reward me with renewed curiosity about their world, and I thank the University of California, Irvine Department of Planning, Policy, and Design for providing a hospitable home base for the last 26 years. Funding for the research sabbatical came from my salary compensation, from the Warmington endowment for peace and international cooperation (thank you Lori and Bob for this essential support), and from a CORCL single investigator innovation grant (SIIG-2014-2015-10). Finally, I extend a note of appreciation and admiration to Ann Rudkin at Alexandrine Press, an editor-extraordinaire who has supported my adventuresome writing style and provided a human touch to the often mysterious book production process.

I acknowledge the following who have granted permission for me to use their images in this book:

| | |
|---|---|
| Cover image: | Hava Law-Yone |
| Figure 1.1: | The United Nations |
| Figure 1.2: | Rand McNally |
| Figure 2.1: | Bimkom |
| Figure 2.5: | Conflict in Cities, Cambridge University (Wendy Pullan and Lefkos Kyriacou) |
| Figure 2.11: | United Nations Office for the Coordination of Humanitarian Affairs – Occupied Palestinian Territory |
| Figure 2.15: | Emek Shaveh |
| Figure 2.20: | Google Earth |
| Figure 2.22: | Google Earth |
| Figure 4.1: | United Nations Office for the Coordination of Humanitarian Affairs, Occupied Palestinian Territory |
| Figure 5.7: | Frederick Boal |
| Figure 5.14: | Mark Hackett and the Forum for Alternative Belfast |

# List of Illustrations

Figure 1.1.   Israel and West Bank.
Figure 1.2.   United Kingdom.
Figure 1.3.   Author in Jerusalem.
Figure 1.4.   Author in Belfast.
Figure 2.1.   Jewish communities in annexed parts of Jerusalem.
Figure 2.2.   Har Homa.
Figure 2.3.   Jerusalem's segregated road system.
Figure 2.4.   Maale Adumim.
Figure 2.5.   Israeli separation barrier and Jerusalem.
Figure 2.6.   Jerusalem separation barrier.
Figure 2.7.   Jerusalem separation barrier.
Figure 2.8.   Jerusalem separation barrier.
Figure 2.9.   Jerusalem separation barrier.
Figure 2.10.  Checkpoint 300 between Bethlehem and Jerusalem.
Figure 2.11.  Jerusalem areas behind the separation barrier – Kafr Aqab and Shuafat refugee camp.
Figure 2.12.  Shuafat refugee camp area.
Figure 2.13.  Kafr Aqab.
Figure 2.14.  Unseeing – at Damascus Gate, Old City Jerusalem.
Figure 2.15.  'City of David' and surroundings.
Figure 2.16.  Jewish settler micro-insertion in Arab Quarter, Old City Jerusalem.
Figure 2.17.  Jewish settler micro-insertion in Arab Quarter, Old City Jerusalem.
Figure 2.18.  Israeli police at Damascus Gate checkpoint.
Figure 2.19.  'Unlicensed' development in Arab neighbourhood of Issawiya, near Hebrew University.
Figure 2.20.  Issawiya.
Figure 2.21.  Jerusalem Old City.
Figure 2.22.  Abu Tor/Abu Tor.
Figure 4.1.   Political geography of the West Bank.
Figure 5.1.   Mural, East Belfast.
Figure 5.2.   Mural, East Belfast.
Figure 5.3.   Cupar Way peace wall.
Figure 5.4.   Cupar Way peace wall.
Figure 5.5.   Cupar Way peace wall.

Figure 5.6.      Workman Avenue gate.
Figure 5.7.      Segregation in Belfast.
Figure 5.8.      Tiger's Bay graffiti.
Figure 5.9.      Participant in loyalist parade, North Belfast.
Figure 5.10.     Alliance Avenue peace wall, North Belfast.
Figure 5.11.     Alliance Avenue peace wall, North Belfast.
Figure 5.12.     Manor Street peace wall, North Belfast.
Figure 5.13.     Tiger's Bay peace wall, North Belfast.
Figure 5.14.     Belfast's 'shatter zones'.
Figure 7.1.      Suffolk, Belfast (1995).
Figure 7.2.      Suffolk, Belfast (2016).

Chapter 1

# National and Urban Co-Production of Conflict and Peace

*A 13-year old boy awakens in the Issawiya neighbourhood of east Jerusalem and faces the grinding and constant feeling of despair, exclusion, hopelessness. It is another day of seeing Jewish houses and apartments, and Hebrew University, dominating the landscape in one direction, and the imposing separation barrier in the other direction. He decides to take a kitchen knife and stabs a Jewish resident of Jerusalem at one of the places in the city where Arab and Jew occupy the same space. He is 'neutralized' immediately by Israeli border police. A 13-year old Catholic boy awakens in the Falls neighbourhood of west Belfast, has never lived a day of conflict having been born five years after the Good Friday Agreement. He sees walls that separate Catholic and Protestant, is intimately familiar with symbols that demarcate nationalist from unionist territories, lives in a hyper-segregated neighbourhood, and attends Catholic school. What he knows of the 'Troubles' comes from his parents and uncles. He likely hears from them about the dysfunctional power sharing Northern Ireland Assembly and that Catholics and Protestants may not be fighting violently, but that they never will be able to co-govern effectively.*

This book highlights peacemaking as a political-spatial iterative process involving national political reform but also urban socio-spatial changes that must embed peace in everyday life. Seeking peace is a social and spatial as well as political process that takes place over an extended period and is co-produced through the interaction of city-based local actors and national elites. I will show how this process of engagement with urban-specific complexities can disrupt the progress of larger peace, and can produce uneven advances, problematic paradoxes, and unforeseen and erratic effects on national goals. I will also show that this difficulty in translating national goals onto local space is not one faced solely by peacemakers, but also confronts governments when they seek hegemonic control of urban and territorial space. The resilient and complex nature of local social and spatial dynamics can resist and confound national objectives – both peacemaking and hegemonic.

In regions hampered by national-level ethnic, nationalistic, and religious conflict, this book focuses on the city and its role in perpetuating or attenuating inter-group conflict. I concentrate on how urban dynamics are both shaped by national political goals and capable of disrupting the implementation of these national programmes. While nationalistic conflict emanates from, and engages with, broader national and international geographies, urban centres are increasingly focal points in military operations, international deliberations, humanitarian efforts, and peacebuilding programmes. Contemporary armed conflicts are almost all intra-state in nature, in marked contrast to the inter-state conflicts of the early twentieth century.[1] Within fracturing states, urban centres assume fundamental importance as territorially strategic and symbolic assets, as exemplified by the active warfare and major loss of life in urban centres such as Homs and Aleppo in the Syrian Civil War and in Mosul in Iraq. With growing warfare in cities, the importance of the urban scale is increasingly a component in military strategies. The U.S. Pentagon, for instance, positions cities as 'human terrain systems' and points to the need for sociocultural understanding and for analysis of the micro-scale human and functional dynamics occurring in complex urban arenas.[2] Counterinsurgency policy has moved out of the mountains and into crowded and connected cities (Kilcullen, 2013). A new military urbanism is focused on the urban system as a conflict zone subject to surveillance amid heightened concerns over security and, in cities of acute conflict, to high-technology urban counterinsurgency forces. As the micro-geographies of everyday urban life become colonized by military control technologies, the city has become a new battleground (Graham, 2010).

With cities the target of collective violence, humanitarian and economic development organizations are increasingly faced with operations within cities and must deal with complex issues of redevelopment, re-housing of war displaced populations, and building back a sustainable physical and human environment often disrupted by ethno-national group-based conflict. Aware that post-conflict urban interventions must be sensitive to complicated, micro-scale, and inter-related issues, agencies such as the United States Agency for International Development (USAID) have organized to provide cross-cutting urban technical expertise to its missions and partners.[3] Meanwhile, the increased focus on 'human security' by the international community advances a more people- and individual-centred notion of security in contrast to traditional state-centric concepts of national security (United Nations Development Programme, 1994). 'Freedom from fear' as a basic element of peace and security is joined in this conceptualization with 'freedom from want' in terms of day-to-day subsistence, employment, education, health care, and shelter. Using this concept of human security, cities and urban policymakers emerge as key platforms and participants in its promotion or denigration. This is so because the planned and unplanned development of cities and the provision of urban services can produce sudden and hurtful disruptions in the patterns of daily life, or in less striking but similarly impactful ways, create over the long term significant urban landscapes of economic disparity and marginalization. The broadened, multidimensional concept of human security moves us from looking solely at the threat and dynamics of overt violence in the city to include types of 'structural violence' that create and maintain urban disadvantage and marginalization. Such structural violence is woven into social, economic, and political systems (UN-Habitat, 2007, p. 51). It 'shows up as unequal power and consequently as unequal life chances' (Galtung, 1969, p. 171; see also Moser, 2004; Iadicola and Shupe, 2003). Exploitation, exclusion, and discrimination at the urban level are forms of structural violence by institutions and powerful private interests that create and perpetuate cities of massive socioeconomic divisions. As such, urban interventions and policies that structure opportunities and costs in cities come to the fore as potential leverage points for building societies of greater inclusiveness and human security. Cities become an essential arena of action in efforts at peacemaking and peacebuilding after traumatic violence and conflict.

My focus on the urban level does not dismiss attention to the national level. Indeed, while the trauma of conflict is increasingly affecting cities and their populations, the state remains an indispensable partner in any political effort to move beyond societal division toward mutual co-existence. The state remains a determinative political container within which the city resides – peace agreements are signed by national leaders, not city officials. What this book's attention to the urban argues is that it is essential to examine the dynamic nature of the relationship between these two important actors – city and state – and how this multi-level co-production facilitates or obstructs opportunities for the promotion of peace and social reconstitution of a society. This is the focus of this book.

I investigate peacemaking as a political-spatial process involving both political institutional restructuring and urban social and spatial changes that embed that peace in everyday life. In this conceptualization, political institutional change that occurs as a result of diplomatic and negotiated peacemaking at the national and international level is necessary but not sufficient for effective and genuine change in society to take place. Such peacemaking must be able to change the urban and spatial dynamics of the city in ways such that peoples' attitudes and behaviours have the opportunity to evolve over time. Urban spatiality can produce significant blocks and rigid obstructers to improvements in inter-group relations or it can create places of affordance and increased tolerance. The reality presented in this book is not one of national political goals being clearly operationalized at the urban level in ways that enhance or weaken peacebuilding. Rather, what I will describe is more complex and paradoxical. National political goals – whether they be partisan and hegemonic in nature or peace-promotive

4   Trajectories of Conflict and Peace

and conciliatory in aspiration – are transmitted to, and implemented in, cities in ways that are multi-threaded, at times internally contradictory, and at other times unintended and contrary to the national goals themselves.

The relationship between the state and the city – between national political goals and mandates and urban spatiality, politics and everyday life – is not a dominant-subordinate one where national political directives are logically transmitted downwards, and operationalized, in urban space. This disconnection between state and city occurs in most places in the world, yet is of a more dramatic and contentious quality in the politically contested environments studied here. The deep societal fault-lines and political dynamics that exist amid political contestation fracture the state and the city in complex, differentiated ways such that the city constitutes a space of semi-autonomy from the state. The city has a politics, history and web of relationships that is qualitatively different than the state. Magnusson (2011, p. 5) usefully points out that the 'spatialities and temporalities of the city' constitute 'an order not susceptible to sovereign authority' by the state. The city and its complex, multi-faceted urbanism is frequently 'uncontainable' in that its politics and everyday dynamics commonly exceed the regulatory effort of the state (Magnusson, 2011, p. 24). Made up of

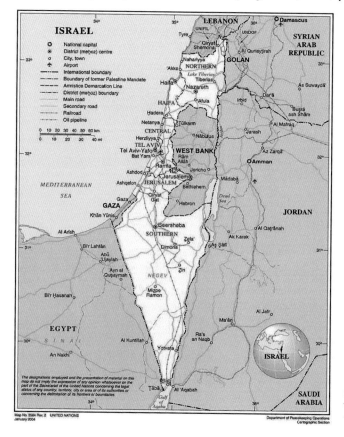

Figure 1.1. Israel and West Bank. (*Source*: United Nations)

National and Urban Co-Production of Conflict and Peace    5

Figure 1.2. United Kingdom. (*Source*: Rand McNally)

numerous self-organizing systems and emergent properties derived from proximity and interdependence, the city and its patterns of interactions defy easy modelling and ordering by the state. The state in its policymaking and interventions seeks to impose order, schematic visions, and regularity (Scott, 1999). Yet, the city presents a mosaic of local histories, geographies, and power relationships that can disrupt and otherwise distort mandates and goals established by the state. 'Seeing like a city' stands in marked contrast to 'seeing like a state' (Magnusson, 2011; Scott, 1999). Urban regimes have an ability to reinforce, alter, or subvert the narratives of state projects.

This book is about the trajectories of urban conflict and peace in the exemplar politically polarized cities of Jerusalem and Belfast – how there has been hopeful change at times and debilitating stasis and regression at other times at both national-political and on-the-ground, urban spatial levels. There exists an interlocking ecology of conflict dynamics in contested areas consisting of national-political, urban-spatial, and interpersonal-psychological domains, and these political and social dimensions intersect and impact each other in non-straightforward ways. Rather than neat categories, these dimensions are domains with porous boundaries, meaning that they not only impact each other but can overlap in messy and paradoxical ways. What gives cities and the agents within them such robustness in these circumstances is that national political goals, whether supporting partisan or peacebuilding objectives, are not commonly able to be operationalized in straightforward ways in urban arenas. This animates the city as an actor able to retard or promote national directives. There are multiple threads of national hegemonic and peacebuilding projects – both become complex and non-sequential in their implementation as they encounter the intricate and micro-scale multidimensionality of the urban system. The city has a rationality that national and regional political interests cannot know, and thus actions in the city can contest and resist the higher-level formulations of national politicians.

At first, Belfast seems small, minor and peripheral compared to the ostensible centrality and potent international significance of Jerusalem. Belfast appears as an anachronistic and out of place conflict between Christian sects in an era of Muslim extremism that is constantly in world headlines. Belfast is a provincial and fringe conflict that was an historic accident; it went well beyond its time. It is a place now without much political violence and with a political agreement since 1998 so the value of studying it appears at first glance to be negligible. Jerusalem, in contrast, feels like a key central node of much of the conflict in the world today; its meaning and value to study is massive. This sense of uneven contrast between the two places seems sensible. Yet, when one removes oneself from the intense lived experience that is Jerusalem, that which feels so expansive and central to the world while there begins to feel like a closed world with little cosmopolitan quality to it; a conflict constantly self-referential with a communally narcissistic sense that is inaccessibly exceptional in the world. At this point, Jerusalem, not Belfast, feels provincial, parochial, and archaic: a stagnant arena of contestation with no sources of fresh input. In contrast, Belfast, in its incremental and difficult moves away from violent conflict, emerges as an important pioneer along the path towards constructing an ethno-nationally inclusive society and city. It is perhaps not a model, but rather constitutes an important illuminator of the obstructions and improbabilities of building peace after violent trauma. In that respect, Belfast, not Jerusalem, feels central to contemporary debates and cosmopolitanism.

While Jerusalem reveals the dynamics of continued violent conflict and its self-reinforcing negative cycles, Belfast exposes the dynamics of a post-violent society and its conflicting institutional and policy imperatives. The sense of unsettledness in Jerusalem is palpable compared to Belfast, although Belfast exhibits its own type of darkness.

## Political, Urban, and Psychological

I examine the trajectories of politically contested urban environments at three levels – national-political, urban, and psychological. The urban arena constitutes the central anchor of this study and I emphasize elements such as the spatial location of antagonistic groups, land control and territoriality, development patterns and trajectories, demographic patterns, location and magnitude of urban violence, borders and boundaries, economic relationships, the location and delivery of public services, and the nature of nongovernmental and civil society groups in the city that seek to embed or transcend inter-group differences. These qualities of the city operate as a mediator between, on the one hand, national political goals and mandates, and on the other hand, the lived and felt experience of urban existence.

Due to the political contestation found in divided societies, the state plays an active role in seeking to manage or control the antagonistic urban area through the formulation of national political goals and mandates. A national governing ideology becomes essential in a contested society because public authorities operating amidst ethnic unrest must adopt an explicit doctrine that justifies and defends their policies amidst societal fragmentation. These national directives commonly take the form of abstract and ideological goals that are then intended to be implemented in the urban field. An ideology is a comprehensive political belief system that embraces an inner logic and seeks to guide and justify organized political and social actions (Bilski and Galnoor, 1980). I focus in this book on the ideology adopted by the state regarding its desired urban outcomes in a society of conflicting ethnic groups. A primary issue facing the state in polarized cities is how its ideological goals interact with the highly salient ethno-nationalist ideologies of its competing populations in urban space. A state's governing ideology can either be ethno-national and exclusive or civic and inclusive (Lijphart, 1977). When there is a single dominating ethnic group in control of the government apparatus, the morally-based doctrines of that ethno-national group regarding sovereignty and cultural identity tend to be determinative of how it addresses the city. In cases during and after the resolution of political conflict, government goals are likely to pursue a civic ideology that seeks to accommodate or transcend ethno-national ideologies.

In the specific cases at hand, fundamental ideologies by higher levels of government have been asserted concerning the status and future of their primary cities. While Israeli goals pertaining to Jerusalem come primarily from its national government, peacemaking goals in Northern Ireland derive from a mix of British national government and Northern Ireland regional government engagement.

In Israel's case, its long held vision for Jerusalem is that it will always be 'united' under Israeli rule. Despite the numerous efforts at finding an Israeli-Palestinian peace beginning in 1993, this assertion has been upheld as sacrosanct by successive Israeli governments. Most Israeli governments have proclaimed that Jerusalem would always be united under Israeli sovereignty, including the areas of East Jerusalem unilaterally annexed in 1967, and have rejected calls to divide the city politically. In 1980, the Israeli Knesset passed the Jerusalem Law declaring Jerusalem the unified capital of Israel. Despite having signed the Oslo Accords, which declared that the future status of Jerusalem would be negotiated, Israeli Prime Minister Rabin (1992–1995) declared that he would never divide the city, saying in 1995 that 'if they told us peace is the price of giving up a united Jerusalem under Israeli sovereignty, my reply would be "let's do without peace"'. Prime Minister Sharon (2001–2006) vowed to keep Jerusalem the 'undivided, eternal capital of the Jewish people'. Current Prime Minister Netanyahu (2009– ) has declared adamantly that 'all of Jerusalem would always remain under Israeli sovereignty', that 'Jerusalem has forever been the capital of only the Jewish people and no other nation', and Jerusalem is Israel's 'eternal indivisible capital'.

Israeli political control of Jerusalem and its urban area is linked to another significant goal of national policy – that of 'security'. Two intertwining forms of this security goal are evident. First, 'military' security focuses on the defensibility of the urban system and concentrates on the location and expansion of military installations and the ability of the road network to provide access to defence units. Second, there exists a 'political' security goal connected to military goals. This type of security broadens beyond strictly military considerations and extends into the civilian sphere – emphasizing growth and development programmes that seek to maintain the demographic dominance of Jews in Jerusalem and its larger urban sphere. In the eyes of Israeli policymakers, such demographic presence decreases the chances that political control will be wrested away from Israel in the future. Military security and political security are intimately connected. As Ochs (2011) observes, while Israeli military sectors address and respond to Palestinian violence, nationalist desires for extending Jewish territory and power propagate actions by non-military developmental sectors which must then be defended militarily.

In its assertion of unilateral and exclusive political control of Jerusalem and its emphasis on military and political security for its Jewish population, Israel's project pertaining to Jerusalem is *hegemonic* and *partisan*.

In the case of Northern Ireland since the 1998 Good Friday peace accord, the goals of a shared future, shared space, and the ending of ethno-national division have been consistently asserted by successive governments in one form or another. In 2005, the Northern Ireland government released the document, *A Shared Future – Policy and Strategic Framework for Good Relations in Northern Ireland*, in which it argued against continued community division between Unionists (Protestants) and Nationalists (Catholics) and for sharing over separation. It stated that, 'the division that perpetuates itself in Northern Ireland is costly both socially and economically. Adapting public policy in Northern Ireland simply to cope with community division holds out no prospect of stability and sustainability' (Office of the First Minister and Deputy First Minister of Northern Ireland (OFMDFMNI), 2005, p. 5). It further underscores that, 'separate but equal is not an option … that parallel living and the provision of parallel services are unsustainable both morally and economically' (p. 20). Subsequent policy documents released by the Northern Ireland government such as *Cohesion, Sharing, and Integration* (2010) and *Together: Building a United Community* (OFMDFMNI, 2013) have emphasized this goal of sharing over continued separation to various degrees.

In addition to shared future goals, Northern Ireland also emphasizes equality and 'good relations' as primary goals guiding future policy. The *Cohesion, Sharing, and Integration* document states that 'equality, fairness, inclusion and the promotion of good relations will be watchwords for all of our policies and programmes across Government' (OFMDFMNI, 2013, p. 3). The 'equality' mandate is set out in the Northern Ireland Act of 1998 (section 75 [1]) pursuant to the Good Friday Agreement. It mandates that government must pursue equality of opportunity between persons of different religious belief, political opinion, racial group, age, marital status or sexual orientation. It further states that promotion of equality of opportunity entails more than the elimination of discrimination and that it requires proactive action to address inequality across groups that currently exists. The 'good relations' goal is spelt out in the following subsection of the act (75 [2]) and states that policies must 'have regard to the desirability of promoting good relations between persons of different religious belief, political opinion or racial group'. While the equality goal seeks to counter societal inequalities, the good relations goal aims at assuring harmony between ethnonational groups in the carrying out of equality and other governmental programmes. We will see how these two goals are not always perceived by antagonistic communities as compatible with one another and have been a source of tension in implementing Northern Ireland's peacebuilding programme.

In its efforts to transcend the ethno-national differences that are causal and correlative of inter-group violence – foregrounding sharing, equality, and good relations as primary goals – the strategy of Northern Ireland government towards urban community divisions is *peace-promotive* and *conciliatory*.

What happens to the national political goals of Israel and Northern Ireland when they encounter the urban environment is the crux of this book's concern. The translating of governing ideology into urban policy is not straightforward. Ideology must be translated into technical prescriptions that seek to move a society, or in this case a city, towards those goals or vision. Yet, a state's governing ideology pertaining to the contested city – often composed of grand visions and abstract declarations – is fraught with ambiguity that may engender multiple interpretations as to which actions are appropriate to achieve chosen ends. The moral and implementation dimensions of ideology have been identified as 'fundamental' and 'operative', respectively (Seliger, 1970). The challenge for societies, and political leaders, is that operative ideology does not automatically proceed from the grand visions or moral ends asserted by fundamental ideology. For example, the moral ends of liberty and equality are espoused by proponents of both liberal economies and communism, yet they propose drastically different means as the way to achieve these ends (Seliger, 1970). In other circumstances, equality between ethnic groups may be espoused as the best way to resolve polarization, yet how it should be achieved in societies where there are significant historic imbalances does not proceed automatically from such overall moral agreement.[4] This incommensurability between national grand visioning and on-the-ground urban realities applies to both hegemonic and peace-promotive national programmes. Consequently, in the Jerusalem case, we would expect to find unforeseen contradictions and consequences from the Israeli project that create complexities and even run counter to larger Israeli goals. In the Belfast case, the conciliatory national programme will face obstructions and counter-forces when seeking to modify ethno-national communities and geographies in the name of tolerance. In this book, I delve into the nature of these national–urban disconnections, their problematical trajectories over time, and what these mean for the success of the larger political programmes.

This analysis of government programmes aimed at cities in contested environments is not restricted to the formulation and content of national political programmes and how such programmes are operationalized within contested urban spatial and physical structures. In addition to political mandates and urban space, I look at the humanistic, interpersonal, and psychological lives of people who live in neighbourhoods, involve themselves in the city's social, cultural, and economic life, and who often must face, during their mundane urban activities, the fact that they are living with 'intimate enemies' who reside in the next neighbourhood, across a visible political border or an invisible psychological boundary, who walk the same streets, take the same public transportation, or co-exist in the same economic or commercial space (Benvenisti, 1995).

The psychological effects and legacies of living in violent and dangerous urban environments are powerful, long lasting, and intergenerational in breadth. Living in constant fear of 'the other' and encountering personal vulnerability to violence and intimidation in everyday life creates a populace strongly resistant to conciliatory changes in city life which they perceive as increasing threat and decreasing personal security. While Jerusalem residents face active and ongoing violence in the form of stabbings, bombings, and shootings, Belfast residents live in a largely 'post-violent' environment, which nonetheless bears the scars and legacies of 25 years of urban civil war. Whether violence is current or historic, urban residents face psychological damage and trauma which reduces the capacity for trust of the other side. Such lack of trust creates a Jewish populace in Jerusalem that tends to align itself with Israeli partisan actions aimed at enhancing security. On the Palestinian side, Israel's domination of the urban landscape of Jerusalem has created substantial marginality, frustration, and hopelessness among the population which is conducive to continued violence and conflict. In Northern Ireland, although 'peace' is nearing 20 years in duration, the trauma of intense historic conflict in the city means that many residents and neighbourhoods in Belfast are resistant to changes in ethno-national segmentation that provided necessary security during the hard years of political violence.

Movement towards peace in the urban environment 'has a significant emotional cost that can cause a whole range of emotions such as fear, anxiety, suspicion, and mistrust in response to the need to readjust' (John Brewer, Professor of Post-Conflict Studies, Queen's University, interview, 19 May 2016). This is true whether peacemaking takes the form of compromises to a hegemonic project or of social and spatial adjustments needed after a peace accord. Peace does not readily produce stability in urban environments; indeed, it introduces new sources and forms of instability and insecurity into the urban system.

In Jerusalem, fear for personal safety in the face of Palestinian resistance to the hegemonic project is a constant feature of Israeli Jewish life in the city, and Jews are deeply afraid for their own lives and for the existence of the state of Israel. Ochs (2011) describes the various forms of security in Jerusalem, including the visible and ubiquitous presence of Israeli border police, walls and blockages that zigzag in and out of city spaces, mesh fencing surrounding school playgrounds, portable police barriers enclosing pedestrian malls, state-employed guards regularly jumping on and off city buses, the presence of gates, closed circuit televisions, hand-held metal detector wands, and the heightened sense of surveillance by Jews going about their everyday life. Israel's Yellow Pages lists 375 different security companies offering guard services with various forms of 'technologies of protection' (Ochs, 2011, p. 11). Any changes to political bordering or sovereignty that would arise from a political agreement threatens Jewish senses of security and safety; in particular, a political division of the city would expose residents in multiple Jewish neighbourhoods to a new political fault-line close to them and heighten their fears of Palestinian violence penetrating their neighbourhoods. Jewish neighbourhoods currently protected through the hegemonic project would overnight become 'frontline' neighbourhoods to Palestinian areas in the city. For Palestinians, daily feelings of deprivation and hopelessness are caused by the hegemonic project. Palestinian life is characterized by dehumanizing and humiliating obstructions in the form of multiple checkpoints bordering the city and the massive separation barrier which separates Palestinians from life in Jerusalem. The road network built for Israeli access, the wall, and constant checkpoints mean that mobility for Palestinians is severely restricted, turning what would normally be a 10-minute walk into a 2-hour drive circumnavigating numerous road closures and restrictions. Many Palestinians also live in constant fear of having their Jerusalem identity card, which allows access to Jerusalem life and services, being revoked by Israeli authorities.

In Northern Ireland, the working classes of both Protestant and Catholic communities are separated by numerous 'peace walls' that reinforce division. Such separation creates in one sense a form of security and safety for residents of the two sides while at the same time concretizing an 'us–them' dynamic in daily life that continues in spatial form to perpetuate wartime antagonisms. Possible changes to this ethno-national segmentation and geography in the name of urban normalization and the advancement of the peace process threatens the two sides and introduces elements of uncertainty and instability to daily life. The spatial form created through years of conflict in Belfast does not change overnight with a peace accord and remains as a significant obstruction and challenge to peacemaking.

Different domains of emotions are involved when seeking peace in a politically conflicted environment: those aroused by the conflict itself; those aroused by the possibility of peace and the psychological adjustments that non-violence or reduced levels of violence provoke; and those aroused by having to live together in some way once the conflict is over (John Brewer, interview, 19 May 2016). Rather than a sequence moving from one domain to another during peacebuilding, these domains overlap in concurrent ways; in particular, the legacy of violence, pain, and trauma associated with violence is present through phases of peacebuilding and must be managed by the peace negotiation process.

## Co-Productions and Trajectories of Peacebuilding

This book examines, over time, the relationship between national peacemaking and urban conflict management. With hostility and competition among groups defined by ethnic, religious and nationalistic identity on the increase across the world, this investigation contributes to our understanding of this phenomenon by focusing on the relationship between national *peacemaking* processes and on-the-ground urban *peacebuilding* outcomes.[5] Unlike the bulk of the extant literature on conflict and peace which emphasizes the national *or* urban arena, this book focuses on the connections between macro-level national policies and the local specificities of urban peacebuilding. Further, I interrogate this relationship at multiple points in time over a two-decade period to identify local and national trajectories of conflict management and how they mutually impact each other.

With Jerusalem (Israel/West Bank) and Belfast (Northern Ireland) as case studies, and employing multiple research methods during seven months of in-country field work in 2015 and 2016, I investigate the connection between national peacemaking efforts (beginning with the 1993 Oslo Accords and the 1998 Good Friday Agreement, respectively) and the spatial, economic, and social changes in the two primary cities during and since these accords. For Jerusalem, this is a record of 23 years; for Belfast, a period of 18 years. I examine urban interventions that address economic development, boundaries and borders, distribution of public services, location and magnitude of urban violence, housing and community development, control and regulation of land, provision and use of public space, and access to local policymaking. I examine how these urban policies – together with broader urban change – have been influenced by national political ideologies and how urban interventions and changes have in turn affected the subsequent evolution of national ideological programmes. The emphasis is on how national ideologies and urban dynamics inter-relate and how this relationship changes over time.

A fundamental premise I interrogate is that national peacemaking and urban peacebuilding endeavours must make progress in (1) complementary ways and (2) over time if there are to be improvements in tolerance and inter-group relations. National peacemaking efforts must be coordinated with urban peacebuilding activities and this coordination must occur over a sustained period of time. National agreements establish a necessary foundation for urban interventions, while urban policies actualize the often abstract principles incorporated in national peace documents. Lacking complementary national and urban progress over time, urban peacebuilding interventions that occur without national peace progress will become isolated experiments that can re-ignite conflict. National peacemaking without urban peacebuilding actions, meanwhile, becomes sterile and divorced from everyday life and challenges, leaving an urban void.

This book contributes to our understanding in the following sub-fields: governance of ethnic difference; urban policy and inter-group conflict and aggression; political transitions; democratization; nationalism; and peace and conflict studies. It fills a gap in the literature on conflict management and peace in its focus on the connection between the broader national and more specific urban components of peace. It emphasizes macro-micro relations in deeply divided contexts and the co-production of peace processes by politicians and policymakers, on the one hand, and by urban stakeholders, on the other.

The study of national peacemaking is commonly located within the domain of political scientists and is focused on getting it right – in terms of institutional and territorial design and political representation of competing groups – at national and international levels (such as Lijphart, 1968; O'Leary and McGarry, 1995; G-Gagnon and Tully, 2001; Chesterman, 2004; Paris, 2004; Roeder and Rothchild, 2005; McEvoy and O'Leary, 2013). But such a focus in the political conflict literature commonly pays minimal attention to the micro-scale processes of urban areas where inter-group relations are felt by city dwellers in tangible ways. In contrast, where there is study of urban areas of conflict, urbanists and public policy scholars emphasize the socio-spatial elements of city life and urban equity strategies (such as Harvey, 1973; Friedmann, 1987; Sandercock, 1998; Fainstein, 2011), and de-emphasize how opportunities or constraints faced by urban policymakers are shaped by, and interact with, larger national political imperatives.

There is an additional literature focusing on politically contested cities vulnerable to violence (such as Bollens, 1999, 2000, 2007; Charlesworth, 2006; Calame and Charlesworth, 2009; Gaffikin and Morrissey, 2011; Pullan and Baillie, 2013; Brand and Fregonese, 2013). Of particular note is an extensive multi-year interdisciplinary research project, 'Conflict in Cities and the Contested State', which examined the connection between the contested city and the state.[6] These valuable contributions help us understand the complexities of politically divided cities embedded in contested states. My contribution in this book extends this research literature in new directions, in particular by focusing on the details of the interaction between state goals and urban implementation, and how this relationship and the urban and spatial dynamics of the cities themselves change over extended periods of time. I seek to uncover mutual, two-way, and conflicting interactions between national political and urban-spatial levels. Just as violent conflict has been found to be jointly produced by the interaction of local actors and national elites (Kalyvas, 2006), this book posits that building peace is a joint product of national aspirations and local, on-the-ground actors and actions. I examine the impacts of peacemaking, or its failure, on the socio-spatial dynamics of the city and *vice versa*. I focus on this interplay of the national and the urban using a detailed and comparative longitudinal analysis of conflict- and peace-inducing processes at these two levels. I emphasize temporality and how dynamics occurring in both the national and urban arenas evolve and mutually impact each other over time. My emphasis on the multi-decade co-production of peace and conflict processes by national and urban actors is distinctive in the literature. It injects a rare longitudinal perspective by the same researcher over two decades of study, utilizing both recent field research and reflections on more than 20 years of study.

From October 2015 to June 2016, I undertook 122 semi-structured interviews in Jerusalem and Belfast with urban professionals, political leaders, community and nongovernmental organization representatives, and academic experts. This recent research adds to my earlier body of work. I have engaged in research on politically contested and polarized cities over the past 23 years and have written four books and a number of journal articles on urban peacebuilding in nine urban areas – Jerusalem, Belfast, Nicosia, Johannesburg, Barcelona, Basque Country, Sarajevo, Mostar, and Beirut (Bollens, 2012, 2007, 2000, 1999). This prior research utilized detailed in-country field research during which I completed 245 interviews with political leaders, urban professionals, community representatives, and academic experts. Drawing on this extensive prior experience and research, I use as an empirical baseline for this book the six months of field research conducted in Jerusalem and Belfast in 1994 and 1995 and more abbreviated research visits in 2001 (Jerusalem) and 2011 (Belfast). This establishes the foundation for rich accounting of changes in national peacemaking and urban peacebuilding dynamics during time periods of 23 and 18 years.[7] Because the early years of these time periods were characterized by existing (Israel/Palestine) and emerging (Northern Ireland) peace processes, this allows me to study how such efforts have permutated and transformed, both in terms of political institutional architecture and on-the-ground urban impacts.

Jerusalem and Belfast, the case study cities, illuminate the dilemmas and challenges faced by cities that are polarized by nationalistic conflict. In polarized cities, political control is contested as identity groups push to create a political system that expresses and protects their distinctive group characteristics (Hepburn, 2004; Calame and Charlesworth, 2009). Such contestation exhibits a lack of trust in normal political channels and is capable of jumping tracks onto aggressive and violent pathways. These cities, and the societies they are embedded in, are characterized by intractable conflict. Such conflict is particularly resistant to resolution because it is viewed as total and existential to participating parties, is violent in nature, perceived as a zero-sum contest, central and highly influential of the public agenda and everyday life, is perceived as unsolvable, demands extensive investment in order to cope with the conflict, and is protracted in duration (Kriesberg, 1993, 1998; Bar-Tal, 2013). In intractable conflicts, a 'conflict supporting narrative' or 'socio-psychological repertoire' develops within a society which legitimates and stimulates violence and the assertion of political power (Bar-Tal, 2013, pp. 130, 254). Such a narrative is functional in helping a group cope with, and explain, the conflict. It strengthens the justness of the group's goals and negates the goals of the rival group, singles out threats and suggests conditions that will ensure a society's security, and glorifies its own group's morality and humanity while viewing it as the sole victim of the conflict. The narrative, propagated by political leaders and the media, creates a specific angle of vision and generates a meaningful and unequivocal perception of the conflict.

With core issues of conflict unresolved in Jerusalem, and not effectively addressed in Belfast until 1998, violence has been a fact of life of these cities. Since September 2000, 1,320 Israelis have been killed by Palestinian violence, most during the second Intifada from 2000 to 2005 but with a recent resurgence since 2015 (Israel Ministry of Foreign Affairs).[8] From 2000 to 2007, there were 140 suicide and other bombing attacks against Israelis, killing 542 individuals (Israel Ministry of Foreign Affairs, 2011). Loss of Israeli life has occurred at a greater rate since 2000 than in earlier periods (348 Israeli deaths in the 1990s; 174 in the 1980s) (Israel Ministry of Foreign Affairs).[9] Meanwhile, from 2000 to 2016, there have been 2,170 Palestinians killed in the West Bank and 7,097 Palestinians killed in the Gaza Strip by Israeli forces and civilians. From 2000 to 2008, Palestinian deaths caused by Israeli security forces or civilians in the West Bank were at an extremely high level, numbering 1,833 (B'Tselem).[10]

During the four months of my field research from October 2015 to February 2016, violence against Israelis was at a heightened level after a period of relative calm from 2005 to 2014. From September 2015 to January 2017, 46 people were killed in terrorist attacks and 645 people injured. There were 169 stabbing attacks and 103 attempted attacks, 126 shootings, 51 vehicular (ramming) attacks and one bus bombing (Israel Ministry of Foreign Affairs).[11] According to the Israeli Shin Bet security agency, 2015 was the deadliest year of terrorism against Israelis since 2008. Unlike earlier patterns of violence perpetuated by Palestinians, most assailants were not linked to organized political groups and were acting more as 'lone wolves' inspired by the general political and economic climate. Many assailants were 18 years of age or younger, quite a few were as young as 13. This new dynamic of individualistic violence is posing new challenges to Israeli security agencies tasked with maintaining security. In 2015,

Palestinian casualties in the West Bank were the highest since 2005 – 145 Palestinian deaths and 14,053 Palestinian injuries (OCHAOPT, 2016). The majority of Palestinian injuries occurred during clashes with Israeli forces and resulted mainly from tear gas inhalation requiring medical treatment, rubber bullets, and from live ammunition.

In Northern Ireland, the 'Troubles' from 1969 to 1998 resulted in 3,489 dead, over 45,000 injuries, and approximately 10,000 bombings.[12] Belfast bore the brunt of this violence. Over 1,000 of the 1,810 fatal incidents from 1969 to July 1983 occurred in the Belfast urban area (Poole, 1990). Forty-one per cent of all explosions from 1969 to 1994 occurred in the Belfast urban area, with almost 70 per cent of bombings of housing occurring in the urban area (Boal, 1995). Attacks on shops, offices, industrial premises, pubs and clubs, and commercial premises were disproportionately concentrated in Belfast. Since the Good Friday Accord, political violence has been at lower levels, sporadic, and traceable to small splinter groups branching off from main paramilitary groups who are sustaining their ceasefires. There have been 100 deaths related to political violence from 1999 to 2014, compared to 564 deaths in the 1990s, 833 in the 1980s, and 1,892 in the 1970s. Since 1999, the number of all incidents of political violence (both lethal and non-lethal) is about 10 per cent of the level seen in the dreadful 1970s (Police Service of Northern Ireland).[13] Although political conflict remains a factor of life in Northern Ireland and there is great uncertainty about whether the society can take the next meaningful steps towards a fuller peace, Northern Ireland in its move away from political violence can be labelled a 'post-violent conflict' society. Contemporary violence in Belfast is not characterized by the 'organized-strategic' political violence of the past, but rather bears the mark of 'disorganized-opportunistic' violence that is a residual effect of the complicated transition to peace (Gaffikin et al., 2016, p. 20).

While the level of violence is an important and tangible indicator of urban conflict or peace, I investigate in this book the broader political and urban contexts that have created the conditions which stimulate or attenuate the incidence of such violence. I endeavour to uncover patterns that exist over time in the relation between (1) the national level of political negotiations and peacemaking and (2) the operational level of local policy that impacts the everyday lived space of contested urban space. I investigate how national considerations may open up or close down possibilities for urban peacebuilding, and how urban actions may impact possibilities for peace at the national level. I examine whether there is incongruity between fundamental national goals and operational forms that such goals take on in complex urban areas full of potential unintentional outcomes. Such incongruity can take place when urban dynamics run counter to national peace goals or when national peacemaking is not adequately reinforced by peace-promotive urban interventions.

This book investigates peace not as a distinct happening linked to a national peace accord but as a process with an extended and problematic trajectory over many years. This approach is essential because, as Darby and Mac Ginty (2000) describe, a peace process is less like climbing a single and visible mountain peak and more akin to navigating a mountain range with complex and unexpected peaks and terrain. Rather than a single thrust or success, making peace involves numerous challenges over time that can cause setbacks, reorientations, and relapses. This book examines one cluster of challenges in particular that can threaten this long distance mountain trek – whether or not there is meaningful urban change that actualizes and operationalizes political peace in authentic and experiential ways.

The theoretical concept of 'path dependence' has been used by social scientists to inform their study of policy and institutional arrangements over time. Path dependence suggests that a sequence of, in this case, urban policy interventions will be dependent on what has come before and the framework that exists to guide urban actions (Malpass, 2011). Development of new policy initiatives will come about only due to critical moments or junctures that reshape national political goals and urban actions that follow from them (Pierson, 2000). Path dependence predicts that institutions and policies will be characterized by periods of relative stability and continuity, punctuated, periodically, by phases of rapid and intense institutional and policy change (Hay, 2002). Nevertheless, the costs of such 'punctuated change' will be high, with the entrenchment of institutional arrangements and biases tending to obstruct easy reversal of prior political goals and policy choices (Levi, 1997). In the cases at hand, two critical junctures of potential radical change are represented by the Oslo Agreement between Israel and the Palestinians in 1993, and the Good Friday Agreement in Northern Ireland in 1998. I examine the influence of these critical agreements on subsequent on-the-ground urban dynamics and how these urban policy interventions have either supported or retarded the advancement of peace outlined in Oslo and Good Friday. My ultimate goal in this longitudinal analysis is to ascertain the relation between national peacemaking and urban peacebuilding and the degree to which there has been temporal congruence, or not, between the two levels of intervention. Both case studies are embedded in long-term and uncertain peacemaking contexts – Jerusalem since 1993 and Belfast since 1998 – and provide insight into continuity and change that occurs over a long time. Because the Northern Ireland peace process has arguably made more progress than negotiations between Israel and the Palestinians, the two cases present different tempos and directions of national peacemaking – the first incremental improvement, the second disrupted and regressive.

I conceptualize peacemaking not as a one-off diplomatic agreement among elites, but rather as a long and complicated process that emerges over an extended period of time. It is the quality and effectiveness of activities and policy initiatives over this duration which will contribute as much, if not more so, to the durability of the peace as the initial political agreement. The insufficiency of negotiated political settlements is exposed by the fact that only a minority of peace agreements survive (Harbom *et al.*, 2006). Negotiated settlements are mostly unsuccessful or they travel from one crisis to another. The corollary of this finding is that the focus of most political accords – on the restructuring of governing institutions and apportionment of political representation – is not sufficient in moving a violence-prone society to a sustainable and tolerant one. Indeed, criticism of the dominant form of peacebuilding supported by leading states, international organizations, and international financial institutions (the so-called 'liberal peace') has focused on its top-down Western orientation towards good governance and institutional reform and its neglect of indigenous micro-level social and economic factors that underpin conflict in the first place (Richmond, 2005; Roberts, 2011; Mac Ginty, 2013).[14] This critique strongly implies that peace and conflict scholars should pay greater attention to the *social* dimensions of peace as well as *political-institutional* factors (Brewer, 2010). These dimensions include, but are not limited to, the capacity of civil society, issues of local ethno-territoriality, income and ownership inequalities, extent and effectiveness of policy interventions into the everyday environment and life chances of residents, the treatment of victims and survivors, and the psychological and emotional capacity of residents to accept change and tolerance. Such a focus on the social dimensions of peacebuilding moves the analytic lens from the front-end of peacemaking and negotiated institutional reform to issues of peace implementation and peacebuilding over an extended time after the accord.

The importance of social dimensions in the maintenance and success of peace implies two further considerations in how best to investigate it: (1) that the city is an important spatial arena of focus because it is there where the experiences of everyday life are most acutely felt in contested societies and where the predominance of social programmes and policies are directed; and (2) that peacebuilding is a hybrid, multi-level process involving national political directives and also local actors, policies, and networks constituted spatially in the city (Mac Ginty, 2010).[15] Effective peacebuilding, accordingly, becomes usefully conceptualized as a political-spatial process that restructures both political institutions and the spatial and social arrangement of inter-group benefits and opportunities in the city. Consideration of both political and social aspects of peacebuilding alerts us to the notion that peace processes are likely to be multidimensional and complex rather than linear and one-dimensional. This is so because peace objectives are implemented across a full range of dimensions (such as political institutional reform, safety and security, equity and fairness, tolerance and sharing), are distributed across numerous actionable issue areas (such as land-use planning, economic and real estate development, social service delivery, housing production, community participation) and, further, are delivered across an intergovernmental web of diverse public authorities acting at both national and urban levels. Consequently, a hybrid peace of national and local influences is likely to have a 'variable geometry' reflecting the multi-level and multi-issue environment within which it operates (Mac Ginty, 2010, p. 397). For some issues, peace may be advancing; for others, it may be stalled or regressing.

The two characteristics of peacebuilding emphasized in this book – (1) that it is a social/spatial as well as political process that takes place over an extended period; and (2) that it is jointly produced through the interaction of local, city-based, actors and national elites – enables a fuller understanding of peace as a process rather than one-time agreement, and as a phenomenon of multi-threaded complexity subject to uneven advances and problematic paradoxes. This promises profound insights compared to viewing peace as a linear process logically unfolding from state to society according to a negotiated agreement. The devil is in the peace implementation details.

Studies of divided cities have led to greater understanding of how an urban area becomes transformed on the ground as the political fabric of a society begins to unravel and fragment. Calame and Charlesworth (2009), most notably, conjecture the existence of a sequence leading up to and solidifying ethnic apartheid in divided cities.[16] This book, in contrast, interrogates a more pro-peace trajectory and explores how urban and national influences intertwine, contradict, and/or complement each other over time during processes seeking inter-group co-existence and peace. While the degree of progress of national peacemaking may create limits or opportunities for urban pro-peace interventions, the magnitude and timing of policies and interventions that take place at the same time at the level of everyday urban life may facilitate or retard possibilities for the advance of national peacemaking.

Positioning peacemaking as a political-spatial process, it becomes clear that if local peacebuilding actions are not occurring in sufficient and responsive ways to support political peace efforts, this will act as a drag on moving the society forward in its aspirations for peace. In some cases, limited tangible peacebuilding changes in the urban arena (in terms of magnitude and impact) after political progress may retard genuinely felt peace and potentially jeopardize it. This is a consideration in the Belfast case. In other cases, when national peacemaking is itself threatened or stalled, urban interventions regarding such key attributes as land settlement, building of divisions, and urban services may occur which harden inter-group antagonisms and endanger future peace efforts. Such a scenario is likely in the Jerusalem case. In the first case, urbanism in practice and outcome is insufficient in its ability to co-contribute to peace. In the second and more damaging case, urbanism intervenes in ways detrimental to the advancement of peace and co-existence. Either way, prospects for developing and sustaining peace become imperilled and subject to relapse.

## How I Conducted this Research

The primary research for this book was conducted from October 2015 to February 2016 in Jerusalem and March to June 2016 in Belfast. I employed four methods: interviews; secondary research of written sources; photo-documentation; and in-depth field observation.

First, I undertook 122 semi-structured interviews (70 in Jerusalem, 52 in Belfast)[17] with urban professionals, political leaders, community and nongovernmental organization representatives, and academic experts. More than 95 per cent of the interviews were audio-taped, with permission of the interviewee. This relative freedom from note-taking during interviews allowed me to focus more effectively on nuances of discussions and guide them in fruitful directions consistent with my specific research interests. In establishing an interview sample, the project drew upon a deep set of contacts in the two cities sustained over a 20-year period, extending back to 1994 and 1995. This core list was supplemented through 'word of mouth' as my on-site interviews developed. The main focus of my interview questioning was on the linkage between national diplomatic movement and the pace and magnitude of urban interventions. I probed interviewees about issues related to the sequencing and timing of national and urban trajectories and how they have influenced each other. I queried them about causation, complementarities, disruptions, incongruences, and contradictions that exist between national goals pertaining to the cities and what was occurring on the ground in the urban arenas.

I also investigated the wide-ranging published and unpublished analyses and data from academic, agency, nongovernmental organization, social media, and popular press sources. Written source material allowed me to check the accuracy and validity of interviewee observations and to compile a richer, more comprehensive view of trajectory dynamics than if I relied on interviews or secondary data alone. I used an integrated approach to data gathering that employed both qualitative and quantitative sources, similar to what has been productive in my past studies of complex conflict environments (Bollens, 2009).

The focus of my interviews and written source research was on the relation between national peacemaking processes and on-the-ground urban changes during several points in time from 1994 to 2016. In order to analyze change systematically over such a long period, I focused on a select number of years within the two-decade period that provided key vantage points for understanding how national and urban processes inter-relate. For the Jerusalem case, I concentrated on 1994 (original field research, soon after the Oslo Accords), 2000 (coterminous with Camp David negotiations), 2003 (Geneva negotiation period), and 2016. For Belfast, the periods of focus were 1995 (original field research), 2000 (formative days after Good Friday Agreement), 2008 (one year after the start of a stable Northern Ireland Assembly), and 2016.[18] On the surface, the Israeli case amidst on-again, off-again and ultimately unsuccessful peace efforts appears to be one of urban retrenchment exacerbating inter-group hardening and segregation over time. In contrast, since the national peace accord in 1998, Belfast aspires to urban reform that would loosen the city's intense hyper-segregation and promote shared co-existence. During interviews and written source research, I specifically analyzed how concrete urban interventions and policies parallel, reinforce, or counter the stated goals of national political leaders regarding the city. I looked for disconnections and contradictions between the national and urban level. I documented the ways that national political trajectories (whether they are progressive or regressive) have been, or can be, disrupted by what occurs at the city level.

I expected disconnections and incongruences because cities are characterized by a multidimensional complexity of political dynamics and local processes that are different from, and can be in contradiction to, the more politically nuanced considerations of national peacemaking. Cities are qualitatively different from states – they are places of inter-group economic interdependency, daily life interactions, spatialized symbolism and territoriality, and spatial proximity of 'intimate enemies'. On the one hand, the realities of individuals needing to function in interdependent urban space may encourage inter-group pragmatic compromises amid broader political stasis. On the other hand, the spatial, economic, and social correlates and remnants of urban strife may distort and corrupt the efforts of well-intentioned national peacemaking. Assuming that cities are micro-scale mirrors of the state – that what is promulgated at the national political level in terms of policy becomes readily and easily translatable onto the urban landscape – produces an analytical blindness in our understanding of the implementation and operationalization of national peacemaking. In the Jerusalem case, during interviews and written source research I explored the possible openings or 'cracks' in the implementation of a national programme aimed at Israeli hegemonic control over Jerusalem. In Belfast, I investigated the on-the-ground blockages faced in Northern Ireland's peacemaking that retard the building of urban tolerance and the psycho-social advancement of the national peace. In the first case, I looked for openings amid despair; in the latter case, obstructions amid progress.

I used two additional methods of research – photo-documentation and field observation – to delve deeper into on-the-ground changes and dynamics of the urban areas. These methods were used to uncover the nature and evolution of activities that occur at the urban scale and to examine how particular urban developments at zones of inter-group interface constrain or facilitate the promotion of inter-group tolerance. I photo-documented specific interface locations – characterized by antagonistic groups operating in physical proximity – in each of the two cities in order to understand the degree and nature of physical changes since 1994. Over 3,200 photographs were taken and categorized in the two cities. These were used with a full inventory of photographs from 1994 and 1995 that established baseline data for contrasting the past with contemporary conditions. I used photo-documentation to illuminate cases where changes in the urban fabric have hardened interfaces between antagonistic groups and also examples where such changes have increased flexibility and openness conducive to greater inter-group interactions.[19] Finally, in order to interrogate the relationship between urban physicality and human behaviour and inter-group interactions, for five areas of inter-group interaction and daily flux in each city I undertook in-depth field observations – using video-recording by smartphone and *GoPro* technology where possible – of the daily ebb and flow of these areas.[20] I documented everyday activity patterns and examined how the physical characteristics of the built landscape impacted on such patterns. I also constructed local histories of each of the sites of interaction and documented whether physical changes occurred relative to national political peacemaking efforts and accords.

I aspire in this book to present facts, opinions, photographs, and observations in ways that bring to life the substantial challenges of living in, and governing, polarized and unsettled cities. In my 23 years of research in contested cities, I have engaged in over 360 interviews with political leaders, planners, architects, community representatives, and academics. During these interviews, many of which were intimate and absorbing, I felt present and aware that the emotional and often controversial things individuals were saying were not being absorbed by me through machine-like neutrality, but rather were interacting with my personal filter and experiences, challenges, and hopes that I had lived through in my life. I realized often that I was less a robotic recorder or inhuman interviewer and more an engaged individual with views and feelings. Consequently, I use both *ethnographic* and *auto-ethnographic* approaches in this book, which means I will describe human social phenomena (the 'other') but also provide at times a reflexive account of my own experiences (the 'self') in these cities and cultures. Auto-ethnography allows the soul to be present in research and foregrounds the often value-laden nature of social science research (Lowenheim, 2010; Doty, 2004; Aydinli

Figure 1.3. Author in Jerusalem.

Figure 1.4. Author in Belfast.

and Rosenau, 2004). It takes seriously the criticism that detached, allegedly objective, and impersonal writing can construct or reify violent or coercive political realities by objectifying contested concepts and giving them an aura of scientific accuracy (Lowenheim, 2010; Doty, 2004). At times, I make transparent to readers my emotions and thoughts as I interacted with my interviewees, their cities, and their political and cultural settings. I delve beneath the surface of local circumstances to illuminate the nuances of politics, planning, and psychology in these contentious places, which are often misunderstood by outsiders. Personal narrative, fragmented and layered writing, short stories, photographic portrayals, and the use of the conventions of literary writing are part of the auto-ethnographic approach that I employ.

This book interweaves ethnography and auto-ethnography, going back and forth between academic rigour and personal narrative in order to construct the complex emotional kaleidoscopes of these polarized cities. The narrative is woven out of my observations, reflections, and interviews. In contrast to the prevailing social science academic tradition that tells you, the reader, that you are not supposed to know who I am, in this book you will find me present and accountable along with the subjects. My interpretations are not always based on pursuit of scientific and universal understanding, but rather seek to make sense of specific encounters, experiences, and complex realities. I endeavour to be probing, thought provoking, self-reflexive, and exploratory of my inner subjective world amidst the outer objective world. This mirrors, I feel, the common experience of urban residents in these cities – a robust, vital, inner emotional and spiritual life existing amidst concrete physical places that have been drained, distorted, dismembered and exhausted by deeply entrenched urban conflict and violence. The essential human contradictions found in urban zones of conflict produce an experience that is vigorously alive and challenging. I believe that an unorthodox treatment of these politically contested cities that combines academic rigour, qualitative interviews, and personal reflection and honesty creates a more compelling and revealing read than a standard academic treatment of the topic which instead would construct order, linearity and sequencing in its interpretation of these cities. Explaining what it was like living and working in these cities – going inside the head of the researcher and those I interviewed – seeks to extend the reader's understanding and connect more intimately with lived experiences.

## National Politics and Urban Dynamics: Preview of Findings

I now present a brief preview summary of main findings. Chapters 2 to 7 will illuminate the details of the Jerusalem and Belfast cases and provide validity for the main conclusions presented here. Four main themes arise from the research, the first two cross-cutting the Jerusalem and Belfast cases, the latter two specific to the two cases. These are: (1) disconnection between national political goals and their urban operationalization; (2) peacebuilding as a process of disruptions and disjunctions; (3) the self-perpetuating dynamics and limits of hegemonic control; and (4) competing demands of political stability and urban peacebuilding.

1. *The translation of national political goals onto the urban landscape – whether they are hegemonic as in the case of Israel's strategy concerning Jerusalem or aimed at co-existent peace as in the case of Northern Ireland's objectives toward Belfast – is a process replete with complexities and contradictions which can thwart and disrupt national goals.*

National political concepts such as 'united Jerusalem' in Israel and 'shared space' in Northern Ireland have become problematized as they are operationalized and enacted in urban space. In the Jerusalem case, certain urban dynamics resulting from state intervention create cracks in Israel's hegemonic goals and the city becomes a block to operationalization of the wider national programme. In the Belfast case, national peacemaking goals become fragmented and stalled as they are operationalized in the stout ethno-national environment that is a residue from 25 years of intense urban conflict and spatial rigidity. This complexity of the national–urban relationship presents positive opportunities for anti-hegemonic actors in Jerusalem and difficult obstructions for peacebuilders in Belfast. In both cases, such national–urban disconnections bring to the fore the importance of considering the city and its unique attributes in efforts to concretize national political goals in the everyday life of its residents. The fact that national–urban disconnections were found in fundamentally different national programmes – one hegemonic, the other peace-promotive – illuminates the resilient nature of urbanism in resisting and confounding national mandates.

National mandates are not easily transferable onto urban space; instead, there exists a political-spatial ecology made up of a complex network of national political policies and on-the-ground urban sectors and interests. A national programme aimed at managing a city is not one of simply formulating national goals and implementing them in urban space, but rather is a political-spatial iterative process of engagement having unforeseen and erratic effects on the national programme. The city and urban region is a semi-autonomous space with its own local dynamics and relationships. This space – full of local history, micro-geographies, and on-the-ground relationships – is not easily understood by national politicians endeavouring to embed either hegemony or peace in the urban space. There is a disconnection between national political and urban spatial levels – between the abstract and the operational. In addition to the insufficiency of the state in understanding urbanism, the nature of the state institutional apparatus – distributed over numerous agents and agencies with multiple and at times conflicting mind-sets – means that state policy intrusions into urban space can work at cross-purposes with overarching national goals. A national political hegemonic or peacemaking programme impacting on the city is not homogeneous, but becomes substantively disaggregated and takes many forms as it encounters the multiple complexities of urban physical and social space. As abstract political programmes confront micro-scale urban dynamics and resistant patterns of community power, their impacts become divergent and even contradictory. Whereas certain state policies produce outcomes consistent with national political goals, other policies and interventions have negative impacts on such goals.

2. *National peace agreements encounter disrupted trajectories in their urban implementation. Peace accords – and also peace negotiation efforts – face complex and problematical challenges due to changing politics, urban spatial dynamics, and obstructive local incidents and influences.*

Restructuring a city takes a long time. Many aspects of cities are obdurate and not susceptible to quick change. In other cases, the urban dynamics of everyday life create resistance to political programmes which seek to order or rearrange basic components of the urban system. Due to the long duration in implementing urban change, national political programmes are susceptible to disruption owing to events and episodes, including but not limited to changes in national governing regimes and priorities, specific incidents such as violence that restrict the advancement of peace, and real and perceived changes in demographic trajectories of competing populations. While national political policies and programmes are important to study in their design and formulation, equally important to understand is how such mandates can become disrupted or reinforced as they are implemented over long and belaboured periods of time. In the two cases at hand, two specific aspects of temporality stand out. In Israel's case, the constant negotiations and lack of resolution appear to play into the hand of the stronger party; there exists a leveraging effect of temporal delaying. At the same time as political agreements and negotiations were opening up possibilities for peacemaking, actions on the ground were strengthening Israel's control over the Jerusalem urban region. In the Northern Ireland case, the 'long peace' has been challenged by disruptive stop-starts in national governing arrangements, in associated interruptions and decay in central political concepts intended to guide urban peacebuilding, and by antagonistic events on the ground which operate in the void of cohesive and directive national policymaking.

3. *Israel has been engaged in a self-perpetuating cycle of hegemonic territoriality in the Jerusalem region, characterized by a sequence of destabilizing partisan actions which stimulate Palestinian resistance and violence, in turn leading to further destabilizing Israeli efforts at consolidation.*

Israel's focus on being constantly under threat of violence and eradication leads it, rationally, to enact urban policies obsessed with security, group protection, spatial consolidation, and the uniting of Jerusalem governance under Israeli rule. Such programmes, however, create massive disequilibria and asymmetries in the urban environment, spawning inflammatory and violence-inciting feelings of hopelessness and exploitation, and objective conditions of socio-economic deprivation and poverty, on the part of Jerusalem area Palestinians. As Palestinians engage in episodes of violence in response, Israel then reacts with further efforts at controlling the Jerusalem area – militarily, politically, spatially, and demographically – thus introducing further destabilizing, dis-equalizing elements into urban space. In short, there exists a self-perpetuating and self-trapping cycle of partisan actions in response to the effects of previous partisan policy. Actions in response to the insecurity felt by the Israeli state have created further conditions of insecurity, in this way acting as a self-fulfilling prophesy (à *la* Merton, 1948). Spatially, these partisan actions constitute a pattern of expanded intrusion into contested political space – both micro-assertions in existing urban fabric and outward intrusions at ever greater geographic scales – which require even stronger security measures to consolidate and defend such actions. Israel's hegemonic project exhibits an insatiable spatial appetite for application at increasing levels of geographic scale. Yet, as the hegemonic project enlarges its spatial scale it becomes increasingly entangled in the volatilities that it produces, revealing the practical and political limits of its territorial goals. In the end, these actions meant to stabilize in the face of destabilization create further disequilibrium in the impacted areas, recreating and extending dynamics which argued for partisan consolidation of space in the first place. This self-perpetuating cycle appears strongly resistant to alternative imaginings and approaches and is jeopardizing the sustainability of the Israeli national political programme itself, while simultaneously foreclosing opportunities for a viable peace between Israel and the Palestinians.

4. *Northern Ireland illuminates the difficult balancing act between political stability and the ability of government to institute changes in urban space to move national peace forward. There exists tension between the necessary requirement of political stability in a post-violence society and the capacity to make meaningful adjustments in urban space associated with, and stimulating of, conflict and violence.*

In order to reach a political peace, the contested and polarized nature of Northern Ireland governance during the years of violent conflict had to be replaced by a functioning government that shares and apportions political power among the antagonistic sides. Because nationalistic conflict is primarily contested sovereignty, political control had to be shared in a way that is at least minimally acceptable to each side. This is a necessary and essential first step on the ladder of peace. Yet, the political stability that has been painstakingly and fitfully created in Northern Ireland creates a political environment that makes it difficult to take further steps up this ladder. Macro-political restructuring based on power sharing since 1998 has inhibited the capacity to make significant change in many of the lives of Belfast's residents living in ethno-nationally segmented neighbourhoods. Political stability and the capacity to make significant urban spatial and territorial changes exist in tension with one another. To maintain political legitimacy and stability in post-violent years, government policy has adhered to middle-ground and ultimately conservative positions that will not antagonize extremists on either side. Yet, such middle-ground policy initiatives face difficulty in addressing the core issues of urban society linked to violent conflict. In Belfast's case, such core issues involve redressing systemic inequalities and its hardened spatial-territorial landscape. Government policy has become stalled in a *status-quo* conflict management approach rather than able to move towards a more progressive conflict resolution approach that can take on the root issues of conflict in urban space. A surprising yet stable governing coalition of the more hard-line political parties from 2007 to 2017 intensified this policy gridlock. The dilemma faced by Northern Ireland is that politically stable governance is needed to move the contested society forward, yet the form this stability took from 2007 to 2017 obstructed the capacity to engage in transformative policymaking. In addition, the institutional design of power sharing in Northern Ireland has been associated with a 'sharing out' of political power across a multiplicity of government departments. This has fragmented policymaking responsibility across different policy domains that need to be integrated in a holistic way to address effectively the multidimensional social and spatial legacies of urban warfare in Belfast.

## Notes

1. The Uppsala Conflict Data Program records forty-nine of the fifty active armed conflicts in the world in 2015 as being intra-state; only the conflict between India and Pakistan is inter-state. Of the forty-nine intrastate conflicts, twenty were internationalized in that one or more states contributed troops to one or both sides (Melander *et al.*, 2016).
2. U.S. Army. Available at: https://www.army.mil/aps/09/information_papers/human_terrain_systems.html.
3. USAID. Available at: http://urban-links.org/.
4. For example, should policy seek equality of opportunity or equality of outcome? Should policy favour removal of discriminatory barriers only or also take remedial action to compensate for past injustices?
5. I and others make a distinction between peacemaking (diplomatic negotiations at the national level aiming to bring two or more antagonistic groups to a political agreement) and peacebuilding (efforts at reconciliation and reconstruction which seek to repair social and inter-group relationships).
6. See: www.conflictincities.org.
7. Both key components of this work – the national–urban connection and its temporal coverage – distinguish it from my earlier work.
8. See: http://mfa.gov.il/MFA/ForeignPolicy/Terrorism/Palestinian/Pages/Victims%20of%20Palestinian%20Violence%20and%20Terrorism%20sinc.aspx.
9. See: http://mfa.gov.il/MFA/MFA-Archive/2000/Pages/Terrorism%20deaths%20in%20Israel%20-%201920-1999.aspx.
10. See: http://www.btselem.org/statistics/fatalities/after-cast-lead/by-date-of-event.
11. See: http://mfa.gov.il/MFA/ForeignPolicy/Terrorism/Palestinian/Pages/Wave-of-terror-October-2015.aspx.
12. Conflict Archive on the Internet (CAIN). Available at: http://cain.ulst.ac.uk/sutton.
13. See: www.psni.police.uk.
14. Paris (2004) adds an additional criticism of traditional peacebuilding – that its tendency to impose rapid liberalization and marketization of post-conflict economies and politics increases the likelihood of renewed violence and instability in post-conflict societies.
15. I adapt Mac Ginty's (2010) ideas concerning hybrid peace. While he applies it to the relationship between international and national actors, I employ it to look at national-local relations.
16. (1) politicizing ethnicity – urban services are delivered in a biased way for a generation or two; (2) clustering – members of a threatened urban community seek out homogeneous neighbourhoods for protection; (3) political up-scaling – ethnic urban enclaves assume emblematic significance in larger nationalist conflict; (4) urban territories are claimed and connected to wider conflict boundary etching – informal and permeable ethnic demarcations emerge along topographic lines, rivers, highways; (5) concretizing – creation of impermeable thresholds, barricades and walls; and (6) consolidating – government or paramilitary actions occur that reinforce partitions, and duplicative urban development and distorted circulation patterns adapt to partitioned realities.
17. In Belfast, in addition to interviews, I was in the audience for ten public presentations by political officials and academic experts. In Jerusalem, I attended five such presentations.
18. The logic behind selecting the intermediate years (2000, 2003, and 2008) is that it is during movement at the national level (whether it be political negotiations or a new government regime) that possibilities for urban advancement increase, thus providing a view into how national and urban trajectories may intersect.
19. I have summarized in Bollens (2013) those policy strategies and tactics regarding physical space which appear suitable to advancing urban peace.
20. Sites in Jerusalem included neighbourhoods close to the separation barrier and security checkpoints, Damascus Gate, economic interaction areas along the old green line, Jerusalem light rail stations used by both Jewish and Arab passengers, and areas in north Jerusalem where a highway corridor used by Arabs/Palestinians is close to Jewish settlements in 'east' Jerusalem. In Belfast, areas included numerous peace wall interface neighbourhoods and areas that are spatial connectors from ethnic neighbourhoods to the central business district.

Chapter 2

# Jerusalem I: Urban Spatial Changes amid Political Impasse

*Jerusalem, Jerusalem, the city that kills the prophets and stones those who are sent to it!*
Matthew 23:37

*Being bound to a city that devours me.*
Albert Antebi, Jewish public activist during Ottoman rule over Palestine<br>(cited in Marcus, 2007, p. 187)

Oh Jerusalem, you seem tighter, meaner, more constricted after so many years of unilateral action, street violence again seeming normalized, there is talk of a third intifada. I feel despair – the city seems colder, tougher, sadder after years of lost hope, more than 20 years since Oslo. Can a society sustain such inequalities and asymmetries? What does a permanent crisis mean? What other region exists where more than 3 million people reside outside of a recognized state. Jerusalem is an asymmetrical, incongruous urban area, a frozen conflict, reinforced through layers and layers of contemporary urbanization. Is this conflict irreconcilable, perhaps not solvable? These are my thoughts as I re-immerse myself in 2015 as a Jerusalem resident after being here in 1994 and 2001. Living in Jerusalem acquaints oneself with the feeling of a consistent low-level, gut-feeling nausea living in such a contested and inflammatory place. I am living in west central Jerusalem on King George Street amid the advantaged population and yet I have a sense of being unsafe, vulnerable, and attackable, that this is unsustainable. The city is larger and more crowded, having grown from 603,000 in 1995 to 850,000 in 2014, the result of the constant competition between Jews and Arabs based on the proposition that demographic growth strengthens political and territorial claims. There is the feeling of irreversibility after the many decades of Israel's hegemonic policies, more and more consolidation of Jewish space, and greater and greater security measures needed to defend this strategy.

The 'wave' of violence began on 3 October when a Palestinian attacker stabbed and killed two individuals – one a rabbi – near the Lion's Gate of the Old City. Violence was to continue throughout the time I was living in the city, and beyond. I arrive 9 October. Aboard a city bus for over an hour, I feel vulnerability, tenuousness, fragility but also the sense of the absolute specialness of this place; the 'centre of the universe' sensation as I describe it to friends and students. On day 4, there are three violent attacks in Jerusalem, one in the Jewish neighbourhood of Pisgat Zeev and two involving border police in the Old City. I witness about fifty police cars and motorcycles rushing through the city on the way to Pisgat Zeev – high alert, high tension, loud, and frenzied. On day 5, three Jews are killed in two attacks. One takes place on bus #78 that runs along the interface with the Arab neighbourhood of Jabel Mukaber.

When I arrive at Hebrew University later that day, an executive secretary is concerned with my wellbeing and observes that, 'we live here, we don't have a choice. You have a choice'. On day 6, in response to violence in the city, border police close off some Arab neighbourhoods within Jerusalem by placing guarded concrete barriers on routes connecting Arab and Jewish neighbourhoods, *de facto* dividing the city held to be 'united' by Israel and raising criticism from right-wing commentators about this precedent. Amid daily violence, Israelis check their smartphones every 15 minutes for the latest attack and news. They are robustly connected, immediate, intimate, and personal in their collective exposure to vulnerability and threats to their personal safety and collective survival. Engaging academically and theoretically with Jerusalem feels like superficial and irrelevant formula-making amid the life-numbing red dust of this daily conflict and tension. Some mornings when I awaken I am just not ready for Jerusalem.

I take a Jewish taxi to the Bethlehem checkpoint #300 at the imposing separation barrier. I walk through the long, tortuous, and monitored checkpoint, through which about 1,500 Palestinian workers pass daily into Israel and endure delays up to five hours during rush hours. I take disallowed photographs of the long and inhuman checkpoint and security apparatus. After getting through, a person near me is mistakenly detained and asked to delete photos from his camera. On the other side, a pre-arranged Arab guide is there to accompany me on my tour of the 'other side' of the wall, which includes the West Bank and even parts of municipal Jerusalem. As we skirt 'B' areas designated in the Oslo agreement (areas of Palestinian civilian governance but joint Israeli-Palestinian security control), red warning signs along the road declare that Israelis are forbidden from entering, per Israeli law, and that their safety cannot be guaranteed by Israel. We enter the Rachel's Tomb area that is walled off on all sides by the Israeli separation wall to assure Jewish access and which is near the Jewish settlement of Gilo. I have a brief interaction with an ultra-orthodox Jew who is praying there and I am informed through a Hebrew translator on site that he described me, a non-Jew, as 'having no soul'. I am only partly successful in fighting off my indignation at this dismissal. My Arab guide and I complete the southern part of our journey by visiting Aida refugee camp, close to Rachel's Tomb and about a mile or 1.5 km north of Bethlehem. Established in 1950 to hold refugees from Jerusalem and Hebron, Aida is a place of high tension and frequent clashes between camp residents and Israeli security forces. In the near horizon are the massive Jewish neighbourhoods and settlements constructed since 1967; extensive ongoing construction is evident in these contentious developments.

We next take a convoluted road system that Palestinians must endure that circumnavigates the numerous Israeli road blockages and checkpoints. As we get to the northern section outside the wall, the separation barrier cuts into municipal Jerusalem, creating a 'no-man's land' of unregulated and high-rise development in the Kafr Aqab area. Although it is within the Israeli-defined Municipality of Jerusalem, urban services are not provided here and there is the sense of it being a wild-wild west with no formal institutions in control. A bit further north the separation wall cuts westwards, establishing the northern hard boundary of Jerusalem. From this border to the fast-growing satellite city of Ramallah is only about 9 miles or 14.5 km. As we skirt the separation wall at the northern limit of Jerusalem, the road network is fragmented, substandard, chaotic, third-world in quality. I witness Palestinian youths after school going forward towards the wall to provoke ever-present Israeli security forces manning the barrier. Although there is a seeming habitual normalcy of the youths' behaviour, my guide warns that when tensions like this arise violence cannot be far off. We turn back towards Jerusalem. We go through the Qalandia checkpoint, the second main route for Palestinians into Jerusalem Municipality. The wait is long as cars inch towards the checkpoint. Evidence of daily conflict is everywhere – burned out parts of infrastructure near the wall and plentiful graffiti honouring Palestinian martyrs and leaders. Not long after departing the Qalandia edifice, I am back in the modern, functioning Jewish urban tissue of Jerusalem, with wide and well-signed roads and busy California-style traffic.

Trekking the southern, eastern, and northern parts of the Jerusalem urban area has taken about six hours. Yet, the distance traversed – as the crow flies – has been modest; I have not been more than 2 miles or 3 km outside the Jerusalem municipal boundaries at any time. The political and physical borders, combined with the fragmented and segregated road system, produce the dramatic effect of being in two different psychological and material worlds within close reach of each other.

Travelling through Jerusalem – both its core and peripheral parts – and witnessing Israel's massive effort to maintain control and security compels me to reflect on what I have observed, and I consider several comments from Israeli military-security officials. Udi Dekel, a retired Brigadier General and former Israeli Defense Forces (IDF) head of Strategic Planning Division, observes that Israel's greater regional strategic situation 'cannot be maintained, and Israel's political-security situation is gradually worsening'. He further claims that 'those who preach united Jerusalem are disconnected from the realities of East Jerusalem' (Institute for National Security Studies, 2015; interview, 3 February 2016). In the documentary *The Gatekeepers* (2012), which probes the perspectives of six former heads of Israel's *Shin Bet* internal security agency, Carmi Gillon (1994–1996) observes that 'we are making the lives of millions unbearable, into prolonged human suffering' and Avraham Shalom (1980–1986) states that 'we have become more cruel – to ourselves but mainly to the occupied population'. These are revealing and troubling revelations and cut to the core of Israel's dilemma in its endeavours to realize its national political hegemonic goals in the urban setting of Jerusalem and its hinterland.

Since the end of World War II, the social and political geography of Jerusalem has shifted fundamentally several times. The multicultural mosaic under the 1920–1948 British Mandate was transformed into a two-sided physical partitioning of the city as a result of the 1948 Arab-Israeli War.[1] For almost 20 years (1949–1967), Jerusalem was a physically divided city separated by a 'green line' that separated the new state of Israel from Jordanian-controlled East Jerusalem and the West Bank. The Six-Day War of 1967, fought between Israel and the states of Egypt (known at the time as the United Arab Republic), Jordan, and Syria, was launched by a series of pre-emptive air strikes by Israel against Egyptian forces mobilizing against the Israeli border in the Sinai Peninsula. The wide-ranging Israeli victories against its antagonists in this war resulted in Israel taking military control over all of Jerusalem and the West Bank. Since 1967, Jerusalem has been a politically contested Israeli-controlled Municipality three times the area of its pre-1967 city (due to unilateral, and internationally unrecognized, annexation) and encompassing formerly Arab East Jerusalem. Despite Israel's political claim of control over all of Jerusalem, the international status of East Jerusalem (and the West Bank) today is as 'occupied territory'. From an urban policy and development perspective, the post-1967 period has had the most significant effects on today's urban and regional landscape.

## Urban Hegemony during Two Decades of Political Impasse

I focus on the spatial and physical trajectories of change in the Jerusalem urban region during the period 1994 to 2016, a period of repeated and unsuccessful attempts at resolving the Israeli-Palestinian conflict. Among the major initiatives were: the Oslo Accords (1993–1995), Camp David Summit (and subsequent 'parameters') (2000), Taba Summit (2001), Geneva Initiative (2003), and the Annapolis Conference (2007).[2] Each of these endeavours treats the governance and sovereignty issues pertaining to Jerusalem in different ways; whereas the initially successful Oslo process remained distant from Jerusalem, the unsuccessful efforts from 2000 onwards more directly considered the possibility of dividing Jerusalem politically.[3]

During my first on-site field research, in 1995, the Jerusalem Municipality, as defined by Israeli borders, had a population of 603,000 and was approximately 70 per cent Jewish and 30 per cent Palestinian (composed of Muslim and Christian populations [see Jerusalem Institute for Israel Studies, 1996]). There was no separation barrier and there existed hope that the Oslo agreement might finally bring the sides together in peace, including an agreement regarding the political status of the city. The *Declaration of Principles on Interim Self-Government Arrangements* ('The Oslo I agreement') was signed by Israel and the Palestine Liberation Organization (PLO) on 13 September 1993 and contained a set of mutually agreed-upon general principles and phases regarding a 5-year 'interim' period of Palestinian self-rule. Land and political autonomy for Palestinians would be exchanged for enhanced security for Israelis and regional stability. The agreement stated, in Article V (3), that the status of Jerusalem was not to be discussed in the negotiations for the interim arrangements but should be one of the subjects left for 'permanent status' negotiations scheduled to occur no later than May 1996.

Subsequent stages of the 1993 agreement were enacted, including (1) self-rule by the Palestinian National Authority (PNA) in Gaza and Jericho, and withdrawal of Israeli forces from those areas; (2) early empowerment in the rest of the West Bank in five specific spheres – education and culture, health, social welfare, direct taxation, and tourism – whose duties were transferred to the PNA; and (3) an interim agreement and elections (Oslo II agreement of September 1995). Oslo II detailed the self-government arrangements in the West Bank and specified the structure and powers, and election procedures, regarding a Palestinian Council. The 1995 agreement map demarcated three areas of the West Bank: *Area A* (seven of the major Palestinian cities where Arabs gained full territorial and security control); *Area B* (village areas where the Palestinians gained territorial control, but security control would be shared); and *Area C* (areas whose status had not yet been determined, including areas Israel deemed to be of strategic security value). The Israeli army redeployed away from Areas A and B in phases, and Palestinian national elections took place in April 1996. Permanent status negotiations were then slated to be held later in 1996 dealing with issues of Jerusalem, refugees, settlements, security arrangements, and borders. However, these negotiations never took place due to serious disagreements over the size and timing of Israeli withdrawals from the West Bank, Israel's construction activities in East Jerusalem and the West Bank, and the PNA's inability to constrain extremists.

*The only way to combat Palestinian resistance is not to step back from the terrorist actions but to maximize friction and to be there on the ground.*

Nadav Shragai, Jerusalem Center for Public Affairs,
interview, 17 December 2015

Amid these emerging political changes affecting the broader geography of the West

Bank, field research in Jerusalem in 1994 documented Israel's hegemonic project concerning the urban area of Jerusalem (Bollens, 2000). Whereas the Oslo peace was producing constructive political changes in the West Bank, this period was characterized by a tightening of Israel's hegemonic control over Jerusalem. A set of implementation tools during the early Oslo years, many part of the Israeli land-use planning system and used since 1967, continued to pursue three main goals related to Jerusalem: (1) facilitate the pace and increase the magnitude of Jewish development to maintain the Jewish/Arab demographic ratio; (2) influence the location of new Jewish development in municipal areas annexed by Israel in 1967 to create an obstacle to 're-division' of the city; and (3) restrict Arab growth and development in the eastern sector to weaken Palestinian claims to Jerusalem (Bollens, 2000).

*For those who say the city is functioning well, I say that a train on a precipice also is functioning. This city is on a precipice.*

Meir Margalit, Former Member of Jerusalem Municipal Council, interview, 27 October 2015

*Jerusalem is a city where no one believes anymore in the impassioned slogans and heroic illusions once inspired by its name.*

Meron Benvenisti, 2007, p. 96

Twenty-one years after initial field research, I return to Jerusalem in 2015 to assess what has changed spatially – and what has not – over these years of on-again, off-again political negotiations over the city's political future. Amid this political impasse, I find that the hegemonic project has produced even greater imprints on the urban region but that there also exist newer dynamics and impacts which add complexity and even contradictions to the Israeli project of control. The overall effect of these dynamics from 1994 to 2016 is the creation of an even more pronounced urban disequilibrium and instability.

The nationalistic competition over Jerusalem has produced a significantly bigger city in terms of population, growing from 603,000 in 1995 to 850,000 in 2014. It is now a city where those I interviewed increasingly describe the existence of '3 Jerusalems' of distinctive populations that lack a common denominator to hold them together – composed of ultra-orthodox Jews (21 per cent), non-orthodox Jews (42 per cent), and Arabs (37 per cent) (Meir Margalit, Former Jerusalem Municipality Councillor, interview, 27 October 2015; Eran Feitelson, Professor, Hebrew University, interview, 25 November 2015).[4]

Based on four months of extensive interviewing and review of planning and policy documents from October 2015 to March 2016, it is evident that Israel's project of control in Jerusalem has continued unabated and has intensified over the past 20 years.

Daniel Seidemann, a preeminent expert on Jerusalem, cites four different methods that Israel uses to shape the city spatially: settlement expansion, enclaving and restricting of the Palestinian presence; the use of infrastructure construction; and the building of the separation barrier beginning in 2003 (interview, 1 February 2016). Demographic planning occurs at three different levels (Yusef Jabareen, presentation, Ben-Gurion University, 2 December 2015): the Israeli state's ideological construction of space; spatial tactics and strategy; and the state's influence on the social-spatial products of planning. These ideological, strategic, and project-specific levels of the hegemonic project intertwine and reinforce one another. The ideologically-driven reshaping of East Jerusalem since 1967 has been implemented through an active network of Israeli development agencies which, combined, constitute a forceful collective project. The unilateral annexation of East Jerusalem in 1967 extended strong Israeli government powers into disputed territory. Israeli law enabled the Ministry of Treasury to expropriate whole areas – both private land and 'state land' – for public purposes. Two state agencies with extensive powers are then able to propose, and shepherd through, large Jewish communities in these expropriated areas. The Israeli Lands Authority performs a critical land banking role after expropriation and influences development through the release of this land for residential, industrial, and afforestation purposes. The Ministry of Construction and Housing is the active agent in creating 'facts on the ground', building housing, infrastructure, and roads using the full financing and development powers of the state. Due to restrictions on the exercise of Palestinian public authority in East Jerusalem, no such collective process of development is possible for Jerusalem Arabs.

According to Peace Now,[5] in 1992, just ahead of the first Oslo Accord, Jewish settlements (neighbourhoods) built on expropriated land in areas of Jerusalem unilaterally annexed by Israel in 1967 were home to 125,800 Jewish residents. By the end of 2014, continued expansion of these areas has led to there being 205,220 residents in these contentious developments in the eastern, southern, and northern sectors of the annexed area (Jerusalem Institute for Israel Studies, 2015). These large developments constructed by the state have been built in locations to prevent political division of the city and to separate Arab East Jerusalem neighbourhoods from each other and from the rest of the West Bank.[6] Several of these large projects continue to expand, most notably Har Homa in southern Jerusalem which splits East Jerusalem from Bethlehem to the south. Whereas prior to 2001 there were about 450 units in this settlement, currently there are 4,500 units with another 1,000 currently being built (Yudith Oppenheimer, Executive Director, Ir Amim, interview, 26 January 2016). Elaborate road infrastructure provides mobility and access to support the Israeli remaking of the urban area. To connect the large Jewish communities in annexed Jerusalem to the rest of the city and to outlying parts of the urban area there has been the construction of an elaborate road system that functionally integrates the Jewish parts of the metropolitan area, splits Arab

36  Trajectories of Conflict and Peace

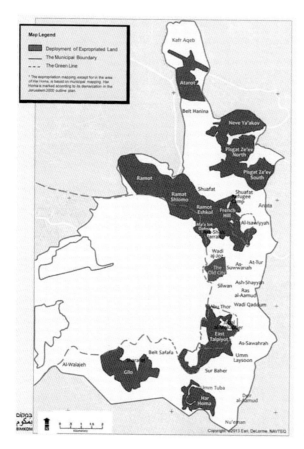

Figure 2.1. Jewish communities in annexed parts of Jerusalem. (*Source*: Bimkom, 2014, Map 2)

Figure 2.2. Har Homa.

Figure 2.3. Jerusalem's segregated road system.

neighbourhoods in some cases, and segregates the road system from Jerusalem's Arab residents.

Of substantial importance to the political future of Jerusalem and the larger region is the Israeli settlement activity that has occurred in the West Bank outside the Israeli-defined borders of the city over the past 20 years. In 1992, 105,400 Jewish settlers lived in the West Bank outside Jerusalem. By the end of 2015, there were 385,900 settlers living there. About two-thirds of Jewish settlers in the West Bank outside Jerusalem reside in three suburban clusters near Jerusalem city – Maale Adumim to the east, Gush Etzion to the south, and Givat Zeev to the north. Combining East Jerusalem and West Bank figures, the number of Jewish settlers living in East Jerusalem and the remainder of the West Bank increased from 231,200 in 1992 to 591,120 in 2015 (Peace Now).[7] This is about 10 per cent of Israel's 6.3 million Jewish citizens. The composition of Jewish settlers has also changed since 1994, with now one-half of settlers being ultra-orthodox Jews (*Haredi*). With high annual growth rates of 7 to 8 per cent, the ultra-orthodox have high demand for housing and are finding it in state-supported settlements in contested space (Gillad Rosen, Senior Lecturer, Hebrew University,

Figure 2.4.  Maale Adumim.

interview, 11 October 2015). The ultra-orthodox city of Betar Illit (south of Jerusalem) is now the largest settlement in the West Bank outside Jerusalem, surpassing 45,000 in population and growing 10 per cent annually (Israel Ministry of Interior).

In terms of the magnitude and location of Israel-promoted development for Jewish residents, the period of 1994–2016 has witnessed intensification and deepening of the Israeli hegemonic project and this has occurred irrespective of efforts at the diplomatic level to find a negotiated solution to the Israel-Palestine conflict. Whereas negotiations come and go, the Israeli project of strengthening Jewish control over Jerusalem and the West Bank has a staying power undeterred by broader politics.

## Israeli Planning Regulatory Regime

The enhancement and promotion by the Israeli state of Jewish development in and outside Jerusalem is one part of the story. The other important aspect is how Israeli public authority has been used to restrict and fragment Arab community development in East Jerusalem. In the early years after unilateral annexation of East Jerusalem and surroundings, Israel expropriated 37 per cent of all of the land in the annexed part for the purposes of building new Jewish neighbourhoods. This amounted to about 26,300 dunams (4.04 dunams = 1 acre or 0.4 ha) expropriated by Israel out of 71,300 dunams in all the annexed part. A further 6,500 dunams – on the outskirts of expropriated areas

– has been left as unplanned (Bimkom, 2013). All told, this directly removed more than 40 per cent of the annexed area from Arab control.

*Planning and architecture are the three-dimensional forms of politics. They are how politics forms in place.*
Yehuda Greenfield-Gilat, Director, SAYA Design, Jerusalem,<br>interview, 19 October 2015

For the areas in the annexed east remaining after Israeli expropriation, the planning and regulatory regime – both in intent and outcome – remains biased and discriminatory against Palestinians and their ability to develop and live in Jerusalem. There are three main types of Israeli plan pertinent to this discussion. *Master plans* are formulated for the larger urban area and set out general guidelines and standards for development. *Outline plans* are done for particular neighbourhoods and set more specific standards pertaining to allowable growth, building volumes, and zoning for different land uses. *Detailed, or re-parcellation, plans* are done to gain building permits for actual construction. According to the 1965 Planning and Building Law, there must be an approved detailed plan in order to legally obtain a permit to expand or build a house, or to develop land for economic purposes. Detailed plans commonly must set aside up to 40 per cent of the land in the designated area for open space and community facilities.

In examining each of these levels of plan as they pertain to the Arab community in East Jerusalem, one encounters explicit and implicit discrimination and bias in both the substance of the plans and the process through which they are implemented.

## City Master Plan

The Master Plan for Jerusalem 2000 (formally *Local Outline Plan Jerusalem 2000*) was first put forward for public review in 2004.[8] As of 2016, it has still not been formally ratified and adopted; yet, it forms the basic planning framework for policy intervention in the city today. Its purpose is to 'offer a new and comprehensive thinking mode towards the creation of a statutory framework according to which the development of the city as the capital of Israel and a metropolitan center can take place...' (Municipality of Jerusalem, 2004). This master plan is intended to fill an enormous vacuum in thinking about the city as a whole. Astoundingly, the last comprehensive and authorized legal document to regulate the city's development was back in 1959 – Plan number 62 – and this took place prior to Israel assuming political control over the full Jerusalem municipal area.

This lack of master planning constitutes a tremendous grey area that exists in comprehensive planning for the city, a grey area that has been used by Israeli planners and elected officials to pursue Israel's hegemonic project. Fundamental to this hegemonic project is Israel's obsession through the decades of maintaining Jewish demographic dominance in the city. Equating demographic strength with political control, the clearest articulation of this Israeli urban strategy was Prime Minister Golda Meir's proclamation in the early 1970s that Israel should do all that is necessary to maintain the numerical ratio of 73 per cent Jewish and 27 per cent Arab population then existing within the municipal borders (Benjamin Hyman, Director, Department of Local Planning, Ministry of the Interior, interview, 9 November 1994; and Israel Kimhi, Former Jerusalem City Planner, interview, 28 October 1994). An inter-ministerial committee in 1973 affirmed this demographic goal and since then subsequent governments, through the Ministerial Commission on Jerusalem, have reaffirmed this demographic goal as a guideline in determining planning policy in Jerusalem.[9] This setting of ethnic demographic percentages as guidelines for planning illuminates clear hegemonic intent and reverses established planning principles that aim to accommodate projected natural population growth of different subgroups within a city.

The Jerusalem Master Plan 2000 addresses this 'demographic balance' goal, noting a ratio of 70 per cent Jews and 30 per cent Arabs that has been adopted in governmental decisions. However, it notes that demographic trends in place since the end of the 1960s distance Jerusalem from this objective. If the demographic trend of recent years continues without any significant change, the Plan projects a population of approximately 60 per cent Jews and 40 per cent Arabs in 2020 and sets this as an achievable goal. It re-asserts the need for 'maintaining a solid Jewish majority in the city' and calls for actions that will reduce negative Jewish migration from the city and draw Jewish residents to the city from other areas in the country through housing and economic opportunities (Municipality of Jerusalem, 2004).[10]

Municipality deliberations on the Master Plan expose two important points. First, that demographic-led planning and policymaking remains primary in Israeli considerations of the city. Second, that demographic trends are overcoming past attempts to maintain the Jewish majority at 70 per cent, despite constant Municipality and government efforts since 1967 to promote Jewish development and restrict Arab growth in the city. According to Israel's own data, the Arab percentage of city population increased from 30 per cent in 1995 to 37 per cent in 2014 (Jerusalem Institute for Israel Studies, 2016, table III/1).[11] 'Israeli planners should understand in looking at this number that their policy has failed', asserts Adnan Husseini (Palestinian Governor of Jerusalem, interview, 25 January 2016). From 1995 to 2014, the Arab population in Jerusalem increased by 134,000, while the Jewish population increased by 113,000 (Jerusalem Institute for Israel Studies, 2016, table III/1). We will see that this magnitude of Arab population growth is not due to hospitable Municipality planning polices and regulations, but to Arabs' ability to bypass a severely restrictive regulatory framework imposed upon them.

## Neighbourhood Outline Plans

Whereas the city Master Plan emphasizes goals and principles at the citywide level, neighbourhood outline plans are done for more particular community areas and specify land allocations and zoning within each area across different types of land use, including residential, commercial, roads, open spaces, and public buildings and institutions. These outline plans are the fundamental building blocks for community development. Twenty-five outline plans have been approved by the Municipality through the years for Arab neighbourhoods of East Jerusalem. An analysis of these plans finds a multitude of elements restrictive of Arab future growth (Bimkom, 2014):

1. Areas deemed for growth in most of the plans are generally limited to the *de-facto* already built up area of the neighbourhood. So-called 'blue lines' in these plans restrict needed outward growth and do not offer meaningful land reserves for future development.

2. Zoning of land as 'open scenic areas' is excessive and curtails space allowed for residential development. In cases where a neighbourhood outline plan includes a larger area than the built-up area, much of the remaining area is commonly zoned as 'open scenic areas'.

3. Limitations on building rights are imposed through strict regulations of maximum allowable building ratios.[12]

4. Sparse road networks in these plans prevent the development of plots that need good road access. Further, routes of roads drawn in Municipality plans disregard the existing road network and often cut deeply into private land.

5. There is inadequate land zoned for public buildings such as community centres, libraries, sports facilities, and other neighbourhood assets that typically constitute responsible and balanced community development.

6. Many neighbourhood outline plans are not sufficiently detailed for the issuance of building permits. Large areas in the plans have been marked as needing more detailed re-parcellation plans, adding another and frequently complex process in seeking building permits even in those areas where a neighbourhood outline plan ostensibly allows for development.

The overall area covered by outline plans is about 23,000 dunams (about 5,700 acres or 2,300 ha), which means that about 40 per cent of land in annexed Jerusalem not already expropriated by Israel in the early years is not covered by plans. The area where there are plans for Arab neighbourhoods is less than one-third of the total annexed area and only about 18 per cent of the full Municipal area (Bimkom, 2014). Within the plans themselves, only about 9,800 dunams are zoned for residential construction, meaning that only 14 per cent of annexed East Jerusalem (8 per cent of the entire municipal area) is available for Arab housing (Bimkom, 2014, 2013; Margalit, 2014). Local plans zone almost as much land for open space as they do for housing (Bimkom, 2013). Further tightening the noose of Israel's regulations is the fact that much residentially-zoned land is already built on. This means that with continued natural increase of the Arab population, housing density is intense. In East Jerusalem, there are 13 square metres of built residential space per person, compared to 24 square metres per person in West Jerusalem (UN-HABITAT, 2015).

## *Detailed, Re-Parcellation, Plans*

Even in areas where Arab development is allowed by neighbourhood outline plans, a further step is often needed in order to obtain actual permission to build. This is the development of a 'detailed plan' for a subarea which details how landowners will allocate plots equitably to meet the Municipality requirement that up to 40 per cent of the area needs to be set aside – expropriated – for public uses such as roads, schools, and community facilities. In Jewish developments, such re-parcellation through detailed plans is relatively easy because land is commonly in public ownership and there exists a publicly supported process of community development – by the Ministry of Construction and Housing – which takes the project to its ultimate fruition. In Arab areas, no such communal process exists, and there are usually no clearly defined private ownership boundaries that are legally 'registered' with the government.[13] Because land registration is a necessary condition for re-parcellation, this constitutes a significant obstacle to obtaining building permits through 'detailed plans'. Additional conditions applied to building permit applications – such as access to an approved road and to adequate sewerage infrastructure – also obstruct building permission due to the undeveloped and inadequate condition of such community infrastructure that in typical cities would be the responsibility of the municipal government. Another source of difficulty in the detailed plan process is that the Municipal requirement that 40 per cent of land be set aside for public purposes ('confiscating land for your benefit') is foreign to Palestinian society. This concept becomes even more problematic when it is being done not by your own people, but by a municipal government seen more as an occupier than overseer. What is a logistical challenge in 'normal' circumstances then becomes a 'political challenge' in such a contested urban situation.

The difficulties of detailed planning, even in cases where neighbourhood outline plans allow development, adds an additional and more opaque layer of Israeli restrictions on Arab development, over and above the more transparent restrictive zoning of the outline plans. The restrictions imposed through outline plans, zoning, and re-parcellation requirements produce radically different patterns in terms of building permits issued. In one detailed analysis of the 2005–2009 period, 81 per cent of building permits issued by the Municipality were for West Jerusalem and Israeli neighbourhoods in East Jerusalem compared to only 19 per cent issued in Arab East Jerusalem (Bimkom, 2014). In terms of housing units allowed by these building permits, only 13 per cent of housing units allowed were in Arab East Jerusalem.[14] While 85 per cent of building permit requests were approved in Israeli parts of the city, 56 per cent of permit requests (603 of 1,087 requests) were granted in Arab East Jerusalem. Even this is an overstatement of the Arab ability to get building permission because an additional almost 500 building permit requests in Arab East Jerusalem were closed before they reached the review process.

Examination of the Municipality planning system across its full spectrum – from the citywide Master Plan to neighbourhood outline plans to detailed plans and the re-parcellation process – clearly reveals the existence of multiple layers of obstacles facing the Arab community that cumulatively results in the strong improbability, if not near impossibility, of Arab development occurring at a level anywhere near what is needed to meet natural demographic growth projections. 'There is not a lack of planning in Arab East Jerusalem, but rather too much planning', states Efrat Cohen-Bar (Planner, Bimkom, interview, 21 January 2016). There exist urban plans for Arab East Jerusalem that are theoretically meant to guide and support future Arab development but, in reality and impact, they are used by Israeli authorities instead to restrict and control Arab development. 'Israel does planning in the language of planning, but we all know that demographic goals are underlying', laments Cohen-Bar. Neighbourhood outline plans that would in typical cities support natural growth and healthy communities, instead, contain myriad stipulations that render the plans unrealizable. Facing the full spectrum of the restrictive Israeli planning system, residents of Arab East Jerusalem are 'trapped in a perpetual state of planning-without-building' (Bimkom, 2014, p. 11). Even in Arab neighbourhoods with a community plan, 'permits are not happening due to either a lack of trust or the fact that our plans do not fit their situation' (Ari Binyamin, Municipality Planner, interview, 16 December 2015). Looking back at the decades of Municipality policies regarding Arab East Jerusalem, Binyamin laments, 'it seems like we believe that if we ignore them, they will disappear; their needs are not part of the equation whatsoever'.

The effect of decades of hegemonic planning applied to Arab East Jerusalem means not only constraints on housing supply but also impoverished communities in terms of urban services and facilities. According to data reported in UN-HABITAT

(2015), there is one kilometre of sewage capacity per 2,800 residents in East Jerusalem compared to one kilometre per 740 persons in West Jerusalem. In East Jerusalem, there is one public park per 6,500 residents compared to one park per 512 persons in the West. There is one kilometre of paved roads per 2,448 residents in East Jerusalem; in the West, there is one kilometre of paved roads per 710 residents. There is one library per 146,000 East Jerusalemites and one library per 19,700 West Jerusalemites. Under spending by the Municipality in East Jerusalem is clear, with between 7 and 11 per cent of the city budget allocated to the eastern Arab sector (UN-HABITAT, 2015; Margalit, 2014). In terms of the average budget for school education, West Jerusalem schools receive twice as much spending per student as East Jerusalem schools.

## The Power of Israeli Planning

The power of the Israeli planning system in Jerusalem to construct these inequalities lies in its near invisibility. Military actions by Israel are obvious but planning decisions take place on the 5th floor of the Municipality building (Haim Yacobi, Professor, Ben Gurion University, interview, 29 October 2015). Yet, these planning decisions have far reaching effects on the built landscape and inter-group disparities. Israeli planning constitutes a restrictive mechanism that displaces and disempowers Palestinian Jerusalemites. Implemented through a dizzying array of restrictive techniques and opaque obstacles, planning constitutes a form of structural violence that creates the enduring structure of an unequal city.

*The engine driving Israeli people is survival.*

Tuvia Tunenbom, 2015, p. 96

Planners who I spoke with privately acknowledged the political elements of their professional life. One interviewee stated that, 'the political agenda is a wall I face. Sometimes I can overcome it; often I can't. But it's always there, it's everywhere – at all layers' (Ari Binyamin, Municipality Planner, interview, 16 December 2015). He further states that 'when you have a political agenda driving things, you don't understand in the Arab parts of the city the person for whom he really is'. He emphasizes that 'there is not a push from the political level to deal with the issues of Arab Jerusalem and we have many ways of blocking development there'. This planner points to another major obstacle when the Municipality tries to plan Arab neighbourhoods. There exists 'a lack of faith and trust. Without trust, you can't really talk. Without the ability to talk, you can't understand their needs. Without this understanding, you can't plan accordingly'. A planner with significant historic experience in the Municipality summarizes the situation – 'you cannot deny that there is political guidance that puts obstacles to development in East Jerusalem' (Israel Kimhi, interview, 3 December 2015).

Another planner laments the disconnection between Israeli bureaucracy and the Arab community, the lack of political initiative regarding planning for Arab East Jerusalem, and the acceptance by Municipality planners that Israeli plans that clearly do not fit Arab community realities will remain unimplemented (Osnat Post, Former Head of Planning Department and City Engineer, Municipality of Jerusalem, interview, 28 October 2015).

In contrast to such acknowledgement of the political context of Jerusalem planning, planners in public settings are prone to using a disingenuous 'mask' of technicality and neutrality. Embedded in the Israeli system, there is reliance on a mind-numbing planning and regulatory vocabulary full of obfuscation and 'double speak'. The existence of plans for Arab East Jerusalem enables the Municipality and government to say 'yes, we have plans' as a line of defence, but in reality there is a tremendous, politically-inspired mismatch between Israeli planning tools and the objective needs of Arab residents and communities.

Meir Turgeman is Deputy Mayor of Jerusalem and Chair of the Local Planning and Building Committee. In a public discussion that involved me and four other panellists (Van Leer Institute, 11 January 2016), his public posture exemplifies well the Municipality public narrative. Taking issue of criticism from the panellists and audience, Turgeman observed the following:

- 'I'm not saying there isn't a gap, but we are trying to reduce it through our actions everyday.'
- 'Every community council in the Arab neighbourhood that works with the Municipality gets services.'
- 'I would like to give them services, but when we send an inspector into their neighbourhood they are subject to be injured and even killed. Then what are we to do?'
- 'Local people are not taking responsibility for their own quality of neighbourhood life. "Two states for two people" is not a response we can work with.'
- 'I differentiate between the Municipality and the Government. I take no responsibility for what the Government does in Jerusalem.'

Within this set of comments we see a compartmentalization of Municipality duties, a blaming of others who are unwilling to engage constructively, and, most importantly, a consideration of his duties independent of the larger political and historic context that strongly frames any interaction between Municipality and Arab residents of Jerusalem. Turgeman may believe everything he is saying and may feel he is doing his best in a difficult situation, but without consideration of the larger political context, his work is ineffective and even irrelevant. At the same time, his narrative positioning allows him freedom of conscience and personal integrity. Whereas Israeli officials like Turgeman tend to talk about trying to address specific Arab needs, many Arab Jerusalemites are likely to be operating in a fundamentally different political frame of reference, one that emphasizes systemic historic injustices and larger political rights and claims.[15]

Positioned within a dominant societal position, a number of Israeli interviewees – across the political spectrum – demonstrated what I call the 'privilege of the hegemon'. The lens and advantage of the superior position enables Israelis to focus on practical and functional considerations of conflict, issues which sidestep or bypass entirely more fundamental issues of rights and sovereignty. This space of freedom of the dominant power facilitates a space of reasoning, rationalization, and practicality not enjoyed by the hamstrung disadvantaged group. Daniel Tirza, the architect of the separation barrier, focuses on the proper location of the barrier 'in the right way so people on the ground can live with it' (interview, 11 November 2015). There is emphasis on the practical micro-scale issues of barrier placement at specific locations, while consideration of the political implications is de-emphasized. This practical focus facilitates a feeling of providing humanitarian support to the subordinate group and provides both a rationalization and legitimation. The elephant in the room – the existence of the separation barrier itself in contested territory – is an assumed reality. Shlomo Hasson, a 'centrist-pragmatist' who has worked with Palestinians for over 20 years, is not immune to the privileges bestowed upon the hegemon. In considering possible political solutions to the conflict, he speaks often at an abstract, pragmatic-functional, and semi-hopeful level (Hasson, Director, Shasha Center for Strategic Studies, interview, 30 November 2015). This type of argumentation stands in contrast to the often despairing assessments of the situation by Palestinian interviewees who emphasize more basic issues of rights, sovereignty, and dignity.

## *Operating within the Israeli Planning Labyrinth*

Those who seek to plan and build for the Arab community face constant and debilitating obstructions imposed by the Israeli planning and regulatory regime. Senan Abdelqader is an Israeli Arab architect who has worked for years trying to present plans to the Municipality that fit the character of Arab development and the needs and aspirations of Palestinians living in the city. He has met with constant delays and postponements from the Municipality – what he labels the 'extreme Israelization and negating of place for Arabs'. 'To be stuck in Jerusalem as an Arab architect or planner is simply suicide', Abdelqader laments, 'it is agreeing to enter the labyrinth and sinkhole' of the Israeli planning and regulatory system (Zandberg, 2015). Long-time Jerusalem observer Mahdi Abdul Hadi (Palestinian Academic Society for the Study of International Affairs, interview, 26 October 2015) describes the difficulties of 'struggling with the system that has been imposed upon you'. A private sector Arab planner with extensive plan-making experience similarly characterizes his work as 'working within the system against the system' (Rassem Khamaisi, Professor, University of Haifa, interview, 29 November 2015).

The development within Arab society of planning capacity that could effectively work within, and against, the Israeli hegemonic project has been partial. Rami Nasrallah is head of the International Peace and Cooperation Center (IPCC), a nongovernmental organization in East Jerusalem which has challenged Israel's urban policies over the past two decades by creating Arab community plans. He points to a basic dilemma faced by Arab society – 'for Palestinians, political rights are proclaimed first and then planning would come after. But for Israelis, planning has always been used as a political instrument. Palestinian leaders see planning as compromising political demands and this explains our failure to develop a parallel agenda of planning'. In their work, IPCC and Nasrallah constantly face the tight zoning restrictions for areas having outline plans, and the difficulty of development outside plan areas restricted by open space designations. To date, Israel has not approved any of the community plans developed by the IPCC. Nasrallah faces difficulties within Arab communities too, the residents of which are more accustomed to incremental, organic growth and view the re-parcellation requirements dealing with land set aside for community facilities as 'confiscation' and 'tools of the colonizer' (Rami Nasrallah, interview, 18 October 2015). In confronting the Municipality with IPCC-assisted community plans, the Municipality comes to Nasrallah with technical requirements that need to be met, 'but we don't run away, we stay. We come with a map and a plan, they can reject it, but we are there, it's just not reactive'. Nasrallah states that working with the Israeli system does not mean that IPCC accepts such control, but rather his efforts are aimed at enhancing Arab responsibility within their own spaces. Nasrallah (interview) recalls that a city engineer once said to him, 'you used to come at us with "occupation, occupation" and we could say "the hell with you". Now you are coming with maps and staying'. Although not successful in having Arab community plans adopted by the Municipality, planning by IPCC makes Arabs more visible within Israel's hegemonic project.

At times, Israeli nongovernmental organizations have attempted to help with planning for Jerusalem Arab neighbourhoods. One effort was in the neighbourhood of Issawiya and involved Bimkom, an Israeli non-profit organization formed in 1999 by a group of planners and architects in order to strengthen democracy and human rights in the field of planning. This effort faced difficulty in gaining public participation by Arab residents in plan-making, especially problematic when an Israeli NGO is involved (Galit Cohen-Blankshtain, Senior Lecturer, Hebrew University, interview, 24 November 2015; Malka Greenberg Raanan, Doctoral Candidate, Hebrew University, interview, 30 November 2015). 'When you work with the "other"', you tend to think of them as unified but in actuality they are quite fragmented', observes Cohen-Blankshtain. In its efforts at gaining genuine and full participation, Bimkom planners frequently needed to rely on traditional neighbourhood leaders who did not always have community support behind them. In addition, although Bimkom tried to make it 'all about planning considerations and not about politics', when Israeli NGOs become involved, 'the process becomes politicized and it moves to the next level of contestation' (Cohen-Blankshtain, interview). In the end, despite many years of plan-making, the Bimkom-assisted plan for Issawiya was rejected by the Municipality. A plan subsequently formulated by the Municipality drew tight limits on outward expansion of the community and this effort also collapsed amid local violence. The plan that currently exists for the community remains non-statutory and not sufficient for the issuance of building permits. More recently, the Municipality has given land to the national government for the proposed creation of a 'Slopes of Mount of Olives' National Park, which would restrict development of substantial amounts of land adjacent to Issawiya.[16]

A further illustration of the tension between Arab development aspirations and the Israeli hegemonic planning programme are privately initiated detailed plans allowed by Amendment 43 to the Planning and Building Law passed in 1995. This was a 'veritable revolution' because until that time only public bodies were entitled to initiate detailed plans (Bimkom, 2014, p. 45). While the 'spot-zoning' amendment to the planning and building law originally resulted from pressures to promote free-market logic in urban planning practices, it unwittingly opened up the possibility for excluded and subordinated residents to pursue a new course of action. Independent plans initiated in Arab East Jerusalem grew significantly, from three in 1994 to 163 in 2011 (Braier, 2013). Although the magnitude of these plans remained marginal compared to need, Braier (2013, p. 2702) observed that putting forth these plans 'destabilizes the proclaimed neutrality of the planning committee since it exposes the ethno-national logic under which the committee operates' and represents a 'quiet encroachment on the bureaucratic apparatus' (p. 2713). This slight opening in the hegemonic planning project also led to creation by Israel of new restrictions that subsequently tightened this opening. In particular, the Jerusalem 2000 Master Plan required that new detailed plans must encompass entire expansion areas, mapped as polygons. This size requirement in effect limited Arab-initiated independent plans because most applicants had neither the resources nor community buy-in to produce such expansive plans (Bimkom, 2014). As residents of the city, Arabs theoretically have two venues for participation – a political channel that is basically closed to Arab Jerusalem residents due to their collective boycotting of municipal elections they deem illegitimate, and a planning channel which can provide an arena of contestation over spatial existence (Braier, 2013; Cohen-Blankshtain, interview, 24 November 2015). The phenomenon of Arab-initiated detailed plans shows both how this arena of contestation can be utilized if provided an opportunity and also how the hegemonic planning project reacts to such openings by imposing additional levels of obstruction.

The characteristics of Israel's hegemonic approach to Jerusalem in 2016 – deeply ingrained in its planning and municipal governance system – are similar to what I observed in 1994 and elicit despair and frustration over the future of a genuinely shared and less violent Jerusalem. Israel's efforts to maintain tight control over Arab East Jerusalem is conspicuous across multiple data points.[17] Whereas the population of Arabs in the city is 37 per cent, their housing opportunities are restricted to only 8 per cent of the city, they receive only about 10 per cent of city spending, and they were granted only 13 per cent of all housing units allowed in the city. Far from being a city where all residents – irrespective of ethnic and religious background – have equality of opportunity in terms of quality of life, Jerusalem instead is an asymmetric, divided city that reflects and reinforces larger power imbalances between Israel and Palestine.

*Between memory and dream, there is no here and now.*

Ari Shavit, 2013, p. 14

[There is the urgent need to] *prevent entrenching a one-state reality of perpetual occupation and conflict that is incompatible with realizing the national aspirations of both peoples.*

Middle East Quartet, July 2016, p. 2

## Complexities and Contradictions in the Hegemonic Project

One witnesses in 2016, however, not just a continuation and deepening of hegemonic practices used by Israel since 1967. On the one hand, there are new features on the ground and newer types of hegemonic action since 1994 intended to solidify Israeli control over Jerusalem. But on the other hand, there are also new urban and spatial phenomena afoot that are creating greater complexities and contradictions in the urban landscape that are not fully consistent with Israel's project of political control. In this section, I delve into four more recent features of the Jerusalem landscape – the separation barrier, micro-penetration of Jewish settler activity in the core of the city, unlicensed Arab housing development, and the growing economic intrusion of Arabs into Jewish spaces. The net effect of these features paints a complex picture of Jerusalem today, one that neither fully supports Israel's hegemonic control nor promotes genuine sharing of the city but rather increases the impossibility of managing the city as it is currently politically organized.

### The Separation Barrier

*Nobody in government wanted to get into the details of the wall; I'm just in the Army – a colonel – not a Minister, and I drew the borders of Israel.*

Daniel Tirza, Director of Separation Barrier Planning Team, interview, 11 November 2015

50  Trajectories of Conflict and Peace

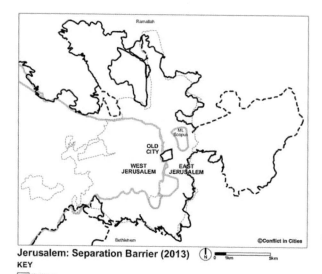

**Jerusalem: Separation Barrier (2013)**
**KEY**
- Green Line, 1949-67
- Israeli Municipal Boundary
- Separation Barrier (Built & Under Construction)
- Separation Barrier (Planned)

Figure 2.5. Israeli separation barrier and Jerusalem. (*Source*: Dumper, 2014, p. 25)

Figures 2.6, 2.7, 2.8 and 2.9. Jerusalem separation barrier.

Jerusalem I: Urban Spatial Changes amid Political Impasse  51

Figure 2.7

Figure 2.8

Figure 2.9

The most visible feature on the landscape today is the imposing separation barrier. This barrier was built in the name of Israeli security but in all likelihood is just as much, if not more, a political line – a type of physical manipulation of territory to solidify future Israeli claims of political control. The barrier cuts off thousands of Palestinians from the city and even cuts into Israel's designated Jerusalem municipal space in a few areas. With thirteen obstructive and heavily-guarded checkpoints in the Jerusalem barrier, it constitutes fortified space by Israel and exposes Israel's capacity and willingness, blatantly and visibly, to manipulate space in the name of control. This raw edge of the barrier is significantly more obvious than the more submerged layers of planning control and manipulation carried out since 1967.

The Israeli 'separation barrier' will consist of a planned 436 miles (702 km) dividing Israeli proper (and more) from the West Bank. The partition is characterized by 25 foot (7.6 m) concrete slabs, electronic fences, barbed wire, radar, cameras, deep trenches, observation posts and patrol roads (Weizman, 2007). With about 62 per cent of it completed as of 2013 and another 10 per cent under construction, only 15 per cent of the wall's length is on the 'green line' that politically demarcates the Israeli state from the West Bank. The remainder is or will be east of the green line and absorbs portions of the West Bank. More than 9 per cent of the internationally disputed West Bank territory (including East Jerusalem) is *de facto* attached to Israel by putting it west of the wall. The wall's placement is estimated to absorb about 85 per cent of the Jewish settlers currently living in the West Bank, including East Jerusalem (OCHAOPT, 2013).

In the Jerusalem urban region specifically, the barrier is over 40 miles (64 km) long and more than 97 per cent of its route does not follow the 'green line' (International Peace and Cooperation Center, 2007). Through the tactical placement of the barrier in the urban region, Israel is partitioning from the city: (1) Arab neighbourhoods currently within the Israeli-defined municipal borders which are now on the 'West Bank' side of the barrier, and (2) Palestinian villages functionally connected to the Jerusalem urban system, while at the same time (3) *de facto* annexing into the city three large Jewish residential blocs built on occupied Palestinian territory east, north, and south of municipal borders. The barrier functionally severs from the city (by placing them east of the barrier or enclaving them within barriers) between 70,000 and 100,000 Palestinians who presently live within municipal Jerusalem (Nadav Shragai, interview, 17 December 2015). Also separated from Jerusalem are another estimated 145,000 Palestinians who have historic ties to the urban centre and who are presently living in villages adjacent to Israel's Jerusalem municipal border (OCHAOPT, 2011).

The separation barrier began construction in 2003 for the stated purpose of security amid horrific violence and loss of Jewish life during the second Intifada. From 2000 to 2004, there were hundreds of attacks by Palestinians on Israeli Jews in Jerusalem, killing 210 people and wounding many more (Shragai, 2015). According to Bhavnani *et al.* (2013), there were 337 incidents of violence in the city from 2001 to 2004, occurring in over two-thirds of Jerusalem's neighbourhoods. The majority of events occurred along the boundary separating Jewish West from Arab East Jerusalem. This magnitude of violence in the early 2000s constituted a threat to the existential daily life of Jews in Jerusalem and in Israel and eventually forced Israel to take action to increase security, despite qualms by nationalist Israelis that the barrier would set a bad precedent in dividing the Israel/Palestine region.[18] 'Israel has been in a state of siege since the second Intifada', observes Eitay Mack (Human Rights Lawyer, presentation, 18 January 2016).[19]

Daniel Tirza is a retired colonel in the Israeli army and was commander of paratrooper units for 30 years. He describes the evolution of thinking regarding the barrier. As terror attacks increased in the early 2000s, there were growing public calls to separate the two sides. However, from 2000 to 2002 the government remained hesitant to act amid different views of where the barrier should be built. By March 2002, a month when 128 Israelis were killed in attacks, the government of Prime Minister Sharon said enough and granted the Army permission to design the barrier. Tirza led a group of thirty-two representatives from all government ministries who deliberated about 'how to do it in the right way so people on the ground can live with it' (interview, 11 November 2015).

There was some consideration of building the barrier along the 'green line' but the team did not regard it a 'holy line' of political demarcation but rather as a temporary ceasefire line. In addition, building the barrier along the green line would locate it along valleys which is not good from a security perspective; 'you always want the high ground'. In the Jerusalem area, it was clear to the team that the barrier needed to separate Ramallah and Bethlehem from Jerusalem. Within Jerusalem, Tirza's team first thought of building the barrier to divide Jews from Arabs within the city; this was consistent with the idea that the barrier was for security and not broader purposes of political demarcation. There was also thought of building it along the Israeli municipal border of the city but this line was also deemed to be arbitrary. In the end, the barrier was built to more expansively take in the three large settlement blocs mentioned above because the government wanted to protect them. Whereas the green line and the municipal border were viewed as abstract lines on a map, the barrier was conceptualized by the team as a route which more realistically reflected the realities on the ground. At the same time, Tirza emphasizes that in the drawing of the route that there was always to be the balancing of Israel's security needs with the rights of people on the ground. Tirza proudly recalls how he lost only five of the 124 petitions against the barrier route lodged by Palestinians in the Israeli Supreme Court.

In a 2004 Advisory Opinion, the International Court of Justice (ICJ) established that the sections of the barrier which run inside the West Bank, including East Jerusalem, together with the associated gate and permit regime, violate Israel's obligations under international law. The ICJ called on Israel to cease construction of the barrier, dismantle sections already completed, and repeal all legislative measures related to the barrier. Israel has not done any of these, and Israeli officials and policymakers responded to criticism of the barrier by pointing out that it was built for security reasons. At this level of argument, the wall is logical. Palestinian suicide and other bombing attacks against Israelis are down since the construction of the separation barrier began. From 2000 to 2004, there were 132 such attacks in Israel killing 502 individuals, while from 2005 to December 2011, there were 18 attacks killing 59 individuals (Israel Ministry of Foreign Affairs, 2011). In the Jerusalem urban region, there was a period of relative calm from 2004 until 2014. Yet, this portrayal of the barrier's positive impact on security may be overstated. The downtick in violence corresponded with dynamics in addition to the presence of the barrier. Mahmoud Abbas had succeeded Yasser Arafat on his death in 2004 and took a different approach to Palestinian terror violence, major sectors of the Fatah organization were cleared out of areas near Jerusalem (such as Beit Jala) by the Israel Defense Forces (IDF), and the IDF gained better intelligence in Palestinian areas of the West Bank. In addition, the barrier itself may not be restricting Arab mobility

Figure 2.10. Checkpoint 300 between Bethlehem and Jerusalem.

into Jerusalem as much as security experts expected. One source cites that between January and March 2013 at least 14,000 Arabs who are without required permits were able to smuggle themselves each day into Jerusalem seeking work (OCHAOPT, 2013). The IDF reports that along the entire barrier length about 50,000 Palestinians enter Israel illegally every day through gaps in it (Lis, 2016). Further, the security barrier did not appear able to stop the wave of violence that gripped Jerusalem starting October 2015. As of March 2016, 44 per cent of Palestinian attackers within the green line were illegal residents (Lis, 2016).

> Yesterday afternoon I'm in Tel Aviv with a retired Brigadier General from the Israeli Army. This morning I am with the Foreign Policy Advisor for the leading Palestinian political party of Fatah. What a difference a day makes – and only 38 miles.

While the Israeli government's stated primary purpose in building the barrier was to increase security, the location of the barrier led many of those I interviewed to consider it a political as much as a security barrier. In this view, the barrier constitutes, in the name of security, a type of physical manipulation of territory that strengthens future Israeli political claims over expanded territory beyond the historic 'green line'. Moshe Amirav, a Primary Advisor during the Camp David negotiations in 2000, calls it a 'political line that symbolizes frustration and defeat' (interview, 12 November 2015). Amir Cheshin, Former Advisor to Jerusalem Mayor, states, 'I have no doubt that the barrier is a political line' (interview, 17 November 2015). And Kareem Jubran, Field Research Director for the B'Tselem nongovernmental organization, notes that with demographic growth pressure by Arabs 'only by building a wall that excludes could Israel re-rig the demographic ratio to what they want' (interview, 26 November 2015). The barrier was built around Jerusalem in such a way that it has consolidated Israel's hold on the city and region, while fragmenting Palestinian life and forcing many Palestinians to emigrate. Even to someone who describes himself as a political centre-right pragmatist, there is recognition that the barrier 'is a political, demographic, and economic wall and that the claim that it is a security barrier was for international audiences' (Noam Shoval, Professor, Hebrew University, interview, 15 October 2015).

> *What allows people not to see? It is fascinating the tools we develop that allow us not to see.*
> Meir Kraus, Director, Jerusalem Institute for Israel Studies, interview, 27 January 2016

> *The separation barrier represents the 'formalization of madness'.*
> Oded Lowenheim, Senior Lecturer, Hebrew University, interview, 17 January 2016

Oded Lowenheim for many years biked each morning for about 7 miles (11 km) along the barrier route from his residence in northwest Jerusalem to the Hebrew University campus in the northeastern part of the city. He recounts his treks in the book, *The Politics of the Trail*. He notes the seemingly arbitrary character of the barrier route as nationalism and ideology intruded into everyday life. Nonetheless, he witnessed the barrier as having significant and debilitating impacts on the daily life of Palestinians. 'The presence of the barrier incriminates you when you are near it, creating layers of meaning that were not there before', he describes (interview, 17 January 2016). Characterized by fence, road, ditch, and patrolled by Israeli security forces, the barrier 'militarizes the place and creates the feeling of it being a dangerous place to avoid'. While Jewish residents in nearby neighbourhoods practice 'blind sight' regarding Arab villages just on the other side of the barrier, Palestinian life is substantially disrupted. Whereas before the barrier Arab workers could walk easily to nearby Jewish neighbourhoods to perform often menial jobs, now they must go to a gate and wait to be escorted across by Jewish employers. Lowenheim once journeyed across the barrier to the Arab village of Beit Surak. To get back to Jerusalem, he needed to take the common route of Arabs into Jerusalem, consisting of a 90 minute circuitous journey through multiple roads that circumvent Jewish-only roads, tunnels, and then through the Qalandia checkpoint in north Jerusalem. Of taking this route he said, 'you feel like what it is to be a Palestinian'. After years of trekking this landscape of pain and scars, Lowenheim no longer bikes the route – it is too much a psychological burden, which he cannot again confront.

Arab villages have gone through radical upheavals in price of land, residence, and travel due to the separation barrier. The 're-topology' of Jerusalem caused by the barrier constituted both a substantial relocation and loss of value away from Palestinian individuals and economy (Savitch and Garb, 2006, p. 153). Israeli policies of separation and exclusion have caused 'warehousing of Palestinian residents in the city and the abandonment of neighbourhoods' (Dumper and Pullan, 2010, p. 1). For Palestinians, a 2004 survey of over 1,200 adults in the Jerusalem urban region documented widespread adverse impacts of the barrier (Brooks *et al*., 2007). Thirty-five per cent of respondents reported experiencing negative economic effects due to the barrier; nearly 60 per cent experience medium or high difficulty in obtaining basic health or education services due to the barrier; and over 46 per cent say the barrier separates them from immediate family. Such walled separation is also producing a hardening of political attitudes. More than 95 per cent of Palestinians surveyed stated that the barrier has deteriorated the political environment and escalated conflict. And, during this time, Palestinian leaders appear to have become more resistant to a two-state solution that they believed in for years, amidst a visceral and deep disillusionment with the peace process (International Crisis Group, 2010).

At times, Israeli actions cause consequences that work against their own political goals of strengthening control of Jerusalem. The location of the separation barrier in the northeastern area of Kafr Aqab and in the eastern area of the Shuafat refugee camp is an example of this conundrum. In these areas, the barrier puts the Jerusalem neighbourhoods of Shuafat refugee camp[20] and Kafr Aqab that are *within* the municipal limits *outside* the wall. This has paradoxically (from Israel's perspective) stimulated development in these places. This is so because planning and building the separation barrier had threatened Palestinians in the urban region with the potential loss of their Jerusalem residency status. Consequently, Kafr Aqab has become the Jerusalem address for those who live in Ramallah; by paying property taxes (*arnona*) in Kafr Aqab, these residents can maintain residency in the city (Fouad Hallak, Policy Advisor, Negotiations Support Unit, PLO, interview, 7 December 2015). From 2006 to 2010,

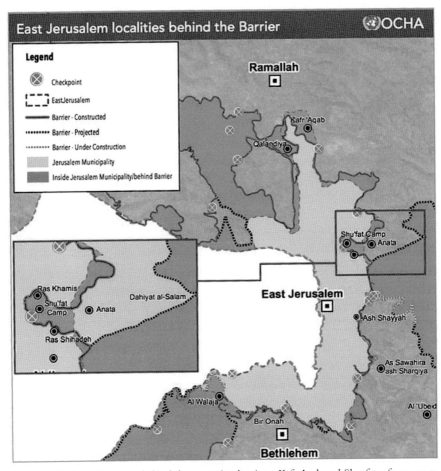

Figure 2.11. Jerusalem areas behind the separation barrier – Kafr Aqab and Shuafat refugee camp. (*Source*: United Nations Office for the Coordination of Humanitarian Affairs, Occupied Palestinian Territory, *Monthly Humanitarian Bulletin*, July 2016)

20 per cent of all recorded residential construction in Arab East Jerusalem took place in Kafr Aqab (Jerusalem Institute for Israel Studies, 2012, table X/14). By 2011, of fifteen Arab neighbourhoods, Kafr Aqab had the second greatest area of square metres of built space (Jerusalem Institute for Israel Studies 2012, tables X/16, X/18). In the first three quarters of 2012, the number of building starts in the Kafr Aqab area accounted for 83 per cent of the total number of building starts in the entire city of Jerusalem. At the beginning of 2013, some 1,282 new apartments were nearing completion, all in high-rise buildings (Ir Amim, 2015). Estimates are that 70,000–100,000 residents now live in Kafr Aqab and Shuafat refugee camp areas within the city but outside the wall (Israel Kimhi, interview, 3 December 2015). Up to 60,000 residents are 'holders of Jerusalem identity cards' which allow them access to the city.[21]

Palestinians have been able to build extensively in these two areas, taking advantage of the fact that since the barrier's construction, the Municipality has abandoned governance in Kafr Aqab and Shuafat refugee camp areas, leading to a wild-wild west atmosphere of unregulated growth (Ir Amim, 2015). As Palestinians living outside city borders have purchased properties in these largely unregulated neighbourhoods in order to maintain Jerusalem residency, this counters Israel's hegemonic demographic mission to weaken the official Arab population count of Jerusalem residents. Further, the migration of Palestinians without official residency status into these areas has produced two dense Arab settlement nodes which are officially within the city.

Figure 2.12.  Shuafat refugee camp area.

Figure 2.13. Kafr Aqab.

In-migration of Arabs caused by the threat of being outside the barrier has increased the density of Arab settlement elsewhere in the city, driven up housing prices, and led some Arabs to migrate into Jewish neighbourhoods in the north, such as Neve Yaakov and Pisgat Zeev. By putting the separation barrier inside the Municipality border in these two locations, Israel's own actions have created consequences that are contrary to their political goals of weakening the Palestinian presence in the city as a path towards protecting Israeli political control.

The explosively growing Kafr Aqab and Shuafat camp areas are also places of extreme neglect, with roads, schools, parks and infrastructure either in an extremely dilapidated condition or non-existent. With no formal institutions governing the area and the Palestinian National Authority disallowed by Israel from operating within the Municipality, under-resourced local popular committees manage the Shuafat refugee camp area along with five civic organizations (Adel Abu Zneid, Member of Fatah Committee in Jerusalem, interview, 27 October 2015). Amidst such a void, Hamas is gaining footholds in the area, particularly within the refugee camp itself. 'We always think we are the smartest people in the room', observes Gillad Rosen (Senior Lecturer, Hebrew University, interview, 11 October 2015), 'but we have manipulated ourselves by creating a problematic "internal frontier" within the city'. Amir Cheshin (Arab Advisor to the Mayor 1984–1994, interview, 17 November 2015) agrees, observing that 'we have shot ourselves in the leg by building the wall inside the city'.

*Each of us needs to see our 'blind spot'; it doesn't matter how much 'truth' you have.*
Isaac Yerushalmi, Co-director, Center for Regional Engagement,
interview, 14 October 2015

*Since we were born, we learned to look and not see parts of Arab Jerusalem.*
Efrat Cohen-Bar, Planner, Bimkom,
interview, 21 January 2016

The separation barrier, intended to cement Israeli control, has instead created unintended consequences for Israel. The specific route of the barrier in the Jerusalem region has had problematic and destabilizing impacts that create complexities in Israel's hegemonic project. Kimhi (interview) takes issue with the spatial consequences to Israel: 'we have put a fence around ourselves and have come back to the pre-1967 situation where Jerusalem is at the end of a corridor, something we tried so hard to overcome after 1967'. Danny Seidemann, Lawyer and Jerusalem expert, views the building of the barrier as 'corking a volcano' having inevitable negative consequences (interview, 1 February 2016). He views barrier building as 'problematic and we are paying now for it, including violence'. The barrier in the Jerusalem region represents an attempt by Israel to consolidate and protect its past settlement building close to the city. It is a project which seeks the unlikely reconciliation of the dual and conflicting imperatives of continued territorial expansion, on the one hand, and the need to protect and consolidate its territorial advances, on the other.

Figure 2.14. Unseeing – at Damascus Gate, Old City Jerusalem.

> **To Unsee the Other**
>
> To unsee the other
> Is a more active disengagement than passively not paying attention
>
> The lens directed at the angle of the other excludes it from view
> Rather than scanning the wider horizon and focusing elsewhere
>
> It is structured neglect rather than considered dismissal
> Premeditated rather than contemporaneous
>
> Unseeing removes the unbearable burden of guilt, of humiliation, of history
> It simplifies and extracts; it keeps the enemy at bay
>
> The gaze of surveillance does not add sight
> But rather a military-security layer through which those excluded become suspect
>
> For the superior, unseeing validates dominance
> For the subordinate, it demarcates a space of dignity
>
> With lack of sight, we gain urban anonymity and illusion of privacy
> Lost is the shared enterprise through which we connect with the other

## *Jewish Settler Micro-Penetration in the City's Core*

Also emergent since 1994 is the increasing Jewish settler penetration of Arab neighbourhoods in and near the Old City. This 'colonial acupuncture' is raising new fault-lines and tension points within inner and sensitive parts of the city (Haim Yacobi, Professor, Ben Gurion University, interview, 29 October 2015). Jewish settler organizations are increasingly engaged in dynamics of territoriality and radicalization in the Old City, 'Holy Basin', and within the existing inner urban fabric of Arab East Jerusalem. The macro-scale forces of nationalism (religious-nationalist ideologies, private religious organizations, government institutions) are intensifying their influence on the micro-scale dynamics of neighbourhoods, streets, religious sites, and archaeological projects. There is the ongoing proliferation of religious and quasi-religious activities and sites by Jewish settler groups linked to national and religious struggles in the city. New religious sites are actively refiguring sacred Jerusalem, radicalization amid sacrality is vigorous and intense, and the core of the Holy City is increasingly becoming an ever-present flashpoint for conflict and violence.

These partisan activities are creating interfaces, psychological fault-lines, and frontiers that pulse through everyday life, generated by sacred epicentres but reverberating outwards along the urban topographies of everyday, secular spaces. Such polarization within the city is not static, but actively manufactured and fabricated. Fault-lines and frontiers are multiplied and intensified by actors through dynamics of radicalization such as land seizures, creation of new religious/sacred sites with dubious and contested legitimacy, politicization of parklands and tourism, and manipulation of archaeological and historical narratives (Pullan et al., 2013). Archaeology is sacralized to further historic claims, religion is anaesthetized to appeal to, and capture, specific audiences, and the sacrality of religion is intertwined with the everyday life of the city (Emek Shaveh, 2015).

Jewish settler organizations are increasingly carving out and extending Jewish versions of contested histories. One example of this manipulation is the establishment of the 'City of David' archaeological park intruding upon the Palestinian village of Silwan in Jerusalem. Managed by a settler organization, David's City's 'purist neo-biblical landscape urbanism, heavy-handed security apparatus and various forms of physical and symbolic dispossession' are creating a deeply antagonizing topography, increasing tension and the potential for violence (Pullan et al., 2013, p. 93). The City of David is an archaeological site of ancient Jerusalem. It is located beneath the Arab neighbourhood of Wadi Hilweh and near the southern city walls of Old Jerusalem. One of the most intensively excavated sites in the wider region, the area is highly controversial because it intrudes on the neighbourhood of Silwan, a predominantly Arab neighbourhood of Jerusalem. Within the City of David compound, Jews now form the majority of the population. A nongovernmental Jewish settler organization, Elad Ir David, has taken the lead in both the archaeological activities and in facilitating the movement of Jewish residents into the area. Elad Ir David operates in a semi-autonomous institutional space, at times operating with support from the Israel government and at other times operating in the absence of the state.

Lea Lipshitz, a guide for Elad Ir David, provides an extensive three hour tour of the City of David to a group of Jewish visitors and new residents (1 November 2015). I feel suddenly that I am part of the Jewish nation as she establishes that each of us as Jews (which I am not) is 'connected in some way' to Jerusalem. We sit for prolonged periods of time along the various stops of the journey as Lea provides religious Torah-based morality and creates a sense of family among those on tour – togetherness and emotional bonding – akin to talking behind closed doors in the comfort of a living room. Private Israeli security personnel are ever-present along the path to protect and keep watch over us. 'I won't talk about politics', Lea states, and then she proceeds to make a joke that the United Nations building we see atop the promenade is one place 'we haven't yet conquered'. The presentation is robustly partisan – the Arabs in the neighbourhood and across the Kidron Valley in the main part of Silwan are barely mentioned. Lea describes the Jewish settlers who live in the City of David area and across Kidron Valley in guarded and monitored enclaves as 'really something' in giving up the comfortable life for what they care about – establishing Jewish presence in this historic area. 'Can you imagine living where you have to have security, soldiers, cameras and where it is hard to park and shop?' Lea asks, as she proudly points across the valley to Israeli flags atop settlers' houses in Silwan and Mount of Olives. The tour ends with a deep contemplation by Lea about what it means to be Jewish in this world of hostility and anger. Members of the tour depart with warm feelings of connectedness and spirit. I leave uneasy.

A second Jewish settler organization, Ateret Cohanim, an organization which purchases properties in Arab neighbourhoods of Jerusalem in order to settle Jews in them, also operates in the Silwan area. This group uses the machinery of the state to take over land in Silwan and the Holy Basin, and is fully supported by the state. Using the state's absentee property law and claiming properties that belonged to Jews before 1948, properties are claimed by the state and then turned over to the settler group. This process does not bring back properties to the original owners, but is being used to make ideologically based property claims in disputed areas.[22]

The state is complicit in settler activity. There has been a longstanding effort by the government and the settlers to create contiguity between isolated settlement enclaves established inside Palestinian neighbourhoods southeast of the Old City (including Wadi Hilwe, Silwan, Batan al-Hawa and Ras Al-Amud). This effort has accelerated and threatens the fabric of these Palestinian neighbourhoods. With increased Jewish settler insertions comes increased Israeli security presence to protect the settlers, introducing new flashpoints and tensions into the dense urban environment. By encircling the Old City, the settlement project is transforming the Israeli-Palestinian conflict from a political conflict into a religious one.

The entire Al-Bustan neighbourhood, the heart of Palestinian Silwan and near the Old City, is under threat of eviction and displacement. Planned as part of an Israeli tourist area that would supplement the City of David, Israel claims that the whole area was held by a Jewish trust before 1948. In 2005, the Jerusalem Municipality tried to demolish eighty-eight homes in this neighbourhood but retreated due to international pressure (Greenberg and Mizrachi, 2010). The Jerusalem Master Plan 2000 designates this area as part of the visual basin surrounding the Old City that is to be transformed into an Israeli national tourist anchor. The Plan allows virtually no development for these neighbourhoods and it zones densely built up areas as open space, setting up the conditions for subsequent demolitions in the name of tourism (Bimkom, 2014).

An additional component of settler activity in the area is the planned Kedem Center which would connect the City of David to the archaeological excavations just south of the Old City. This would create one complex of continuity for Jewish claims in the area, strengthening the hold of settler activity amid contested Palestinian neighbourhoods. This private plan by Elad Ir David runs counter to rules against building this close to

64   Trajectories of Conflict and Peace

Figure 2.15. 'City of David' and surroundings. This area of intensive excavation and Israeli control is just south of the Old City and the Haram al Sharif/Temple Mount. Areas 3-13 are associated with the 'City of David' compound. Area 2 is the proposed Kedem Center. Areas 14-15 are planned tourist areas in what is now the Al-Bustan neighbourhood of Silwan Village. (*Source*: Emek Shaveh, http://alt-arch.org/en/interactive-map/)

the Old City. Nonetheless, the Kedem Center as envisioned would be a 16,000 square metre visitors compound built over an active excavation site. Although the project was initially downsized due to criticism by left-wing nongovernmental organizations, the Israeli Minister of Justice intervened, overrode technical advice from her own office, and reopened the process, making the whole planning process a 'farce' amid the desire of the Municipality to increase tourism and its political claims in the area (Yudith Oppenheimer, Ir Amim, interview, 26 January 2016). The current Mayor of Jerusalem has endorsed the Kedem Center as part of his project to increase tourism to 10 million per year. 'With visions like the Kedem Center, you end up with another intifada', observes Oppenheimer. 'How will that support his vision for 10 million tourists?', she asks.

Amid political contestation, partisan Jewish organizations are working to establish, extend, and reinforce their claims in contested space. There is the strategic manipulation of historical and archaeological narratives by these groups in the Muslim and Jewish Quarters of the Old City and in areas just outside the Old City. This micro-scale contestation is dynamic – the 'nature of everyday piety in Jerusalem is fluid, inventive, often raucous, sometimes violent ... and oriented to its own exclusivity' (Pullan *et al.*, 2013, p. 191). Such contestation is not set in stone and unmoving but subject to constant extension into new urban micro-sites. Amid the larger Israeli-Palestinian political impasse is a city core of constantly new fault-lines and nationalist micro-territories that further unsettle and destabilize it as a place of mutual coexistence. The creation of frontiers that promote one group and are characterized by an 'us–them' dynamic, traditionally conceptualized by political science scholars as taking place in remote peripheries, is taking place in Jerusalem within dense centres of proximate antagonistic populations. The partisan activities of spatial manipulation that are occurring within Jerusalem's core exist within a context of indeterminate public authority. In particular, Jewish settler organizations at times are sponsored by formal state channels and at others operate in murky interstitial spaces. In short, they have been able to use gaps in urban authority to enact their agendas in highly contentious areas such as the Muslim Quarter and outside the Old City near the Palestinian village of Silwan. Indeed, it is the indeterminacy of authority structure that enables them to operate so fruitfully in pursuing their partisan goals.

Jewish right-wing and settler activity reaches into the very core and most combustible part of Jerusalem – the Old City and the sacred Haram al Sharif/Temple Mount compound. In the Old City, increased Jewish settler occupation of units in the Muslim Quarter is adding additional fuel to the fire of nationalistic conflict. Settlers commonly assert claims to properties owned by Jews prior to 1948 as a way to get a foothold in the Quarter. After occupation, they frequently fly Israeli flags high above the walking streets and live behind protected and monitored gates and doors. This micro-insertion of hardcore settlers into Arab neighbourhoods is a 'provocation' that

66  Trajectories of Conflict and Peace

Figures 2.16 and 2.17. Jewish settler micro-insertion in Arab Quarter, Old City Jerusalem.

Figure 2.18. Israeli police at Damascus Gate checkpoint.

aggrieves the dignity of the other side (Eran Razin, Director of Institute of Urban and Regional Studies, Hebrew University (interview, 11 October 2015).

Most combustible of all interventions are increased right-wing claims and activities on the Haram al Sharif/Temple Mount (hereafter Haram/Mount). This is one of the most provocative and sensitive issues and is activating friction points between Israeli and Palestinian populations, the Arab nations surrounding Israel, and the Muslim world generally. For over a hundred years, a '*status quo*' has been maintained according to which the Haram/Mount is an area reserved for Muslim prayer and the Western Wall adjoining it is a prayer area reserved for Jews. Over the last 10 years, there has been increased activity by Jews determined to strengthen the status of the Haram/Mount complex as a Jewish religious centre and to marginalize the claims of Muslims to the complex (Ir Amim, 2013). Hundreds of national religious Jewish pilgrims have ascended the Haram/Mount, including groups of rabbis, women, members of the Israeli legislative Knesset, and soldiers in uniform. The goals of 'Temple Movement' activists are diverse, from those advocating the use of political, cultural, and educational actions to enable Jews to pray on the Haram/Mount to extremists who call for the destruction of Islamic shrines and construction of a third Jewish Temple in their place (Ir Amim, 2013). Of particular strength is a form of Jewish national religious radicalism which seeks to rebuild the Jewish Temple on the Haram/Mount as a way to establish a new national and religious order defined by Jewish unity, stability, and eternity. Palestinians feel threatened that the gradual penetration by Jewish visitors of the Haram will increasingly draw in the Israeli security apparatus to the Haram in order to protect them, and lead to a 'gradual Hebronization' of the Haram[23] (Michael Dumper, Professor, University of Exeter, interview, 10 February 2016).

In September 2015, clashes between Palestinian youths and Israeli security forces erupted at the compound amid fears among Muslims that Israel was planning to change the rules governing the site, a charge which Israel has denied. The Haram/Mount tinderbox had earlier formed the catalyst for the second Intifada, which started in September 2000 when then Prime Minister Sharon made a visit to the Haram al Sharif compound, an act seen as highly provocative and which led to Palestinian demonstrators throwing stones at police and then being dispersed by the Israeli army using tear gas and rubber bullets. The period of wider conflict started at the Haram/Mount lasted more than 4 years, claiming over 3,000 Palestinian and 800 Jewish lives.[24] The flashpoint nature of the Haram/Mount was evident again in July 2017 when Israel, in response to the killing of two Israeli policemen by Israeli Arab assailants on the Haram/Mount, instituted airport-style walk-through metal detectors manned by Israeli security forces at entrances to the Haram/Mount. This unilateral action stimulated mass Palestinian protests, unrest and violence in East Jerusalem, and resulted in multiple deaths in Jerusalem and elsewhere.

> *Together with my Palestinian companion, we start walking down a lonely street in Hebron, abandoned by all except Israeli Defense Forces. Two soldiers approach, fully body-armoured and carrying Tavor assault rifles pointed at us. They stop 15 feet from us, intently gaze upon us, and tell us to drop our wallets in front of us and back away. They ask us why we are on this street. All power was with these two young 20 year olds on this deserted street with no sympathetic observers. We were alone. Besides feeling vulnerable and trapped by this power imbalance, what struck me the most – and what was most frightening – was that when I looked at the eyes of these two soldiers I saw fear and an equal amount of vulnerability. Fear registered on the face of a soldier pointing an assault rifle at you is an alarming experience. We back away and slowly head back in the direction we came.*

## Arab 'Unlicensed' Development

A further conspicuous feature among the differences in 2016 compared to 1994 is the amount of 'unlicensed' Palestinian development in Jerusalem. Such growth in the city is evident in Palestinian areas such as Issawiya, A Tur, Ras al Amud, Jabel Mukaber, Sur Bahir and most extensively, as I have described, in the Kafr Aqab and Shuafat refugee camp areas outside the separation wall. The magnitude of this type of development creates complexities and contradictions in the urban landscape that are not consistent with Israeli political objectives.

Palestinian development of 'unlicensed' housing in Israeli-defined East Jerusalem is overwhelming the Israeli legal and regulatory system aimed at containing and restricting it. According to Israeli data, the Arab percentage of city population increased from 30 per cent of city population in 1995 to 37 per cent in 2013.[25] From 1995 to 2014,

Figure 2.19. 'Unlicensed' development in Arab neighbourhood of Issawiya, near Hebrew University.

Figure 2.20. Issawiya. (*Source*: Google Earth image)

the Arab population in Jerusalem increased by 134,000, while the Jewish population increased by 113,000 (Jerusalem Institute for Israel Studies 2016, table III/1). This growth in Arab population in the city is not being accommodated through increased housing opportunities for them in the city authorized by the Municipality; indeed, such opportunities are severely restricted by Israel. Rather, growth is being supported through unlicensed housing construction deemed 'illegal' by the Israeli planning and regulatory system. The most cited figure for the number of unlicensed units in Arab East Jerusalem is 20,000, which would mean more than 30 per cent of all Palestinian units in Jerusalem are not authorized by the Israeli state. In the period 2001–2010, 70 per cent of all new Palestinian construction was estimated to be unlicensed (IPCC, 2013). During those 10 years, IPCC estimates that while 3,800 dwelling units were granted by the Municipality in Arab Jerusalem, more than 9,000 unlicensed units were constructed. This is the inevitable result of authorized housing supply not meeting objective need; IPCC estimates that while about 380 units were permitted by the Municipality each year between 2000 and 2010, housing need exceeds 1,650 units per year. From 1967 until the end of 2012, only 4,300 building permits were granted in Arab neighbourhoods in Jerusalem (Bimkom, 2014). On average, each of these permits is for four units. This means that about 17,200 units were permitted over a 45-year period. This amount of licensed development is nowhere close to that needed to accommodate the increase of over 230,000 Arab residents in the city that occurred over this period.

The magnitude of unlicensed development is causing difficulties for Israel's hegemonic project because it is supporting continued growth in the Arab population in the city. One possible response would be house demolition by Israel of unlicensed housing in Jerusalem. Indeed, housing demolition does occur sometimes. However, the wholesale demolition of thousands of unlicensed units would be politically difficult because Israel would be destroying large amounts of urban fabric in what it deems 'unified' Jerusalem. The significant destruction of urban settlements which Israel has accomplished in more peripheral Gaza, or in Lebanon in 2006, is politically and practically unlikely within Jerusalem. While state governments have more leeway to engage in hard-edged tactics in their remote frontiers, such action becomes problematic in more core areas within their states (Ron, 2003).

*There is no possibility of Israel stopping this 'illegal' building. Israel has lost the larger battle of Jerusalem.*

Efrat Cohen-Bar, planner, Bimkom,
interview, 21 January 2016

The fact that Arab growth in the city has increased during a time of strict Israeli controls over formal development is remarkable and exposes a major vulnerability and crack in Israel's hegemonic project. 'For a long time now', observes Meir Margalit (Former Jerusalem Municipal Councillor), 'the Municipality has lost control over what is happening on the ground' (interview, 27 October 2015). In a circumstance where Palestinians' formal right to develop is obstructed by Israel through myriad layers and types of regulations, unlicensed development is the main way for Palestinians to meet their needs, and it is done incrementally and in ways not always visible to Israeli authorities (Abeer Al Saheb, United Nations Human Settlements Programme, interview, 1 December 2015). Municipal officials know that unlicensed housing is increasing, but for the most part look the other way. In certain Arab neighbourhoods in Jerusalem, Israeli police do not even allow housing inspectors to enter the area due to security concerns. Osnat Post, Former Municipal City Engineer, states that 'although the Municipality has the legal means of blocking these developments, they can't stop them' (interview, 28 October 2015). The Municipality 'restricts Arab development theoretically, but not practically' (Amir Cheshin, Former Advisor to Jerusalem Mayor, interview, 17 November 2015).

This phenomenon of unlicensed housing construction is not due to a collective and organized strategy on the part of Palestinian authorities because such interventions are banned by the Israeli state, but rather is the result of hundreds of individual and family household actions that are, cumulatively, creating a dispersed pattern of unlicensed development activity which is bypassing and overwhelming Israeli control mechanisms aimed at suppressing and restricting Arab growth. Operating outside formal planning channels, this Palestinian development in Jerusalem is primarily residential and suffers from lack of road networks, community and public spaces, and economic activities. However, in terms of the politically loaded demographic numbers game, Arab unlicensed growth is creating a stalemate that is thwarting goals of Israeli control.

*Every square meter in East Jerusalem is a plot of politics.*
UN-Habitat, 2015, Executive summary

The extent of unlicensed development in Arab East Jerusalem is a significant and complicating feature in the urban-scape and projects a substantial and growing demographic presence of Palestinians in the city. Such informality is a necessary and logical response to the lack of development opportunities sanctioned by the Israeli system. The extent of informal, 'illegal' Arab development over the past two decades is meeting, at least partially, objective needs for housing and is creating Palestinian facts on the ground that bolster their political claims. It is consistent with the Arab strategy of *sumud* (steadfast perseverance) aimed at maintaining Palestinian's presence on their land. However, the fact that this development is not sanctioned and informal in nature has consequences for the quality of Arab existence in the city. Unlicensed development frequently occurs in haphazard, *ad hoc* patterns and is unsupported by community assets such as parks, community centres, employment opportunities, utility connections, and adequate roads. Such impoverished and unbalanced community development creates ghettos and slums lacking in real opportunity and is associated with deep feelings of hopelessness and despair (Judith Oppenheimer, *Ir Amim*, interview, 26 January 2016). Even if peace takes hold someday in Jerusalem, the socioeconomic deprivation in Arab East Jerusalem that has developed amid Israeli restrictions may lead to nightmarish and chaotic conditions of crime and poverty that destabilizes peacebuilding. If there ever is peace, 'we don't know what we will find on the other side' (Oppenheimer, interview, 26 January 2016).

At the wider metropolitan Jerusalem scale, there has also been extensive Arab development since 1994 in places outside the Israeli Municipality of Jerusalem. Such development – in places like A Ram, Dahiyat al Bareed, Al Izariya, Abu Dis, Sawahira, and Al Ubeidiya, and most extensively in the city of Ramallah – is consolidating the Palestinian presence at this larger metropolitan scale such that one estimate puts the demographic ratio of the metropolitan region at 50 per cent Jewish and 50 per cent Arab (Israel Kimhi, interview, 3 December 2015). This is of potential political importance because some peacemaking initiatives envision a metropolitan level of governance as part of a solution. Israel's restrictive urban planning policy in Jerusalem has pushed Palestinians towards forced suburbanization and created a ring of Arab development just outside municipal borders beyond Israel's regulatory reach.[26] This suburban zone serves as a 'middle ground' between West Bank towns and restricted Jerusalem. A Ram, just outside the Israeli Jerusalem municipal border in the north, emerged as a new growing suburb linking Jerusalem and Ramallah and hosts many Palestinian ministries not able to operate within Jerusalem (IPCC, 2008). Al Izariya and Abu Dis to the east also grew, but to a lesser extent. To the southeast, considerable development has more recently occurred in Sawahira and Al Ubeidiya. Most pronounced has been the development of the city of Ramallah from a smaller edge city and regional centre into a nation centre and *de facto* administrative home of the Palestinian National Authority (Khamaisi, 2006). Ramallah today is an area of significant outside investment and modern development and constitutes a strong Palestinian presence and competing power based just 9 miles (14.5 km) north of the Jerusalem's municipal border.[27]

Focusing attention back within Jerusalem, one finds that the demographic-political competition is strikingly asymmetric in terms of institutional capacity – a contest between a well sponsored and coordinated Israeli hegemonic project and a poorly coordinated and largely individualistically motivated Palestinian development dynamic. That such a competition is producing a type of political stalemate is a testament to the Arabs' deep connection and need to reside in the Holy City. Nevertheless, the Palestinian capacity to exert a collective and governmental strategy regarding Jerusalem is severely constrained – both by Israeli restrictions on the exercise of Arab public authority in the city and an inability, through the years of limited Palestinian autonomy, of the Palestinian National Authority to mount an effective collective strategy for Jerusalem.

Palestinians have had in place the structures of national government since after Oslo. Due to Israeli locational restrictions, the Palestinian National Authority (PNA) and many national ministries are based in Ramallah, while the Jerusalem Governorate in charge of affairs in the city and the wider region extending eastwards to Jericho is located just outside, and close to, the separation barrier in the village of A-Ram. An official of the negotiation support unit of the Palestine Liberation Organization has an office in the village of Dariet Al Barid, which paradoxically is technically outside the Municipality but inside the separation barrier. Further, located within the Municipality borders is a nongovernmental civil society unit – the Palestinian Academic Society for the Study of International Affairs – which constitutes an informal meeting ground for Palestinian scholars and officials.

Although East Jerusalem is a central platform and source of contention for Palestinian sovereignty, it is evident when talking to Palestinian officials that Palestinian authorities lack an overall national strategy or vision in terms of how to consolidate their position in Jerusalem. A report by a Palestinian think tank is critical, stating that 'a coherent strategy for the future of the city by the Palestinian leadership remains absent' (Arafeh, 2015, p. 5). This report further states that the Palestinian National Authority has demonstrated a lack of genuine investment in Jerusalem since Oslo in 1993 and this has led to an 'effective abandonment of the population to fend for itself' (Arafeh, 2015, p. 1). The Authority allocates a negligible budget to the city; the budget allocated in 2014 to the Ministry of Jerusalem Affairs and the Jerusalem Governorate was only 0.4 per cent of the total PNA budget for that year (Arafeh, 2015, p. 5). The PNA 'is very focused on Oslo areas A, B, and C in the West Bank and is very hesitant to work in areas where they don't have control', observes Foaud Hallak (Jerusalem Policy Advisor, Negotiations Support Unit, Palestine Liberation Organization, interview, 7 December 2015). This lack of concerted effort for East Jerusalem appears to be a significant missed opportunity. The formulation of a development plan or vision for Arab East Jerusalem, although it is likely it would be rejected by Israel, would have important benefits. It could create a proactive strategy and move the PNA away from constantly reacting to Israeli hegemonic initiatives, coordinate Palestinian investments and urban programmes, bring different Palestinian stakeholders together under a common plan, and provide a spatial representation to international and Israeli negotiators of what a sovereign Arab East Jerusalem would look like on the ground.

*In order to penetrate hegemony, one must work at the margins of the occupation. Palestinians need more of a collective effort which would increase these 'margins'.*

Yosef Jabareen, Technion Institute of Technology, presentation, 2 December 2015

*An occupation regime has soft spots. We should increase costs to Israeli society of the occupation regime, not attack directly the regime's hard spots. We need to think in terms of the soft power that we have.*

Husam Zomlot, Ambassador at Large, State of Palestine Presidency,<br>interview, 4 February 2016

There exists a difficult challenge in liberation movements between higher political negotiation work and on-the-ground planning activities. Often, such as in the Palestinian case, national political objectives take priority while formulations of urban and regional growth and spatial planning efforts are relegated to secondary status projects that are to occur after successful political negotiations. Husam Zomlot (Ambassador at Large, State of Palestine Presidency, interview, 4 February 2016) observes that the 'right to develop', which includes planning and visioning, is often promoted by the international community as an incentive or complement to peacemaking that comes after signed agreements. Yet, acknowledges Zomlot, a more effective approach by liberation movements would be to view the right to plan and develop not as a complement or gift of peacemaking, but as an inherent right that stands on its own and is formative of, and should take place along the path towards, a peaceful settlement. In this view, Palestinian capacity building in planning and development work would come not as an after effect of a larger peace, but be independently developed as part of the path towards such a peace.

After Oslo, work on urban planning was done within the Ministry of Planning and International Cooperation from 1994 to 2002 (Nabeel Shaath, Member of Fatah Central Committee, interview, 4 February 2016). A Palestinian plan for the Jerusalem region emphasized three rings – the inner city, adjacent areas in the city, and areas of influence outside the city – and recommended ways to increase continuity of Palestinian settlements and connect them through transport mobility (Ministry of Planning and International Cooperation, 1998*a* and 1998*b*) (Samih Al-Abid, Deputy Minister of MOPIC 1994–2003, interview, 11 February 2016). Yet, this momentum appears to have waned and become fragmented over the years. The death of Jerusalem leader Faisal Husseini in 2001, who worked to build up a network of Palestinian institutions in East Jerusalem to act as a type of shadow municipal structure, dealt a severe blow to Palestinian efforts in East Jerusalem. The lack of an equally strong local leader to succeed Husseini, together with Israel's closing of the Orient House centre of local Palestinian activity, left a local and debilitating void. Within the PNA, a Ministry office for Jerusalem was established after Oslo to concentrate PNA efforts but was closed in 2010.

Two agencies of the Palestinian National Authority are currently involved in the physical planning of Palestinian areas: (1) the Ministry of Planning and Development formulates national and regional plans; and (2) the Ministry of Local Government

(MOLG) provides support for localities and cities. The MOLG is tasked with creating local structure plans and could theoretically develop a development plan or vision for East Jerusalem, but it is handicapped by a lack of qualified and skilled urban planners and by Israel's restriction on its reach into East Jerusalem (Abdelhamid, 2006). The Ministry of Planning, meanwhile, has become more oriented towards working with donors and project based finance rather than spatial planning (Fouad Hallak, interview, 7 December 2015). Consequently, there exists a significant unmet need for Palestinians to create an organized approach to creating Palestinian 'facts on the ground' which would counter Israel (Hallak, interview). Such an approach could first develop planning capacity in 'B' areas of the West Bank where there exists Palestinian civilian authority (such as in A Ram, Abu Dis, and Izariya) and then transfer that expertise into independent plan-making in East Jerusalem. Because the Israeli regulatory regime has vacated Kafr Aqab and Shuafat refugee camp areas outside the separation barrier, these locations constitute specific opportunity spaces for Palestinian efforts to enhance social-spatial connections between these 'grey areas' and Arab neighbourhoods both outside and inside the barrier. Yet, there has been little progress in developing such a strategy of social-spatial integration.

The Palestinian government's ability to put brakes on the Israeli hegemonic project remains hampered today by a lack of collective strategic engagement with the city. A recent examination of Palestinian efforts concerning Jerusalem describes 'poor coordination, overlapping and duplication, an inconsistent stop-start implementation of programs, all dressed up with empty rhetoric full of sound and fury' (Dumper, 2014, p. 181). Husam Zomlot, in our interview, acknowledges that 'at this point in time people are in a survival mode; it is hard to get ahead of the game in terms of planning and strategy'. Instead of a collective development vision or plan for Jerusalem that could guide Palestinian efforts, Palestinian engagement relies on a set of tools and programmes that provide financial, legal, and moral support to Jerusalem residents. These tools are not insubstantial in their impacts on Arab Jerusalemites' ability to withstand Israeli hegemony, but appear fragmented, reactive, and at times even conciliatory to Israeli hegemony.

One key document outlining these tools and programmes is the Palestinian Strategic Multi-Sector Development Plan (SMDP) for East Jerusalem (Office of the President, November 2010). The Palestinian National Development Plan 2014–2016 (Ministry of Planning and Administrative Development, 2014) does not contain a development plan for Jerusalem and cites the SMDP as the main reference document for East Jerusalem. The National Plan does seek to 'assist residents of East Jerusalem and those affected by the separation wall to obtain and safeguard appropriate housing connected to electricity and water supplies', but is otherwise quiet on specific issues of Jerusalem. The SMDP is more explicit, seeking to respond to the 'need for new and sustained investment to safeguard East Jerusalem's critical role as the capital city of the emerging state of Palestine'. A European Union contribution to the SMDP supports community services in Jerusalem in a way 'to contribute to improve Palestinian communities' access to and protection of their social, political, and economic rights in selected neighbourhoods in East Jerusalem'. The 3-year SMDP directs funding at social protection and development, economic development, and human rights. About one-half of funding comes from the private sector and another half from government funding and external aid (Palestinian National Authority, 2011).

In terms of housing provision in East Jerusalem, the PNA is restricted by Israel and cannot intervene directly in supporting the development of new housing. No systematic Palestinian government assistance for new development in East Jerusalem is possible, in marked contrast to the massive Israeli state sponsorship of new housing development that exists in Jerusalem. The Palestine Housing Council, a non-profit organization, provides housing loans to East Jerusalem residents but only if the recipients have been granted permission to build by the Jerusalem Municipality. This conciliatory approach to Israeli control is due to the Council's financial interests in assuring payback of its loans. The PNA does provide financial support for some who have built without licences so that they can apply through the Israeli legal system to retroactively obtain legal status. This type of 'backtracking' is meant to stave off possible demolition (Husam Zomlot, interview, 4 February 2016). Yet, this intervention is project-specific and limited in scope.

In addition to being hampered by Israeli restrictions on government activity in Jerusalem, Palestinian investment of its own resources is too limited to compete with Israeli investment or meet the significant needs of Palestinian residents in Jerusalem. There are, however, external funding sources which add to the effort (Adnan Husseini, Governor of Jerusalem District, PNA, interview, 25 January 2015). The Al Quds Committee of the Organization of the Islamic Conferences is a large donor of funding for housing renovation, education, and health (Dumper, 2014). The Welfare Organization, a large Palestinian non-governmental organization, invests in revitalization of the Old City, and the Islamic Development Bank contributes to health and educational facilities, including in the refugee camps within the Municipality (Shuafat and Qalandia). A significant role is played by the Waqf Administration in East Jerusalem, which is a branch of a Jordanian ministry and employs hundreds of clerics, teachers, and other personnel and has invested substantial sums in the restoration of the al-Aqsa Mosque and Dome of the Rock. The Waqf is responsible for thirty-eight schools in East Jerusalem providing education to more than 12,000 students (Dumper, 2014). 'Believe me, there has been a lot of money spent in Arab East Jerusalem', notes planner Samih Al-Abid (interview, 11 February 2016), 'but unfortunately you cannot see it and I don't know why'.

*You can't say that pain associated with a 2000 year identity is more than pain from a 100 year identity. Pain is pain, it doesn't matter to individuals who are feeling this pain.*

Jay Rothman, Professor, Bar Ilan University,
interview, 13 January 2016

Stepping into the void of planning capacity in East Jerusalem, the United Nations Human Settlements Programme (UN-Habitat) has become the international window into the area. Funded by the European Union, the 'Urban Planning Support Programme for Palestinian Communities in East Jerusalem' has been undertaken by UN-Habitat and local partners. In 2015, it published *Right to Develop: Planning Palestinian Communities in East Jerusalem,* in which it advocates for 'more inclusive socio-cultural planning practices in response to Palestinian rights, claims, and aspirations' (p. 62). It argues for a form of 'resolution planning'; that alongside efforts to resolve the conflict and end Israel's occupation, the PNA should 'develop a comprehensive, integrated, inclusive, and beyond all action-oriented strategy for development planning in East Jerusalem' (p. 62). It states that 'more strategic options aimed at reinforcing Palestinian steadfastness in East Jerusalem should take center stage'. Among its suggested actions are increased land registration, creating local development standards to fit Arab growth styles, and focusing on incremental housing and economic development, capacity building, and alternative forms of community planning.

Taking note that local based planning initiatives in East Jerusalem are 'currently sporadic and lack an overall clear spatial growth agenda' (p. 1), the UN-Habitat report proposes an 'all-East Jerusalem spatial planning framework' that is more responsive and effective. Such a planning framework would undoubtedly encounter strong Israeli resistance and is thus pragmatically proposed as a policy recommendation not requiring a new regulatory framework subject to Israeli review and obstruction. Such a plan would not even be placed before Israeli authorities, but rather is based on the right of Palestinians to the city, the right to develop, and the right to vision. This is consistent with Jabareen's (2015, p. 6) theoretical argument that, when the state in control does not provide for the basic rights of an ethnic group, the 'right to necessity' provides its own legitimation to the group facing discrimination. This approach is supported by Israeli scholar Hubert Law-Yone (Senior Lecturer, Technion Institute, interview, 14 February 2016), who asserts 'that we need more than modification of a restrictive system, we need a whole different approach'.

UN-Habitat's *Right to Develop* stakes out an important role for Arab spatial planning in contested East Jerusalem and, while steering clear of directly confrontational language *vis-à-vis* Israel, it nevertheless proposes a type of Palestinian planning with greater capacity to challenge Israel's hegemonic control. This approach appears as a 'third seam' or middle-ground strategy that is neither dependent on the formal Israeli planning regulatory system nor accepting of continuing the substantial unorganized and chaotic unlicensed development of the past decades. I probe Abeer Al Saheb (Manager, East Jerusalem Portfolio, UN-Habitat, interview, 1 December 2015) about the political implications of UN-Habitat's approach. Admitting that unlicensed development is '*de-facto* already a response' to Israeli regulations, she suggests that 'you want to encourage that, but you also want to make sure there is a kind of shadow system that governs such development and that is done in a way not to attract attention'. Palestinians need to coordinate among themselves and to engage at planning coordination at a larger scale in order to 'maintain their existence in the city'. Planning efforts encompassing all of East Jerusalem would help establish development rights, assist economic development, and be better able to provide public benefits such as open space, community facilities, and roads (the latter a major impediment to Arab development under Israeli regulations).

Figure 2.21. Jerusalem Old City.

Along the same lines as UN-Habitat, the Israeli nongovernmental group Bimkom systematically outlines a strategy of alternative, resident-initiated planning for East Jerusalem (Cohen-Bar and Ronel, 2013). It proposes bottom-up planning based on resident knowledge of land ownership patterns and actual neighbourhood conditions and suggests a set of planning tools that can regularize houses built without permits, provide flexible guidance for development, and provide land for public purposes through local landowner agreements. At the same time, appropriate top-down principles at the general planning level would be maintained, although applied in more flexible ways cognizant of existing neighbourhood conditions. Rassem Khamaisi (Professor, Haifa University, interview, 29 November 2015) practices this type of community planning in his work with Arab Jerusalem neighbourhoods. He labels it '*de-facto* planning' that is not authorized by the state but provides norms and standards that the community can use as guidance for future growth. This type of planning seeks to bridge the gap between real community needs and the often complex language of planning, and seeks to create a climate of understanding for Palestinians who are mistrustful of how planning has been used by Israel. In his work, Khamaisi proposes planning that is more context-oriented, creatively adapting planning tools to fit the needs and limitations of the community, rather than using the modernist and tightly regulatory techniques imposed by Israel.

The type of planning strategy recommended by UN-Habitat and Bimkom, and practised by Khamaisi, seeks to establish a more organized spatial orientation to guide Arab communities in Jerusalem so that development not technically permitted by Israel can take place with greater logic and order. Such community-based neighbourhood upgrading would be likely to follow standards different from those currently allowed by top-down Israeli regulatory control and be more responsive to the actual conditions and needs of Arab neighbourhoods. In essence, this approach resides at the fine line between an alternative type of local capacity building and directly confrontational counter-hegemonic planning. The controversial nature of this approach – neither playing by Israel's rules nor accommodating *laissez-faire* chaotic Arab development – is noted by Husam Zomlot in interview – 'if the Jerusalem governor attempts such a middle approach, his office will likely be closed. This is the balancing act we are playing'.

## *Economic 'Intrusion' of Arabs into Jewish Spaces*

In addition to the separation barrier, settler micro-penetration, and Arab unlicensed development, another feature of Jerusalem different from 1994 is the growing penetration by East Jerusalem Palestinians into Jewish parts of Jerusalem in order to gain access to services, employment, and goods. Due to the inadequate provision of urban services in Arab East Jerusalem, Palestinians increasingly need to use services and spaces in Jewish neighbourhoods. This is upsetting to certain Jewish neighbourhoods as the identity of those using services shifts. In one case, because of the lack of services in the Arab neighbourhood of Issawiya close to Hebrew University, Arabs have increasingly used commercial and post office facilities in the Jewish neighbourhood of French Hill. In response, a Jewish resident group in that neighbourhood pressured the Municipality to increase investment in Issawiya, based on the thinking that 'from a functional perspective, if they have their own spaces, then they won't come into ours' (Galit Cohen-Blankshtain, Senior Lecturer, Hebrew University, interview, 24 November 2015). This example of Jewish residents advocating increased attention to a nearby Arab neighbourhood illuminates the distorting and destabilizing effects of Israel's hegemonic project on the city at large.

Similarly, the lack of employment opportunities in East Jerusalem – due to planning restrictions and its walled separation from the West Bank – has led to a situation where 35,000 East Jerusalem Palestinians work in Jewish parts of the city on a daily basis. Based on a travel survey of 6,000 Arabs in Jerusalem conducted in 2010, an estimated 28 per cent of the Arab labour force in Jerusalem works in West Jerusalem, while another 9 per cent works in Jewish parts of East Jerusalem (Marik Shtern, Jerusalem Institute for Israel Studies, interview, 27 January 2016). It is estimated that 71 per cent of construction jobs in the entire city in 2015 were held by Arabs, 57 per cent of transportation jobs, 40 per cent of jobs in the hotel, hospitality, and food sector, 34 per cent of retail jobs, and 29 per cent of industrial jobs (Shtern, 2017). A large percentage of these jobs are in West Jerusalem and in the Jewish parts of East Jerusalem. The Arab workforce in the city is increasing, growing from 21 per cent of the workforce in the city in 2006 to 28 per cent in 2014. Amid the political uncertainties over the past 20 years, there has been a major economic shift in the city due to the restricted employment opportunities found in East Jerusalem. However, although there is growing economic mixing, social and psychological separation remains the norm in workplaces – which Shtern (interview) labels 'polarized integration'.

On the one hand, this economic interdependence in Jerusalem is consistent with the Israeli narrative that the city is unified because it creates a dependent Palestinian work population and thus furthers Israeli control. But, on the other hand, this growing interdependence and intrusion of Arabs into Jewish parts of Jerusalem is threatening to the contemporary Zionist rationale of separation (Shtern, interview). Jewish radicalization – in the form of 'don't hire Arabs' and 'don't buy there' pamphlets – is increasingly common in the city. Paradoxically, the hardcore approach to urban hegemony that has restricted opportunities for Arabs in East Jerusalem is now reacting to the economic mixing that such restrictions helped cause. The inherent contradiction within the Israeli partisan ideology – that Jews want a united city but don't want mixing – is illuminated. Also problematic from the Israeli view is that the Israeli economy in Jerusalem is now more dependent on Palestinian labour and thus more vulnerable to labour disruption such as might happen due to political strife.

In addition to economic mixing, there also exists increasing Arab use of Jewish consumption spaces. Such Arab use of Jewish commercial areas increases territorial sensitivities as groups look out for their collective identity, security, and ownership of space (Shtern, 2016). Estimates are that one-third of the customer base in the Mamilla Mall near the Old City is Arab (while 60 per cent of the shopkeepers are Arab), while

15 per cent of the customers are Arab in the Malha Mall in West Jerusalem (Shtern, interview; Shtern, 2016). The reaction by Jews to this penetration depends on the spatial location of the Mall. Because Malha is more firmly within Jewish space, Arab consumers there are viewed more negatively (although shopkeepers have more positive assessments because it increases their consumer base). In the Mamilla Mall closer to the Old City and the zone between Jewish and Arab space, attitudes tend to be more tolerant.

One study illuminates in greater detail what this everyday life of mixing feels like. A study of 157 middle-class, mostly younger secular Jews, ultra-orthodox Jews, and Israeli Arabs (Malka Greenberg Raanan, Hebrew University, interview, 30 November 2015) found Jerusalem is 'divided into three cities in some respects' and that 'ethnonational power relations structure space in terms of sense of belonging and sense of fear'.[28] At the same time, she finds urban space to be complex in the way it is perceived and used. Those Arab women surveyed spent up to 40 per cent of their time in Jewish space, for education, work, shopping, and entertainment.[29] Rather than spaces of encounter being truly shared places of mutual interaction, spaces where Jews and Arabs mix are more appropriately described as 'co-presence in the same space' (Raanan, interview). Arab women, present in Jewish space, do not view it as compliance in terms of becoming more Israeli, but rather as 'quiet encroachment on space' where they can feel their own identity and assert their right to the use of the space. Interestingly, these Arab women also feel a certain 'freedom from the supervised patriarchal space' of their own communities. At the same time, the power relations embedded in the city are constantly structuring activities in Jerusalem; 'occupation has affected the everydayness of urban life' in the city. 'It's not two different cities and functional integration is similar to many cities', observes Noam Shoval (Professor, Hebrew University, interview, 15 October 2015). At the same time, this functional integration is in marked contrast to the broader political, nationalistic, and religious fault-lines which divide the city. Two worlds co-exist – one functional, the other nationalistic and political (Shoval, interview).

The increased use by Jerusalem Arabs of medical and social services, and of public transportation, in Jewish parts of the city brings to light the possibility that there may be a creeping institutionalization of Israeli sovereignty over the Arab population – a type of 'practical Israelization' (Oren Shlomo, presentation, Ben-Gurion University, 2 December 2015). This state soft power is more submerged than the more visible and blatant power exerted through the spatial planning system and represents a newer regime of control. In this circumstance of 'trapped urbanism', Jerusalem Arabs have little choice but to engage with the Israeli state in order to survive day-to-day (Shlomo, presentation). At the same time as contesting the legitimacy of Israeli rule through the collective act of not voting in municipal elections, Jerusalem Arabs engage in struggles over urban service issues; organized national struggle co-exists with struggles over urban civil issues.

A legitimate question is whether such urban engagement in Jerusalem is slowly eroding the Palestinian national project of political autonomy. A poll of Arab East Jerusalemites (Pollack, 2011) gained much currency in the Israeli media in its finding that 35 per cent of respondents would prefer Israeli citizenship instead of Palestinian citizenship should there be a two-state peace agreement.[30] There were also many references in interviews with Israelis that the number of Jerusalem Arabs applying for Israeli citizenship, and the number of Arab students taking Israeli matriculation exams, are both increasing. Such data imply that the Palestinian political project may be eroding. Yet, a closer look at these data reveals that such a conclusion may be unwarranted. First, Dan Miodownik (Professor of Political Science, Hebrew University, interview, 19 January 2016) takes the Pollack survey to task for using an unrepresentative sample that is more middle income, more educated, and more Christian than the full Jerusalem Arab population. Each of these characteristics is likely to be associated with attitudes of less resistance to the Israeli state and thus produces an over-inflation of Jerusalem Arab desires regarding possible Israeli citizenship. Regarding actual Arab applications for Israeli citizenship, although data indicate recent increases, the larger picture must not be lost. Since 1967, there have been approximately 12,500 applications, a mere 4 per cent of the total Arab population in Jerusalem (Daniel Seidemann, Jerusalem Lawyer and Expert, interview, 1 February 2016). Similarly, although increasing, recent figures show that only 5 per cent of graduating Arab seniors in the city took the Israeli matriculation exam (Kashti and Hasson, 2016). Indeed, a larger reality points to a clearly different trajectory – only eight of the 180 schools in Arab East Jerusalem teach the Israeli curriculum (Kashti and Hasson, 2016). Based on data regarding citizenship aspirations and student behaviour that indicate whether there is Israelization of the Arab population in the city, it appears that the Israeli state's wish for such assimilation is at odds with the reality on the ground. Despite intrusion of Arabs in Jewish Jerusalem for jobs, goods, and services, the national struggle for Palestinian political autonomy on the part of Arabs appears intact and resilient.

## Conclusion

*Ninety-nine per cent of the people in Jerusalem live with the reality of the border of the 2-state solution already. But they live it in the service of occupation and an unsustainable reality rather than in the service of a political agreement.*

Daniel Seidemann, Director, Terrestrial Jerusalem,<br>interview, 1 February 2016

Despite consistent and intensifying Israeli structural efforts to strengthen its hold over Jerusalem, the Palestinian presence in and around the city in terms of residential development is greater today than in 1994. Israel is not winning the competition and the situation represents more of a stalemate. This brings into question the ability of the Israeli governing regime to 'control' a city through partisan demographic-based policy. Forty-eight years of such policies have not gained Israel true control over the city and inherent tensions in the Israeli project are exposed. Strict land-use planning controls are so extensive in their ability to constrain sanctioned development that it creates Palestinian resistance and successful efforts through unlicensed development to bypass the regulatory regime. The demographic goal related to Israel's political aspiration of having a unified Jerusalem remains in force, but its operationalization in the urban environment produces impacts that are inconsistent with this goal, and in other cases creates complexities and uncertainties from an Israeli perspective. Separation imposed through the barrier has distorted the natural growth dynamics of the urban area, threatening Palestinians with loss of Jerusalem residency status and stimulating significant growth outside the wall but inside the Municipality. Further, limitations on employment opportunities for Palestinians in Arab East Jerusalem have created economic mixing in parts of the city, which complicate efforts to create a Jewish Jerusalem.

The Israeli hegemonic project pertaining to control of Jerusalem is strategic and powerful, yet at the same time it produces tensions and contradictions that threaten achievement of hegemonic goals. 'This is a puzzle', observes Yudith Oppenheimer (Executive Director, Ir Amim, interview, 26 January 2016), 'we don't see the problems we are creating. Hardcore Zionists are bringing the Zionist dream to its collapse, so preoccupied they are with the illusion of power'. Hegemonic control and urban complexity run at cross purposes; decision-makers focused on operational control 'do not understand the complex dynamics of an urban organism' (Daniel Seidemann, interview, 1 February 2016).

The city in 2016 is divided in all but name. The reality is that there exists a *de facto* binational urban state regime, strongly partisan, asymmetric and unilateral. The retired Brigadier General of the IDF, Udi Dekel, observes unreservedly that 'there is a two-state reality in Jerusalem' (interview, 3 February 2016). Internal, confidential polling by the Institute for National Security Studies, mentioned by Dekel in our interview, indicates that fully 75 per cent of the 800 Israeli Jerusalemites surveyed perceive that the city will not be unified in the future; only 25 per cent envision a unified city under Israel control. Former Municipality planner Israel Kimhi notes that the city is unified economically and functionally, but that 'it is psychologically divided'; that many Jews are afraid to visit Arab East Jerusalem because it is 'a different place' (interview, 3 December 2015). 'The younger Israeli generation', observes former Municipal Councillor Meir Margalit (interview, 27 October 2015), 'is starting to realize that parts of the city are not Israel'. The urban region of Jerusalem appears to be an unsustainable situation that, lacking political resolve, may last a long time because Israeli hegemonic dynamics seem locked in place. As discussed in Chapter 4, political

Figure 2.22. Abu Tor/Abu Tor. This image of two neighbourhoods that reside next to each other, but on opposite sides of the 'green line' that divided the city from 1949 to 1967, shows the disparity in living conditions that currently exist between Jewish Abu Tor and Arab Abu Tor. Israel has governed Jerusalem as a unified city for almost 50 years and extreme disparities persist. (*Source*: Google Earth image)

and material asymmetry is creating Palestinian frustration and violence which creates further consolidation and tightening of control by Israel. There exists an unfortunate downward cycle, perpetuated by a focus on the violence and conflict generated by the disequilibrium rather than on the root issues of political sovereignty conflict. The Israeli hegemonic project is not achieving its goals of political and emotive unification of Jerusalem.

## Notes

1. The 1947 United Nations Partition Plan had envisioned a Jewish state encompassing 56 per cent of Palestine, an Arab state encompassing 43 per cent of Palestine, and an international zone (*corpus separatum*) for Jerusalem. Arab states rejected this proposal for granting too much area (including districts of Arab population) to the Jewish state. After the Arab-Israeli War of 1948, Israel controlled 78 per cent of Palestine, constituting the borders of contemporary Israel.
2. There were also more recent negotiations led by U.S. special envoy George Mitchell in 2010–2011 and by U.S. Secretary of State John Kerry 2013–2014.
3. In Chapter 3, I address how these national peacemaking initiatives influenced on-the-ground dynamics in the Jerusalem urban area.
4. Population figures come from the weekly supplement of *Globes* (in Hebrew), 22 October 2015. Note that the non-orthodox Jewish group itself contains distinctive subgroups within it – 'traditional religious' and 'secular'.

5. See: www.peacenow.org.
6. According to international law, areas in East Jerusalem unilaterally annexed by Israel are considered to be part of the West Bank.
7. Peace Now: http://peacenow.org.il/en/settlements-watch/settlements-data/jerusalem. Peace Now compiles settler population in the West Bank outside Jerusalem from the Israel Central Bureau of Statistics. For Jewish population within annexed Jerusalem, data come from the Jerusalem Institute for Israel Studies.
8. Although this citywide planning document is formally referred to as the Jerusalem 'local outline plan', for the sake of clarity and to distinguish it from neighbourhood outline plans, I will use the alternative term 'Master Plan' when referring to the Jerusalem 2000 plan.
9. The Inter-Ministerial Committee to Examine the Rate of Development in Jerusalem (1973).
10. The English version of the Master Plan is not paginated. Demographic discussion occurs in Section 7, Population and Society.
11. Population figures for Jerusalem more recent than 2014 are not available.
12. Building ratios are the allowable built square footage divided by the area of the land plot. Maximum building ratios are generally 25–50 per cent of the area of the plot, with the exception of village cores where the allowable ratio is 70 per cent. These ratios are significantly lower than found in Jewish neighbourhoods of the city.
13. Arab ownership patterns are a legacy of substantial land being held in community or state ownership under British or Jordanian control. About one-half of the Arab sector in Jerusalem is 'unregistered' in terms of private ownership.
14. Multiple housing units can be allowed by a single building permit.
15. This disjunction between Jewish and Arab perspectives on city management has parallels with conflicts between whites and African-Americans in the United States. While whites respond to specific conflict events (such as white police mistreatment of a black person) by focusing on the specific event, African-Americans usually consider a deeper history and the wider context of American discrimination and inequality within which the event occurred (Forester, 2009).
16. Another method of countering Israeli hegemony in the city, which has been used at times by Israeli nongovernmental organizations, is to seek court rulings that the extreme disparities in service provision between the two parts of the city are not legally defensible. One case, showing that playground acreage in the Arab neighbourhoods of Shuafat and Beit Hanina was 3 per cent of that existing in nearby Jewish neighbourhoods, resulted in a finding of discrimination by the Municipality amid an 'extreme unreasonable' level of disparities (Yosi Havilio, Former Legal Advisor, Municipality of Jerusalem, 2000–2010, interview, 2 November 2016). The Municipality must now build ten playgrounds in these neighbourhoods over the next 3 years. An earlier successful case, with the Association of Civil Rights in Israel and Ir Amim NGO as plaintiffs, found the under-provision of public schools in Arab East Jerusalem to be legally indefensible and mandated a 5-year public school building programme to address the problem. Havilio (interviews) feels that such a legal approach to remedying housing disparities in the city would be a harder task because it would be based on a more general argument rather than examining disparities between specific and proximate neighbourhoods.
17. Chapter 4 details how the hegemonic project also extends outwards to the wider geographic spaces of the Jerusalem region and the rest of the West Bank.
18. In Israel overall, during the second Intifada of 2000–2005, there were 887 Israeli civilians killed and 5,676 Israeli civilians wounded (International Institute for Counter-Terrorism, https://www.ict.org.il/).
19. Presentation before Ecumenical Accompaniment Programme in Palestine and Israel (EAPPI), Old City Jerusalem.
20. This area includes adjacent neighbourhoods of Ras Khamis, Ras Shehadeh, and Dahiyat al-Salaam ('new Anata').
21. According to the Jerusalem Envelope Administration, an administrative body established for neighbourhoods beyond the barrier (Ir Amim, 2015).
22. The opportunity for Jews to claim pre-1948 properties is not available to Arabs wanting to claim pre-1948 properties in such Jerusalem Jewish neighbourhoods as Baka or Katamon.
23. Hebron, location of the traditional burial site of biblical patriarchs and matriarchs and viewed as

a holy city in Judaism and Islam, is home to 500–750 Jewish settlers in a city of about 215,000 Palestinians, necessitating a major Israeli Defense Force presence, control of the old quarter by Israeli forces with eighteen military checkpoints, and the barring of Arabs into the city's former principal commercial corridor.
24. In October 2016, the United Nations Educational, Scientific, and Cultural Organization (UNESCO) approved a resolution which set off strong Israeli criticism when it emphasized the Muslim heritage of the Haram/Mount area and downplayed its historic significance to Judaism.
25. It is significant to note that this official count of the Arab population in the city by the Central Bureau of Statistics does not include the unknown number of Palestinian residents who live in the city without official residency status (Jerusalem Institute for Israel Studies, 2014).
26. Most of these areas are classified by the Oslo II agreement (1995) as either B or A, which allows for Palestinian civilian control. Political demarcation of the West Bank outside Jerusalem is further discussed in subsequent chapters.
27. Although Ramallah is only 13 miles (21 km) from the centre of Jerusalem, due to checkpoints and barriers, the trip in a car commonly takes about 50 minutes during rush hour times. Urban development in contested societies can create competing power centres in proximity. Ramallah's development as a political power centre close to Israeli-controlled Jerusalem bears similarities with Beirut, Lebanon, where the development of the Shiite Muslim Hezbollah suburb of Haret Hreik just south of the city of Beirut competes with that central city traditionally of strong Sunni Muslim influence.
28. The study used two hour interviews, mental mapping, and questions about activity patterns. Note that the study sample is biased towards the middle class and that Arab interviewees were Israeli citizens. The study nonetheless provides insights into the perceptions of mixing in Jerusalem. Spaces of encounter included the city centre, Hebrew University, industrial estate, hospitals, the two major Malls of the city, the Promenade extension, and the Light Rail system, which is used by about 130,000 travellers per day (about 30 per cent of whom are Arab).
29. In contrast, in an earlier study, Raanan and Shoval (2014) describe the activity patterns of secular Jewish women as living in a bubble largely removed from exposure to Arabs.
30. Arab inhabitants in annexed parts of Israeli-defined Jerusalem are considered by the Israeli state to be residents of the city if they meet certain residency requirements, but not citizens of Israel (unless they apply and receive such status). As residents, Arabs can vote in Jerusalem municipal elections but have chosen for the most part to boycott elections because they do not view Israeli municipal authority as legitimate.

Chapter 3

# Jerusalem II: Interlocking Trajectories of National Politics and Urban Dynamics

*East Jerusalemites paid a heavy price as a result of the Oslo peace accord.*
Mansour Nsasra, Lecturer, Ben Gurion University of the Negev,
interview, 4 February 2016

*Growing up in Jerusalem in the early 1990s, I never knew that the occupation was a twenty minutes' drive from my house.*
Etay Levy (pseudonym), Israel Defense Forces Soldier, 2008–2009,
interview, 18 January 2016

*Growing up it felt like one city. With the (first) Intifada, all of a sudden it was very clear that there was an 'East Jerusalem' and there were neighbourhoods that were off limits. This was a shock as a child. Now, East Jerusalem is not my city – both normatively and functionally. It shouldn't be my city. I understand this.*
Gillad Rosen, Senior Lecturer in Geography, Hebrew University,
interview, 11 October 2015

The spatial changes and dynamics in Jerusalem discussed in the previous chapter uncover changes since 1994 that reinforce the hegemonic Israeli project but also add complexity and at times contradict the Israeli project. Today, Jerusalem is a messy reality that is neither the unified city of Israeli aspirations nor the politically shared city of Palestinian hopes. This chapter examines how the numerous Israeli-Palestinian national negotiations that have occurred since 1993 have influenced urban spatial dynamics and how such on-the-ground changes have impacted possibilities for a genuine national peace. I discuss the intertwining and dynamic relationship between national political deliberations and spatial changes and how this interaction has influenced opportunities for the promotion of peace between Israelis and Palestinians. Peacemaking is examined here not just as a single diplomatic event but as a political-spatial process – political in its restructuring of political institutions and power and spatial in its impact over time on the distribution of inter-group benefits and opportunities in the city. Seeking peace is a spatial-social as well as a political one; it takes place over an extended period and is jointly produced through the interaction of local, city-based, actors and national elites. I emphasize peace as a process rather than an agreement, constituting a phenomenon of multi-threaded complexity subject to uneven advances and problematic paradoxes.

In the case where there exists a national political agreement (such as the Oslo agreement of 1993), the implementation of peace at the spatial, on-the-ground level informs us of the progress of a peace agreement. National peacemaking without consistent and visible urban peacebuilding actions to reinforce political goals faces the threat of becoming sterile documents divorced from everyday life and challenges, leaving an urban void. Incongruity between fundamental peacemaking goals and the operational forms that such goals take on in complex urban space jeopardizes peace. If urban dynamics are detrimental to urban tolerance and co-existence, prospects for sustaining national peacemaking become imperiled and subject to relapse. In the case where national peacemaking is stalled (which has been the case in Israel and Palestine since at least 2000), urban interventions regarding key attributes as land settlement, building of divisions, and urban services can incite inter-group antagonisms and endanger possibilities for future peace efforts.

*Jerusalem is complex, wonderful, horrible, magical, mind-boggling, mind-numbing, multi-layered, psychologically a heavy burden. It is the most problematic, intense, and unresolved of the cities I have studied over the past 24 years.*

Author's journal notes, 24 November 2015

Israeli-Palestinian negotiations have been numerous during the period under study and are as follows:

| | |
|---|---|
| Oslo Accords | 1993/1995 |
| Hebron Protocol | 1997 |
| Wye River Memorandum | 1998 |
| Sharm el-Sheikh Memorandum | 1999 |
| Camp David Summit (Clinton parameters) | 2000 |
| Taba Summit | 2001 |
| Arab Peace Initiative | 2002 |
| Road Map | 2003 |
| Geneva Initiative | 2003 |
| Agreement on Movement and Access | 2005 |
| Annapolis Conference | 2007 |
| Mitchell-led talks | 2010–2011 |
| Kerry-led talks | 2013–2014 |

I emphasize the Oslo Accords, Camp David Summit (and Clinton 'parameters'), and the Geneva Initiative as key deliberations. Each of these addresses the governance and sovereignty issues pertaining to Jerusalem in different ways; one clear pattern is that whereas the initially successful Oslo process remained distant from Jerusalem, the unsuccessful negotiation efforts from 2000 onwards more directly discussed issues related to the possible political division of the Holy City.

One clear observation is that national political settlements (in the case of Oslo) and national negotiation efforts (in the case of Camp David and Geneva) have not been supported by on-the-ground changes in the Jerusalem urban region that would reinforce and embed such national peacemaking efforts. There exists an intertwining relationship between national political deliberations and socio-spatial dynamics and changes in the Jerusalem urban region. Jerusalem has not stayed still amid national political activity; rather, national peacemaking and negotiation efforts have influenced changes in the social, spatial, and security aspects of Israeli control in Jerusalem. The pattern, however, is one of antagonism between national peace efforts and local dynamics in Jerusalem. At the same time that national settlements or negotiation efforts open up possibilities for Israel-Palestinian mutual coexistence, dynamics at the local level have run counter to these possibilities and increased consolidation of Israeli control in the urban region. This pattern of peacemaking possibilities at the national level and consolidation of Israeli control at the local level is evident throughout the period since 1994 and explains the dim prospects for peace that exist today.

Israeli interventions in the Jerusalem urban region have retarded, blocked, and resisted the possibilities for peace outlined in Oslo and discussed in subsequent unsuccessful national negotiations. Rather than the city being a pragmatic platform for peacebuilding that would operationalize peaceful coexistence, Jerusalem has constituted an ideological straightjacket that has stunted opportunities for genuine peaceful coexistence. Instead of the city being a constitutive agent promoting peaceful and equitable interaction between Israelis and Palestinians, Jerusalem has existed as socio-political quicksand – manipulated by state actors and right-wing groups in ways that retard possibilities for a truly shared city. Amid the slow progress and eventual dissolution of the Oslo agreement, and amid the political stasis that has existed through Camp David, Taba, and Geneva, the city has been a place of constant flux and change that has restricted possibilities for peaceful resolution at this important urban level. The city has been a key foundation during this time, but this role has been as a drag on peace rather than supportive of national peace possibilities. At the same time that diplomatic processes are initiated or contemplated, the city became increasingly politicized and subject to symbolic manipulation by Israeli actors who create on-the-ground operations that retard hopes for peace. Such actions in the Jerusalem urban region (and in the remainder of the West Bank) reveal the real story from 1994 to 2016, not the promises extended or discussed by Israel during the numerous peace negotiations.

## Oslo

The *Declaration of Principles on Interim Self-Government Arrangements* ('The Oslo I agreement') in 1993 was the first time that Israel ever agreed to negotiate on Jerusalem. However, the agreement stated, in Article V (3), that the status of Jerusalem was not to be discussed in the negotiations for the interim arrangements but would be one of the subjects left for 'permanent status' negotiations scheduled to occur no later than May 1996. While interim arrangements established limited autonomy and empowerment for Palestinians in some areas of the West Bank,[1] permanent status negotiations dealing with issues of Jerusalem, refugees, settlements, security arrangements, and borders never seriously took place due to strong disagreements over the size and timing of Israeli withdrawals from the West Bank, Israel's construction activities in East Jerusalem and the West Bank, and the PNA's ability to constrain extremists.

Israel's commitment in Oslo to negotiate on Jerusalem – albeit at a later date – created a race to establish facts on the ground by Israel that consolidated its control over the urban region. The threat of negotiating on Jerusalem in the future – together with the postponement in Oslo of actually negotiating on the city – created an environment ripe for Israeli hegemonic actions in the city. Although the status of Jerusalem was theoretically now open for negotiation, Israel engaged in a series of actions on the ground to change the reality of the city. One visible intervention was the construction of the Har Homa neighbourhood in the annexed part of the city. This settlement was of strategic importance to Israel because it would prevent Palestinian territorial continuity in southern Jerusalem, by both blocking the growing together of the Arab neighbourhoods of Beit Sahour and Sur Baher, and by separating Jerusalem from Bethlehem to the south. Land confiscations for this settlement were started in 1995, during the early years of Oslo, but held up in court. By 1997, however, Prime Minister Netanyahu approved construction. This started a momentum that has continued into the present. Har Homa has expanded significantly, growing from about 450 units prior to 2001 to about 4,500 units in 2016, with another 1,000 units in process of being built (Yudith Oppenheimer, interview, 26 January 2016). Because Har Homa began after, not before Oslo, it is considered a major thorn in the side of Palestinians and a significant affront to the spirit of Oslo.

Har Homa was not the only on-the-ground change during the Oslo years that was obstructive to peace possibilities. A number of interventions by Israel occurred that effectively separated Jerusalem from the rest of the Palestinian West Bank and weakened Jerusalem as a centre of Palestinian life. Prior to Oslo, at the time of the first Intifada (1987–1993), Jerusalem was the *de facto* capital for Palestinians and was the home of Arab leadership and media (Hillel Cohen, Senior Lecturer, Hebrew University, interview, 11 November 2015). Of considerable importance was the influence of Jerusalem Palestinian leader Faisel Husseini, considered at the time to be a possible future leader of the Palestinian people. As early as 1987, Husseini and Moshe Amirav, Advisor to then Likud Prime Minister Shamir, had discussions about the future status of the city. The feeling between the two was that 'if we can find an answer to Jerusalem, everything else will be less difficult' (Moshe Amirav, interview, 12 November 2015). The two men spoke of a possible '2 cities, 2 capitals' scenario with the Old City shared under the 'sovereignty of God'.[2] With the emergence of Oslo and progress at the national political level, the paradoxical impact was the weakening of Jerusalem as a Palestinian centre and detachment of it from the rest of the West Bank (Israel Kimhi, Jerusalem Institute for Israel Studies, interview, 3 December 2015). Rather than Oslo being accompanied by a strengthening of Arab Jerusalem that would accommodate mutual coexistence in the city, Israeli actions in the Oslo years have had the effect of alienating and separating Arab East Jerusalem from the rest of the West Bank and handicapping it as a focus of Palestinian institutional and social life. While Arab residents of East Jerusalem have commonly had a unique identity among Palestinians of the greater region – due to their proximity to Israeli institutions and services – Israeli actions after Oslo made this difference even more significant while at the same time making life harder in Jerusalem (Cohen, interview).

In the mid-1990s, Israel instituted numerous checkpoints along the Jerusalem border intended to regulate the flow of Arabs from the West Bank into the city. An integrated system of checkpoints between Jerusalem and the West Bank was created in 1993, with fourteen permanently staffed Israeli checkpoints along the city borders to monitor and restrict Arab mobility (B'Tselem, 2008). In addition, Israel imposed restrictions on Palestinian institutions operating in East Jerusalem. A 1994 law restricted Palestinian institutions in the city 'to prevent the Palestinian Authority or PLO diplomatic or government activity … within the borders of Israel that was not consistent with respect for the sovereignty of the State of Israel'.[3] This restriction stunted the development of Arab governance in the city, including many of the institutions established post-Oslo, and necessitated their location instead in areas outside the city. Further, in 1993, the Israel Ministry of Interior published new regulations revoking the Jerusalem residency status of those Palestinians who lived outside the city (Margalit, 2014).[4] In 1995, the 'Center of Life' policy was established by Israel, authorizing the confiscation of Jerusalem residency status from Palestinians who were unable to prove that Jerusalem had been their 'centre of life' for the previous 7 years by producing documents (such as tax receipts, education certificates, employment records, and utility bills) that demonstrated continuous residency in the city (Palestinian Academic Society for the Study of International Affairs, 2013).[5] Further restricting Arab life in Jerusalem are restrictive 'family reunification' policies which make it difficult for non-resident spouses, children, and relatives of East Jerusalem permanent residents to gain official residency in the city.

As a result of these Israeli actions after Oslo, Jerusalem became a different place for Palestinians – with tightly controlled mobility, impotent institutional capacity, and a populace consistently under threat of losing their right to reside in the city. At the same time as Oslo at the national level was moving slowly towards greater Palestinian autonomy and self-governance in the West Bank outside Jerusalem, the city as a centre for Palestinians was being restricted and eroded. After Oslo, Jerusalem lost its primary place in Palestinian life. The 'peace' promised by Oslo in actuality fragmented Palestinian life in Jerusalem, cordoning off the city from the rest of the West Bank. 'We detached East Jerusalem socially, politically, and psychologically from the West Bank', observes Amir Cheshin (Former Advisor to Jerusalem Mayor, interview, 17 November 2015), but for Palestinians 'they are one unit, Israelis don't understand this'. Post-Oslo Israeli actions moved forward Israel's strategic objectives of political control by separating and weakening Arab East Jerusalem.

The fact that Jerusalem was postponed as a negotiation issue in the 1993 Oslo accord – and eventually never seriously addressed – has been the subject of much deliberation. On the one hand, there is a legitimate justification that Oslo was first to develop trust between the two sides through an incremental process of granting Palestinian autonomy. As the process continued and confidence between the two sides built, the premise of this view was that such trust building would then build the momentum for addressing the stickier issues including Jerusalem. A more direct criticism of the Oslo accord was that too much was left unresolved and that it was an intentional bypassing of core issues. Insider Moshe Amirav (interview) states adamantly that Oslo was 'a meeting of cowards' and Prime Minister Rabin was afraid of Jerusalem.

No matter the justification for Jerusalem's relegation in the original Oslo accord, what is clear is the practical effect that its removal had on spatial and political changes within the city. The constant negotiations and lack of resolution has 'enabled Israel to fully exploit its decidedly more powerful position' and allowed Israel to use its superior power to tighten its control over the Holy City (Benvenisti, 2007, p. 117). The incompleteness of the Oslo process allowed for the continuance of Israel's hegemonic project in Jerusalem (Jay Rothman, Professor, Bar Ilan University, interview, 13 January 2016). Instead of preserving Jerusalem as a place of possible future co-existence, Oslo 'opened up competition over the city' and Israel, having the stronger hand, proceeded to take actions to pre-empt and pre-determine final status negotiations over Jerusalem (Mansour Nsara, Ben Gurion University, interview, 4 February 2016). This highlights the fact that irresolution and indeterminacy in national diplomatic politics is not neutral, but can provide the necessary time and void in institutional authority within which the stronger actor can continue to exercise unilateral actions. 'Managing, as opposed to resolving, a conflict is usually in the interests of those in control', Michael Dumper usefully points out (Presentation at Dar Isaaf Nashashibi, Jerusalem, 4 February 2016). The extended nature of the Oslo process did not put things on hold on the ground (as some envisioned and hoped) but rather gave Israel the time to consolidate further its hold over Jerusalem and to separate it – socially, economically, politically, and psychologically – from the remainder of the West Bank. Israel has used temporality – the passing of time – as a leveraging mechanism.[6]

## Camp David, Clinton Parameters, and Geneva

*Look what has happened on the ground during all these negotiations.*
   Nabeel Shaath, Commissioner of International Relations Palestinian Authority,
interview, 4 February 2016

With Oslo's indefinite postponement of Jerusalem negotiations, the first substantive official discussion of Jerusalem did not take place until a new effort at negotiations at Camp David (Maryland, USA) which began in July 2000. This summit represented a potential turning point in political progress because Israel, for the first time in its history, publicly agreed to explore the possibility of politically dividing the city.[7] Israel's adamant and long-held stance that Jerusalem was always to be united under Israeli control was 'shattered' by Prime Minister Barak at Camp David, and the Israeli taboo against redrawing Jerusalem borders and against the transferring of Arab neighbourhoods to Palestinian authority was broken (Klein, 2007). Despite Israel's opening stance that opposed the possibility of Palestinian sovereignty anywhere within the municipal borders of Jerusalem,[8] this evolved during negotiations to propose Palestinian sovereignty in 'external neighbourhoods' of Jerusalem, in two quarters of the Old City, and autonomy or partial sovereignty in 'internal neighbourhoods'[9] (Lehrs, 2013). In the end Camp David failed, according to most observers, due to irrevocable differences about governing authority over the Haram al Sharif. One Israeli insider, who met with PLO Chairman Arafat prior to the Camp David negotiations, recounts Arafat's view on Jerusalem – 'our fight for Jerusalem and the Haram/Temple Mount has to do with our place in the Arab world. We don't have anything, not even territory. All we have is the Haram' (Moshe Amirav, interview, 12 November 2015). Concerned with history and his place in the wider Arab world, Arafat in the end refused to accept any proposals about the status of Jerusalem that did not meet his minimal condition of Palestinian sovereignty over the Haram Al-Sharif.

   In December 2000, two weeks before the end of his term, American President Clinton – an active participant at Camp David – put foward an American proposal on Jerusalem and other permanent status issues. These 'Clinton parameters' took a modified two-state approach to the larger territorial issues, with Israel to withdraw from 94 to 96 per cent of the West Bank and territorially compensate the Palestinians from Israel's sovereign territory. In return, Israel would be able to annex the large settlement blocks surrounding Jerusalem to the north, east, and south. In Jerusalem proper, Clinton declared that 'Arab areas are Palestinian and Jewish ones are Israeli.

This would apply to the Old City as well'. This implies political and administrative separation of the two sides of the city, although the nature of the intracity boundary was left open as well as issues of how to create territorial continuity for both sides in a situation where the city is a mosaic of segregated neighbourhoods that span west and east. Of special note is that Israel accepted Palestinian sovereignty over 'internal' neighbourhoods close to the Old City, something they were resistant to in Camp David. In the Temple/Haram, it was proposed that Palestine would be sovereign but would honour the deep Jewish historic connection to the site. Both sides accepted Clinton's ideas in principle but added reservations. Even though the Clinton parameters lend themselves to differing interpretations, they have become accepted benchmarks, and negotiation proposals since then have been variations of those parameters.[10]

The failure of Camp David negotiations led to political and local spatial dynamics obstructive of peacemaking. Feeling under threat prior to and during Camp David, the right-wing opposition in Israel acted to block progress. One important partner in Prime Minister Barak's government (the ultra-orthodox 'Guardians of the Sephardim' or Shas Party) left the coalition, leaving Barak without a majority and weakening his capacity to take action. At the local level, the right-wing opposition acted to 're-explode' Jerusalem as a way to block progress (Menachem Klein, Senior Lecturer, Ban-Ilan University, interview, 21 October 2015). As noted in the previous chapter, the most significant inflammatory event occurred when opposition leader Ariel Sharon visited the Temple Mount in late September 2000. Surrounded by hundreds of Israeli riot police, Sharon and a handful of Likud politicians marched up to the Haram al-Sharif, the site of the Dome of the Rock and Al-Aqsa Mosque, the third holiest shrine in Islam. The appearance of Sharon, whom the Palestinians regarded as a symbol of Israeli aggression, on the Haram instigated large riots in the Old City. After Palestinians on the Temple Mount threw rocks over the Western Wall at Jewish worshipers, Israeli police fired back, eventually switching to live ammunition which killed four Palestinian youths. Violence continued in the Old City thereafter and throughout the West Bank, and the second (or Al-Aqsa) Intifada had started a 4-year period of intense Israeli-Palestinian violence that would cost thousands of Israeli and Palestinian lives.

In addition to Israeli political manoeuvrings which obstructed the peace opportunities posed by Camp David and the Clinton parameters, another phenomenon would begin in the shadow of these negotiation efforts – increased efforts by right-wing groups to insert Jewish settlers into Arab neighbourhoods and into the Muslim Quarter of the Old City. These groups appealed to the symbolic value of claiming all Jerusalem for Jews and acted through their spatial tactics to increase tension in the city, further disrupting opportunities for peacemaking. Assisted by government, settler movement into Arab neighbourhoods was done in the spirit that 'everything should be done to prevent the Clinton parameters' (Klein, interview).

Local actions such as the Sharon visit and tactical actions such as Jewish settler micro-insertion into Arab areas occurred in response to the threat of negotiations and effectively obstructed progress. Amid national diplomatic openings, local actions were leading to a downward spiral of violence and reinforcement of the Israeli hegemonic approach to the city. A trap had been created – Israeli urban-based reactions to the threat of negotiations and possible political division of the city increased instability in the city, which then stimulated violent Palestinian response, the net effect of which was to hinder the possibility of effective negotiated outcomes. The power of local-spatial dynamics to thwart national peacemaking is evident.

Amid the violence of the second Intifada (2000–2005), an accord between Israeli and Palestinian negotiators was prepared in secret for more than 2 years. The official document, the Geneva Accord, was published December 2003.[11] Although it received broad international support, it was heavily criticized by then Prime Minister Sharon. The Geneva Accord follows much of the logic of the Camp David summit and Clinton parameters, imagining a two-state solution, with territorial modifications, applied both to the broader West Bank geography and to the city of Jerusalem. Despite Geneva, the intense and ongoing violence and loss of life in the second Intifada had by then created a debilitating momentum which overwhelmed any possibility for a negotiated peace to be accepted. In response to the security threat, Israel engaged in further tightening of its control over Jerusalem. The physical wedge between Jerusalem and the West Bank – first established with Israel checkpoints in the post-Oslo years of the mid-1990s – was strengthened as military roadblocks into the city were made permanent. In addition, on the death of local Arab Jerusalem leader Faisal Husseini in 2001, the local political life of East Jerusalem was further shuttered, with the Orient House – the headquarters of the PLO in the 1980s and 1990s – permanently shut down by Israel. Amid the frightening violence of the Intifada, Israel tightened the screws over its control of the city. As terror attacks increased in the early 2000s, there were growing public calls to separate the two sides through the building of a physical barrier. From 2000 to 2002 Prime Minister Sharon remained hesitant to act amid different views of where the barrier should be built and also because he faced right-wing opposition within his own camp to dividing greater Israel. Nonetheless, by March 2002, a one month period when 128 Israelis were killed by attacks, Sharon and his government had had enough, bowed to mounting pressure, and granted the Army permission to design the barrier. The building of this separation barrier over the next decade, as discussed earlier, has had a massive and incapacitating impact on Israeli-Palestinian political relations. By 2005, the process of walling off and disembowelling the city of Palestinian capacity was in full force, creating the structure of severe political-spatial disequilibrium evident during my 2016 research. To this day, the barrier is a palpable and disheartening sign of the failure and defeat of peace prospects in the region.

*Welcome to your new home, we have been waiting for you for 3000 years. This is your heritage – ever since and ever more.*

> Advertising poster, David's Village luxury apartment complex built for wealthy overseas Jewish residents, Mamilla District (located along the green line)

From Oslo to Geneva and beyond, national peacemaking has been bedevilled by local on-the-ground dynamics that were either insufficient to support political progress or acted as major retardants to peace prospects. Oslo's incremental process failed to deliver socio-spatial and material wellbeing to Palestinians in Jerusalem but instead was associated with increased restrictions on Palestinians and the institutional and functional separation of Arab Jerusalem from the rest of the West Bank. As Oslo opened up possibilities, changes on the ground were consolidating Israel's hegemonic power over the city. Camp David and the Clinton parameters provided opportunities for national peacemaking, yet were associated with inflammatory local processes instigated by obstructive actors who felt under threat from political scenarios that would politically share the city. By the time of Geneva, local violence resulting in part from past negotiation failures were lethal impediments to national peace progress and in the end initiated the largest Israeli infrastructure project in its history to separate the two sides physically and *de facto* expand Israeli control over major settlement zones in the West Bank.

The trajectories of national peacemaking and urban dynamics are interlocking. What happens at the national political level – whether actual agreements or prospective peace deals – has impacts on what goes on at spatial and social levels and, in Jerusalem, these urban dynamics have had obstructive influences on the success of negotiated peacemaking. The city became a platform for symbolic manipulation by partisan actors, which condemned national peace prospects to the dustbin of ineffectiveness and eventual irrelevancy.

Alongside the episodic ups and downs of peace negotiations and local counter-actions exists the longer-term and largely uninterrupted Israeli project of settlement expansion both in and outside Jerusalem. From 1994 to 2016, there has been the continuous building by Israel of Jewish neighbourhoods in contested parts of Jerusalem and Jewish settlements throughout the rest of the West Bank. As noted in the previous chapter, the number of Jewish settlers living in East Jerusalem and other parts of the West Bank increased from 231,200 in 1992 to 591,120 in 2015 (Peace Now). Within Jerusalem, a total of 205,220 Jewish residents in 2014 lived in annexed parts of East Jerusalem, compared to 125,800 in 1992. Combined with sustained restrictions on Arab development and life in Jerusalem, the Israeli settlement project has created a spatial structure of immense disequilibrium that is deleterious to peace prospects between Israel and the Palestinians. In marriage counselling, psychotherapists caution antagonistic partners to pay attention to the concrete actions of each partner as appropriate guides, rather than focusing on what each side says. Applying this approach to the case at hand, it is clear that Israel has not been a willing partner moving in the direction of a genuine peace.

## Palestinian Reactions

Palestinian responses to the Israeli hegemonic project have varied over time from frustration and ineptitude to wide-scale violence and destruction. As Israel acted after Oslo to weaken Palestinian governmental influence in East Jerusalem and to separate East Jerusalem from other parts of the West Bank, local Palestinian capacity in Jerusalem to counter Israeli actions has been ineffective and anaemic. The predilection of national governmental, and the Fatah political party, leadership outside Jerusalem has typically emphasized national political issues rather than urban tactics or strategies, leaving a void in the ability of local Jerusalem Palestinians to organize resistance to Israeli programmes and plans. 'Palestinian leadership on Jerusalem has been disappointing', remarks Palestinian activist Riman Barakat (Former Co-Director, Israel-Palestine Center for Research and Information, interview, 22 November 2015). Place-based resistance in Jerusalem has been commonly overshadowed by Fatah's emphasis on national political issues of sovereignty and political control. Both in 2016 and in 1994, the feeling among many Palestinians I interviewed was that their national leadership believed that larger negotiations involving sovereignty, borders, and right of Palestinian return must first be successful before local issues of land development and growth can be addressed.

My interviews with national Palestinian leadership do not disabuse me of this sense of local incapacity in dealing with Jerusalem. Adnan Husseini is the Palestinian Governor of Jerusalem District and the cousin of Faisal Husseini. Sixty-eight years old, his personal history as an elder Palestinian is linked to established institutions and family. During our discussion, he exclaims a deep historic sense of injustice. When I probe him about specific strategies that the PNA employs in countering Israel in Jerusalem, he begins to speak of specific actions, but then returns to broader themes of occupation and historic domination (Adnan Husseini, interview, 25 January 2016). His recounting of the wider historic context feels like a type of defeatism at times, as if he is so used to losing out to Israel that he cannot afford the hopefulness of contemplating Palestinian counter-actions on the ground. This attitude appears as if ingrained in him after living through continuous assertive actions by Israel; like a reflex after so much losing and feeling his side is not being heard. I sense that this attitude of historic injustice and hopelessness may be linked to the common criticism of the PNA as emphasizing national platitudes but not on-the-ground counter-strategies and actions. Samih Al-Abid acknowledges the costs of having local issues of growth and development overshadowed by national negotiators' attention to larger political issues. Al-Abid was Deputy Minister of Planning and International Cooperation for 12 years and was involved in Camp David and Annapolis (2007) negotiations. In both negotiations, he emphasized to his compatriots the importance of having control over land and territory ('I wanted the land, the space'). Yet, Palestinian negotiators emphasized that all the issues of a comprehensive peace accord needed to be dealt with concurrently and this approach ultimately failed, leaving Palestinians today with full autonomy over only 18 per cent of the West Bank outside Jerusalem. Al-Abid's priority was territory; 'once you have the space, you have the capacity to move and function. Once you have land and space, it no longer is a political issue but becomes a planning issue, of how to develop. Then negotiations over the other issues would be different'. He explains, 'Palestinian politicians at that time didn't understand the importance and power of planning' (Samir Al-Abid, interview, 11 February 2016). Jerusalem, so important to the Palestinian political cause, has ironically become submerged as a place of political resistance as the national leadership stays above the fray with national political claims and slogans.

The outbreak of intense violence and hostility during the second Intifada was stimulated by the acute tension created by Sharon's visit to the Haram, yet the pressure had been building prior to September 2000. Palestinian popular discontent, the failure of the Camp David summit, and the pressure by extremist groups such as Islamic Jihad and Hamas to use force all prepared the ground for the outbreak of violence (Klein, 2003). The loss of Israeli and Palestinian lives from late 2000 to 2005 was extensive, and violent conflict took on a self-perpetuating logic and energy that buried any chance for national peacemaking. Hundreds of Israelis died as a result of horrendous mass-casualty suicide bomb attacks in Jerusalem and other cities. Thousands of Palestinians were killed in operations by the Israel Defense Forces, sometimes during targeted assassination projects. The trajectory of violence disrupted, invaded, and intersected with the mundane trajectory of everyday life (Hatuka, 2011). The chaotic reality that is Jerusalem was further compounded by violence.

The record of Israeli-Palestinian peacemaking since 1993 shows peace to be a complex emergent process that must necessarily engage elements at both national political and urban spatial levels. It further exhibits how peacemaking operates amid an unstable equilibrium always susceptible to disruption. By the first half of the 2000–2010 decade, the Israeli-Palestinian region was reaching breaking point, with seemingly unsustainable levels of violence continuing. A critical juncture was at hand. Palestinian violence and the threat it posed to Israeli society were increasing Israeli counter-responses which strengthened its hegemonic hold over Jerusalem and the region. These actions – tougher and wider Israeli security operations, increased cordoning off of Jerusalem from the rest of the West Bank, continued Jewish development in and outside Jerusalem – were anathema to possibilities that any national peacemaking effort would be successful. Yet, violence was also increasing pressure on both sides to re-engage with each other in negotiations, at least over a ceasefire if not over a larger peace.[12] The combined impacts of this intense period of violence were thus incompatible. Violence was an instigator of both increased pressure for renewed negotiations and a strengthening and consolidation of Israel's hegemony that hinders possibilities for negotiations to be successful. The interlocking and mutually obstructive relationship between national politics and socio-spatial dynamics at the local level is evident in examining the destructive spiral associated with violent conflict.

Examining more specifically Arab East Jerusalem during these years of violent conflict, one witnesses a void in local Palestinian leadership and thus Israeli officials had no local representatives to talk to who could potentially dampen down city-based violence. This void was the intentional product of Israeli restrictions on Palestinian governance in the city, first instituted during the Oslo years, culminating with the closing of Orient House in 2001, and continuing today. This local void was exacerbated by the emphasis of the national Palestinian leadership (both the PNA and Fatah) on national, not local, issues. This void incapacitated any ability for there to be local agreements to stem violence or for there to be non-violent place-based resistance by Palestinians in Jerusalem, leaving the door open to Palestinian extremist sentiment and influence.[13] Israeli building of settlements in and around Jerusalem continued without effective local protests by city-based counter-movements. Without any local mediating influence, Jerusalem increasingly became an open 'arena attracting non-Jerusalem actors for nationalistic reasons' (Menachem Klein, interview, 21 October 2015). Perpetrators of Palestinian violence in Jerusalem, despite increasingly stringent Israeli security operations, continued to come from outside the city as well as from within.

The political impact on Arab East Jerusalem of national peacemaking stasis and of sustained violence and instability was clearly marked in 2006, when the more extreme political party of Hamas won in East Jerusalem elections for national Palestinian leadership. What Israel feared most – a strengthening of extreme political elements within Jerusalem – was itself a product of Israeli restrictions on political activity in the city. Lacking urban leadership and increasingly cut off from Ramallah-based Fatah political influence, Arab East Jerusalem was becoming increasingly conservative and reactionary. In certain neighbourhoods, such as Sur Baher and Umm Tuba, Hamas is stepping in to deliver services not provided by the Municipality (Israel Kimhi, interview, 3 December 2015). The local void opened the door not just to Hamas but also to other adherents of political Islam to exert influence in the city. Compared to before 2000, Al Aqsa Mosque has increasingly become an 'identity centre' or epicentre for Arab East Jerusalem politics (Menachem Klein, interview). Facing despair, Palestinian political dynamics in the city have more and more aligned with Islamic movements. The Islamic Movement in Israel began to mobilize around Al Aqsa by bussing its faithful into Jerusalem for Friday prayers and it also started to protest Israeli actions in such places as the inner neighbourhood of Sheikh Jarrah, and against Israeli projects in the city (such as the Museum of Tolerance to be built partially on a Muslim cemetery) seen as threatening of Arab heritage (Pullan *et al.*, 2013).[14]

## Jerusalem as Battleground

Jerusalem, instead of providing a potential moderating influence based on local agreements and accommodations, has instead become a battleground between exclusionary and rigid perspectives not conducive to political accommodation. Among the Jewish population, at the end of 2014, 34 per cent of the population was ultra-orthodox and another 33 per cent was religious ('observant' or 'traditional-observant' Jews, as measured by the Israel Central Bureau of Statistics); these proportions are significantly higher than for the country as a whole (9 per cent and 24 per cent, respectively)[15] (Israel Kimhi, Jerusalem Institute for Israel Studies, press release for Jerusalem Day 2016). This has created a politically conservative Jewish Jerusalem, with only about 20 per cent of the Jewish population holding political left or centre attitudes (Marik Shtern, Jerusalem Institute for Israel Studies, interview, 27 January 2016). On the Palestinian side, the continued Jewish hegemonic development of settlements and Jewish settler activity in contested areas of the city is countered by a growing Islamization and radicalization. Israel's continued domination and partisan governance of the city, together with national Palestinian leadership's hesitancy to engage locally without a wider peace, has created a void filled by a growing extremist Islamization.

The local political impact of the continued failure of national peacemaking has hamstrung the capacity of the city to act as a place of local political accommodation potentially stimulating of a larger national peace. Rather than a possible constitutive agent promoting accommodative interaction, Jerusalem has become, more and more, an ideological straightjacket as Israeli settlement activity and the building of the separation barrier locks the city into rigid competition and a never-ending cycle of Israeli consolidation in the name of security and Palestinian extremist actions and violence in the name of defence.

## Notes

1. In 1996, area A (full Palestinian autonomy) comprised 3 per cent of the land area of the West Bank, exclusive of East Jerusalem, area B (Palestinian territorial control with security shared between Palestinians and Israelis) 27 per cent, and area C (Israeli control) 70 per cent. As of 2016, primarily due to the 1998 Wye River Memorandum, these percentages were 18, 22, and 60 per cent, respectively.
2. 'I was the first person to talk to the Palestinians in a serious way and it was with Shamir's permission', recounts Amirav. These were secret negotiations and when news broke that Likud and the PLO were in secret talks about a demilitarized Palestinian state, these talks were abruptly terminated.
3. Knesset law, 'Implementation of the Agreement on Gaza and Jericho (Restrictions on Activity)', 1994. Because Palestinians do not *accept* East Jerusalem to be part of Israel, this law is held as invalidly applied to East Jerusalem.

4. Many Jerusalem Palestinian couples, due to high home prices in Jerusalem, had suburbanized to communities just outside the city border (in places such as A-Ram, Anata, and Abu Dis). Although living just outside the city border, the life of most of these households remained connected to the city in terms of economic and social life. These households were now threatened by loss of Jerusalem residency status and restrictions on their mobility into Jerusalem proper.
5. From 1967 to 2014, over 14,000 Palestinians have had their residency status revoked by Israel, see: http://www.btselem.org/jerusalem/revocation_statistics.
6. This dynamic can be seen in the contemporary lack of resolution regarding Palestinian authority in the West Bank. The carving up of the West Bank area into A, B, and C zones has created Palestinian enclaves of authority cut off from one another and continuation of direct Israeli control over most of West Bank territory. Whereas full Palestinian authority in the West Bank would terminate Israeli security operations in the territories, this lack of progress in granting full authority to the PNA in the West Bank allows Israeli surveillance and intelligence agents to act widely in the territories (Udi Dekel, Israeli Institute for National Security Studies, interview, 3 February 2016).
7. Israel's post-Oslo consideration of possibly dividing the sovereignty of Jerusalem did not actually start with Camp David, but had earlier been considered in secret negotiations between Israeli negotiator Yossi Beilin and Palestinian negotiator Abu Mazin (Mahmoud Abbas, now PNA President) which took place soon after Oslo, in 1994–1995, as an attempt to move forward discussions of Jerusalem under Oslo (Klein, 2003). Not officially published until 2000, this understanding would have expanded the city's territory, created an umbrella municipality for the Jerusalem area, and established two sub-municipalities – one Jewish and other Arab – which would provide services to their respective parts. Based on a functional approach to authority in the city, the understanding would have basically preserved the unity of the city but on a variable basis, demarcating different levels of division within the city (Klein, 2003). The assassination of Prime Minister Rabin in November 1995, and the election of a Likud government in May 1996, prevented this plan from being realized.
8. This opening stance allowed for the establishment of a Palestinian capital in the villages of Abu Dis or Anata outside municipal borders and the granting of limited municipal authority for Arab neighbourhoods in East Jerusalem (Lehrs, 2013).
9. Although not explicitly itemized, 'external' neighbourhoods more distant from the Old City are often thought to include Beit Hanina and Shuafat, while 'internal' neighbourhoods nearer to the Old City include Sheikh Jarrah, Abu Tor, and Silwan.
10. Taba in 2001 and Annapolis in 2007 wrestled with how the parameter approach could be implemented, in particular focusing on where to place the border within Jerusalem, how each of the two sovereign cities within Jerusalem would be geographically integrated, and how to resolve the status of the Old City and the Holy Basin surrounding it.
11. A detailed expanded version of the Accord, with annexes, was published in 2009.
12. During the second Intifada, in addition to the 2 years of secret negotiations resulting in the 2003 Geneva Initiative, the Roadmap for Peace plan was put forth in 2003 by the 'Quartet' of the United States, Russia, European Union, and United Nations. A summit between Abbas and Sharon in February 2005 is viewed as demarcating the end of the second Intifada.
13. The ability of local leaders in cities and towns to moderate violence has been shown by Varshney (2002).
14. The Islamic Movement in Israel was banned by Israel in November 2015.
15. The proportion of the Jewish population in Jerusalem that is secular or 'traditional but non-observant' is 33 per cent, substantially below the national average of 67 per cent. Estimates of the Jewish population in Jerusalem that is 'secular' are put as low as 17–20 per cent.

Chapter 4

# Jerusalem III: The Self-Perpetuating Cycle of Israeli Hegemonic Territoriality

*Despite its numerous esoteric and celestial attributes, Jerusalem's magical and mystical quality is amazingly accessible to all seekers at a certain level of recognition. It engages one in the centuries-long attempt to understand humankind and its relationship to the unknown. Jerusalem draws you in and welcomes you to the transcendent and stimulates the senses and the soul at a core level. Jerusalem is for everyone to share this magic in one's own way. Efforts to obtain and demarcate this connection for one's own will fail because Jerusalem grants its gift to all who seek it. – In peace, shalom, salaam.*

Author's journal notes, 17 February 2016

In his ground-breaking article, Sack (1983, p. 55) defines territoriality as an 'attempt to affect, influence, or control actions, interactions, or access by asserting and attempting to enforce control over a specific geographic area'. He also asserts that territoriality can engender more territoriality and more relationships to mould, that it has a momentum of its own in creating inequalities, and that it can backfire, leading to a reduction of control, disorganization, alienation, and hostility. In this chapter, I examine the political geographic process of Israeli hegemonic territoriality in Jerusalem and the West Bank, focusing on three keys aspects of the enterprise: the self-perpetuating tendency of Israeli territoriality; the requisites of bordering and bounding; and the problematic limits faced by Israel in intervening in its West Bank peripheral frontier. This chapter illuminates the self-perpetuating cycle, practical complexities, and political limits of the hegemonic project. Israel has been engaged in a project of territoriality since 1967 in a concerted effort to secure control in Jerusalem and the West Bank. However, I conclude that this project has, instead, destabilized and *de facto* divided Jerusalem's urban system. Further, the Israeli project has exhibited an insatiable spatial appetite for application at increasing geographic scale. As the hegemonic project enlarges its geographic scale, it has become increasingly entangled in the volatilities that it produces, revealing both the practical and political limits of hegemonic territoriality. The far-reaching geographic reach of Israel's hegemonic project has forced new practical complexities upon Israeli policymakers – concerning the future political status of the Israel/West Bank region and Jerusalem and the tactics needed to protect settlements in the face of continuing instability and violence.

## Territoriality in the City of Jerusalem

Israeli actions since 1967 have, at one level, increased Israeli political control of the city. Growth strategies have sustained a solid, albeit declining, Jewish majority within municipal borders drawn by Israel. At the same time, the location of new neighbourhoods has created a contiguous Jewish presence throughout the city and thus a degree of functional and demographic unification for Jewish residents. More recently, a separation barrier has been constructed that cordons off Arab East Jerusalem from the West Bank. These actions have created a landscape conducive to Israeli political control of the city and have made political division of the city increasingly problematic and unlikely. Outside the city borders, 'thickening' strategies pertaining to building and expansion of three major suburban settlement blocs in the West Bank create the spatial foundations for future Israeli consolidation of territorial claims. Such a project constitutes a 'civilian occupation' reinforced by police and security personnel (Segal and Weizman, 2003, p. 15). This leads even an Israeli political opponent of this territorial strategy – a leftist Knesset member – to comment when looking out at the urban landscape from one of the city's promenades 'but you must admit, it is so clever' (reported by Yudith Oppenheimer, interview, 26 January 2016).

*A city is always a realization of the stories that it tells about itself.*

Sharon Rotbard (2015)

Yet, the landscape of domination is one of internal frictions and vulnerability which increase, not decrease, inter-ethnic instability. Domination and partisan planning become exposed as strategies within conditions of ethno-political contest, not as solutions to ethnic polarization. Indicative of the continuing unstable conditions that exist in Jerusalem is the recent wave of violence that has centred on the Jerusalem area. Tension rose first in September 2015 in East Jerusalem with protests, clashes and violence spreading to the West Bank outside Jerusalem. From September 2015 to January 2017, there have been 46 Israelis killed and 645 injured. Palestinian violence included 169 stabbing attacks and 103 attempted stabbings, 126 shootings, 51 vehicular ramming attacks, and one bus bombing. These attacks have been carried out primarily by young lone extremists, most of them from East Jerusalem but some from the West Bank, who have generally not been operatives of established organizations but rather young individuals inspired by the general political climate (Israel Ministry of Foreign Affairs).[1] With Palestinian youths acting out of hopelessness and despair, such violence points to the pervasive effects of decades of Israeli hegemonic actions in the city and exposes practical limits to the sustainability of such a political programme.

Israel's ability since 1967 to control Jerusalem politically is built on fragile foundations. The major friction produced by hegemonic territorial planning within the city is due to extended and expansive Jewish penetration into disputed and contested territory in annexed parts of the city. With political competition over disputed territory came Israel's perceived need to penetrate Palestinian territory in the city as a way to strengthen its sovereignty argument. Yet, over time, the means towards achieving the political control goal – that of penetration – has created spatial conditions of instability that militate against Israel's capacity to control the urban environment. In an effort to counter such instability, Israel then engages in subsequent rounds of penetration and spatial consolidation in order to control an urban fabric of complex ethnic geographies and unstable interfaces. Yet, such actions further manipulate ethnic geographies, creating new spatial axes of tension in the city rather than addressing the political-spatial causes of intergroup conflict.

*As we strengthen our hold on Jerusalem, there is increasing terror all around.*
        Yehonathan Golani, Director, Planning Administration, Ministry of Interior,
                interview, 27 December 1994 (cited in Bollens, 2000)

Political territorial competition since 1967 has brought Jewish and Arab communities spatially closer together in Jerusalem. Demographically-based planning in pursuit of political control meant that the location of new Jewish neighbourhoods was just as important to Israel as the pace and extent of development. Thus, the new neighbourhoods after 1967 were built in 'east' Jerusalem across the old green line. If Israel solely desired to safeguard a Jewish majority in the city, West Jerusalem areas could have accommodated extensive Jewish growth in relatively safe environs separate from East Jerusalem. With the goal of political territorial control over the larger annexed city, however, spatial penetration and consolidation of the east became vital. Thus, Israeli expansions fingered into and fragmented Arab urbanization but at the same time attempted to stay separate through the use of extravagant infrastructure systems and natural geological divides.[2] Israel wanted to penetrate the wider Arab fabric while still remaining separate. Yet, Israeli partisan policies aimed at penetrating East Jerusalem increases Jewish vulnerability and Israeli residents find that major portions of the city are off-limits to them due to insecurity and fear. The greater the territory that Israel has sought to control politically in the contested urban environment, the less capacity it has to control fully the urban environment. This, in turn, stimulates further unilateral actions by Israel – both geographic and military – in efforts to sustain its political claims. The fallacy of the territorial project is that its goal – political control – appears feasible, but only comes at the expense of an urban stability required for the exercise of genuine control. The implementation of hegemonic territoriality has created urban conditions that erode the urban stability required for the exercise of authentic control.

The physical and symbolic extension of Israeli territorial claims into disputed areas creates a landscape that exacerbates intergroup tension and potential conflict. Significant Israeli intrusions into eastern Arab Jerusalem increase potential violent interfaces between Israeli and Palestinian communities and appear counterproductive to Israel's goals of building and safeguarding a Jewish Jerusalem. The extensive spatial reach of Jewish neighbourhoods adjacent to marginalized and fragmented Arab villages provides multiple and indefensible interface points where the potential for interpersonal and intergroup conflict increases.[3] These interfaces are spatial focal points where politically-constructed material and psychological inequalities are most visible and inflammatory.

Volatile interfaces are evident along the old green line/border that divided the city from 1949 to 1967, along interfaces between Jewish and Arab neighbourhoods created in annexed parts of Jerusalem, along the 1967 Israeli municipal border, and at checkpoints of the separation barrier whose construction began in 2003. These are areas of frequent tension due to the proximity of Arab and Jewish residents and the frequency of Jewish-Arab interactions. The potentially antagonistic neighbourhoods on the narrowest ground are those along the old 1949 'green line' border. The physical division of Jerusalem from 1949 to 1967 often separated close neighbourhoods that since 1967 exist vulnerably along the old seam line area. In the violence of 2015 and 2016, many stabbing attacks took place near the old seam line, at and near the Damascus Gate area in East Jerusalem. In other cases, post-1967 Israeli building over the green line penetrated near to existing Arab villages. The contact points along interface areas east of the 1949 green line are the product of Israel's efforts to extend its political claims and fragment the north–south Arab axis of villages. The final set of interfaces represents contact points along the 1967 outer border of Israeli-defined Jerusalem and at separation barrier interfaces. These types of interfaces are paradoxical because the Israeli-delineated municipal border and the separation barrier, meant to separate peoples, have actually drawn the two sides closer in space due to the land-use competition over Jerusalem. For example, much of A-Ram's growth can be attributed to its location just outside the Israeli-defined municipal border and its ability to act as a safety net for Arabs unable to live in Israeli-defined Jerusalem due to housing restrictions. And the robust development of Kafr Aqab and Shuafat refugee camp areas is because of its proximity to the separation barrier. Borders and barriers, far from separating and sealing, have created increased interaction and points of conflict between the antagonistic groups.

*The division of urban space to separate one group from another is a colonial fantasy. In a city, there will always be interaction and mixing.*

Haim Yacobi, Professor, Ben Gurion University of the Negev,<br>interview, 29 October 2015

*Victory is creating a better political reality, not in conquering. We win every battle, but we lose the war.*

Ami Ayalon, Head of Shin Bet (1996–2000),<br>*The Gatekeepers*, documentary film, 2012

Because Israel's hegemonic project within Jerusalem has produced instability that militates against its success, it has no seeming end point or completion. Penetration and consolidation of Jewish development in the city creates urban disequilibria and tensions which, consequently, necessitate further hegemonic consolidation and measures seeking to control the urban environment. This quandary faced by Israel was visible during the wave of violence starting in 2015. In response to daily knifing attacks on the streets, Israel instituted forty new checkpoints and roadblocks *within* the city (affecting the mobility of 138,000 Palestinians in nine neighbourhoods) in order to regulate Arab entry into Jewish parts of the city (OCHAOPT, 2016). This action by an Israeli government, which constantly proclaims the unified nature of the city, was an awkward admission of the *de facto* contested and divided nature of the real city.[4]

Despite decades of consistent hegemonic action in the city, Jerusalem remains divided functionally and psychologically. Hegemonic actions have increased Jewish spatial and political claims to disputed territory, penetrated and fragmented Palestinian communities and villages, and substantially restructured the physical landscape of the Holy City. These strategies have drastically divided the social fabric of the urban system. With a former head of the strategic planning division of the Israel Defense Force acknowledging that 'there is a two-state reality in Jerusalem', the limits of Israel's territorial approach to the city are revealed (Udi Dekel, interview, 3 February 2016).

## The Urban Demands of Peace

The distorted and unequal disequilibrium of contemporary Jerusalem presents those seeking peace in the region with significant obstacles. For Israel to engage effectively in a peace process with tangible benefits for Jerusalem Palestinians, it will need to step back from a hegemonic project which, despite incomplete and partial success, has argued successfully for its continued application based on the unstable conditions it creates. I recount an earlier statement (from Nadav Shragai, Jerusalem Center for Public Affairs, interview, 17 December 2015) because it is a central tenant of the hegemonic project and it resonates with a large share of Israeli Jews – that it is 'proven the only way to combat Palestinian resistance is not to set back from terrorist actions but to maximize friction and to be there on the ground. To assure safe Jewish access, you can't do this from remote control or from a "parameter", you have to be on the ground'. In the face of constant Jewish-Muslim tension over the course of more than a century, and extreme periods of violence since 1980, this stance is understandable.

Shragai predicts dire consequences should Jerusalem be politically divided as part of a negotiated peace. 'Two sovereignties over one city is a sure way to continue the conflict', he posits, as Jewish neighbourhoods located along the dividing line would be exposed to wide scale terror and shooting after political division. These neighbourhoods would become 'frontline' border areas, and the 'Lebanonization' of Jerusalem would result.[5] This would continue the cruel irony that as the Oslo 'peace process' advanced, more Jewish lives, not fewer, were lost due to political violence.[6] He forecasts out-migration of Jews from these neighbourhoods and from Jerusalem, entirely due to violence, with Palestinians more and more moving to the Israeli side of the border to ensure access to city benefits. 'Division would defeat our goals of having more Jews and less Arabs in Jerusalem; indeed, we would see just the opposite', Shragai predicts. 'When I was a boy, I was told I would see peace', he recalls (note: Shragai was born in 1959 and his grandfather was Mayor of Jerusalem from 1948 to 1951); 'I'm not delusional about the prospects for peace now'.

Liberal formulations of peacemaking in Jerusalem must confront this belief system that equates political compromise with renewed hostility and the defeat of Israeli goals pertaining to a Jewish Jerusalem. This perspective asserts that political sharing of Jerusalem would lead to lack of personal safety and threatened group security; thus, Israeli political control and security must be assured through demographic domination on the ground. This is the core of the belief system supporting the Israeli hegemonic project.

*We didn't come here to be a minority. It's not South Africa. We are here on moral grounds and we cannot compare ourselves to Palestinians.*

Eran Razin, Professor, Hebrew University, interview, 11 October 2015

This equating of security with on-the-ground strength and hegemony is a belief held not only by right-wing Israelis. Eran Razin (interview, 11 October 2015), a self-described 'centrist realist' and a member of the Labor Party, notes that the current hegemonic situation is likely to be unsustainable, yet also notes the 'imbalance of power here protects both sides, that proportionate power would tend to bring more destruction and death, and that if there was a greater balance of power Palestinians would engage in behaviour destructive to both sides'. Given the substantial decades-long investment in its hegemonic project, how can the Israeli state step back from further exercise of this project and further consolidation of its position on the ground amid violence and the feeling of threat to its existential existence as a state and people?

*The current situation is like a cancer on Israeli society as a pluralistic state; there is a loss of collective spirit and moral sense.*
Yehuda Doran, Former Member of Shayetet 13 (S'13) (Israeli Navy Seals), interview, 7 November 2015

Yet, the counter-argument to the hegemonic project has considerable merit: that the project has created urban and regional conditions that jeopardize Jewish security and thus is counter to its political objectives; that continued hegemony is not sustainable amid substantial and destabilizing Palestinian material and political marginalization; and that contemporary Jerusalem, despite Israel's decades-long efforts, is in fact a divided city in all but name. Given these continuing conditions of instability, there have been initiatives among Israeli officials that modify the long-held stance equating security with hegemonic control over all of Jerusalem. Even in the hardened political environment of Israel, concepts and goals that drive political strategies are susceptible to modification, adaptation, and evolution over time amid difficult conditions. This was seen in the Camp David negotiations in 2000, when Israel for the first time entertained the idea of sharing, or dividing, sovereignty in the Holy City. In this possibility, Israeli security was viewed as possibly more effectively maintained through the granting of some Palestinian autonomy or sovereignty in the city, rather than the continuation of Israeli hegemonic authority in the city. This was a significant fracturing of the Israeli stance of a 'unified' Jerusalem and showed that even ideas thought by many as sacrosanct can experience modification in negotiations. It should be noted that as late as 2008, after the significant violence of the second Intifada and during the regime of relative hardliner Prime Minister Olmert's administration, the Annapolis proposal called for most large Arab neighbourhoods in Jerusalem to be under Palestinian sovereignty. And further, as recent as the Mitchell-led talks of 2010–2011 and the Kerry-led talks of 2013–2014, the spirit of the Clinton parameters – which divided sovereignty in the city – remained a guiding framework. This shows a continuing and sustaining modification of Israel's thinking concerning hegemonic control of the city.

Future political strategies aimed at building peace in the city may be unable to compensate in the short term for the significant and pervasive instability rooted in the city's spatial and social structure. Should any gradual political empowerment of the local Palestinian community in Jerusalem take place as part of a permanent settlement, the city's spatial structure may in the short term encourage an increase in traumatic urban events in certain parts of the city. Political scientist Dan Miodownik (Hebrew University, interview, 19 January 2016) uses statistical modelling to explain the likelihood of violence in Jerusalem's neighbourhoods. Using models calibrated to account for current levels of violence, he assesses the consequences of reorganizing the political and spatial dimensions of the city. Compared to the baseline 'business as usual' scenario, he predicts under the Clinton parameters option that the overall number of violent events would decrease by 33 per cent and the number of violent neighbourhoods would decrease by 10 per cent. However, violence that would take place would cluster in neighbourhoods along the newly created divide and be concentrated in areas under Israeli control, including parts of East Jerusalem that would be annexed by Israel under the Clinton parameters. Neighbourhood interface areas in the Jerusalem region would provide magnets for Arab activists who reject the terms, or the basic idea, of a Jerusalem settlement with Israel. Thus, although the overall level of violence would lessen, its spatial incidence would cluster in particularly hard-hit Jewish neighbourhoods, but at levels less than the baseline 'business as usual' scenario. The targeting of specific Jewish neighbourhoods is consistent with Shragai's earlier dire prediction, yet of importance here is the forecast that the overall level of violence would be reduced. The critical questions then are – can Israeli political leaders sustain peace efforts sharing Jerusalem sovereignty in the face of violence hitting specific Jewish neighbourhoods? Or, would the local violence associated with Palestinian sovereignty lead to Israeli military actions to solidify the security of Jewish neighbourhoods and restrict the exercise of Palestinian power in the city?

Continued violence in the city after a negotiated settlement over shared sovereignty in Jerusalem, albeit at lower levels, illuminates the challenging issues of dealing with the implementation of a peace agreement – in short, urban peacemaking is a process that involves risks. Rather than thinking that a peace agreement will solve all problems of the city and then perceiving recurring violence as a sign of the failure of the agreement, it appears more realistic to anticipate these problems, factor them into the overall peacemaking equation, and work to sustain the agreement in the light of these foreseeable problems. The severe socio-spatial disequilibrium of contemporary Jerusalem, and the volatilities it produces, will not disappear overnight with an agreement, but linger on and continue to create problems even after a peace agreement has been negotiated. The hope is that with time, the urban system would begin to stabilize as the disequilibrium is attenuated.

Peacemaking when applied to, and operationalized in, the urban arena has distinct spatial micro-scale consequences (both positive and negative) which can make peace implementation at the urban level more problematic than implementing peace at broader geographic scales where antagonistic communities have greater breathing space. Again, similar to what we witness in the implementation of Israel's hegemonic project in Jerusalem, any prospective movement towards peaceful resolution in the city would probably reveal the intertwining and complicating trajectories of national political goals, on the one hand, and their implementation in urban space, on the other.

*We failed in taking over Jerusalem.*
> Moshe Amirav, Advisor to Prime Minister Barak at Camp David Negotiations, interview, 12 November 2015

*If we have failed after more than 45 years, let's think of someone else who will govern and manage East Jerusalem.*
> Amir Cheshin, Arab Advisor to Jerusalem Mayor 1984–1994, interview, 17 November 2015

Security and urbanism are contrasting projects in a politically contested city. The goal of ensuring security in an urban arena demands clear-cut boundaries, checkpoints, compartments that can be sealed, and the control and monitoring of movement. Urbanism, in contrast, necessitates openness, sharing, and unfettered mobility to gain the advantages that come with urban economic and social interactions and interdependency. In shaping a possible political reformulation of Jerusalem, the objectives of security and openness are typically in conflict (Israel Kimhi, interview, 3 December 2015). The idea of Jerusalem as an 'open city' that is politically divided, and whether it can meet the requisites of both urbanity and security, has been discussed as part of larger negotiations as far back as 1987. At that time, Israeli envoy Moshe Amirav met Jerusalem leader Faisal Husseini and discussed a plan for an open metropolitan area hosting two cities and two capitals (Amirav, interview, 12 November 2015). In addition, the goal of creating a politically divided but functionally integrated Jerusalem was the foundation of professional talks, coordinated by the Jerusalem Institute for Israel Studies and the Palestinian International Peace and Cooperation Center, which took place throughout the 1990s.[7] 'Even in the worst days, we were always working on this possibility', recalls participant Israel Kimhi (interview, 3 December 2015). In the Camp David negotiations in 2000, Amirav and Shlomo Hasson proposed Jerusalem as an 'open city' with two municipalities – one Jewish and one Arab. This formulation was included in the paper, 'Jerusalem in the Final Status Accord', which supported Prime Minister Barak in his deliberations and was published by the Prime Minister's office (Moshe Amirav and Shlomo Hasson, interviews, 12 November 2015 and 30 November 2015). More recently, the Israel Palestine Center for Regional Initiatives (IPCRI)[8] published a report in 2014, 'Two States in One Space', which envisioned two states with separate sovereign borders but with freedom of movement. The Jerusalem/Al Quds Metropolitan Authority (JAMA) would contain about 800,000 people and be constituted as a 'Capital Region' of joint sovereignty. There would be a security cordon running around JAMA, but inside the metropolitan area there would be freedom of movement and demilitarization (Riman Barakat, Former Co-Director, IPCRI, interview, 22 November 2015).

Each of these 'open city' ideas for Jerusalem seeks to reconcile Israeli national political demands for security with the requisites of urbanity, and to create a synthesis between political-territorial imperatives and the economic and infrastructure functionality of the urban sphere. From an Israeli security perspective, such an 'open city' would need to be separated from outside negative forces through a strong security cordon surrounding the urban area (Udi Dekel, interview, 3 February 2016). Inside the city, intelligence and police work, cameras, and newer technological tactics could be used to ensure stability and functionality with the hope that over time common interests would bring people together. However, to support this open functioning city, there would need to be external control of its borders.

Even within the open city, Israeli security concerns would probably dictate a security barrier within the city to maintain stability. And the need for Palestinian political autonomy in Jerusalem might necessitate, at least in the short term, a clear political boundary within the city. 'There will need to be a hard border in Jerusalem, but the minute that border is created, it's the day it will start to unravel because the city will begin to heal', suggests Daniel Seidemann (Lawyer, interview, 2 January 2016). 'Reconciliation and healing don't begin until a divorce is completed', he explains, 'and a divorce will be completed here when there is an ugly border.' The intrusiveness of such a political barrier could be attenuated through creative architectural design. For example, buildings could have dual entrances and exits so that users would not feel the division (Kimhi, interview). Electronic checks could be used in the road network, although Israeli security agencies would probably want more severe checkpoints to monitor mobility. In the Old City, open gates would connect the Muslim Quarter to Palestinian Jerusalem and the Jewish Quarter to Israeli Jerusalem. If such a system works in the Old City, this idea of connectivity could be expanded to the larger jurisdiction (Kimhi, interview). Architect Yehuda Greenfield-Gilat (interview, 19 October 2015) laments that 'policymakers are often unable to spatially imagine what they are negotiating over' and he has offered visions of how Jerusalem could be divided in order to maintain security. Instead of one-dimensional or two-dimensional interventions to counter violence such as walls and settlements which stimulate tension, he suggests that there are more sophisticated and flexible three-dimensional systems that could ensure needed mobility while maintaining security. One proposal, envisioning the northern Road 60/Road 1 as a 'binational road with light rail as a natural urban security barrier', was incorporated into the Jerusalem Annex to the Geneva Accord in 2003.

*Israeli political leaders have an axiomatic, almost Jesuit, devotion to an article of faith about the city and are completely cut off from the realities on the ground that exist.*

Daniel Seidemann, Terrestrial Jerusalem, interview, 1 February 2016

The 'open city' proposal for Jerusalem seeks to address the difficult balance between security and urbanism and provides alternatives to the dominant Israeli narrative that security is to be assured only through hegemonic control and strength. To the extent that Jerusalem is the central stumbling block in Israeli-Palestinian negotiations, this vision of an open but politically divided city may loosen the obstructive hold Jerusalem has on larger negotiations. For this conceptualization of an open, functionally integrated, but politically divided Jerusalem to mature, however, the power of ideological systems that obsess on the symbolism of the city will need to provide room for a more realistic assessment of the logistical and practical strategies for dealing with the chaotic reality of contemporary Jerusalem.

## Territoriality in the West Bank outside Jerusalem

Since 1967, Israel has established 127 settlements in the West Bank; in addition, there are about 100 'outposts' erected by settlers without official authorization (OCHAOPT, 2012). In 1996, pursuant to the Oslo II agreement, the West Bank was territorially divided into three sections for what was intended to be an interim period. As of 2016, these territories were:

- Area A = Palestinians have full territorial and security control. Eighteen per cent of the West Bank land area, includes eight Palestinian cities and their surrounding areas, with no Israeli settlements.

- Area B = Palestinians have territorial control, but security control is shared between Israelis and Palestinians. Twenty-two per cent of West Bank land area. This area includes 440 Palestinian villages and their surrounding lands, and no Israeli settlements.

- Area C = Israel maintains full territorial and security control. Sixty per cent of the West Bank land area. This area is comprised of Israeli settlements, outposts, and 'state land'. As of 2015, an estimated 385,900 Jewish settlers lived in Area C in Israeli settlements and outposts. In 2013, approximately 300,000 Palestinians lived in Area C, scattered over 532 residential locations.

Although Area C was to be gradually transferred to Palestinian jurisdiction in accordance with the Oslo II agreement, less than 20 per cent of it has been transferred,[9] and since the mid-1990s it has instead become a location of major Israeli settlement development. Israel has retained complete control of this area, including security and all civil matters such as land allocation, planning and construction, and infrastructure provision. To build settlements in the West Bank, the Israeli government has used

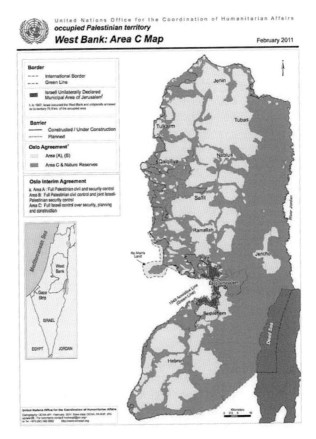

Figure 4.1. Political geography of the West Bank. (*Source*: United Nations Office for the Coordination of Humanitarian Affairs in the Occupied Palestinian Territory)

various means of land seizure. The primary method has been to transfer to Israeli control areas that were Jordanian government land or whose ownership was not formally registered as 'state land'. Other methods include the seizing of 'abandoned' land of refugees and others who have left the West Bank and the closure of land for military purposes. The Coordinator of Government Activities in the Territories (or COGAT), whose West Bank branch is headed by an Army Brigadier-General, is a unit in the Israeli Ministry of Defense responsible for implementing the Israeli government's policy in Area C. It constitutes the civilian authority for residential zoning and infrastructure and is responsible for addressing the needs of Israeli settlements. Local governance of settlements in the West Bank is exercised by six regional councils, thirteen local councils, and four city councils. For large land areas, Israeli regional councils, established in 1979, dominate the planning of land-use zones, roads and nature reserves, and have been used by Israeli authorities to channel services and benefits to Jewish settlers.

Fully 70 per cent of Area C has been demarcated by Israel as within settler municipal boundaries, where permits for development are denied to Palestinians. Palestinians cannot build in Area C without an army permit which is, according to a World Bank report, 'almost impossible' for Palestinians to obtain (Niksic *et al.*, 2014, p. 13). Israel has not approved master plans for over 90 per cent of Palestinian villages located within Area C. Where master plans do exist, the limited building area in these plans commonly excludes from development potential land surrounding Palestinian villages and typically does not designate areas for public purposes such as schools or medical clinics. In addition to land for settlement building, approximately 21 per cent of Area C is closed military zones and another 9 per cent is designated as nature reserves.

Israeli settlements in Area C have been allocated vast areas, far exceeding their built-up sections. Unlike the restrictive planning policy in place for Palestinian development in Area C, settlements enjoy the support of detailed planning and advanced infrastructure. Although the West Bank is not part of Israel's sovereign territory, the settlements and the settlers are subject to Israeli law. As a result, settlers enjoy all the rights of citizens in a democratic state, just as do Israeli citizens who live within the State of Israel. In contrast, Palestinians live under martial law in Area C and are severely restricted in their ability to impact policymaking affecting territory in which they live. The territorial division into Areas A, B, and C in 1995 was to have been a temporary step in a process of incremental transfer of greater amounts of West Bank territory to full Palestinian control. Nevertheless, this 'temporary' arrangement has remained in force for over 20 years and has provided a politico-territorial foundation for the substantial aggrandizement of the Israeli settlement programme and restrictions on Palestinian demographic growth. Of the full West Bank territory (including A, B, and C), 43 per cent of the land area has been allocated to Jewish settlement local and regional councils. Virtually all the land declared by Israel as public or 'state land' (27 per cent of the West Bank) has been allocated to settlements.

The extensive settlement of the West Bank outside the City of Jerusalem is intimately connected to Israel's hegemonic project pertaining to Jerusalem itself. The core and periphery are interconnected in Israel's overall political strategy of territoriality. Due to incompleteness in the achievement of territorial control of Jerusalem, the hegemonic project has an insatiable spatial appetite for further application at increasing geographic scale. This is because territorial control sought by Israel at the urban scale exposes the country to vulnerability at the next more expansive scale – in this case, in the metropolitan area and the greater West Bank. This dynamic is consistent with Sack's (1983) proclamation that territoriality tends to engender more territoriality. Israeli policy that has sustained a Jewish majority within 'Jerusalem' confronts an outer metropolitan region that is more Arab than Israeli.[10] Consequently, metropolitan aggrandizement through building suburban settlement blocs becomes a necessary extension of the Israeli partisan strategy as a means of consolidating its hold on parts of the larger region as a way to protect Jewish Jerusalem. Combined with nationalistic thirst for a greater Israel, the hegemonic project also extends itself geographically into the far reaches of the West Bank. Yet, penetration on the metropolitan fringes and in the rest of the West Bank exposes Israel even more to the same dynamic of penetration and resistance as found within Jerusalem proper.

As the Israeli hegemonic project enlarges its geographic scale, it becomes increasingly entangled in the volatilities that it produces. In the West Bank outside Jerusalem, approximately 2.5 million Palestinians and 385,900 Jewish settlers 'inhabit the head of a pin' (Weizman, 2007, p. 4). With continued territorial incursions in the West Bank, Israel becomes responsible for Jewish security in more frontier areas that face greater exposure to Palestinian resistance and violence. In the face of such vulnerability, the hegemonic strategy builds more settlements and enacts greater security measures to protect these frontier areas. The Israeli settlement project shows no signs of abating. According to the Israel Central Bureau of Statistics,[11] the number of new 'building starts' in settlements in the West Bank outside Jerusalem increased by 26 per cent in 2015 compared to 2014. In 2016, the number of new building starts rose another 40 per cent compared to 2015; ground was broken on 2,630 new housing units in the West Bank outside Jerusalem (Israel Central Bureau of Statistics). This was the second highest number of construction starts in the past 15 years, according to Peace Now. Yet, what is produced by this extensive settlement activity is not a stable equilibrium but a disrupted and increasingly contested larger geography.

Humanitarian need and vulnerability are at heightened levels for Palestinians. The UN Office for the Coordination of Humanitarian Affairs in the Occupied Palestinian Territory cites the major driver of Palestinian humanitarian vulnerability in the West Bank as Israel's protracted occupation, asserting that settlement related activities have 'undermined the living conditions of Palestinians and rendered them increasingly vulnerable' (OCHAOPT, 2016, p. 18). The West Bank is fragile across multiple economic, societal, environmental, political, and security dimensions as measured by the Organization for Economic Co-operation and Development (OECD, 2016). Approximately 600,000 Palestinians in the West Bank and Jerusalem face severe humanitarian need (Palestinian Central Bureau of Statistics, 2014). Violence in the West Bank has intensified as settlement activities continue. In 2015, the number of Palestinian and Israeli casualties in the West Bank and Israel was the highest since 2005 – 145 Palestinian deaths and 14,053 Palestinian injuries in the West Bank; 25 Israeli deaths and 304 Israeli injuries in the West Bank and Israel (OCHAOPT, 2016). The majority of Palestinian injuries occurred during clashes and resulted mainly from tear gas inhalation requiring medical treatment, rubber bullets, and from live ammunition from Israeli forces. Violence by Israeli settlers against Palestinians in the West Bank remained a fact of life, resulting in 97 Palestinian casualties in 2015, 107 in 2014, and 92 in 2013.

In efforts to protect Israeli territorial settlement incursions into the West Bank, a substantial amount of territorial bordering and bounding by Israel is needed to demarcate functional safe zones for Jewish settlers. As of December 2015, there were

543 closure obstacles in the West Bank – 70 checkpoints staffed by Israeli Army and/or Border Police with observation towers, 26 partial checkpoints that operate periodically, 77 concrete roadblocks, 179 earth mounds, 63 road gates normally closed, 48 road gates normally open, 50 road barriers of continuous fencing along roads to prevent Palestinian access to roads used by Israeli settlers, 22 earth walls, and 8 trenches (OCHAOPT, 2016). In addition, Israel has dedicated considerable financial resources to creating and maintaining this system of asymmetry and hegemony. Investments in settlements, security, separation barrier construction, and the building of a regional road network to service Jewish settlements have been extensive (Hever, 2013; Bar-Tal, 2013). The civilian costs of the settlements are estimated at $530 million per year (Bassok, 2003), totalling $17 billion from 1967 to 2010 (Levinson, 2010). Added to this are substantial military and police expenditures needed in the West Bank to provide security to the settlements, estimated to be between $500 million and $1 billion per year (Bar-Tal, 2013).

Territorial control sought by Israel in the West Bank has been elusive, subject to both self-created instabilities and ever-widening geographic applications. Control through penetration and expansion has sacrificed the security of ethnic separation and propelled Israel down a path of ever-increasing and ever-destabilizing incursions into contested areas in pursuit of political control. The volatility produced by the hegemonic project has commonly argued for its recharged intensification and for increased geographic extension to new territories of conquest.

*In this endless struggle, how can you gain control?*

Michael Romann, Tel Aviv University,<br>interview, 16 December 1994 (cited in Bollens 2000)

Lack of larger political resolution between Israel and Palestinians enables Israel to exploit fully its more powerful position and continue its efforts to tighten its control over the territories within Jerusalem and in Area C. Although Israel faced oversight of its settlement activities during the Obama Administration and has put on hold its development of the contentious 'E1' area near Jerusalem and its expansion of Maale Adumim east of Jerusalem, it continues construction that is internal to already existing settlements, such as in Gilo and Har Homa in Jerusalem (Gillad Rosen, Senior Lecturer, Hebrew University, interview, 11 October 2015). An additional tactic by Israel is allowing Jewish settlements in the West Bank built 'illegally' to be later retroactively legalized and supported by the state (Kareem Jabran, Field Research Director, B'Tselem, interview, 26 November 2015). Among the 100 'illegal' outposts mostly established within the last two decades by settler groups, about one-third have been or are in process of being retroactively legalized in a 'quiet but methodical' effort by the government (Kershner, 2016). In early 2017, the Israeli Parliament gave the government the authority to legalize retroactively thousands of homes in West Bank settlements and dozens of unauthorized hilltop outposts that sit on privately owned Palestinian land (Mitnick, 2017). Significantly, this constituted the first time that Israeli Knesset laws have been directly applied to lands in the West Bank outside Jerusalem, heretofore under the legal authority of Israel's military.

Israel's project asserting political control over the West Bank and the unification of Jerusalem is linked to the significant national goal of ensuring security. Born out of wars and conflict and surrounded by Arab countries, Israel's preoccupation with security is understandable. While 'military' security focuses on the defensibility of the urban system and concentrates on the location and expansion of military installations and the ability of the road network to provide access to defence units, there exists a 'political' security goal connected to military goals. This type of security broadens beyond strictly military considerations and extends into the civilian sphere – emphasizing growth and development programmes that seek to maintain the demographic superiority of Jews in Jerusalem and its larger urban sphere. Military security and political security are intimately connected. As noted earlier, 'while Israeli military sectors address and respond to Palestinian violence, nationalist desires for Jewish territory and power propagate actions by non-military developmental sectors which must then be defended militarily' (Ochs, 2011).

Israel must address two types of political security: group security linked to the protection of Jews as a distinctive group, and personal security involving protection of Jewish individuals. Jerusalem's security for the Jewish population as a whole is addressed through the maintenance of a Jewish demographic majority, political unification of the city, and the presence of Jewish residents throughout the city's geographic area and wider metropolitan area and beyond. Group security is to be sustained through barring the physical or political division in the city and through the extensive settlement of the West Bank to ensure greater Israeli spatial control. Yet, the settlement policies selected to operationalize the Israeli goal of group security in Jerusalem and in the West Bank have created a landscape conducive to heightened political contestation and violence that decreases Jewish personal security. The means towards achieving political control and group security is endangering individual Jewish lives by engendering volatile urban inequalities and vulnerable interfaces. Nationalistic goals of political control and group security exist at odds with the goals of ensuring security at the personal level. The continued exertion of Israel's tactics of domination and Palestinian resistance to them in the West Bank is producing a 'tragic process of cumulatively radicalizing violence' (Weizmann, 2007, p. 15). Since September 2000, 1,320 Israelis have been killed by Palestinian violence, most during the second Intifada in 2001–2004 but with a recent resurgence since 2015 (Israel Ministry of Foreign Affairs).[12] Loss of Israeli life has occurred at a greater rate since 2000 than in earlier periods (348 Israeli deaths in the 1990s, 174 in the 1980s).[13] Meanwhile, since 2000, there have been over 2,000 Palestinians killed in the West Bank by Israeli forces and civilians (341 in the 2009–2016 period; 1,833 from 2000 to 2008) (B'Tselem, 2008).[14]

## The Limits of Israel's Territorial Project

*Most of us after many years tend to the left. We see the reality – we are knocking ourselves against a wall.*
Israel Kimhi, Former Director of Planning Policy, Jerusalem Municipality (1973–1985),
interview, 3 December 2015

Palestinian violence that occurred in 2015 and 2016 was more individualistic in nature and less connected to extremist group mobilization. This different type of violence has initiated a new thread in Israeli thinking about the sustainability of its hegemonic project in Jerusalem. During my field research in late 2015 and early 2016, violence against Israelis was again at an intense level. From September 2015 to January 2017, there were hundreds of stabbing attacks and attempts, shootings, and vehicular ramming attacks, resulting in the loss of forty-six Israeli lives. These attacks have been carried out primarily by young lone extremists, most of them from East Jerusalem and some from West Bank, who have generally not been operatives of established organizations but rather young individuals inspired by the general political climate (Israel Ministry of Foreign Affairs).[15] Many assailants were 18 years old or younger, quite a few were as young as thirteen. Such individualistic and unorganized violence not connected to organizational networks is harder for Israel security agencies to control and combat because it is not traceable to group mobilization, and points to the pervasive effects of decades of Israeli hegemony and marginalization. This dynamic is consistent with an emerging understanding of violence as behaving like an epidemic, having characteristics of clustering, spread, and transmission (OECD, 2016). In the violent environment that has characterized the West Bank through the decades, violence becomes accepted as a normal aspect of life and youths, in particular, adopt violent proclivities as a learned behaviour (Spano *et al.*, 2010; DuRant *et al.*, 1994; Kelly, 2010). Spawned by widespread hopelessness and marginalization among young Palestinians in the West Bank and Jerusalem, the less trackable form of Palestinian violence since 2015 constitutes one indicator of the limits of sustainability of Israel's hegemonic project.

*I sometimes need to show my Israeli driver's license 3 or 4 times a day to an 18 year old with a gun.*
Adnan Husseini, Palestinian Governor of Jerusalem District,
interview, 25 January 2016

This new dynamic of individualistic, non-group based violence is pointing to the effects of Palestinian mass deprivation and marginalization that has resulted from decades of Israeli hegemonic control and it is posing new challenges to Israeli security agencies tasked with maintaining security. This new dynamic of violence is personified by an 11-year old boy who killed a Jew. When asked why, he stated 'I was sitting in my little village ... and I was jealous' (Raphie Etgar, Chief Curator, Museum on the Seam, interview, 17 November 2015). There exists in Palestinian areas an 'atmosphere' and 'spirit' born of hopelessness that is conducive to individual action (Hillel Cohen, Senior Lecturer, Hebrew University, interview, 11 November 2015). In her research on young Palestinian activists, Albana Dwonch (Researcher, interview, 18 November 2015) finds that their activism is not connected to political party or organizations, that they come together for specific purposes (often neighbourhood issues), dissolve, and then come together again in different configurations. These young activists prefer loose networks to fixed groups and operate outside formal structures. At times they even face resistance by Palestinian authorities because their protests extend to criticism of Palestinian leadership. Palestinian scholar Mahdi Abdul Hadi observes that, 'the Oslo generation of young people today acts individually – no flags, no sense of belonging, they don't want representatives and leaders. They always think they have an answer, but there is little dialogue with others' (interview, 26 October 2015).

Individualistic violence – youths engaged in knife attacks and stone throwing – is less controllable due to its non-systematic nature. Although macro-scale explanations for this violence remain rooted in sovereignty conflict, the micro-scale dynamics of this recent violence add another layer of complexity in terms of the reasons behind it and how Israel is to counter it (Dan Miodownik, interview, 19 January 2016). This is a type of violence that the Israeli state cannot 'see', surveil and target, as it can violence aligned with group mobilization. 'You can't control individualistic violence not rooted in organizations', observes Udi Dekel (Former Head of Strategic Planning Division of the IDF, interview, 3 February 2016). As the hegemonic project of Israel has taken on new forms through the years, it appears that violent acts of resistance have also evolved in nature.

The phenomenon of Palestinian youths acting out of hopelessness and despair highlights the widespread effects of decades of Israeli hegemony and domination. 'There is no way you can oppress a people for 50 years without negative consequences', observes Israeli activist Ronny Perlman (Machsom Watch, Presentation at Ecumenical Accompaniment Programme in Palestine and Israel team meeting, 18 January 2016). Relative deprivation, marginalization, and frustration have been created and solidified through Israel's spatiality of dominance. The disadvantage imposed upon Palestinians has been more than material conditions and encompasses severe damage to Arab self-esteem. 'The social aspects and social-psychological depletion caused by poverty has been underestimated by Israel through the years', explains Avner de-Shalit (Professor of Political Science, Hebrew University, interview, 20 January 2016). Due to the nature of contemporary Palestinian violence, the Israel Defense Force is becoming increasingly aware that Palestinian deprivation and the lack of economic livelihood in Arab East Jerusalem and the rest of the West Bank is increasingly a cause behind contemporary Palestinian violence (Dekel, interview). Israeli elites, including security agencies, are beginning to push back against the hegemonic project, pointing to the unsustainability of the current situation and the dangers of perpetual occupation (Daniel Seidemann, interview, 1 February 2016). The prospects for a real peace, asserts Seidemann, 'depends on how bloody and painful it is going to be for us to perpetuate occupation'. During the horrific days of the second Intifada, security agencies were necessarily focused on the operational details of maintaining control and had little time to develop a broader strategy (Seidemann, interview, 1 February 2016). That now is starting to change as security agencies recognize social and economic deprivation as contributors to instability and violence. Security personnel 'are out there exposed in their daily life and we see how problematic it is to cut off their economic mobility and close off areas after violence', continues Dekel. To further Israel's own interests, it then becomes logical, according to this narrative, to invest more in Arab East Jerusalem for reasons of stability and functionality, to 'open tracks for the dispossessed', and to provide a certain autonomy for Palestinian local leadership and young people in Jerusalem (Dekel, interview, 3 February 2016).

This less trackable form of Palestinian violence, spawned by widespread hopelessness and marginalization among young people, is forcing some Israeli policy sectors to consider socio-economic betterment of the Palestinian people, and the provision of hope, as necessary correlates of maintaining security. Even a staunch advocate of a united Jewish Jerusalem, such as Nadav Shragai (interview, 17 December 2015), acknowledges that 'you can't control territory while disregarding the people on that territory', asserting that Israel should be tough on Jerusalem Arabs in terms of security but lenient in providing civilian benefits in the city. 'We should treat Jerusalem Arabs like Jews in the city in terms of schools, clinics, playgrounds, roads, and other services', Shragai notes, 'tactically it is wrong to deny them services because it brings more Palestinians into hostility'. 'What we learned from Oslo', comments Daniel Seidemann (interview, 1 February 2016), 'is that you can't have a stable political agreement where humanitarian issues are left out'. Seidemann continues, 'occupation is a disease of the occupied and a disease of the occupier; we are at the point now where it is a "metastasizing occupation"'. Yudith Oppenheimer (Ir Amim NGO, interview, 26 January 2016) looks ahead – because of the conditions it has created on the ground, 'our system of control will not collapse in one day, but there will be a gradual process of self-destruction that will spur momentum for change within Israeli society'.

In addition to violence spawned by decades-long marginalization, the Israeli hegemonic project is also increasingly facing new political limits to its continued implementation. The aggrandizement of the Jewish settlement project into the West

Bank is producing a debilitating new political reality in Israel today, pointing to the political limits of the territorial project. With over 385,900 Jewish citizens now residing in the West Bank outside Jerusalem, the possibilities for an effective two-state solution are increasingly being extinguished. The continuing policy of settlement construction and expansion is 'steadily eroding the viability of the two-state solution' and 'raises legitimate questions about Israel's long-term intentions' (Middle East Quartet, 2016, p. 5). Increasingly problematic in the face of settlement blocs outside Jerusalem is the ability of a two-state formulation to integrate East Jerusalem into a greater Palestinian Jerusalem metropolis in such a way as to produce continuity of Palestinian territory (Daniel Seidemann, interview, 1 February 2016). Yet, Israel's capacity to create facts on the ground that thwart the two-state option is also creating difficulties for its own hegemonic project. As described in Klein (2010), these facts on the ground are shifting the attention of Israeli policymakers from articulation of borders in a two-state solution to the challenges of inter-group ethnic management in a *de facto* one-state reality. One response to this new reality is consideration of a binational one-state strategy, a political option being publicly considered (see Tarazi, 2004; LeVine and Mossberg, 2014; Mitnick, 2016) and discussed by several of my interviewees – both Israeli and Palestinian. Yet, moving to a binational democratic one-state having genuine Palestinian participation would expose Israel to the fact that such a state would over time assume a Palestinian demographic majority, endangering the 'Jewish' nature of Israel today.[16] Israel is thus caught between a two-state solution increasingly problematic due to Jewish settlements in the West Bank and a binational, democratic one-state solution that would threaten Jewish majority control.

Given the substantial decades-long investment in its hegemonic project in Jerusalem and the West Bank, it is difficult to envision the Israeli state stepping back from further exercise of this project amid violence and the feeling of threat to its existential existence as a state and people. Debilitating any movement towards peace in the region is the possibility that the 'geography of the occupation is irreversible', that there is a socio-spatial structure in place in the form of settlements that will be close to impossible to remove (Haim Yacobi, Professor, Ben Gurion University, interview 29 October 2015). However, Israel's project has created urban and regional conditions that jeopardize Jewish personal security and the future political status of Israel as a Jewish state; it has produced substantial and destabilizing Palestinian material and political marginalization; and it has created a contemporary Jerusalem that, despite Israel's decades-long efforts, is in fact a divided city in all but name. These all highlight the limits imposed by the *realpolitik* of Israel's hegemonic strategy.

Acknowledging these realities and limits, there have been initiatives among Israeli officials that modify the long-held stance equating security with hegemonic control over all of Jerusalem. Goals and objectives that drive Israeli political-territorial tactics are facing greater self-examination. As previously mentioned, since the Camp David negotiations in 2000, Israel has shown greater openness to the idea of sharing, or dividing, sovereignty in the Holy City. In this discussion, Israeli security is viewed as possibly being more effectively maintained through the granting of some Palestinian autonomy or sovereignty in the city, rather than the continuation of Israeli hegemonic authority in the city. This increasing introspection in Israel's thinking concerning hegemonic control of the city points to acknowledgement of the limits of its hegemonic project in achieving its political objectives. Another significant indicator of Israel's evolution in tactical thinking is its creation, beginning in 2003, of the barrier to separate Israeli citizens from Palestinians. Rather than relying solely on a settlement expansion project, which penetrates into and geographically extends the Jewish presence in the West Bank, the construction of the separation barrier recognized the need, in the face of Palestinian violence and resistance, to consolidate and protect existing and prospective settlements. Although it faces criticism that it constitutes another form of unilateral annexation, the building of the barrier nonetheless redirects one strategy of domination (territorial penetration) towards another (territorial consolidation) (Weizman, 2007). Rather than focusing on continued penetration of West Bank territory through settlement building, Israel's building of the barrier in the Jerusalem region seeks to consolidate and protect its past settlement building close to the city. Yet, the separation barrier has introduced an additional and complicating element in Israel's hegemonic project. It brings to the fore the 'impossible politics of separation' in disputed political geography, with the barrier 'desperately struggling to separate the inseparable' (Weizman, 2007, pp. 161 and 15). The separation barrier constitutes the most visible manifestation of the conundrum facing Israel in its territorial project – the dual and conflicting imperatives of continued territorial expansion, on the one hand, and the need to protect and consolidate its territorial advances, on the other.

Israel's engagement in a decades-long project of hegemonic territoriality in Jerusalem, its urban region, and the wider West Bank exposes the self-perpetuating proclivities, practical complexities, and political limits of the hegemonic project. As it continually deepens and extends its reach into the volatile and shifting geographies of peripheral West Bank, the contradictions and limits of the hegemonic project become more exposed. Consistent with Simone's (2010, p. 40) observation that peripheral activities can be 'potentially destabilizing of the center', the impacts of Israeli interventions in the contested periphery of the West Bank uncover the political limits of hegemonic territoriality as physical and demographic realities force new practical complexities upon Israeli policymakers – concerning the political future of the Israel/West Bank region and Jerusalem city and the tactics needed to protect settlements in the face of continuing instability and violence.

Israel's hegemonic project has produced an atmosphere of destabilizing hopelessness on the part of Palestinians and has, through its near-erasure of the two-state solution, created a political conundrum concerning the future political status of the

West Bank. Whether acknowledgement by the Israeli state of these realities will lead it to grant Palestinians greater political autonomy or sovereignty in the future – both in Jerusalem and in the West Bank – is an important challenge faced by Israeli political negotiators. The 'interim' political geography of the West Bank that created three zones of differentiated control has remained in force for over 20 years, enabling Israel to continue to strengthen its territorial project in internationally disputed lands. Far from achieving its political objectives, however, such territorial aggrandizement has created a complex and destabilizing environment that spawns Palestinian resistance and Israeli counter-actions in a self-perpetuating dynamic. Without progress on larger Israeli-Palestinian peace, the West Bank exists *de facto* as a 'discriminatory binational regime from the Mediterranean to the Jordan River' (Menachem Klein, interview, 21 October 2015) and will continue to regress into a 'semi-permanent counterinsurgency frontier' for Israel (Ron, 2003, p. 201).

## Jerusalem and the West Bank Since 1994

*There is a crack, a crack in everything.*
*That's how the light gets in.*

Leonard Cohen, Anthem, 1992

Israel's hegemonic project in Jerusalem has created a city consistent in many ways with its goals of political control ('unification') and security. Through a comprehensive programme of land planning and development, reinforced by police and defence forces, Israel has accomplished the following:

- Maintenance of a Jewish majority and Israeli political control;

- Establishment of major Jewish settlements within the annexed part of the city which entrenches Jewish presence as facts on the ground;

- Creation of three major settlement blocs outside municipal borders which is predetermining future political negotiations;

- The building of a separated network of roads and tunnels which connects Jewish settlements in the city to those outside, creating a Jewish metropolitan network;

- Severe restrictions on Arabs' ability to develop their communities in East Jerusalem, producing a fragmented and disconnected set of Arab neighbourhoods hampered by restricted mobility and lack of economic opportunities;

♦ The institutional separation since Oslo of Arab East Jerusalem from the rest of the West Bank;

♦ Limitations on Arab mobility into Jerusalem, first through security checkpoints in the mid-1990s followed by erection of the separation barrier in the mid-2000s.

In many ways, Israel's use of urban planning and policy as a partisan tool is one of the most effective examples in the world in achieving its societal goals. Land planning and development have been used as key tools in the implementation of political goals in comprehensive, forceful, impactful, and consistent ways throughout a period of 50 years. Urban policy has advanced major goals related to military security in the urban landscape and has furthered group security for the Jewish population in the Jerusalem urban area, albeit at the expense of personal security.

Notwithstanding these important impacts in securing Jerusalem for Israeli Jews, there are important cracks in the hegemonic project as it has been operationalized in Jerusalem's complex and dynamic urban environment. Amid domination, there are aspects of urbanity and openness which run counter to the partisan project. At times, implementation of the hegemonic project by Israel has created unintended effects that are complex and contradictory to Israel goals of political control and security. Despite 50 years of partisan urban policy:

♦ Informal, unlicensed Arab development of housing in the city has been able effectively to bypass and overwhelm the restrictive Israeli planning and regulatory system;

♦ Arab population in the city is increasing relative to Jewish population; the Jewish-Arab population ratio is significantly less than the demographic goals of Israel;

♦ Arab penetration of Jewish Jerusalem has increased – economically, commercially, and in terms of access to urban services;

♦ In-migration of Palestinians into Jerusalem has increased due to the building of the separation barrier, strengthening the Arab demographic profile in the city;

♦ Two major new nodes of Palestinian development within the Municipality but outside the separation barrier have developed, bolstering the Arab demographic profile;

♦ There is growing Islamization of Palestinian life in the city in response to the void in Palestinian local governance produced by Israeli restrictions on political organizations in East Jerusalem;

- A new type of Palestinian violence against Jews has emerged which is individualistic in nature, not connected to group mobilization, and thus less trackable by Israeli security agencies, calling into question the sustainability of a hegemonic project which has created widespread despair and hopelessness among Palestinian youth;

- There is fracturing of Israeli's historic negotiation stance against politically dividing Jerusalem and its equating of security with political unification of the city, starting with Camp David (2000) and proceeding through to this day in the form of the common use of the Clinton parameters as a benchmark for future negotiations.

To summarize Chapters 2 to 4, findings highlight the disconnection between national ideological goals and urban implementation, the intertwining trajectories of national politics and urban dynamics, and the internally problematic nature of Israel's territorial project.

The Israel case exposes the fact that the translation of national hegemonic political goals is not a straightforward process when applied to a complex and dynamic urban centre. Rather, it appears as a political-spatial process replete with complexities and contradictions which can thwart and add uncertainties to the achievement of national goals. The national hegemonic programme aimed at transforming the city in ways to assert Israeli political control has encountered disruptions and the programme has evolved in complex and unforeseen ways due to changing politics, complex and contradictory urban dynamics, and the unanticipated impacts of partisan actions. The hegemonic project is not homogeneous in its outcomes as it is implemented in a dynamic and resilient urban landscape. It has produced many outcomes – territorial expansion and consolidation, separation, economic interdependency and 'intrusion', resistant 'informal' Arab development, tensions between Palestinians and Israeli security personnel at separation barrier interfaces and checkpoints, ghettoization and marginalization, and financially onerous settlement and security expenditures – and these are not all consistent with hegemonic goals. There exist cracks in the hegemonic project, margins and soft spots in it where its implementation creates opportunities for obstruction and resistance.

National political settlements (in the case of Oslo) and national negotiation efforts (in the cases of Camp David and Geneva) have not been supported by on-the-ground changes in the Jerusalem urban region that would reinforce and embed such national peacemaking. There exists an intertwining or interlocking relationship between national political deliberations and socio-spatial dynamics and changes in the Jerusalem urban region. The on-the-ground conditions of Jerusalem have not stayed in place amid national political impasse. Rather, national peacemaking efforts influence changes in the social, spatial, and security aspects of Israeli control in the city. At the same time that national settlements or negotiation efforts opened up possibilities for

Israel-Palestinian mutual coexistence, the impact of Israeli actions at the local level have run counter to these possibilities and increased consolidation of Israeli control in the urban region. The power of local-spatial dynamics to thwart national peacemaking is evident. Further, the destructive spiral associated with violent conflict exposes the interlocking and mutually obstructive relationship between national peacemaking and socio-spatial dynamics at the local level. Rather than the city being a pragmatic platform for peacebuilding that would operationalize peaceful coexistence, Jerusalem has constituted an ideological straightjacket that has stunted opportunities for genuine peaceful coexistence.

The self-perpetuating cycle of hegemonic control in the Jerusalem urban area has created a spatial reality characterized by destabilizing partisan actions which stimulate Palestinian responses – both violent acts and resistance in the form of 'unlicensed' development. These Palestinian reactions in turn lead Israel to engage in more efforts at territorial consolidation, which further destabilize and perpetuate tension and conflict. There has been the creation of an urban fabric not of security and stability, but of disequilibrium, nationalistic and increasingly religious conflict, vulnerable interfaces, and inter-ethnic instability. Israel's spatial strategies in pursuit of its goal of political control of the city expose tensions and contradictions in its hegemonic project. Over time, the means towards achieving the political control goal – that of penetration – have created spatial conditions of instability that militate against Israel's capacity to control the urban environment. The fallacy of partisan planning is that its goal – political control – comes at the expense of urban stability required for the exercise of political control and the maintenance of security. Further, due to the incompleteness of the partisan project in Jerusalem, the hegemonic project has an insatiable spatial appetite at increasing levels of geographic scale. Yet, penetration on the metropolitan fringes and in the rest of the West Bank exposes Israel even more to the same cycle of penetration, resistance, and consolidation found within Jerusalem proper. As the hegemonic project enlarges its geographic scale, it becomes increasingly entangled in the volatilities that it produces. The self-perpetuating cycle of Israel's hegemonic approach to Jerusalem and the West Bank both exposes the limits of such an approach and provides the rationale for its continued and more destabilizing application. Lacking political leadership capable of breaking out of this destructive dynamic, the *de facto* binationalism that exists in the area encompassed by Israel and the Palestinians will continue in the form of destabilizing quasi-domination of one nation by the other (Benvenisti, 2007, p. 48).

## Notes

1. See: http://mfa.gov.il/MFA/ForeignPolicy/Terrorism/Palestinian/Pages/Wave-of-terror-October-2015.aspx.
2. More recent Jewish settler micro-scale penetration into Arab neighbourhoods in and near the Old City – often involving insertions within existing Arab areas – abandons Israel's traditional

approach of penetration-with-separation and introduces considerable volatility into the local environment.
3. The problematic nature of Israel's territorial project in Jerusalem is further heightened by its inability to restrict Arab 'unlicensed' development in the city, as discussed in Chapter 2.
4. Owing to these implications, most of the roadblocks were gradually removed after a few weeks.
5. 'Lebanonization' here refers to the hostility between Muslim and Christian militias in the city of Beirut, leading to the disintegration of the city as a coherent identity during the Lebanese Civil War of 1975–1990.
6. Jewish deaths in Israel and the occupied territories due to political violence were 75 in 1995–1996, 83 in 1994–1995, and 66 in 1993–1994; compared to 50 in 1992–1993, and 36 in 1991–1992 (Trounson, 1996). The figures are from September to September; their original source is Jerusalem-based Peace Watch. Jewish deaths in Israel proper during those years, in particular, rose dramatically.
7. The author participated in two of these professional sessions – held in Delft, Netherlands and in Sarajevo, Bosnia-Herzegovina.
8. Formerly the Israel/Palestine Center for Research and Information. The report can be found at: http://www.ipcri.org/index.php/publications/research-and-information/191-two-states-in-one-space-research-paper.
9. Wye River Memorandum, 1998.
10. Israel Kimhi (Jerusalem Institute for Israel Studies, interview, 3 December 2015) estimates that the metropolitan functional region of Jerusalem is about 50:50 Israeli/Palestinian. Outside the Israeli-defined borders of the city but within the metropolitan region, he estimates the population to be about 28:72 Israeli/Palestinian.
11. 'Dwellings, by stage of construction, district and construction initiator'. March 2016.
12. See: http://mfa.gov.il/MFA/ForeignPolicy/Terrorism/Palestinian/Pages/Victims%20of%20Palestinian%20Violence%20and%20Terrorism%20sinc.aspx.
13. See: http://mfa.gov.il/MFA/MFA-Archive/2000/Pages/Terrorism%20deaths%20in%20Israel%20-%201920-1999.aspx.
14. See: http://www.btselem.org/statistics/fatalities/after-cast-lead/by-date-of-event.
15. See: http://mfa.gov.il/MFA/ForeignPolicy/Terrorism/Palestinian/Pages/Wave-of-terror-October-2015.aspx.
16. Population estimates for the year 2035 forecast that the total population in Israel and Palestinian territories combined will be 54:46 Palestinian to Jewish (Israel National Security Project; www.israelnsp.org). Currently, it is approximately 50:50.

Chapter 5

# Belfast I: Building Peace in a Post-Violent Conflict City

In the ugly and traumatizing years of the violent 'Troubles' (1969–1998) that gripped Northern Ireland, peace in Belfast was viewed as a possibility by only a few. The strong alignment of religious identities with political and national loyalties led to the seeming intractability of the conflict. Protestants assert their claims to continued political association within the United Kingdom, and their allegiances were with Britain, which since 1972 had exercised direct rule over Northern Ireland. Catholics, on the other hand, consider themselves more Irish and committed their personal and political loyalties more to the Republic of Ireland to the south. The border between Northern Ireland and the Republic of Ireland, established in 1920, created a secure Protestant majority in the north by including six of the nine counties of the historic province of Ulster. A double minority syndrome trapped Northern Ireland in an unrelenting dilemma – Protestants were an island-wide minority threatened by possible unification of Northern Ireland and Ireland, while Catholics were a minority within Northern Ireland threatened by Protestant and British direct rule.

In 2016, now almost 20 years after the groundbreaking peace agreement that has for the most part stopped violent conflict, there is joy and relief as a peace has come which some never thought would be possible. Political violence has decreased substantially and the major paramilitaries have formally disarmed. Ethno-national disagreements have been channelled for the most part from violent expression into the political forum. However, it is also a 'peace' that feels qualitatively different from what people envisioned and hoped peace would feel like. To many it feels more like a post-violent conflict society rather than a post-conflict society of transformative normalization. Indeed, some wonder whether there really is a peace – there is still political animosity and deep suspicion, significant fits and starts in institutionalizing new forms of local democracy and shared governance, sustained rigidity of exclusionary ethno-national geography in Belfast, and paramilitaries and dissidents stirring trouble. Instead of the optimism and hope of peace, feelings are more ambivalent, unresolved and uncertain.

Northern Ireland fundamentally changed in 1998, when a historic shift in Northern Ireland governing institutions and constitutional status was specified in the April 1998 *Agreement Reached in the Multi-Party Negotiations* (i.e. The 'Good Friday Agreement'). This agreement, approved by over 70 per cent of Northern Ireland voters in May 1998, allowed the transfer of day-to-day rule of the province from Britain ('direct rule') to a locally-elected Northern Ireland Assembly in which Protestants (Unionists/Loyalists) and Catholics (Nationalists/Republicans) share power ('local rule').[1] Major legislative decisions require concurrent majorities from both sectarian groups.[2] A seemingly unending series of obstructions to peace progress (most prominently, paramilitary decommissioning and police reform) from 1998 to 2007 resulted in on-again, off-again local rule by Northern Ireland elected officials. From 2007 to early 2017, the Northern Ireland Assembly and Northern Ireland Executive achieved its first period of sustained local rule, but this period of political stability did not come until 9 years after the breakthrough peace agreement. The Good Friday Agreement also states that Northern Ireland is to remain within the United Kingdom as long as a majority in the province wants to remain there. Further, the Agreement created new multi-party forums to placate both sides. In response to Catholic desires, the new Assembly and the Irish Parliament are part of a North-South Council to coordinate and encourage cross-border cooperation. To reassure Protestants, a Council of the Isles links the governments in Northern Ireland and Ireland with the British government and with the Scottish Parliament and Welsh Assembly.

In contrast to the Israel case, Northern Ireland has succeeded in creating a peace agreement that included the core political issues underlying violent conflict and which has effectively countered regression back to political violence.[3] The 'organized-strategic' political violence of the Troubles has given way to lesser amounts of 'disorganized-opportunistic' violence that appear to be residual of a complicated transition to peace (Frank Gaffikin, Professor, Queen's University, interview, 15 March 2016). In the 15 years after negotiated peace (1999 to 2014), there were 100 security-related deaths; this is far lower than the 564 deaths from 1989 to 1999, 833 from 1979 to 1989, and 1,892 from 1969 to 1978 (Police Service of Northern Ireland). The difference between Israel and Northern Ireland is fundamental and of great magnitude and allows us to consider the role of urbanism in a 'post-peace' transitioning environment, rather than amid unresolved conflict. While Jerusalem reveals the dynamics of continued violent conflict and its self-reinforcing negative cycles, Belfast exposes the dynamics of a post-violent society and its conflicting institutional and policy imperatives. The active sense of unsettledness in Jerusalem is palpable compared to Belfast, although the latter exhibits its own type of volatility.[4]

My daylong exploration of the city in 2016 with Gerard McGlade, of Black Cab Tours, exposes the micro-territorial local histories, memorials, and legacies of the Troubles that remain robustly inscribed in the city's landscape. The experience resembles being in an open-air art gallery or living museum. In Protestant-majority East Belfast, political murals shout for attention. I am informed that six brigadiers from loyalist paramilitary groups are in charge of local territories and they divide the turf. Murals extolling the major loyalist paramilitaries – Ulster Volunteer Force (UVF), Ulster Defence Association (UDA) and the Ulster Freedom Fighters (UFF) – stake claims to blocks, street corners, and neighbourhoods. Intimidating murals portray balaclava-masked men armed with submachine guns aimed threateningly towards the viewer.[5] One mural celebrates Michael Stone, who in 1988 attacked Catholic mourners with hand grenades and pistols during a funeral at Belfast's Milltown Cemetery for three Irish Republican Army (IRA) fighters. The loyalist community in Belfast is fragmented and loyalist-loyalist fighting (especially between the UVF and the UDA) since the Good Friday agreement has claimed many lives. McGlade explains that, 'loyalist paramilitaries are still active and that the brigadiers make money out of keeping things alive through extortion and recruitment' (interview, 14 March 2016).

Figures 5.1 and 5.2. Murals, East Belfast.

*Growing up Orange (Protestant) was like a womb – it provided comfort but also alienation from others. I downloaded the language of the urban vocabulary, the culture of religious contempt, the blood sacrifice of our forefathers, and community rituals were a powerful influence. This all enlarged the prejudice zone.*

Ken Newell, Former Minister of Fitzroy Presbyterian Church (1976–2008), presentation, 22 May 2016

We move from East Belfast to the western part of the city and travel down the Shankill Road, which is the Protestant 'heartland' of Belfast, itself now divided between UVF and UDA sections. 'In proud memory of Lt. Jackie Coulter', states a mural in a depopulated neighbourhood, '2nd Battalion UDA, murdered by the UVF'. Further on is evidence of the effect of peace – an old inflammatory mural has been replaced by a peace-promoting sculpture, courtesy of the 'Re-imaging Communities programme' funded by the Northern Ireland Arts Council and the Shared Future Consortium. We make our way to the largest and most notorious 'peace wall' in the city – the one along Cupar Street which separates the Shankill from the 'heartland' Catholic community of the Falls. Gerard laments how this has now become a 'tourist trap' – the site of frequent tours given by former paramilitary members to interested tourists who want to experience and learn about the bloody conflict years. Near the top of the Cupar peace wall is the Workman Avenue gate that closes off the street, a gate that is opened once each year so that loyalist parades can take place along Catholic Springfield Road

Figures 5.3, 5.4, and 5.5. Cupar Way peace wall.

Figure 5.6. Workman Avenue gate.

on 12 July, a date which commemorates the victory of Protestant King William of Orange over Catholic King James II at the Battle of the Boyne in 1690 and the start of the Protestant ascendancy in Ireland

*Paramilitaries are not just in balaclavas who come out at night, but come out (infused) in parades, murals, bonfires, and flags. The presence of these organizations are legitimated and valorized in communities.*

Neil Jarman, Research Fellow, Queen's University, interview, 23 May 2016

We now are fully within Catholic West Belfast. The murals along Falls Road are more celebratory than blatantly confrontational. Irish language is evident on signs, building and street names, and memorials. When we move further to the west into the neighbourhood of Ballymurphy, where Republican dissident groups opposed to the Good Friday peace are active, the murals become more politically assertive. A large and fortressed police station dominates the landscape along Springmartin Road. In the Milltown cemetery, I traverse a special section dedicated to Republican heroes and martyrs from the years of violence, including the burial site of Bobby Sands, whose death after a 66-day hunger strike of Republican prisoners at the Maze prison in 1981 drew worldwide attention and activated a surge in IRA recruitment and activity. Plaques throughout the special section commemorate several 'massacres' of IRA members by British agents and forces.

At the end of the emotionally exhausting tour of Protestant and Catholic territories, Gerard wants to emphasize that 'this is what we lived; this is the reality; killings and violence'. The Northern Ireland government wanted to sponsor these tours at one point, but the tour guides refused their support because the government, in efforts at peacebuilding, wanted them to do 'fairy tale tours' that would whitewash the past. In Belfast, the past is still present, constituting a significant and ever-present obstacle along the path to peace in Northern Ireland.

Violent conflict has been transmuted into 'war by other means' now, which surely is preferable (James Anderson, Professor of Political Geography, Queen's University, interview, 22 March 2016). Yet, manifested in the form of inflammatory murals, dividing walls, and political antagonisms, the identity dimension in Belfast remains robust and resistant to change that is needed to transform a war-torn city into a post-war city of greater normalcy. Symbolic contests and disputes continue over the naming of buildings and bridges, parades and protests, playing of national anthems, wearing of sports shirts, names of sports grounds, displays of various types of lily and poppy, displays of portraits, images of banners and murals, painting of street paving stones, commemorative events, funerals, statues, bonfires, visits of dignitaries, display of uniforms and badges, names of places – parks, streets, cities, towns – and the displaying of flags (Dominic Bryan, Institute of Irish Studies, Queen's University, interview, 12 April 2016).

*Working for the BBC (British Broadcasting Corporation) for 17 years during the Troubles, I recall checking under my wife's car every morning* [for explosives] *and telling the kids that I was looking for the cat.*

Brian Rowan, Journalist and Author,<br>interview 1 June 2016

There is also the curious and illuminating phenomenon that since peace there has been an *increase* in the number of physical partitions ('peace walls' and other sectarian interface barriers) built to buffer antagonistic groups. The barriers consist of corrugated iron fences, steel palisade structures, brick or steel walls, and many were constructed during the years of urban sectarian violence. They are located in interface areas where there was the potential for rival and nearby communities to engage in conflict. Sixteen primary partition walls were identified in a 1991 survey (Environmental Design Consultants, 1991). Such urban fortification was made necessary by the violent nature of civil war in Belfast. From 1969 to 1998, the 'Troubles' in Northern Ireland produced 3,459 dead, over 45,000 injuries, and approximately 10,000 bombings.[6] Belfast bore the brunt of this violence. Over 1,000 of the 1,810 fatal incidents from 1969 to July

1983 occurred in the Belfast urban area (Poole, 1990). Forty-one per cent of all explosions from 1969 to 1994 occurred in the Belfast urban area, with almost 70 per cent of bombings aimed at housing occurring in the urban area (Boal, 1995). Attacks on shops, offices, industrial premises, pubs and clubs, and commercial premises were disproportionately concentrated in Belfast.

Since the end of most hostilities in 1994 with an IRA ceasefire, there has been a measurable increase in the number of security barriers, as documented by the non-sectarian Community Relations Council (2009a) and the Belfast Interface Project (2012). Although there are differing interpretations as to what constitutes an interface barrier, it is nonetheless clear that the partitioning of the city has increased, not decreased, since 'peace'. The uncertainty of the peace process has intensified defensiveness by sectarian communities. It is probably a profound understatement of the Community Relations Council to observe that 'peace has proved to be a more complex and difficult process than can be imagined by pictures of former enemies united as leaders of a new dispensation' (Community Relations Council, 2009b).

*I don't want someone to tell me, 'but you have to understand'. I don't need this ... I understand everything. I just need someone to get inside my story.*
Alan McBride, reflecting on the killing of his wife in the Shankill Road bombing by the IRA in 1993, presentation, All Souls' Church, Belfast, 16 April 2016

The political implementation of the 1998 Good Friday Agreement has been a rocky road, characterized by fits and starts in institutionalizing a stable Protestant-Catholic power sharing governing arrangement. The 1998 agreement put Northern Ireland on a new track, bringing local rule to the province after 26 years of 'direct rule' by Britain. 'Direct rule' from Westminster was imposed to override the discriminatory Protestant-led Northern Ireland government that existed from 1920 to 1972 and was tasked with holding together the province during the fragmenting and difficult years of violent conflict. Good Friday allowed for the 'devolution' of day-to-day rule of the province from Britain to a 'consociationalist' directly-elected 108-seat Northern Ireland Assembly and cabinet-level Northern Ireland Executive in which Protestants (Unionists/Loyalists) and Catholics (Nationalists/Republicans) share power both in terms of the proportionate distribution of ministers and in decision-making rules which require concurrent majorities within both sectarian camps on significant community issues.[7] To ensure power sharing at the top, the First Minister and Deputy First Minister must come from opposing sides of the sectarian divide. The First Minister is a representative of the political party gaining the most votes in elections, while the Deputy First Minister represents the political party from the other identity getting the most votes. Since 1998, the First Minister has been a Protestant, the Deputy First Minister a Catholic. Ministerial positions in the Northern Ireland

Executive are allocated to parties with significant representation in the Assembly. The number of ministries to which each party is entitled in the Northern Ireland Executive, composed of ten departments, is determined by the D'Hondt system of proportionate representation. In effect, all major parties through power sharing can be part of government. Further, the Executive cannot function if either of the two largest parties refuses to take part.

The path towards creating a sustainable devolved power-sharing government has been tortuous. During five occasions – 2000, twice in 2001, from 2002 to 2007, and in 2017 – devolution was suspended due to conflicts over paramilitary decommissioning and police reform, and most recently over a mishandled renewable energy programme. During the first four suspensions, Northern Ireland departments reverted back to the responsibility of British direct rule ministers from the Northern Ireland Office. In addition, political control of the Northern Ireland Executive has shifted over time. From 1998 to 2002, the two moderate political parties (the Protestant Ulster Unionist Party (UUP) and the Catholic Social and Democratic Labour Party (SDLP)) controlled the top positions based on voting. Leaders from these two parties had played central roles in negotiations leading up to Good Friday and the UUP-SDLP partnership was viewed as potentially leading to compromise and moderation. Yet, with devolution obstructed and then suspended for 5 years, the composition of the Executive when re-established in 2007 was of a radically different nature. New elections enshrined the two more extreme political parties as government leaders: the Protestant Democratic Unionist Party (DUP) (of hard-liner Ian Paisley), and Sinn Féin (the political party of the paramilitary Irish Republican Army). This shocking coalition between long-time enemies is described variously as a 'non-aggression pact', 'wrestler's embrace', and as a 'coalition of the unwilling' (Neil Galway, Lecturer, Queen's University, interview, 19 May 2016; Paul Nolan, Director of Northern Ireland Peace Monitoring report, interview, 9 May 2016; Jennifer Irwin, Chief Executive Director, Northern Ireland Community Relations Council, interview, 15 April 2016). Remarkably, this shared leadership by the two hardline parties produced the longest period of political stability since the 1998 peace. However, as will be discussed, this governing arrangement constituted a significant barrier in terms of making critical changes in Belfast's hardened territoriality and community deprivation. Political stability has been purchased but at the expense of lost opportunities in moving towards the needed transformation of urban realities in Belfast.

## Peacebuilding and Urban Realities

Good Friday fundamentally restructured government in Northern Ireland and has produced a framework of shared power between former enemies. The significance of this accomplishment should not be underestimated. One needs only to look at the

Israel/Palestine case to understand how far Northern Ireland has progressed politically in addressing core issues of political control and sovereignty. This, however, is only part of the story. Peacebuilding is a political-spatial process that involves not just political reorganization but also urban spatial interventions that seek to operationalize peace in places where antagonistic sides live, work, and cope in tight urban space. And, nowhere in Northern Ireland is the spatial challenge of operationalizing peace as great as in the tight sectarian urban spaces of its major city of Belfast.

Since the Good Friday peace accord, the Northern Ireland government has put forward meaningful and potentially impactful urban goals addressing the future of Belfast. The objectives of *shared future, shared space*, and the ending of ethnic-religious division have been consistently asserted by successive governments in one form or another. In 2005, Northern Ireland government released, *A Shared Future – Policy and Strategic Framework for Good Relations in Northern Ireland*, in which it argues against continued community division between Unionists/Protestants and Nationalists/Catholics and advocates for sharing over separation. It states:

*The division that perpetuates itself in Northern Ireland is costly both socially and economically. Adapting public policy in Northern Ireland simply to cope with division holds out no prospect of stability and sustainability in the long run.*
Office of the First Minister and Deputy First Minister for Northern Ireland, 2005, p. 4

It further underscores that, 'separate but equal is not an option ... that parallel living and the provision of parallel services are unsustainable both morally and economically' (p. 20). Subsequent policy documents released by the Northern Ireland government such as *Cohesion, Sharing, and Integration* (2010) and *Together: Building a United Community* (2013) have emphasized this goal of sharing over continued separation to various degrees. Most ambitious of government goals pertaining to the legacy of separation in Belfast is the proclamation by the Northern Ireland Executive in 2013 that all interface barriers and peace walls will be removed by mutual consent by 2023.

In addition to shared future goals, Northern Ireland emphasizes *equality* and *good relations* as primary goals guiding future policy. In the *Cohesion, Sharing, and Integration* document, it states that:

*equality, fairness, inclusion and the promotion of good relations will be watchwords for all of our policies and programmes across Government.*
Office of the First Minister and Deputy First Minister for
Northern Ireland, 2010, p. 3

The 'equality' mandate is set out in the Northern Ireland Act of 1998 (section 75 [1]) pursuant to the Good Friday Agreement. It mandates that government must pursue equality of opportunity between persons of different religious belief, political opinion, racial group, age, marital status or sexual orientation. It further states that promotion of equality of opportunity entails more than the elimination of discrimination and that it requires proactive action to address inequality across groups that currently exists.

The 'good relations' goal is spelled out in the subsequent subsection of the Act (75 [2]) and states that policies must be carried out that 'have regard to the desirability of promoting good relations between persons of different religious belief, political opinion or racial group'. While the equality goal seeks to counter deeply ingrained social and religious inequalities, the good relations goal aims at ensuring harmony between sectarian groups in the carrying out of equality and other governmental programmes. I will describe how these two goals are not always perceived by Protestants and Catholics as compatible with one another and have been a source of enduring tension in implementing Northern Ireland's peacebuilding programme.

In its efforts to transcend the sectarian differences that are causal and correlative of inter-group violence – foregrounding sharing, equality, and good relations as primary goals – these strategies of the Northern Ireland government aimed at community divisions attempt to be *peace-promotive* and *conciliatory* and are a radical departure from the decades of discriminatory Protestant rule (1920–1972) and the period of British 'direct rule' (1972–1998), which focused conservatively on stability and maintenance of the *status quo* amid destabilizing political violence. Yet, the distorted urban spatial realities of Belfast that were created and reinforced during the Troubles constitute significant obstructions to the implementation of these new peace-promotive political goals.

## Belfast in the Early Years of Peace

The Belfast that existed in the early years after Good Friday was one of robust sectarian segmentation and deep socioeconomic deprivation in its working-class 'heartland' neighbourhoods, the ever-present and ominous presence of peace walls and interface barriers, lingering community violence both a legacy of the Troubles and due to the uncertainty of what peace would entail, major challenges of community policing and security, and the sustaining presence of inflammatory symbols and events on the ground – most prominently political murals, parades, and bonfires. In the years prior to and during the peace process, Belfast was also a city in demographic flux, with a seismic shift in population and a change in the balance of power from Protestants to Catholics in the local City Council. After decades of Protestant majorities, the city by 2001 was reaching parity between those having a Protestant community background (48.6 per cent) and those of Catholic community background (47.2 per cent) (Northern Ireland Statistics and Research Agency, 2011).[8] The ascendance of the Catholic population demographically since 1981 is explained by their greater natural birth rates and by out-migration of Protestants from the city to adjacent suburbs. By 2011, the majority/minority positions had switched in Belfast, by then composed of 49 per cent Catholic background and 42 per cent Protestant background.[9]

In the early years of peace, the city of Belfast's population (277,000 in 2001) was at a level approximately two-thirds its size in 1961 (416,000).[10] The population had dramatically declined during the 1970s and 1980s due to political violence and economic disinvestment. A large part of the population decline of the city can be attributed to suburbanization of the Protestant middle class. While the city's population was declining substantially from 1961 to 1991, first ring suburbs gained more than 80,000 residents while second ring suburbs gained almost 90,000 residents (Boal, 2006).

Traditionally a city of Protestant-Catholic residential segregation, separation intensified into a level of 'hyper-segregation' amid the horrific violence of an urban civil war. Such segregation was instrumental in furthering community feelings of security in the face of extremely abnormal living conditions. Community divisions (along with peace walls built to reinforce separation) became spatial reflections of the underlying political and religious conflict. A significant intensification of segregation occurred between 1971 and 1991, levelling off during the 1990s. In 2001, of the 51

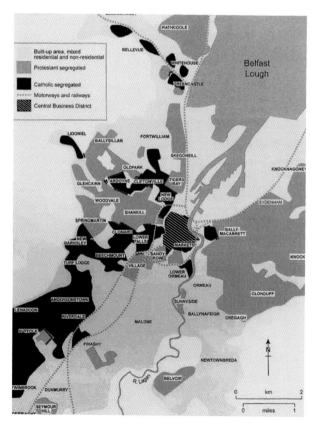

Figure 5.7. Segregation in Belfast. (*Source*: Boal and Royle, 2006, figure 4.17)

electoral wards in the City of Belfast, 65 per cent (33) contained 80 per cent or more of one religion, while 43 per cent (22) contained 90 per cent or more of one religion. Analysis using a smaller geographic scale – that of the Super Output Area (SOA),[11] which is more sensitive to block and neighbourhood patterns, shows a similar level of separation in 2001 as ward analysis, with 60 per cent of these smaller geographies made up of a single religion constituting 75 per cent or more of the population (Gaffikin *et al.*, 2008). Segregated, predominantly working-class neighbourhoods were home to a disproportionate amount of social housing sponsored by government and this constituted a segregating influence. Ninety-one per cent of tenants of Northern Ireland Housing Executive housing in Belfast live in estates where one religious community identity is 80 per cent or more (Shuttleworth and Lloyd, 2009, 2007).

Residential segregation is, in itself, neither negative nor positive. Indeed, hyper-segregation is explainable in the context of Belfast's history of violence, intimidation, and the forced displacement of populations that occurred in the early years of the Troubles. Segregated neighbourhoods, beyond providing needed security, could potentially be associated with healthy community functioning and livelihood to the extent that segregated residents have access to economic opportunities and community assets either in their community or in the wider city. Yet, this is clearly not the case in Belfast. The most segregated communities in the city are also the areas with high levels of socioeconomic deprivation and urban poverty. In 2001, twenty wards in the city were among the 10 per cent most deprived of all wards in Northern Ireland (Northern Ireland Multi Deprivation Measure, NISRA).[12] About 35 per cent of the city's population lived in these segregated, deprived wards (Gaffikin *et al.*, 2016).

In addition to community socioeconomic deprivation, another debilitating aspect of Belfast's sectarian segregation is that it is frequently demarcated by interface barriers. The Belfast Interface Project (BIP, 2012) has comprehensively documented these barriers, which snake a path some 12 miles (19 km) in length between Protestant and Catholic areas. The most obvious and ominous barriers are the so-called 'peace walls' made of solid and high walls and sometimes metal fencing above. Other types of barriers are made of different styles of metal fencing, a mixture of fences and vegetation used as buffers, and the permanent and occasional closing of roads (BIP, 2012). These structures have most often been constructed and/or are owned by the Department of Justice or the Northern Ireland Housing Executive. It is informative to note that of the 99 total barriers documented, while 32 of these for which construction dates are known were built before 1990, 26 others were constructed during the 1990s when efforts at national peacemaking started to crystallize and culminated in the 1998 peace accord (14 of these were constructed from 1995 to 1999, a period when political violence was attenuating due to the 1994 IRA ceasefire).[13] In the years before and right after Good Friday (1996–2000), there was significant community instability and disturbances while 'peace' was going on, especially associated with loyalist parading; this instigated a process of securing territory through barrier building during the uncertainty of the transition to peace (Neil Jarman, Research Fellow, Queen's University of Belfast, interview, 23 May 2016).

The walls and barriers reflect the wider political conflict but also appear to stimulate independent negative effects on residents living nearby. Interface communities host concentrated forms of disadvantage: unemployment, voided housing, lack of access to community services, high levels of physical and mental health disability, high rates of youth suicide, heightened paramilitary presence (especially in loyalist communities) and increased propensity of youths to engage in at-risk behaviour, including violence (Murtagh, 1994).

Madeleine Leonard, a Sociology Professor at Queen's University (interview, 12 May 2016) has surveyed hundreds of teenagers (14–16 year olds) who live in interface neighbourhoods. She has examined how the conflict has become spatialized, and how the physicality imposed by interface barriers makes it difficult for youths to think outside their group. She finds that whereas parts of the city (mostly middle-class areas) may be moving forward, youths in mainly working-class interface neighbourhoods are significantly shaped by the physical territoriality. For many teenagers, peace walls do not stand out as unusual because they have been there since they were born; nonetheless the barriers determine their behavioural patterns and attitudes by marking what is in and out of their territory. Leonard refers to the 'routine banality of separateness of everyday life' in these neighbourhoods – the routine ways that territorial restrictions become normalized in the everyday way of seeing and not seeing. Territorial sectarian markers such as murals and memorials provide a sense of security for these teenagers – a streetwise geography. At the same time, deprivation in these places allows youths to be more easily manipulated to engage in sectarian activities such as parades and flag-waving. While certain public discourses (such as shared space) seek to transform sectarian space, the tight territorial spaces of these neighbourhoods do not enable these discourses to have a local impact. The routine everyday life in interface areas is spatialized and territorialized.[14]

## *Evolution in Government Strategy: From Maintenance of the Status Quo to Sectarian Acknowledgement*

The explicit recognition by Northern Ireland government of the sectarian nature of separation and inequality found in documents such as the *Shared Future* programme in 2005 is an important turning point along a long evolutionary road in public sector consideration of sectarianism. The period of British direct rule utilized, with minor exceptions, an urban policy approach that was largely silent on sectarian divisions (what I called a 'colour-blind' approach in my 1995 research and described in Bollens, 2000). This approach prioritized stability, neutrality, and maintenance in efforts to manage and contain the conflict. More active interventions that would address and seek to transform sectarian division were viewed as potentially inflammatory in the face of ongoing political violence. This protection of the *status quo* defended a rigid and sterile territoriality of segregation, and reinforced in the name of stability the physical and psychological correlates of urban civil war.

A plan developed in 1987 is representative of the strategy adopted during Direct Rule. The *Belfast Urban Area (BUA) Plan 2001* (DOENI, 1990) neglects issues of sectarianism by defining them as outside the scope of planning. The Department of the Environment for Northern Ireland (DOENI), in its plan adoption statement (DOENI, 1989, p. 2) 'notes the views expressed on wider political, ecological, social or economic matters'. However, it states that it is not the purpose of a strategic land-use plan to deal with social and economic aspects. The Department had earlier expressed this view at a public inquiry when it stated that the contentious 'non-planning' issues of housing and social service delivery are outside the agency's specific domain (DOENI, 1988). Not one of the strategic objectives of the plan explicitly addressed an ethnic or sectarian issue (DOENI, 1990, p. 16). Echoing earlier plans, it largely accepts sectarian divides in stating that 'this strategy acknowledges the wishes of residents to continue living within their own areas'. Even the bread-and-butter of land-use planning work – the forecasting of total and subgroup populations – is excluded from the plan, probably because of its ethnic and political sensitivity.

*De-politicization of planning can itself be a mechanism that continues and reinforces division and conflict.*

Milena Komarova, Research Fellow, Queen's University, interview, 24 March 2016

In order to maintain sectarian segregation as a means towards stability, the government's approach at times was more than 'hands-off' and was complicit in the creation of the segregated and territorialized city. Security agencies sometimes played a key role in shaping the redevelopment of the city during the 1970s and 1980s (Cunningham, 2014, 2016). Security agencies used the concept of 'defensive planning' as a counter-insurgency strategy. A 'Standing Committee on Security Implications of Housing Problems in Belfast' (SCH) composed of security representatives of the local police force (Royal Ulster Constabulary), British Army, and development agency officials, advised on the development of social housing and roads and steered development in ways to contain religious communities within their traditional boundaries (Cunningham, 2014). Containment of sectarian territory was viewed as a stabilizing influence amid active violence. Social housing was placed firmly within territorial boundaries, major roads were built to disconnect sectarian trouble spots in West and North Belfast from the city centre area (creating 'shatter zones' of separation), and cul-de-sac designs were incorporated into new residential subdivisions in ways that insulated and disconnected them from adjacent neighbourhoods (Cunningham, 2014; Mark Hackett, Forum for Alternative Belfast, interview, 29 March 2016). De-densifying urban renewal projects applied to inner working-class communities – both Protestant and Catholic – in the 1970s and 1980s resulted in a major loss of units in neighbourhoods such as in the Lower Falls, Lower Shankill, and Inner East Belfast. Today, these inner areas contain a population of about 32,000, compared to approximately 100,000 in the 1960s (Mark Hackett, interview). 'It suited government to de-densify these troublesome areas and cut them off' through urban renewal and extensive road infrastructure (Mark Hackett, interview). Disconnection and separation as a means of maintaining security helped build 'socio-material pathology' into the urban landscape (David Coyles, Lecturer, University of Ulster, interview, 4 April 2016).

For the Catholic community, such a government approach to the sectarian divide further concentrated social and economic inequalities and perpetuated housing disadvantage and other structural inequalities with roots in historic discrimination practices of the Protestant majority Northern Ireland government that existed prior to the institution of direct rule in 1972. For the Protestant community, such depopulation and disconnection heightened a psychological sense of alienation – still existing today – that they were intentionally targeted by government planners and left behind, a feeling best exemplified by the title of a well-known treatise, *The Rape and Plunder of the Shankill in Belfast* (Wiener, 1976).

As peace has taken hold, public discussions and documents have shown an increased ability to consider what was silenced in public documents during the years of violent conflict. In examining numerous public initiatives and plans from cessation of the height of political violence in 1994 until the present, one sees an evolution of government attitudes from accommodating and reinforcing sectarian divisions to a more open and explicit consideration of the need to transform sectarian geographies.

The period 1995 to 2000 was a key transitional time when fundamental political tectonic plates were shifting. In the mid-1990s in the City of Belfast, as part of the Making Belfast Work economic initiative, multi-sectoral dialogues and consultations openly acknowledged the impact of contested space on city residents (Gaffikin and Sweeney, 1995). Then, starting in 1995, the City of Belfast engaged in a City Vision process during which participating individuals, including paramilitary representatives, 'communicated outside their ghettos for one of the first times' (Frank Gaffikin, Professor, Queen's University, interview, 15 March 2016). The Belfast City Partnership Board, created during this process, envisions a city, 'where people are valued more than territory or the ideology that they hold … a city determined to move beyond the habit of hate to discover new ways of creatively living with difference'. The Board's final plan (Belfast City Partnership Board, 1999) adopted the vision of a 'Mutual City'.

Meanwhile, at the larger regional level, a planning process involving 500 community and voluntary organizations discussed issues of sectarian division and the role of planning (Gaffikin *et al.*, 2000). The impact of these discussions is evident in the final regional plan of 2001, called *Shaping Our Future: Regional Development Strategy 2025* (Department of Regional Development [DRD]), which recognized that 'internally, Northern Ireland is a deeply divided and polarized society. Evidence suggests that community divisions have deepened in recent years. This has obvious implications for planning, especially when rational planning choice is often constrained by a strong sense of community "ownership of territory"' (DRD, 2001, p. 9). The successor regional plan, *Regional Development Strategy 2035* (DRD, 2010), includes goals aimed at lessening separation and inequality in the city, including the creation and enhancement of shared spaces and the direction of regeneration efforts into areas of disadvantage and social exclusion.

At the city level, formal plans began to acknowledge sectarian realities. In the *Belfast Masterplan 2004*, the City Council stated the commitment to 'tackle even unpalatable and difficult issues' (Belfast City Council, 2004, p. 6). In the more recent *Belfast Masterplan Review 2012*, the report acknowledged that 'there has been little if any positive impact on the city's poorest communities' (Belfast City Council, 2012, p. 6). It further recognizes the spatially disconnected nature of the city – 'the city's "shatter zones" remain a challenge to accessibility and wider integration. Projects that seek to reduce the physical severance between the Centre City and the surrounding residential areas should concentrate on these "shatter zones" surrounding the Core of the city' (Belfast City Council, 2012, p. 14). It emphasizes that connectivity of disadvantaged neighbourhoods to the city centre is critical to ensure equality of opportunity and services for those living in segregated areas.

At the metropolitan level, engagement with sectarianism is particularly important because it was at this level of planning that the government provided the land-use context for planning in the city and established a framework of allocations, site specific designations, policies, and zoning.[15] The greater specificity of this planning means that it confronts the micro-scale issues of sectarianism more directly than other plans. The *Belfast Metropolitan Area Plan (BMAP) 2015* (DOENI, 2014a) comprises an extensive 166-page document detailing land-use designations for the city in its Belfast District Plan. It notes that 'many challenges ... remain for the City – in particular community division, social and economic disadvantage...' (p. 6). It acknowledges the disconnected nature of the Belfast landscape: 'many of the gateways into Belfast City Centre can be characterless places dominated by the road infrastructure. Key sites around these junctions have often been inappropriately developed or remain undeveloped' (p. 22). It designates over 750 acres (304 ha) in the city for development but avoids the implications of these allocations on Protestant and Catholic communities. Using colour-blind language, it describes that 'sites are selected to allow for the efficient use of land within the urban footprint, to provide choice in the housing market and to include existing commitments. Other factors influencing site selection include access to public transport, and the need to minimize any detrimental impact on the environment'. These are criteria that one would find in professional deliberations in most cities throughout the world. Yet, Belfast with its robust territorial demarcation of Catholic and Protestant space is not like most other cities; 'land is not a neutral resource' in Belfast (Wallace, 2015, p. 88).

The allocation of land for future development in Belfast brings government agencies to the brink of a central challenge. The static and restrictive territorial boundaries that exist in the west, east, and northern parts of the city have created two cities in effect: one part is Catholic, growing in population, but experiencing lack of land for growth in areas typically considered Catholic; the other is Protestant, stagnating in population, and containing areas of underutilized and vacant land. In a normal city, neighbourhood evolution is often a natural progression, with a growing ethnic group replacing another ethnic group over time. Yet, during the decades of violent conflict, such evolution of Protestant areas into Catholic areas was simply not possible. To maintain political stability, increasing needs for Catholic housing owing to greater population growth could not be met by building new dwelling units in traditional Protestant territories or by locating Catholic residents in existing units there. Because of the difficulty of finding non-contentious sites outside traditionally Protestant areas, the ability to meet Catholic need has been severely constrained. This was so even though many Protestant areas had experienced depopulation and contained significant vacant land and high vacancy rates. With the advance of peace, the question becomes at what point, if ever, can there be a more natural progression of neighbourhood religious composition that would challenge the strict territoriality created out of violent political conflict.[16]

The allocation of future growth by the Belfast Metropolitan Area Plan does not touch on the sectarian issue directly but is important because it forecasts where development should occur to accommodate overall city needs. Whether such growth is allowed to take place by existing Protestant communities weary of Catholic 'invasion' into their territory – and who is to live in these new developments – is of fundamental importance to the city's future. In order to advance peace, the pressure to move the city along a path of greater normalization is growing.

A significant institutional change occurred in 2014 when responsibilities for local planning were transferred (*devolved*) to city councils. This was the first time that Belfast City Council has had local planning powers since Direct Rule took them away in 1972. To guide local councils in their engagement with planning, in late 2015 the Northern Ireland government issued a 'Strategic Planning Policy Statement' [SPPS] (DOENI, 2015) to set strategic directions for new councils. One of its five core planning principles is 'creating and enhancing shared space' and it defines shared space as 'places where there is a sense of belonging for everyone, where relationships between people from different backgrounds are most likely to be positive and where differences are valued and respected' (p. 18). It recommends that the planning system 'assist in the removal of barriers to shared space and maximize the accessibility of all areas within our community' (p. 18) and that 'planning authorities should aim to use the range of planning powers they possess to create environments that are accessible to all and which enhance opportunities for shared communities' (p. 70). A guide for local councils published the previous year, *Living Places: An Urban Stewardship and Design Guide for Northern Ireland* (DOENI, 2014b), identifies in photographic detail 'bad places' that are susceptible to antisocial behaviour and damage to external perceptions. These areas include unoccupied, unmaintained, unconnected, unsafe, and unwelcoming spaces. The legacy of division and disconnection evident in Belfast is described as a 'hangover' from the violent conflict era that should be constructively addressed in planning (DOENI, 2014b, p. 13).

The Programme for Government Framework, released in 2016, is a key document that indicates the priorities and directions of Northern Ireland Executive spending programmes and policies (Northern Ireland Executive, 2016). In its elucidation of intended outcomes and indicators to assess progress in achieving outcomes, the Programme's outcome 14 states that 'we are a shared society that respects diversity'. Among the myriad indicators of progress, two are important for their sectarian implications. Indicator 31 is to 'increase shared space' and is to be measured by the 'percentage of residents who think that leisure centres, parks, libraries and shopping centres in their areas are 'shared and open' to both Protestants and Catholics'.[17] Indicator 35 is to 'increase reconciliation' and is be measured by the 'percentage who feel their cultural identity is respected'.

In evaluating the numerous local, regional, metropolitan, and national plans and programmes that have been advanced during the run-up to, and since, the Good Friday Agreement, it is clear that public authorities in Northern Ireland have come a long way from the silence of the Direct Rule days to contemporary acknowledgement of sectarian realities and legacies and the need for policy to confront and address these distortions. However, this advancement comes primarily in the form of policy language and rhetoric. Difficult challenges face public agencies when these policy statements and goals hit the ground and must be implemented in the hard and narrow territories of Belfast. Peacebuilding policy objectives must constructively intervene in an urban environment where the 'spatial legacy of the conflict together with over forty years of planning and regeneration has delivered a city that is fractured, disjointed, and poorly managed' (Gaffikin, *et al.*, 2016, p. 60).

These challenges will be increasingly faced by local city councils, now tasked with local planning responsibility amid contested territoriality. Good Friday specified that local governments must engage in two types of plans: a 'community plan' and a 'local development plan'. The community plan, called in the capital city the Belfast Agenda, was in draft form and undergoing public consultation in early 2017. This is to be a joint vision for Belfast in the year 2030, created in partnership with key city partners, residents and community organizations. It is to address social issues, spatial planning, and the shaping of place in ways that will improve the wellbeing of city residents. The vision is to be backed up with budgetary and spending priorities, and the plan will set out measurable medium- and long-term goals for social, economic and environmental improvements for Belfast over the next 15 years. The local development plan (LDP) is to deliver the spatial aspects of The Belfast Agenda, provide a 15-year plan framework to support economic and social needs in the city, and allocate sufficient land to meet the needs of the city.

The future LDP, in particular, promises to be where the rubber hits the road as local government is faced with operationalizing spatial terms such as 'shared space', locating and allocating 'available land' in contested areas, and seeking to reduce inequalities while maintaining good relations. Each of these tasks confronts local officials with contentious issues about how to move Belfast forward amid obstructive local forces borne during violent conflict and still rooted in sectarian neighbourhoods.

## Political Goals and Urban Implementation

Political negotiations between antagonistic groups – whether in a momentous peace agreement or in subsequent policy documents aimed at building peace – are of extreme difficulty. With opposing sides, having ideologically opposed perspectives and narratives, coming to the negotiating table in Northern Ireland, the language incorporated into political and policy agreements becomes necessarily abstract in order to accommodate their differences under one umbrella. A 'creative ambiguity' in terminology is used to facilitate political compromise (Colin Knox, Professor, University of Ulster, interview, 7 April 2016).[18] This 'discursive and ambiguous language of the peace agreement was necessary so that all could sign on' to the Good Friday Agreement, observes Brendan Murtagh (Queen's University, interview, 21 March 2016). The Good Friday Agreement was an attempt to realize a set of principles – an idealistic process – that sought to reframe the context by creating a set of constitutional and political structures to address and contain the violence (Duncan Morrow, Chief Executive Officer, Community Relations Council 2002–2011, interview, 16 May 2016). High principles of reconciliation, peacemaking, and consent were emphasized, but there was less attention in the Good Friday Agreement as to how specific policies would address core issues of injustice and inequality.

The power-sharing structure of government established to contain the conflict de-emphasized, or formulated as abstract goals, those issues of societal transformation that would move the society, and the city of Belfast, forward into a post-conflict future (Duncan Morrow, interview). The power-sharing arrangement of the Agreement, written by external actors and acquiesced to by internal parties, responded to the needs to manage and contain the political conflict, while being more abstractly conceptual in elucidating concrete steps to be taken to address the deeply unequal and separate nature of Northern Ireland society (Adrian Guelke, Professor, Queen's University, interview, 16 March 2016). Political-institutional aspects of peacemaking were necessarily foregrounded, while considerations of the social dimensions of peacebuilding were backgrounded (Brewer, 2010). In terms of institutional structures created by the Good Friday Agreement, the requisites of power sharing meant that the design of new structures within government were guided more by the need to facilitate political accommodation than by what would be most successful in delivering public services and effective public policy (Colin Knox, Professor, University of Ulster, interview, 7 April 2016). Power sharing, in its institutionalized allocation of political power proportionately across groups, is built on an understanding that antithetical identities cannot be integrated (Knox, 2010). Yet, there is the need for social transformation of a society after violent conflict and this is not supported through the consolidation of identities but rather their bridging through cross-community peacebuilding efforts.

The social goals that were incorporated pursuant to the Good Friday Agreement proposed admirable intentions while remaining at a level of abstraction that creates uncertainty in their implementation. The 'equality' mandate states that promotion of equality of opportunity entails more than the elimination of discrimination and that it requires proactive action to address existing inequality across groups that currently exists. The 'good relations' goal spelled out in the same act, meanwhile, asserts that policies must be carried out in a way that inter-group harmony is sustained. A difficult balancing act is evident. The equality goal seeks to counter societal inequalities and thus would benefit historically disadvantaged Catholics more than Protestants due to existing patterns of inter-group disparities. At the same time, the good relations goal aims to ensure that discord between sectarian groups is avoided in the carrying out of equity programmes. Equity programmes disproportionately benefiting Catholics are to take place while ensuring that Protestants are not so antagonized by government policies that inter-group relations deteriorate. An additional primary social goal incorporated into post- Good Friday Agreement policy documents and consistently highlighted by successive governments in one form or another involves promoting a 'shared future' for Northern Ireland. Often included within this goal of countering sectarian division has been the objective of creating 'shared spaces'. The 2005 *Shared Future* document by Northern Ireland government argued against continued community division and advocated sharing over separation (OFMDFMNI, 2005). Continued accommodation of community division was viewed as jeopardizing the stability and sustainability of peace, with government asserting that the 'separate but equal 'approach to urban policymaking was contrary to peacebuilding goals (p. 20). Yet, the goals of shared future and shared space were not accompanied by specific articulation of how such objectives were to be implemented.

These goals of shared future, equality, and good relations are commendable. Few would disagree with the general objectives of increasing mutual sharing, remedying inequalities, and seeking harmony and tolerance in relationships between individuals and groups. Yet, as indicated above, these goals remain at a level of abstraction which creates tensions and political difficulties in their actualization. The problems created by abstraction in political and policy goals become even more acute when these high principles are to be operationalized in the complex environment of a city such as Belfast. There is an inherent difficulty in connecting the political to the urban; national politicians have a hard time understanding the complexity of the urban system. In contrast to a political level that tends to remain at the high level of principles and goals, intervention in contentious places like Belfast requires a more detailed calibration of the myriad conflicting imperatives found in the city. Political discussions in the Northern Ireland government often exist at a 'symbolic, rhetorical level' not directly useful for implementation at the 'urban and specific level', laments James Anderson (Professor, Queen's University, interview, 22 March 2016).

*We have had a lot of changed language and empty signifiers since 1998, but they are not challenging the fundamental impulses of balkanization and sectarian bias and at times may be legitimizing them.*

Frank Gaffikin, Professor, Queen's University,<br>interview, 15 March 2016

It is a challenging trek when moving from shared future, equality, and good relations goals to their actualization in Belfast. Operationalization of abstract political goals in cities such as Belfast does not automatically proceed from grand visions, but instead faces difficult trade-offs and balancing acts when confronting the urban complex. These goals confront a sectarian divided city of structural inequality reinforced by numerous interface barriers. The physical legacies of the Troubles are numerous: disconnection, partition, enclosures, dead spaces, walls, policeable and controllable space, symbols, and territoriality. These spatial and physical legacies of violent conflict create an obdurate physical environment not easily modified or disrupted. Supporting the durability of such legacies are various local actors who feel they gain more by existing conditions than in changing them. In Belfast, these include paramilitary legacy groups and dissidents who control sectarian territories through their involvement in community organizational infrastructure, local elected officials who are electorally wedded to their own sectarian districts, residents who feel secure in their segregated neighbourhoods and fear integration and sharing with the 'other', and community groups whose constituencies and funding pathways are within single-community channels.

The operational translation of national political goals onto Belfast becomes a process replete with on-the-ground complexities, contradictions, and manipulations that distort and disrupt national objectives. The ambiguity of the peace process needed to facilitate political agreement leaves 'huge embedded contradictions' in their implementation (Brendan Murtagh, Queen's University, interview, 21 March 2016). 'After all the fuzzy technologies of politics needed to get us across the line for Good Friday', adds Murtagh, 'now comes the time to work out what these concepts really mean on the ground'. How much should equality programmes be pursued if they are perceived as benefiting one community more than the other? How are good relations between antagonistic groups to be maintained when seeking to change a social and spatial fabric that is viewed by many as assuring security and community identity? How, and in what forms, is sharing to take place in a city where sectarianized territoriality remains robust? Due to the abstract, even ambiguous goals used by political leaders, these peacebuilding concepts become susceptible to different interpretations and manipulations, becoming at times 'political footballs' as they are implemented in contested urban space (Colin Knox, interview, 7 April 2016).

*We have a grossly inefficient housing market in Belfast. We need 140 hectares (346 acres) of land to house Catholics in West Belfast. On the Protestant side, we have 144 hectares of land vacant. They are 100 metres (320 feet) apart. But we have to pay top dollar for sites in the Catholic west boundary area when we own sites 100 metres away that we can't do anything with.*
Jennifer Hawthorne, Head of Income and Communities, Northern Ireland Housing Executive (NIHE), interview, 14 April 2016

The fundamental challenge facing policymakers in Belfast is that the persistence of sectarian territoriality in the west, east, and northern parts of the city has created two cities in effect. As previously mentioned, one part is Catholic with a growing population, but experiencing limited land for growth in areas typically considered Catholic; the other is Protestant, stagnating in population, and containing areas of underutilized and vacant land. John McPeake, who worked for the Northern Ireland Housing Executive for 22 years (and was its Chief Executive from 2011 to 2014), describes the 'dual faces of housing need' in Belfast (interview, 25 May 2016). Catholics have greater objective need for new housing due to their growth rate and historic deficits in the provision of housing supply in their neighbourhoods – this is evident when looking at demand for social housing. There are significantly more Catholics than Protestants on the waiting list, they score higher points in terms of eligibility and existing 'housing stress', and they spend longer times on the waiting list (McPeake, interview, 25 May 2016).[19] But due to the difficulty of finding suitable non-contentious sites for new Catholic housing in areas outside traditional Protestant neighbourhoods, the ability to meet Catholic need is severely limited. On the other hand, the current Protestant housing stock needs revitalization due to its inadequate condition, unfitness, and disrepair; Protestants argue for more housing construction, jobs, and services in their communities to bring back the vitality that has been lost in the past decades. The two communities – beset by territorial boundaries which preclude normal urban functionality – experience different community needs: objective needs on the Catholic side, needs for community revitalization and viability on the Protestant side.

The contrasting and qualitatively different community needs – in effect, two cities in one – create a difficult matrix when policymakers seek to intervene in the city. Duncan Morrow (Chief Executive Officer, Community Relations Council, interview, 16 May 2016) refers to this as the 'deep structural reality' created out of conflict, pointing to how the nature of division is structured at multiple levels – narrative, history, religion, sports, education, behavioural, territorial, and cultural. The social structure of the Troubles was underpinned not just politically but sociologically in terms of segregation, education, and structural inequalities. When peacemaking goals such as shared future, equality, and good relations are operationalized, they face these deep fractures in the urban system. Peace implementation faces a rocky road when political agreements and compromises hit the ground of Belfast's spatial and territorial realities.

The three primary goals of equality, good relations, and shared space are perceived by local political leaders and community activists as not necessarily compatible with one another and have been a constant source of tension in implementing Northern Ireland's peacebuilding programme. Since the Catholic population faces greater levels of socioeconomic deprivation and objective housing need (Gaffikin et al., 2016), the challenge becomes how to distribute more resources to the Catholic population without it disturbing good relations between the two groups. The redevelopment of the closed Girdwood Barracks site in north Belfast is an illuminating case in point. This 14 acre (5.7 ha) site, formerly the largest British army base in Northern Ireland, is close to both Catholic and Protestant neighbourhoods and redevelopment plans thus ignited a long-running sectarian dispute over prospective uses. On the one hand, the plan sought to build a greater amount of housing to be used by Catholics in order to meet projected demand. On the other hand, Protestant leaders argued that such housing at a large scale would facilitate Catholic intrusion that would negatively impact on adjacent Protestant areas, degrade good relations between the two sides, and eliminate the possibility for shared space in the area. This project shows how 'equality' and 'shared future' can be taken up by each community as convenient leverage for their own advocacy (Gaffikin et al., 2016). The Protestant side argued that the pursuit of equality, which effectively supported a greater Catholic presence on the site, was contrary to promotion of good relations and a shared future.[20] In contrast, the Catholic side argued that sustainable good relations could not occur without implementation of equality policies. The Girdwood project was eventually built, but with significantly less Catholic housing than objective need would dictate and with the building of a new 'community hub' facility wedged in between the two communities which effectively reproduced sectarian spatial divisions rather than transcending them (Frank Gaffikin, Professor, Queen's University, interview, 15 March 2016).

The dynamic exposed at Girdwood is one that exists throughout the city when policymakers seek to intervene in the city post-Good Friday Agreement. The identification of land suitable for future development, where to build new and revitalize existing housing, the location of community recreation and health facilities, the intended removal of peace walls and other interface barriers, and development of sites for economic purposes each confront the sectarian physicality and distortions of the spatial landscape and deeply rooted and obstructive antagonistic forces on the ground. The ability of robust sectarian territorialities and constituencies to obstruct peace implementation efforts leads to the 'sense that we acquiesce to community divisions rather than address them' (Mike Morrissey, Community Economic Consultant, interview, 12 April 2016).

Government-funded social housing for Belfast low-income residents constitutes a particularly difficult issue facing policymakers in the Northern Ireland Housing Executive (NIHE). Since over 90 per cent of social housing in the city is currently segregated, decisions regarding the location of new social housing, and who will live there, can be an important influence in creating a city where the two sides are less geographically segregated (Jennifer Hawthorne, Head of Income and Communities, NIHE, interview, 14 April 2016). Consistent with both shared space and good relations goals, there is the need to have greater amounts of shared, or integrated, housing in the city. Building greater amounts of shared housing is essential in assisting the two sides to learn to live together and in breaking down sectarian territoriality. Theories such as the contact hypothesis assert that increased contact between antagonistic groups helps reduce prejudice by dispelling myths and stereotypes about the 'other' and enabling the formation of positive relationships (Allport, 1954). It is clear that a post violent conflict city cannot move forward in a social-psychological sense if housing remains deeply divided.

*Loyalist paramilitaries are absolutely still in place, as much as they ever were and you have to ask yourself, why?*

Jennifer Hawthorne, Head of Income and Communities, NIHE, interview, 14 April 2016

Yet, efforts to build integrated housing in Belfast run up against the sharp edge of embedded and obstructive sectarian territoriality. Eighteen years after Good Friday, many neighbourhoods in Belfast remain the protectorates of strong community voices who seek to maintain the *status quo* of separation. 'People are still sitting in single-identity communities often with the strong presence of paramilitaries', notes Hawthorne (interview). Housing intimidation of minorities – often by loyalist paramilitaries or Catholic dissidents[21] – that seeks to drive them out of majority-held housing estates remains a fact of life. The NIHE is acutely aware of the sectarian nature of their estates, compiling a map of all paramilitary symbols and areas of displacement due to intimidation. Such sectarianism is visible and obvious; 'even the dogs in the street know' (Hawthorne, interview). Estates are commonly controlled by the two loyalist paramilitary groups – the UDA and the UVF (themselves in conflict) – and by Catholic dissident republicans. For those estates and communities 'in transition' and not fully controlled by one group, power struggles occur with increased intensity of intimidation and homelessness and the insertion of aggressive loyalist bonfires and murals. In these areas, 'we have hardened men back in the murals again' (Hawthorne, interview).

The 2013 government document *Together: Building a United Community (TBUC)* (OFMDFMNI, 2013) tasked the NIHE with building ten 'shared new build' estates in Northern Ireland.[22] Most of these are in Belfast. One direct method of integrating housing would be to use explicit quotas that would ensure a mix of Catholics and Protestants in these estates. Yet this use of quotas is not allowed by the Northern Ireland Equality Commission. Without this option, the NIHE must rely on decisions of where to build shared housing in an attempt to integrate. The effort is to locate these estates in areas that might produce mix – areas where one community is not more than 70 per cent of neighbourhood population (Jennifer Hawthorne, interview,

Figure 5.8. Tiger's Bay graffiti, Belfast (UFF is a loyalist paramilitary organization).

14 April 2016). At the same time, however, the NIHE throughout its entire history has used a strict needs-based approach to allocating social housing as a way to overcome past distrust of government housing allocations (John McPeake, NIHE, interview, 25 May 2016). Thus, government is faced with a difficult balancing act – trying to develop mixed housing estates in a situation where the use of objective need criteria would allocate housing significantly more to Catholics than to Protestants. 'We build shared new build in areas of highest need, and these tend to be in Catholic areas', observes Hawthorne, 'we meet need; we are not here to build houses for Protestants when need does not support this'.

The core of the dilemma involving integrated, shared housing exposes again the policy cross-currents in seeking to transform Belfast's sectarian geographies. Responding to the equality mandate, new social housing must accommodate the greater objective need of Catholics. Yet, shared space and good relations goals would entail ensuring a religious mix in these estates greater than would be produced using strict needs-based criteria.

*Divisions here were 300 years in the making. You're not going to solve them in 10 or 20 years.*
John McPeake, NIHE (1982–2014),
interview, 25 May 2016

Because it seeks to weaken sectarian segregation, the construction of shared housing estates commonly faces resistance by extremists. If located close to Protestant areas, threats and spray-painting by the UVF of 'No Fenians' on buildings have occurred.[23] Shared estates elsewhere become captured by republicans through threats and the flying of the Irish Tricolour flag. To its credit, the NIHE is attempting openly to counter such obstructions. All shared housing developments are publicly branded as government endeavours. Although there is an argument that a less explicit approach to shared housing might be more effective and not elicit such extremist disruption, such a 'stealth' approach is frowned upon by community relations experts in the NIHE who say it is now time to confront extremists more publicly. There is the perceived need to face extremists and not modify government actions to accommodate them: 'in a post-conflict society, at a certain point the stealth approach is no longer the right way forward' (Hawthorne, interview).[24]

## Shared Space

The most spatially specific peacemaking goal of government arising from the Good Friday Agreement has been the promotion of 'shared spaces' where Protestants and Catholics co-exist without fear of threat and intimidation. In a city where 'ethnic space' is inscribed through segregated and territorially bound neighbourhoods, the development of such shared spaces constitutes a central and significant challenge. Whereas the city centre is increasingly viewed as a successful shared space devoid of sectarian paraphernalia, the segregated spatial geography of working-class areas remains robust. Further, many residents of these working-class neighbourhoods face psychological detachment and physical separation from the shared spaces of the city centre (Mark Hackett, Forum for Alternative Belfast, interview, 29 March 2016). The creation of shared spaces in working-class areas remains challenging because it is about breaking down the barriers of territory and developing spaces that both communities can have access to and share. The Girdwood example discussed earlier shows how attempts to create shared spaces become highly problematic amid contesting communities. It is an achievement for government to state, abstractly, the goal of sharing spaces; it is another feat altogether to actually construct such accessible and shared spaces. In the Girdwood case, the construction of a community recreation hub has been criticized as creating a 'more benign peace wall' that separates more than bringing together adjacent Protestant and Catholic neighbourhoods (Frank Gaffikin, interview, 15 March 2016). Rather than building a facility that connected to the organic needs of the neighbourhoods, the high-quality community centre with international funding was just 'plopped down' in the area without real connectivity to the two communities nearby (Mark Hackett, interview, 29 March 2016; Ken Sterrett, Senior Lecturer, Queen's University, interview, 23 March 2016). Without buy-in and support from neighbouring communities, the community centre risks reinforcing, rather than transcending, sectarian segregation.[25]

The 'shared space' goal suffers from a level of abstraction which does not denote a methodology about how it is to be achieved in contentious geographies. Without greater specification, the goal becomes susceptible to political appropriation and manipulation by sectarian interests. In the Girdwood case, Protestant opposition to Catholic housing on the site to meet objective need was based on a claim that this amount of Catholic housing in the area would denigrate shared space objectives because there would be Catholic 'intrusion' and the creation of a flashpoint (Frank Gaffikin, interview, 15 March 2016). This is a disingenuous, politically motivated capturing of the shared space ideology to support one community's desire for sustained segregation. Instead of basing their claims on overt sectarianism, Protestant opponents were able to wrap themselves within the peacemaking goal of shared space to support their ultimately successful claims to downsize the amount of housing built for Catholics.

A tenuous relation exists between the shared space concept and how it is to be materialized in the city (Milena Komarova, interview, 24 March 2016). At a conceptual and theoretical level, shared space is hard to define, let alone operationalize on the ground.[26] The goal has thus been far stronger in discourse than in actual execution; indeed, there are 'few mechanisms in the planning system by which you can develop shared space' (Komarova, interview). In discussion with Keith Sutherland

(Development Policy and Plans Manager, Belfast City Council, interview, 14 April 2016) about this assertion, he shows caution in using shared space as a goal. 'Planning cannot create shared space, only people can', he observes, 'you could create a perfectly accessible physical environment but this will not necessarily change how people use the space'. Without consideration of adjacent communities, and their sense of territorial ownership, there exists the 'danger that when planners try to create shared space that we create neutral space that is antagonistic to all sides'.

The least difficult method to counter ethnic space is by creating neutral and bland spaces which are not inviting to either side, yet shared space implies more – an everyday sharing of space that is safe and inviting, not identifiable as belonging to one group or the other, and purpose-based with programming of frequent activities to encourage interaction (Callie Persic, Urban Development Officer, Belfast City Council, interview, 14 April 2016). The activities that take place on site and who is running them are important components of shared space. High-activity shared spaces can be victims of their own success, with one community over time able to control the space through greater use. A group can also secure control through gaining operational control of a community facility. 'People are looking for opportunities to claim space and you can't design that out' simply through planning, observes Keith Sutherland (interview). Physical design of shared space is one element, but operational control and activity patterns are also important to the ultimate success of a space as truly shared across groups.

An important consideration in efforts to create shared spaces in Belfast is the location of new community facilities *vis-à-vis* sectarian territories. If these facilities are established within sectarian segregated communities, the urban context of the facility will lead to the site not being neutral and welcoming to one of the groups, the so-called 'chill factor'. Starting in 2005, Belfast opened seven new 'Wellbeing and Treatment Centres' which sought to distribute health services throughout the city beyond the traditional hospitals. Gaffikin *et al.* (2016) report that four of these centres were located in areas of high religious segregation (two of the facilities located in more mixed areas were built in less sectarian South Belfast). Although the buildings were of considerable high quality and their internal design was welcoming, the location of the four in areas of high religious segregation obstructs their ability to be truly accommodating of both groups. An alternative approach – of locating these facilities in mixed areas accessible to both groups – would have more effectively addressed the territorial realities that remain in the city today.[27]

When articulating a future where space in Belfast is to be more shared, policymakers must confront the presence of intimidating single-identity events and symbols such as parades, flags, and murals. Each of these phenomena is a significant demarcation of sectarian identity, and contains assertive nationalistic content antagonistic to the vision of a shared and tolerant society. They confront government with challenges of how to respect community traditions while at the same time creating non-intimidating and shared spaces.

Parades and marches, mostly loyalist, are a common occurrence in Belfast and Northern Ireland. Taking place mostly around the July commemoration of the Battle of the Boyne, triumphalist loyalist parades assert the right to use and access space throughout the city and, prior to the Good Friday Agreement, frequently travelled intentionally near or through Catholic communities as a way to assert their rights. In 1997, an independent, quasi-judicial Parades Commission was established to regulate the routes that these parades could take. If a parade is deemed as potentially 'contentious' due to its route's proximity to Catholic neighbourhoods, the Commission restricts the routing and/or regulates the playing of triumphalist music near specific hotspots. With the exception of a particular contentious time in 2012–2013, loyalist parades have since become more low-key, with semi-formulaic restrictions by the Parades Commission (Neil Jarman, interview, 23 May 2016). The major sponsor of loyalist parades, the Orange Order, has refused to engage with the Commission and basically walked away from the process, resulting in a 'frozen dispute' of *de facto*, but not willing, acceptance (Jarman, interview). Parades remain, however, as potentially inflammatory events in Belfast, as witnessed in 2012–2013 when conflict over the flying of the Union Jack flag on City Hall led to a contentious parade season, resulting in the physical injuring of one in ten police officers who became 'human shock absorbers' of the conflict (Jarman, interview).

Figure 5.9. Participant in loyalist parade, North Belfast; is this man ready for peace?

The flying of flags and banners similarly demarcate sectarian and nationalistic space. Whether the Union Jack, the Irish Tricolour, or numerous other symbols aligned with sectarian identity and paramilitaries, flags are commonly positioned in housing estates and on lampposts in sectarian heartlands and at contentious sites along roads and intersections. Multi-party talks in 2013 (the so-called Haass-O'Sullivan talks) failed to make progress on how to address flags, considering both informal mechanisms that would encourage self-regulation and more formal regulation through legislation (Nolan and Bryan, 2016). Although there are existing laws on the books that make it illegal to fly flags on lampposts along roads or on government social housing structures, police remain hesitant to involve themselves in implementing this law (Dominic Bryan, Director of Institute of Irish Studies, Queen's University, interview, 12 April 2016). The most formidable challenge associated with flags came in December 2012, when the Belfast City Council voted not to fly the Union Jack on City Hall year-round, but only on eighteen designated days during the year. This enraged the loyalist community and led to numerous protests, demonstrations, and a volatile parading season. While most were peaceful, there were some extremely violent incidents, with the police force bearing the brunt of the injuries. The cost of the policing due to the 'flags dispute' was estimated at over £18 million ($22 million) (Nolan, 2014).

Political murals in the city having sectarian and paramilitary references constitute visual claims on territory and create intimidating and chilling effects in the city. In order to address the most inflammatory of these murals, the primary government approach has been to work with community groups and to fund efforts to take down or modify the most antagonistic murals. The Building Peace through the Arts: Re-Imaging Communities Programme of the Northern Ireland Arts Council funds efforts by artists to work with local communities to tackle the most visible murals of sectarian and racist content (Wallace Consulting, 2016). Some modifications and take-downs of inflammatory murals were noticeable in my 2016 research compared to 1994. Yet, these success stories appear as a small minority. Inflammatory political murals remain a fact of life in Belfast, particularly in Protestant neighbourhoods; indeed, at times even increasing in number during volatile periods. Painting a realistic picture of the mural re-imaging project in loyalist areas, one observer equates it with 'legal extortion' by the government that enables churches and community groups to get the consent of paramilitary groups (Gerard McGlade, Black Cab Tours, interview, 14 March 2016).

In the sectarian neighbourhoods of Belfast, there is no more potent and visible indicator of the anaemic condition of shared space than the peace walls and interface barriers that divide one community from another. In an eye-catching declaration, the Northern Ireland government, in its 2013 *TBUC* report (OFMDFMNI, 2013), stated its goal of removing all interface barriers in the city by 2023. This is a significant and forceful stance by government. Nonetheless, it has left many observers wondering how such an intervention will take place and the effect it may have on communities

Figures 5.10 and 5.11. Alliance Avenue peace wall, North Belfast.

adjacent to the barriers. One local nongovernmental group observes, 'seeking the removal of barriers is in some ways an easy call to make, examining what this might mean, supporting and preparing communities to consider the option is a much harder challenge' (Belfast Interface Project, 2015, p. 1). People I interviewed expressed concerns about implementation. Several pointed to the fact that interface barriers have performed a function in providing security amid unstable conditions of violence and that merely removing them would expose and intensify the myriad problems of adjacent communities.

The barriers themselves are perceived by many as not the problem, but rather a symptom of the structural imbalances and distortions of the city. Barriers are seen as a symptom of a dysfunctional urban system, not the problem *per se* (Frank Gaffikin, interview; Mark Hackett, interview). A long time Belfast expert views peace walls and barriers as constituting 'dikes' that have held back the pressure on each side (Frederick Boal, Professor Emeritus, Queen's University, interview, 25 May 2016).

Figure 5.12. Manor Street peace wall, North Belfast.

Figure 5.13. Tiger's Bay peace wall, North Belfast.

In removing barriers, one must understand that urban partitions are the end-result of an extended sequence of local events and actions which debilitated the area in terms of normal functioning (Calame and Charlesworth, 2009).[28] Without attention to the underlying problems of territoriality, conflict, and community deprivation which produced the peace walls, removing the barriers risks being insufficient, if not contrary, to peacebuilding goals. 'You can't just take down a peace wall because you then create dead space and deprivation. You need also to regenerate the area as well as build relationships between groups', asserts Claire Hackett (Falls Community Council, interview, 11 April 2016). There is the need for a multi-dimensional planning strategy in addressing barrier removal, one that pursues wider regeneration of interface areas as a complement to barrier removal (Neil Jarman, interview).

An Attitudes to Peace Walls Survey in 2012, commissioned by Northern Ireland leadership, points to hesitancy on the part of interface community residents to barrier removal (Byrne *et al.*, 2012). Whereas 76 per cent of the general population of the city would like to see the walls come down now or in the near future, this percentage falls to 58 per cent for residents in interface communities. Further, whereas 38 per cent of the general population believes that peace walls are necessary because of the potential for violence, this percentage increases to 69 per cent for residents living near them. Concerns of interface community residents were underpinned by expressed fears of potential 'loss' of community, fear of violence, and fear that the police would be unable to maintain law and order should there be community unrest once the walls are removed. Although stated in *TBUC* as an essential component in barrier removal, government engagement with community representatives (including those representing single-identity interests) is seen as problematic. Local groups were not brought into the process that led to *TBUC*'s top-down declaration and thus 'they resist the macro level initiative at the micro level because they feel a loss of engagement' (Colin Knox, interview). Local residents feel their quality of life depends on the maintenance of barriers and 'they feel they are part of somebody else's plan rather than feel they will be empowered' (Kim Walsh, Community Planning Project Officer, Belfast City Council, interview, 24 May 2016.)

*Can you build a peace behind walls? You can't. Nor can you remove those walls and say 'now we have peace'. When the walls come down, what do we put in its place? Now we have a chance.*
            Brian Rowan, Journalist and Author, interview, 1 June 2016

The removal of barriers – a visible spatial and social legacy of the Troubles – is clearly an important part of urban peacebuilding and the creation of shared space in Belfast. This is not in doubt. However, the articulation of this public goal in the form of a top-down declaration shows the obstacles faced when attempting to implement it amid the sectarian complexity of the city. Similar to the goals of equality, good relations, and shared space, the devil is in the operational details of how a laudable public goal such as barrier removal is to be achieved. Political pronouncements are not enough; urban peacebuilding involves sensitive spatial, social, and psychological elements which must be addressed in carrying out such goals. Political aspirations are necessary but must be matched by engaged consideration of peacebuilding as a political-spatial iterative process unfolding over time amid contested physical and social legacies.

 Another complication in seeking to build a shared Belfast is that the shared space concept suffers from myopia because it sidesteps the fact that the city is fundamentally unshared across socio-economic sectors of the population. Whereas the middle- and higher-income residents of Belfast have good access via automobile mobility to the full range of services and facilities of the city centre, working-class communities of *both* religious backgrounds face barriers and obstacles that hinder their easy access to the benefits of the city centre. The broader spatial environment of Belfast privileges the more affluent that have cars and disadvantages working-class residents in terms of their pedestrian and public transport access to city centre (Mark Hackett, interview, 29 March 2016). Large road infrastructure, blighted areas, car parks, and vacant land encircle the city centre and cut off access to those without a car. These 'shatter zones' of separation, in part intentionally created by planners and officials to disconnect the city centre from violent neighbourhoods during the years of the Troubles, constitute today a significant structural impediment to fuller sharing of the entire city (Mark

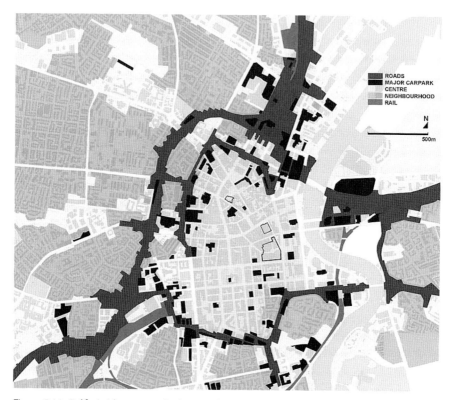

Figure 5.14. Belfast's 'shatter zones'. (*Source*: 'The Unshared City No. 1', *Shared Space 2011*, Mark Hackett and the Forum for Alternative Belfast) *https://www.forumbelfast.org/projects/shared-space-2011.php*.

Hackett, interview). Efforts to create shared space in working-class and interface neighbourhoods are essential, but shared space strategies that do not also address how the city is fundamentally unshared across income classes as well as sectarian affiliation misses the bigger picture. Consequently, development of shared spaces in the sectarian neighbourhoods should be complemented by public strategies that counter the broader structural and spatial conditions of unequal accessibility across the whole city.

## Disconnection between National and Urban

This chapter has revealed the challenges faced in implementing national political goals in the city. Efforts by policymakers to intervene in Belfast in ways to support peacebuilding reveal the difficulties of connecting often abstract political aspirations to tangible urban changes that can modify spatial sectarianism and normalize the city. The examples described in this chapter show that on-the-ground translation of commendable national political goals – equality, good relations, and shared space – aimed at creating co-existent peace is a process bedevilled by complexities and contradictions that obstruct and distort national goals. A national programme aimed at reforming a city is not one of simple goal formulation and straightforward urban implementation, but rather a difficult political-spatial process of engagement with urban realities having unforeseen and erratic effects on the national programme. The basic challenges and contradictions faced by public authorities 20 years ago – how to intervene in a city with two sectarian and segregated communities having different trajectories and needs – have now become ingrained and enshrined in the peace agreement and political programmes; the contradictions have reached a higher level of politics.

When the formal peace process, composed of high-level political diplomacy and significant achievements in political restructuring, faces implementation on the ground, it intersects with the myriad local dynamics and obstructions created during the years of violent conflict (Neil Jarman, Research Fellow, Queen's University, interview, 23 May 2016). Peacemaking is revealed as not taking place solely within the political domain, but as a political-spatial iterative process subject to significant impediments as it is implemented on the ground. As political concepts such as equality, good relations, and shared future are operationalized in specific places with distinct local histories in the urban arena, each peacebuilding intervention constitutes 'test-grounds' for how far political peacemaking can affect meaningful and necessary material change in the local landscape (Milena Komarova, Research Fellow, Queen's University, interview, 24 March 2016). Efforts to change the built environment constitute 'spatial points of visibility' where national and local interests collide: 'a working space between national and lived experiences' (Komarova, interview). In this contentious relationship between political aspirations and on-the-the ground realities, Belfast constitutes an essential, yet highly problematic, component of peacemaking in Northern Ireland.

## Notes

1. Among Protestants, 'Unionists' favour more moderate political approaches in seeking continued alignment within the United Kingdom, while 'Loyalists' are more prone to violence and extreme actions in defence of this alignment. Among Catholics, 'Nationalists' are more supportive of constitutional means for achieving unification, while 'Republicans' are more sympathetic with physical force as a legitimate means towards separation from the United Kingdom.
2. The division in Northern Ireland is more accurately labelled as 'ethno-national' because it involves not just religious and ethnic identity but national identity and allegiance. Nevertheless, I will continue to use here the historically- and commonly-used descriptor 'sectarian' to describe the Northern Ireland conflict.
3. It is important to note, however, that Good Friday did not resolve the question of national alignment, but rather created an electoral pathway by which citizens in the future can potentially vote to join Northern Ireland to the Republic of Ireland.
4. The uncertainty of Northern Ireland politics has intensified after my early 2016 field research due to three events. First, on 23 June 2016, United Kingdom voted to leave the European Union (EU). The so-called 'Brexit' decision threatens to re-establish a firmer border between Northern Ireland and the Republic of Ireland, which will remain in the European Union. Voters in Northern Ireland were strongly against leaving the EU, 56 per cent to 44 per cent. Northern

Ireland has been the beneficiary of significant funds from the EU over the past decades. Second, in January 2017, the power-sharing government collapsed when the Republican Deputy Minister resigned from his post. If a power-sharing agreement between the two religious groups cannot be achieved, governance of Northern Ireland will revert back to direct rule by Britain. Third, in June 2017, the Democratic Unionist Party entered an agreement to support the minority Conservative Party government in England, raising concern among Republicans about London's ability to act as a neutral agent in Northern Irish affairs.

5. Balaclavas (named after the Battle of Balaclava, 1854) are hoods covering the whole head and neck except for parts of the face, typically made of wool.
6. Conflict Archive on the Internet (CAIN); see: http://cain.ulst.ac.uk/sutton.
7. Consociationalism is a type of power sharing that seeks to reconcile societal fragmentation along ethnic and religious lines through methods such as a grand coalition, mutual vetoes, and proportionality of authority. Its goals are governmental stability, the survival of the power-sharing arrangements and of democracy, and avoidance of violence. The model is most closely associated with political scientist Arend Lijphart (1977) and is currently used in Lebanon and Bosnia-Herzegovina, among others.
8. Protestant majorities in the city of Belfast were 62:38 as recently as 1981; it was 57:43 in 1991. For Northern Ireland as a whole in 2001, population was 53 per cent Protestant background and 44 per cent Catholic background.
9. By 2011, the Northern Ireland population was 48 per cent Protestant background and 45 per cent Catholic background.
10. Northern Ireland Statistics and Research Agency (www.nisra.gov.uk/census). In 2011, Belfast city population was 286,000. Expansion of city boundaries due to council reform in 2015 has increased the city population to 334,000.
11. There are 152 statistical Super Output Areas in Belfast City, compared to 51 electoral wards.
12. The Multi Deprivation Measure uses seven clusters of indicators: income, employment, health, education, services, living environment, and crime.
13. Another seven interface barriers were constructed in the 2000s. For thirty-four barriers, date of construction was not obtainable by researchers.
14. This has lasting effects on individuals. One interviewee, a 45 year old man from Protestant East Belfast, relates that 'even now, I would feel very uncomfortable in the (Catholic) Falls neighbourhood' (Gareth McAleese, community member, interview, 25 March 2016).
15. With the devolution of planning powers to local councils in 2014, many of these functions are now to be undertaken by local governments.
16. The Equality Impact Assessment required as part of BMAP notes the sectarian implications of BMAP land allocations in Belfast, pointing out that disproportionately more developable space zoned for housing and employment is found in areas traditionally characterized as 'Protestant'. Belfast City Council estimates that about 80 per cent of easily accessible and developable land in Belfast is in traditionally Protestant/Unionist areas (Keith Sutherland, Development Policy and Plans Manager, Department of Planning and Place, Belfast City Council, interview, 20 April 2016).
17. As measured in the Northern Ireland Life and Times Survey.
18. A famous case of creative ambiguity from the U.S. is the passage of the historic Housing Act of 1949, which used general goal language to garner support from both economic developers and low-income housing advocates: 'seldom have so many angels danced on the same small pin'. The lack of specificity in the Act bedevilled its implementation throughout its 25-year history.
19. In Belfast, the waiting list for social housing includes about 11,000 households and is about 60:40 Catholic:Protestant (Jennifer Hawthorne, NIHE, interview 14 April 2016). For applicants on the waiting list experiencing 'housing stress' (serious housing need due to overcrowding, insecurity of tenure, or threat of homelessness), Catholics constitute about 80 per cent of candidates (John McPeake, interview).
20. Although Section 75 of the Northern Ireland Act enshrines both equality and good relations as goals, the Equality Commission has stated that the pursuit of the latter objective should not validate failure to comply with the primary goal of delivering equality (Gaffikin et al., 2016).
21. Although Catholic paramilitaries are no longer present, Catholic 'dissidents' who oppose the GFA have grown significantly in certain neighbourhoods, such as Ardoyne and the Lower Falls area.

22. Since 1995, the NIHE no longer directly constructs social housing; that is now done by a set of housing associations. The NIHE still determines the need for existing units and determines where shared new build housing is located. Before 1995, the NIHE built about 7,000–8,000 new social housing units per year throughout Northern Ireland. Housing associations currently build about 2,000 units per year (John McPeake, interview).
23. 'Fenians' is a demeaning term for Irish Catholics and supporters of Irish nationalism.
24. My field research in 1995 found that in the few cases when government intervened to modify sectarian space that its approach was not openly stated because of fear of arousing local opposition and violence (Bollens, 2000).
25. One interviewee, off the record, spoke of the sense on the ground that the Gridwood community hub is becoming 'Catholic space'; that residents consider it as land that traditionally would be considered Catholic.
26. One attempt to more fully define 'shared space' is by Gaffikin (interview). In contrast to 'neutral space', which pretends that divisions do not exist, shared space more openly acknowledges division and sets out deliberately and proactively to create spaces of interaction and dialogue that recognize and respect difference.
27. During the years of active conflict, government commonly located community facilities on each side of the sectarian divide, leading to expensive duplication of services to accommodate sectarian realities.
28. Steps along this sequence include politicization of ethnicity, homogeneous clustering, political up-scaling, boundary etching, concretizing, and consolidation.

Chapter 6

# Belfast II: Peacebuilding as Process – Disrupted Trajectories and Urban Outcomes

*Should what was sufficient post-settlement continue or are we at a different point now? Are we moving away from conflict or are we looking back?*
  Jacqueline Irwin, Chief Executive Officer, Northern Ireland Community Relations Council, interview, 15 April 2016

The previous chapter described the difficulties in translating national goals onto the urban arena. Further complicating this relationship in Northern Ireland is that the process of peacebuilding itself has been subject to dramatic disruptions and discontinuities. I focus in this chapter on the temporal disjunctions of peacebuilding, examining it as a process that has occurred over an 18-year period of significant political changes and subject to fundamental challenges. The national political programme of peacebuilding, aimed at transforming the city, has encountered disruptions and obstructions due to changing political leadership, local responses to peace goals, and unforeseen events and episodes that challenge national goals. The peacebuilding process has not been a singular, coordinated process but rather one that has been multi-threaded and characterized by differentiation across types of peace outcomes.

This portrayal of peacebuilding as temporally disjunctive and dynamic and as substantively disaggregated and multi-threaded contrasts with views of peacebuilding that assume a singular process where 'state' and 'society' move through relatively well defined phases towards greater tolerance and normalization. Using an urban analytical lens, which focuses on what happens when national goals hit the ground locally, helps illuminate the complicated nature of peacebuilding and achieves a depth of understanding not accessible to studies that focus solely on the larger national politics of peacebuilding. John Darby,[1] renowned expert on the Northern Ireland conflict, helped us understand peacebuilding not as a single peak but more as a mountain range of multiple peaks. I add to this understanding by suggesting that the process not only is analogous to trekking a mountain range over an extended period of time, but that the peaks have qualitatively different challenges and characteristics; at times, a peace process must sustain itself by circumnavigating around certain peaks and at other times mountains are subject to landslides which stall and disrupt progress. The translation of national political goals to the urban spatial level takes many different forms and is influenced by such factors as the dynamics and disruptions of political control, type of policy issue involved, inherent ambiguity and reformulation of political goals, and the degree of resistance or acquiescence by local community agents.

## Disrupted Peacebuilding

*The underlying momentum of the peace process was strong in 2012.*
Paul Nolan, 2013, p. 5

*The moral basis of the 1998 peace accord has evaporated. The fundamental divisions remain unchanged.*
Paul Nolan, 2014, p. 11

The path towards creating a sustainable devolved power-sharing government has been tortuous and subject to major disruptions and discontinuities. It actually took 9 years for the Good Friday Agreement to stabilize politically and institutionally (Bertie Ahern, Prime Minister, Republic of Ireland, presentation, 31 May 2016). Prior to 2007, on four occasions – 2000, twice in 2001, and from 2002 to 2007 – devolution was suspended due to conflicts over paramilitary decommissioning and police reform, and Northern Ireland departments reverted back to the responsibility of direct rule ministers from the Northern Ireland Office in London. And, when local rule stabilized between 2007 and 2017, it was led by a governing coalition unexpected by experts and insiders.

From 1998 to 2002, the two more moderate political parties (the Protestant Ulster Unionist Party (UUP) and the Catholic Social and Democratic Labour Party (SDLP)) controlled the top positions based on voting strength. Leaders from these two parties played central roles in negotiations leading up to Good Friday and the UUP–SDLP partnership was viewed as potentially leading to compromise and moderation in governing. Yet, with devolution obstructed and then suspended for 5 years, the composition of the Executive when re-established in 2007 was of a radically different nature. Between 2002, when local rule collapsed, and 2007, when Northern Ireland government was re-empowered, the political universe of Northern Ireland flipped dramatically (Cochrane, 2013). New elections in 2007 enshrined the two more extreme political parties as government leaders – the Protestant Democratic Unionist Party (DUP) (of hard-liner Ian Paisley), and Sinn Féin (the political party of the paramilitary Irish Republican Army). From 2007 to early 2017, this leadership coalition of opposites produced political stability not seen in the first 9 years after Good Friday.[2]

It was amid this on-again, off-again cycle of disruptive political change that major policy documents were produced articulating peacebuilding goals for Belfast and Northern Ireland. In 2005, during suspension of local rule in Northern Ireland, the report, *A Shared Future – Policy and Strategic Framework for Good Relations in Northern Ireland*, was released. This document, citing the social and economic costs and moral unsustainability of continued community separation between Protestants and Catholics, argued against continued community division and advocated sharing over separation (OFMDFMNI, 2005). *A Shared Future* constituted a significant, flagship policy on community relations which sought, together with equality and good relations goals within the Good Friday Agreement itself, to guide policymaking in Belfast towards a different future. Viewed as a fundamental turning point in terms of how government would address and counter sectarianism, it was based on significant consultation with the non-profit community sector composed of grassroots peacebuilding organizations[3] (Jacqueline Irwin, Community Relations Council, interview, 15 April 2016). Yet, paradoxically, the document was written by the direct rule Northern Ireland Office during a time when local rule was suspended. It thus was a curious combination of features: a direct rule document with strong community consultation but lacking participation by locally elected officials frozen out of the process by local rule suspension.

Following the re-instatement of local rule in 2007 and the emergence of the DUP–Sinn Féin leadership coalition in the Northern Ireland Executive, the *Shared Future* document faced scrutiny by locally elected officials and was held to be suspect due to its direct rule authorship.[4] Consequently, local rule elected politicians took up the task of revising and reworking the document, producing in 2010 *Cohesion, Sharing, and Integration (CSI)*. *CSI*, the first vision of peacebuilding issued by locally elected officials, was a major disappointment to many in its 'rinsing out' of objectives dealing with community relations, sharing, and integration (Jacqueline Irwin, interview). Criticisms were numerous: that it had little to say about sharing and integration (Todd and Ruane, 2010); that its language was vague and unhelpful to implementation (Chartered Institute of Housing, 2010); and that it was useless due to its lack of substance (Belfast Interface Project, in Cochrane, 2013). Particularly disheartened was the local community sector, whose perspectives were earlier included in the direct rule *Shared Future* document but minimized in the local rule *CSI* document. An irony is apparent – that the transition from direct rule to local rule resulted in less, not more, involvement by local community representatives. Whereas *Shared Future* was promulgated by officials not directly elected by Northern Ireland citizens but nonetheless incorporated significant bottom-up input from local community groups, the *CSI* document was a product of locally elected officials largely without bottom-up community sector input.

The move towards democratization of Northern Ireland governance produced a policy document more removed from, and less meaningful to, the local community sector. The *Together: Building a United Community* (*TBUC*) (OFMDFMNI, 2013) document, the second major directive by local rule elected officials, continued this practice of little community sector consultation and has existed as a directive lacking the type of community sector buy-in needed for its implementation.

The fragility of Northern Ireland's political architecture for most of the period 2000-2010 led to a loss of momentum in the development of key urban and spatial directives, and disrupted the constructive movement on peacebuilding interventions needed to operationalize the GFA in ways that would begin to transcend sectarian constraints. The checkered evolution of political directives during transition from direct rule to local rule exposes the enigmatic nature of democratization and policy development in a complex political environment. Rather than a full flowering of local initiative incorporating citizen and community sector perspectives often anticipated by proponents of democratization, local rule documents after 2007 took on hierarchical qualities as locally elected officials cordoned off for themselves the policymaking domain from community sector representatives. This also reveals how political goals and concepts pertaining to peacebuilding are susceptible to political manoeuvring and disruptions (as different political actors with different interests became involved over time), and how political change influenced and weakened the formation and acceptance of key policy directives aimed at guiding peacebuilding. The disruptive nature of the temporality of peacebuilding is revealed. The instability of Northern Ireland political arrangements not only disrupted the development of the peacebuilding discourse and policymaking at the national level, but also obstructed progress that was occurring in Belfast. The major City Vision process in Belfast from 1995 to 1999 included a broad swath of shareholders, reached consensus about how to move forward, and developed a vision of a 'Mutual City'. Yet, this effort existed outside a strong national political structure which could support its implementation. Despite local consensus, the political impasse at the national level, together with restricted local government power at that time, left the City Vision process hanging in the wind and ultimately unable to be implemented (Frank Gaffikin, interview, 15 March 2006). The important role of local peacebuilding arising from the municipal level was incapacitated by the instability of national governance and politics.

In the transition to local rule democracy in Northern Ireland, there was the decay and erosion of key political peacebuilding goals. A clear weakening of institutional discourse dealing with shared future and shared space occurred as *A Shared Future* turned into *CSI* and then *TBUC*. Many integrationist policies pursued under direct rule, especially in community relations, were sidelined by local politicians (Knox, 2011). One observer notes that direct rule documents have over time tended to be more substantive and challenging of the sectarian *status quo* than have local rule pronouncements (John McPeake, interview, 25 May 2016). 'Commitment towards an objective like shared housing', for example, 'has been there but has waxed and waned depending on the political context within which policy documents are written' (McPeake, interview). Direct rule documents, one step removed and less beholden to sectarian constituencies, have had the freedom to be more challenging of the *status quo*. In contrast, democratization resulted in the empowerment of local politicians more tied to sectarian constituencies and more restricted in their capacity to articulate elements of a shared future. This became even more problematic with the political ascendance of the DUP and Sinn Féin in 2007, which empowered two political parties with robust sectarian bases and clashing views about how to build a shared Belfast. Although this coalition provided political stability from 2007 to 2017, it weakened institutional discourse regarding peacebuilding goals and directives. The two hardline parties were able to agree on policy principles only at an abstract, ambiguous level, lacking firm policies that could operationalize national goals.

The association between local democracy and the inability to rise above sectarianism has significant implications for the peacebuilding project in Northern Ireland. Two paradoxes are evident. First, the movement from direct rule to local rule has obstructed, not facilitated, peacebuilding. Second, the consociational power-sharing model of governance has politically evolved in ways that counter expectations of advocates of power sharing. The hope embedded in power-sharing arrangements is that, over time, cross-cutting coalitions will form which will moderate strict political sectarianism – that over time more moderate political interests will form and gain political power. In the Northern Ireland case, just the opposite occurred. It was the more moderate parties (the SDLP and the UUP) that led early negotiations leading to the Good Friday Agreement and which gained political control in the early years of devolved government. Hope existed that this would facilitate effective governance and policymaking based on moderate political parties coming together in government. This did not happen, and after 5 years of suspended local rule, it was the more extreme parties (Sinn Féin and DUP) which gained political control as the electorate saw these two parties as better able to protect each side's interests. Rather than leading to moderation over time, power sharing in Northern Ireland has evolved from moderate to more extreme political leadership.[5]

A counterintuitive effect of devolved local rule in Northern Ireland has been its effect on civil society in the country, and specifically in Belfast. Because of the absence of genuine local political power during the direct rule years before Good Friday and amid the dysfunctionalities associated with violent conflict, a robust set of community-based and voluntary organizations formed during the Troubles to make up for the 'democratic deficit' in Northern Ireland. This community/voluntary sector was funded at high levels by international sponsors and direct rule governments as a way to build grassroots peacebuilding capacity in the absence of more formal political power at the local level. Some of these organizations are single-identity with sectarian constituencies and engage in community development, but many are cross-community in nature, engaged in community relations and seeking to bridge the sectarian divide, forming important on-the-ground footholds in efforts to further cross-community initiatives. In Belfast alone, the city database contains 1,200 community groups; at a May 2016 workshop sponsored by the city, between seventy and eighty different organizations were present (Kim Walsh, Community Planning Project Officer, Belfast City Council, interview, 24 May 2016).

With extensive on-the-ground knowledge of local community dynamics, this active civil society would seem to be a necessary and important player in the development of post-Good Friday Agreement public policymaking aimed at intervening in, and attempting to transcend, the sectarian divisions of the city. They represent a key fabric of democracy connecting citizens to government. One might logically assume the transference of political power from external to local rule would empower this sector as democracy is brought to the land. Yet, evidence points in just the opposite direction – towards a weakening and disempowerment of community institutional infrastructure.

Macro-level political reorganization of the Good Friday Agreement has increasingly sidelined the role of the civil society (Colin Knox, interview, 7 April 2016). During direct rule, community and voluntary organizations in Belfast had good access to administrators and permanent secretaries owing to the absence of functioning local government. With the emergence of formal peace, elected representatives at national and local levels have dislodged civil society organizations and their ability to construct peace from the grassroots. As the peace process unfolded with the establishment of formal local rule institutions, government institutions have created mechanisms and channels within their new institutional spaces and have drawn resources away that in previous years were in the domain of civil society (Claire Hackett, Falls Community Council, interview, 11 April 2016; John McCorry, Executive Director, North Belfast Partnership, interview, 23 May 2016). A certain degree of reallocation of resources to institutionalized public authority is appropriate as local rule government becomes normalized and takes on more functions. However, in the Northern Ireland case, civil society organizations have faced significant cutbacks in funding support. Having long involvement in grassroots activism, many of these organizations now feel they are under-resourced and under-valued. Civil society capacities, vital in gaining community buy-in to government peace strategies and meaningful change on the ground, have been weakened. Backlash from a community sector which feels it is not included in peacebuilding is evident in the form of resistance to government programmes such as *Cohesion, Sharing, and Integration* (OFMDFMNI, 2010) and *Together: Building a United Community* (OFMDFMNI, 2013), and the government's goal of removing all interface barriers by 2023.

The thinking by post-Good Friday Agreement political and civil servants is that peace has become sufficiently embedded that there is less need for an activated community sector (John McCorry, interview). Once peace broke out, government increasingly defined the problem more as violence than sectarianism; resources have thus been targeted more at violence prone areas and less at the larger structural issue of sectarianism (Duncan Morrow, Former Chief Executive Director, Community Relations Council, interview, 16 May 2016). This has resulted in a squeezing of civil society and a diminishment of resources. For those at the community level seeking to build bridges across sectarian communities, this has meant less support for a non-political space where new ideas could be explored, and pilot projects tested, concerning shared space. At the same time that bridge-building capacity at the community level has been weakened, polarizing sectarian forces have been able to create their own mechanisms and channels within the new institutional spaces of Northern Ireland local rule government (John McCorry, interview).

This institutionalization of sectarian political power, no longer moderated by a strong civil society, has produced differential impacts across the two traditions. Catholic Republicans have been more able than Protestants to bring their community expertise into Northern Ireland government and formalize their community activities within government channels. Their capture of resources has been considerable in the areas of social enterprise and job creation. Sinn Féin's command and control style of organization has resulted in efficient service delivery and a good degree of internal coherence (John McCorry, interview);[6] such coherence is due to its strong community capacity-building during the Troubles. Alienated from the state, Sinn Féin used grassroots activity both to take the place of the state and, at other times, to negotiate with the state (Claire Hackett, interview). In contrast, Protestants operating at the grassroots have been less able to bring their interests into formal governmental channels. They are fragmented internally, and feel left behind by the peace process and detached from elected Protestant political leadership (John McCorry, interview). Operating within this alienated space, the influence of loyalist paramilitaries at the community level has remained a troubling fact. Community leaders in Protestant working-class neighbourhoods are often those with links to paramilitaries, and constitute the 'powers that be' (confidential interview). Loyalist paramilitary representatives claim their role in safeguarding community rights under the new government and constitute significant blocks in efforts to counter sectarianism. 'They are now more open and walk around the streets wearing their knock off Armani suits', describes a community leader (confidential interview). Some lead legitimate social programmes, but many others use the 'front of community workers' to engage in illegal activities such as drug racketeering (confidential interview). Loyalist paramilitary leaders have become community enforcers in many neighbourhoods, with loyalist paramilitary organizations incorporated into the management of community projects (Paul Nolan, interview, 9 May 2016).

This differential incorporation of sectarian interests into the new institutional spaces of Good Friday has significant implications for future peacebuilding efforts at the community level. In the new Belfast, the two traditions are not operating from parity in terms of institutionalized political capacity.

## Outcomes of the Peace Process

*The fragility of the peace process has increased because of the continuing absence of a policy on division. The continuing absence ... [has] left the political establishment vulnerable to the shocks developed by particular incidents and events.*

Paul Nolan, 2013, p. 7

Due both to disruptions in peace policymaking and local resistance to peace goals, the nature of the peacebuilding process in Belfast has been unsteady, incremental, and uneven in outcomes. As national goals hit the sectarian grounds of the city, it intersects with resistant sectarian geographies and place-based interests and personalities. Lacking a coordinated and forceful set of interventions, the peace process 'churns' along in erratic and jagged ways (Neil Jarman, interview, 23 May 2016). There exists a constant ebbing and flowing in the relationship between everyday life and ethno-national politics, occurring at different times and in different spaces (Milena Komarova, interview, 24 March 2016). Indeed, peacebuilding does not appear as a singular process, but as consisting of multiple threads moving at different trajectories, each one confronting distinctive dynamics and magnitudes of local resistance. Peacebuilding efforts have produced 'a set of choppy contradictions in terms of indicators and outcomes', with advances seen in some areas and stagnation in others (Jacqueline Irwin, interview, 15 March 2016). There is a non-uniform 'granularity' of the peace process in terms of local outcomes (Jacqueline Irwin, interview).

The process reveals the 'duality of peace-building' (Bar-Tal, 2013, p. 359), where the context and many of the characteristics of conflict remain at the same time as the appearance of some signs of a new emerging peace. The *Northern Ireland Peace Monitoring Report* (*PMR*) notes this duality: 'two conflicting realities co-exist in Northern Ireland, and run alongside each other in ways that can be difficult to understand' (Nolan, 2014, p. 15). It questions further: 'is the peace process now set to backslide, or is there a positive momentum that can keep moving it forwards?' (p. 15). Earlier, the *PMR* pondered the question, 'is Northern Ireland moving toward a shared future, or is it falling back into older patterns of separation and antagonism? Evidence can seem to point in both directions' (Nolan, 2012, p. 13). Fifteen years after the Good Friday Agreement, the *PMR* describes the peace process existing vulnerably at a fundamental precipice.

It is clear that Northern Ireland has moved significantly from violent conflict to a post-violent conflict society. There were 100 deaths related to political violence from 1999 to 2014, compared to 564 deaths in the 1990s, 833 in the 1980s, and 1,892 in the 1970s. Since 1999, the number of all incidents of political violence (both lethal and non-lethal) is about 10 per cent of the level seen in the dreadful 1970s (Police Service of Northern Ireland).[7] This lessening of political violence is a significant achievement. What is less clear, and problematic, is whether there has been sufficient movement from a 'negative peace' (the absence of violence) to a society of normalization and transformation.[8] It is a society where political violence has attenuated, but one that remains handicapped by substantial sectarian-based sources of conflict and resistance that thwart movement towards a more 'positive peace' of tolerance and reconciliation. 'We have come a long way, but I doubt that the arrangements and processes we have put in place will be able to deal with our needs and problems comprehensively', observes long-time community planner Mike Morrissey (interview, 12 April 2016); 'we have not yet reached a point where the peace process is self-sustaining because we don't have a way yet to engage with the roadblocks'. The fundamental question facing Northern Ireland is whether peace can be maintained without a more progressive societal transformation that would counter and weaken sectarian obstructions.

The uneven advance and differentiated progress of Northern Ireland's peacebuilding is brought out in the comprehensive *Peace Monitoring Report* (Nolan, 2012, 2013, and 2014), which uses four main indicators in its evaluation – sense of safety, equality, cohesion and sharing,[9] and political progress.[10] Paul Nolan, the author of the *PMR*, observes that there has been the greatest amount of progress dealing with equality, in particular dealing with non-discrimination and employment owing to the 1998 Fair Employment Act. He asserts that the least progress has been made in the political domain, with fundamental sectarian differences obstructing the development of constructive policymaking. The other two domains – safety and cohesion/sharing – exhibit some advances along with difficult lingering problems (Nolan, 2014). In terms of safety, political violence is infrequent, crime rates are down, sectarian hate crimes have lessened from over 1,400 in Northern Ireland in 2005 to 889 in 2013, and support for policing has increased. However, sectarian hate crimes remain at a high level, intimidation on housing estates remains a fact of life, domestic violence levels are the highest in the United Kingdom, paramilitaries and dissident republican activities remain embedded within certain communities, and peace walls and interface barriers remain as reminders of the insecurity that community residents still feel. While few interface barriers have come down, numerous new interfaces were constructed during the period leading up to Good Friday and during the early peace years. Twenty-six barriers were constructed during the 1990s, of which fourteen were built from 1995 to 1999, a period when political violence was attenuating due to the 1994 IRA ceasefire. And, another seven interface barriers were constructed in the 2000s.[11] In the volatile North Belfast area, where sectarian geographies resemble a checkerboard pattern, of the thirty-five barriers with known date of construction, seventeen have been built since 1995 (Belfast Interface Project, 2012).

In terms of cohesion and sharing, residential mixing in some parts of Belfast is counterbalanced by continued segregation in working-class communities, the number of children in integrated schools remains stubbornly low (6.5 per cent), murals and bonfires continue to bedevil the urban landscape, and the percentage of individuals surveyed who 'think community relations is better than they were five years ago' fell from 62 per cent in 2010 to 51 per cent in 2012 (Nolan, 2014). Even the progress in equality (in non-discrimination and employment) is stained by problematic realities. Poverty has increased on all measures in Northern Ireland, and in Belfast it is concentrated in socially deprived and segregated sectarian working-class neighbourhoods.

An important spatial indicator of the progress of coexistence since peace is the degree to which the city's heightened residential segregation has moderated as violence attenuates and people feel less threatened in their neighbourhood environments. Examining data from 2001 to 2011, the picture is mixed and equivocal. There is some decline in overall segregation measures, but this may be related more to new immigration and changes in how people identify in terms of religion than a genuine mixing of Catholic Nationalists and Protestant Unionists (Gaffikin et al., 2016). The *Peace Monitoring Report* registers a 'decline in segregation – although an uneven one, with little change in the most segregated areas such as East and West Belfast...' (Nolan, 2013, p. 120). Ninety-one per cent of social housing tenants still live in estates in Belfast where one identity is 80 per cent or more (Nolan, 2013).

Based on my independent research of 2011 Census data, 37 per cent of the fifty-one electoral wards in Belfast have 80 per cent or more of one religion and 18 per cent have 90 per cent or more of a single identity (this compares to 65 per cent and 43 per cent, respectively, in 2001). Using the smaller unit of analysis of the 'super output area' (SOA), we see that Catholics remain segregated while formerly Protestant areas are undergoing change. In 2011, 22 per cent of SOAs in Belfast contained 90 per cent or more Catholic and 32 per cent had a Catholic population greater than 75 per cent. This is approximately the same level of Catholic segregation in 2001 as reported in Gaffikin *et al.* (2008). The Protestant story is different. By 2011, there were no SOAs in Belfast where Protestant proportions were 90 per cent or higher, while 19 per cent of SOAs registered 75 per cent or more of Protestants (this compares to 18 per cent and 29 per cent, respectively, in 2001).

A closer look at data reveals what may be happening to explain declines in Protestant segregation levels in Belfast during the 2001–2011 decade. Six of the ten wards in Northern Ireland showing the greatest declines in Protestant population from 2001 to 2011 were in Belfast – Duncairn, Woodstock, The Mount, Ravenhill, Island, and Bloomfield (Nolan, 2014). In these formerly strong Protestant areas of East and inner North Belfast, housing vacated by Protestants during the decade is increasingly being occupied by 'new immigrants' from countries such as Poland and Lithuania. As such, decline in Protestant segregation is less a phenomenon of internal migration and genuine mixing between established Catholic and Protestant residents and more an impact of declining Protestant neighbourhoods where Protestants are replaced by new immigrants to the country. An additional complicating factor is that individuals have become less likely to register a religious affiliation in Census reporting, with more people identifying 'no religion'. Internal migration figures do not seem high enough to account for reduction in Protestant segregation. Rather, it appears to be a 'complex mixture of outside immigration, decaying Protestant communities, combined with changes in people's self-identified religious affiliation' (Ian Shuttleworth, Senior Lecturer of Geography, Queen's University, interview, 23 March 2106).

Overall declines in city segregation registered between 2001 and 2011 appear to obscure lingering and problematic aspects of Belfast life. De-segregation is more a feature of middle-class neighbourhoods than working-class areas (Brendan Murtagh, interview, 21 March 2016). And in those cases where working-class areas registered segregation declines, it appears less a genuine mixing of established Catholic and Protestant residents and more due to outside immigration and changes in how individuals identify religiously. In addition, the possibility exists that these formerly Protestant areas will slowly transform into Catholic areas and that 2011 constitutes a transition point along a path of re-segregation in the future.

Residential segregation remains 'remarkably high in the north and west of the city where these areas had also the most intense exposure to political violence' (Gaffikin *et al.*, 2016, p. 46). Dissimilarity indices of segregation in West Belfast (79 in 2011; 85 in 2001) and north Belfast (61 in 2011; 69 in 2001) remain stubbornly high.[12] Equally troubling is that segregated neighbourhoods are also those registering the highest levels of socioeconomic deprivation. Eighteen of the most deprived wards in Northern Ireland in 2011 are in Belfast, and these wards have remained on the list of most deprived since at least 1991 (Gaffikin *et al.*, 2016). Three-quarters of these deprived wards had populations that were 70 per cent or more of one religion, exposing the 'intractable persistence of urban poverty and social and religious segregation' (Gaffikin *et al.*, 2016, p. 52). Of these segregated and deprived wards, nine are Catholic and six are Protestant.

A detailed look at two of these deprived wards illuminates the difficult conditions of these areas. The Falls neighbourhood, whose population consists of 88 per cent Catholic background, is the second most deprived ward overall in Northern Ireland (out of 582 total wards), 4th most deprived in income, 3rd most deprived in employment, most deprived in terms of health deprivation and disability, 4th most deprived in educational and training, and sixth most deprived in terms of crime and disorder (Northern Ireland Statistics and Research Agency 2011). The Shankill neighbourhood, 85 per cent Protestant, is the fourth most deprived ward overall in Northern Ireland, 6th most deprived in income, 11th most deprived in employment, 5th most deprived in health deprivation and disability, and Northern Ireland's most deprived ward in terms of education and training. This concentration of multiple types of disadvantage produces a debilitating environment corrosive of community and individual behaviours and attitudes and creates a dynamic where poverty becomes self-perpetuating and inter-generational. Insular and cut off from larger opportunities in the urban area, these environments of disadvantage create feelings of extreme despair and alienation on the part of its residents.[13]

Such despair is devastating in its effects. Murtagh (interview, 21 March 2016) has studied young unemployed individuals in these communities who are not in education or training programmes and finds wide-ranging effects – including family breakdown, drug consumption, mental breakdown, growing propensity to be influenced by community extremists, hopelessness, and increased rates of suicide. Their expectations are close to zero, they don't know the city, lack an identity, and are drifting. He describes the powerful influence of poverty and deprivation in producing a fatalism that is enduring and inter-generational. Madeleine Leonard (Professor Sociology, Queen's University, interview, 12 May 2016) cites Belfast as having the worst child poverty rate in Europe, the highest level of mental and physical disability in the United Kingdom, and unsettling rates of youth suicide.

The persistence and durability of deprivation in working-class sectarian neighbourhoods reveals that the peace process has not made positive impacts where it matters most. Although the Northern Ireland peace process has put into place inclusive political institutions, 'it has failed to meet public expectations for a "peace dividend" from those most affected by the conflict' (Knox, 2014, p. 3). This disconnection between the benefits of peace and long suffering sectarian neighbourhoods constitutes a fundamental dilemma facing urban policymakers in the future. The existence of this concentrated deprivation, in contrast to other areas of Belfast which are more mixed and of higher incomes, presents the distinct possibility that there really are two cities in Belfast – 'one more diverse, more affluent and more peaceful; the other still locked in traditional enclaves, prone to violence and whose deprivation has been relatively untouched by four decades of urban programmes designed to alleviate poverty' (Gaffikin et al., 2016, p. 44). In 2011, there were still 280,000 individuals in the wider Belfast urban area (56 per cent of the area's population) living in a ward that was either predominantly Catholic or predominantly Protestant (over 70 per cent or more single-identity), while 35 per cent of the city's population lived in wards of persistent and debilitating socioeconomic deprivation, which were also typically segregated (pp. 44, 50).

These outcomes – spanning across measures of safety, equality, cohesion and sharing, and political progress – demonstrate that peacebuilding is a difficult enterprise after decades of violent conflict. More than 15 years after formal 'peace', there existed a quagmire of choppy and contradictory findings in terms of the impacts of peace on the wider society. Evidence can support both the portrayal of Northern Ireland as advancing towards a fuller peace and the darker view that it is at a precipice, vulnerable to stagnation and regression.

## The Emotional Costs of Peacebuilding

In the focus on how post-Good Friday Agreement national political change has affected the possibilities for urban peacebuilding, I have thus far emphasized Belfast's local spatial realities as roadblocks to a more genuine peace. Yet, there is another realm that should be considered in looking at the process and progress of the peace process: the social and psychological adjustments that must be made by citizens for Northern Ireland and Belfast to move forward into a more constructive, less sectarian future. Whereas earlier I have focused on spatial and organizational factors that structure lived experience in Belfast, I next turn toward how individuals may or may not be ready for the emotional and psychological demands of peaceful co-existence. I turn from the spatial legacies of the Troubles to its potent emotional legacies.

*Post-conflict societies do not experience time in a serial way, but concurrently where past and present co-exist.*

John Brewer, Professor, Queen's University, interview, 19 May 2016

The social-psychological and emotional correlates of peacebuilding are significant aspects of societies in transition (Bar-Tal, 2013; Brewer, 2010). Without social and psychological adjustments on the part of citizens, a formal peace agreement runs the risk of producing a 'cold peace' lacking in reconciliation and ultimately unsuccessful in societal transformation (Bar-Tal, 2013, p. 401). John Brewer (Professor of Post-Conflict Studies, Queen's University, interview, 19 May 2016) speaks of the 'emotional costs of peace' that incite a range of emotions such as fear, anxiety, suspicion, and mistrust in response to the need to readjust. He articulates three domains of emotions: (1) those aroused by the conflict itself (a legacy that needs to be managed in the peace process); (2) those aroused by peace (emotional adjustments that non-violence or reduced levels of violence provoke); and (3) those aroused by having to live together once the conflict is over.

The 1998 peace of Northern Ireland has elicited reactions that demonstrate the difficulties of emotional adjustment. During a period of peace transition and the ending of armed conflict (1996–2000), there emerged a considerable amount of community violence amid the insecurity and uncertainty of the peace process (Neil Jarman, interview). The threat posed by peace also produced physical changes in the city that sought to increase community security – in particular the growth of interface barriers. Amid the sense of insecurity associated with peacemaking, the 'strategic identity dimensions' of community life (flags, parades, murals, bonfires) have become activated as communities assert their presence (Dominic Bryan, interview, 12 April 2016). Since the Good Friday Agreement, the number of sectarian parades has increased significantly in Northern Ireland, growing from 2,100 in 2005 to 4,600 in 2013 (Nolan, 2014). Events such as Belfast's change in Union Jack flag flying on City Hall became potent sources of intense conflict and instability as Protestants viewed it as a bellwether of more fundamental dislocations in the future. Peace has also elicited intra-group feuding and violence, such as seen in intra-loyalist antagonisms, as the pressures of peace break open internal fault-lines within a community. Peace brings forth feelings of winners and losers, supporting the view that there is one group in ascendance and another in decline. It confronts a society with asking who were the 'victims' of violent conflict. Clearly, peace is not a smooth transition but is a hard and difficult road, forcing people to try to make sense of the violent conflict and to understand what it means to live in peace with the 'enemy'.

*Reconciliation cannot be rushed; it is a process, a journey with miles to travel. The peace process is an emotional and psychological roller-coaster.*
Martin McGuinness, Former Deputy First Minister, Northern Ireland (2007–2017), Former Member of the IRA, presentation, Queen's University, 22 March 2016

Of particular cogency in peacebuilding are 'legacy' issues that 'deal with the past'. Decades of violent and bloody conflict leave a society wondering about its meaning and seeking redress for wrongs done by individuals. For a society to truly transform itself over time, there must be some reconciliation over the past. Yet an undue obsession with the past can also thwart the capacity to move forward. John Brewer (interview) describes Northern Ireland as having a 'pathological memory culture obsessed with remembering'. He uses a metaphor to describe this – it is similar to driving a car while looking only through the rear view mirror and inevitably ending up in a crash. Instead, there is the need to look forward through the windscreen. Whereas a rear view mirror provides only a concentrated backward view that only one person can see, looking forward through the windscreen provides a wider perspective through which all can look through. Brewer is not advocating forgetting about the past and recognizes that 'there will always be remembering', but rather for responsibly and constructively addressing the past as a way to move towards a more shared future – what Brewer labels 'remembering forwards'.

Legacy issues, or dealing with the past, remain a fundamental stumbling block 18 years after formal peace. Brewer (interview) observes that legacy issues in post-conflict societies typically arise in the latter stages of the peacebuilding process, amid the long and difficult process of learning to live together and occurring at seemingly low ebbs in the peace process when peoples' expectations of change have been disappointed. The past is the last thing that gets addressed in peace processes, which tend to leave the thorniest issues to the last. Brewer suggests that if truth is addressed in earlier phases of peacebuilding, it tends to be partial. He claims 'Truth never initiates a peace process, it completes it' (interview). The essential dilemma in dealing with the perpetrators and victims of the Troubles is the choice between the demands of justice and the demands for truth recovery. The more that prosecutorial processes are employed in the pursuit of justice, the less likely the main actors will be open about past events. On the other hand, a lessening of the threat of legal consequences may open up greater storytelling and fuller versions of the past but leave demands for justice unfulfilled. As of today, there is still no collective process in place to deal with the past. Without any formal process, 'the conflict is being re-fought at the level of 'popular memory' which is selective and constructed' (Liam O'Dowd, Professor, Queen's University, interview, 15 March 2016). Without a process for dealing with the past, O'Dowd adds, 'politics always reverts back to remembering'. The social risks of inaction on legacy issues are that the 'daily drip of allegations will poison our society' (Sean Murray, Northern Ireland Assembly Policy Evaluation Division, comment response in seminar, 14 March 2016). It becomes nearly impossible to debate about a shared future when sides are still arguing about the past.

There have been various approaches discussed concerning dealing with the past. They include: (1) amnesty for all security-related crimes before 1998; (2) a truth and reconciliation commission broadly based on the South Africa model; (3) a truth recovery process in which witnesses would be required to give evidence, but with immunity from prosecution; and (4) a truth recovery process which would also allow for prosecutorial actions. In an atmosphere where victim issues are highly politicized, there is the need for neutral listening spaces outside formal political channels. Many observers believe the legacy process needs to be shaped by an entity outside Northern Ireland's political parties who are implicated in the violence and engage now in a 'war of narratives [that] has replaced the war of weapons' (Nolan. 2014, p. 163). Politicians should not be allowed to shape the legacy process to fit their own ends. 'It can't be about winners and losers', observes Brian Rowan (interview, 1 June 2016), 'trying to win in the peace what wasn't won in the conflict'. Appropriate understanding of the realistic goals of a legacy process is also important, with Rowan adding: 'we are not going to be able to unravel the tangled mess of the conflict period and be able to say, "this is what happened". To think we will get one agreed narrative is simply "pie in the sky"'.

Political progress has been made in Northern Ireland in the establishment of democratic institutions and power-sharing governance, but there has clearly been less progress on the social side of the peace process involving healing, reconciliation, and the restoration of broken relationships. If unable to find some mutually agreed method of confronting the past, political interests in Northern Ireland will continue to live the present through the past, and peace will remain unreconciled and unfinished.

This chapter has focused on the temporalities of peacebuilding in Northern Ireland, highlighting it as a process that unfolds over time and is subject to disruptions and disaggregated outcomes. The 'long peace' has been challenged by disruptive stop-starts in national governing arrangements and by fundamental changes in political leadership, by interruptions and decay in central political concepts intended to guide urban peacebuilding, and by antagonistic events and dynamics on the ground which operate amid the void of cohesive and directive national policymaking. The difficult translation of abstract political language onto the urban landscape, documented in Chapter 5, becomes intensified further as the process of peacebuilding is disrupted and obstructed. In addition to being temporally interrupted, the peace process is characterized by its multi-threaded and granular nature, with distinct spatial, social, and psychological threads moving at different trajectories of success, some advancing while others stagnate. Further, as peace has institutionally advanced with devolution, a counterintuitive diminishment of the vital grassroots civil society layer of democracy is evident. The political-spatial iterative process of peacebuilding is challenged by both the difficulty of connecting national goals to urban realities and by the discontinuities inflicted upon the process as it evolves over time amid unstable political terrain. Eighteen years after its enactment, peace in Northern Ireland remains a problematic and unfinished achievement.

## Notes

1. For details of John Darby's life and work see: https://www.theguardian.com/theguardian/2012/jul/31/john-darby-obituary.
2. In early 2017, Northern Ireland government was again suspended when Republican deputy minister Martin McGuiness pulled Sinn Féin out of government.
3. The community/voluntary sector is made up of numerous local organizations involved in community development and cross-sectarian community relations. This sector was a major player during Direct Rule (1972–1998) due to the 'democratic deficit' of local government impotence. Such civil society is viewed as playing an important role mediating between local residents and formal political leadership.
4. One interviewee suggests that the forceful nature of *A Shared Future* can be explained by direct rule officials in Westminster intentionally producing documents they knew would be unpopular with locally elected officials as a way to say 'if you don't like it, get into government again' (Angus Kerr, Director of Planning Policy Division, Department of the Environment for Northern Ireland, interview, 19 April 2016).
5. Experiences of power sharing in Lebanon and Bosnia-Herzegovina also show problematic trajectories, with the locking in of sectarian power and policy gridlock more evident than moderation and compromise.

6. An exception to this Republican organizational coherence is Republican 'dissidents' located in neighbourhoods such as Ardoyne.
7. See: www.psni.police.uk.
8. 'Negative peace' and 'positive peace' are concepts first employed by Johan Galtung (1969).
9. Measured by the extent to which people 'recognize each other as fellow citizens' – the extent to which there is a sense of hostility or a society of openness, pluralism, and inclusiveness (Nolan, 2014, p. 16).
10. Measured by the extent to which political opponents use dialogue to arrive at mutually satisfactory outcomes.
11. The Belfast Interface Project (2012) documents a total of ninety-nine interface barriers in the city. Thirty-two barriers were constructed before 1990. Date of construction for thirty-four barriers was not obtainable by researchers.
12. The index is an overall measure of segregation that varies from 0 (complete integration) to 100 (complete segregation) and is interpretable as the percentage of one group which would have to move out of the area for there to be complete integration.
13. The role of concentrated poverty and segregation in structuring future disadvantage has been documented in the US (Massey and Denton, 1993).

# Chapter 7

# Belfast III: The Competing Demands of Political Stability and Urban Peacebuilding

*Breakthrough agreements are the beginning not the end of a peace process.*
Jonathan Powell, 2011

*Scratch the surface not too deeply and you find that little has been resolved.*
John McCorry, North Belfast Partnership,
interview, 23 May 2016

I have examined the difficulty of implementing broad national peacebuilding goals amongst the complex spatial legacies of conflict that exist in Belfast, and have highlighted how the process of peacebuilding has become disrupted and slowed by national political reverberations. This chapter incorporates aspects of both earlier chapters and delves in greater detail into the institutional architecture of Northern Ireland governance and the dialectic that exists between political sustainability and the ability to enact meaningful changes in Belfast's obstructive spatiality. This tension between institutional stability through power sharing and impactful policymaking adds one more layer of obstruction to peacebuilding.

Power sharing is the common prescription for reconciling antagonistic groups in places deeply divided by national, ethnic, or religious conflict (McEvoy and O'Leary, 2013). It seeks to reconcile societal fragmentation along ethnic and religious lines through methods such as grand coalitions, mutual vetoes, and proportionality of authority. The model is associated with Arend Lijphart (1977) and is currently used in Lebanon, Northern Ireland, Belgium, and Bosnia-Herzegovina, among others. Accommodationist strategies associated with power sharing favour the formal public recognition and organization of ethnic and religious groups and acknowledge that group differences are often resilient and durable (O'Leary, 2013). When such differences are not malleable, attempts either to assimilate or integrate groups politically are seen as unjust. Critics of power sharing in ethnically divided societies, on the other hand, assert that it shapes political processes to produce greater incentives to act in ways that threaten democracy and peace (Roeder and Rothchild, 2005) and that it is more likely to keep 'deadly and destructive hope alive' (Roeder, 2005, p. 80).

In societies emerging from active warfare and political violence, power sharing is positioned by a number of analysts as an indispensable element of post-conflict stabilization. At the same time, however, there are compelling needs in such societies to engage in transformative policymaking that addresses the societal inequalities, distortions, and residuals of the active conflict period. A tension arises at this juncture. While power sharing tends to enshrine and reinforce antithetical identities, social transformation objectives require cross-community dialogue and peace-building initiatives on the ground (Knox, 2010). Whereas power sharing emphasizes a structural/institutional approach to political stability, social transformation advocates assert the importance of micro-level and community-based behavioural approaches towards reconciliation and the building of bridges across antagonistic communities (Oberschall, 2007 and Taylor, 2006). Critics of power sharing assert that, left on its own, an accommodationist power sharing structure will more likely regulate rather than transform a conflict (Taylor, 2006).

Northern Ireland illuminates the difficult balancing act between political stability through power sharing and the capacity of government to institute changes in urban space to move national peace forward. It shows that there exists tension between the necessary requirement of political stability in a post-violence society and the capacity to make meaningful adjustments in urban space associated with, and stimulating of, conflict and violence. In order to stop the fighting, political compromises and restructuring are needed at the highest levels of society. The contested and polarized nature of governance during the years of violent conflict needed to be replaced by a functioning government that shares and apportions political power among the antagonistic sides. Because political conflict is rooted in nationalistic aspirations and contested sovereignty, in order to begin the process of peace, sovereignty had to be shared in a way that was at least minimally acceptable to each side. This is a necessary and essential first step on the ladder of peace. Yet, the political stability that was painstakingly and fitfully sustained in Northern Ireland from 2007 to 2017 produced conditions that made it difficult to take further steps up this ladder. The dilemma faced by Northern Ireland is that politically stable governance is needed to move a contested society forward, yet the form this stability assumed from 2007 to 2017 obstructed the capacity of government to engage in transformative policymaking.

*You cannot have a process of successful conflict transformation while you leave issues of poverty, inequality, and social injustice alive.*

John Brewer, Professor of Post-Conflict Studies, Queen's University, interview, 19 May 2016

## Conflict Management through Power Sharing

The Good Friday Agreement of 1998 was directed first and foremost at containing the horrific violence of the past three decades. To stem the violence, a power-sharing consociational model of government was established through constitutional provisions and political structures. The power sharing arrangements were a function of conflict management written by external actors and acquiesced by internal parties (Adrian Guelke, Professor of Comparative Politics, Queen's University, interview, 16 March 2016; Guelke, 2012). Political control was shared across Protestant and Catholic communities through proportional representation, allocation of government leadership and ministerial positions across sectarian parties, and Assembly voting rules which require endorsement from both sides of the divide on important policy matters. Incorporated into the Good Friday Agreement were transformative principles such as reconciliation, peacemaking, and consent, but these were necessarily translated through *realpolitik* institutions (Duncan Morrow, interview, 16 May 2016). A consociational structure created in order to get political buy-in coexisted alongside principles of a shared future and reconciliation. The aspiration was that compromise based on political realities would create an environment through which a shared future could be pursued. Once the containment of the conflict was achieved politically, the expectation was that policymaking would evolve towards achieving transformative principles. A politically stable local rule government was needed. Without it, the chances for constructive policymaking with real impacts on the ground would become minimal if not non-existent. The frequent breakdowns in power sharing that occurred in the 1998 to 2007 period, with local rule suspended by Britain four different times, attests to the fragility of the power-sharing model in Northern Ireland and how disruptions in local rule governance have hampered urban peacebuilding.

'Northern Ireland is more fragile than South Africa', observes Guelke (interview), 'because the nature of the settlement between ideologically opposed parties is inherently difficult'. The 'nature of the walkaway' from the Good Friday Agreement allowed each side to retain the notion that inherent in political compromise was victory (Duncan Morrow, interview). Unionists could claim to their constituents that the agreement led to Republicans putting away their guns and signing up to shared government. Meanwhile, Nationalists could claim that the Good Friday Agreement allows, in the future, for the achievement of their political goals – specifically that shared governance is a transitional step towards a united Ireland.[1] Uncertainty about the ultimate political status of Northern Ireland – the core of the political conflict in the first place – remains and this intensifies lingering clashes between the two sides over basic political narratives. The two sides, accordingly, often become stuck at the symbolic level and seek to maintain their own community's narrative and its continuity with the past, rather than contemplating how to move forward and transform inter-group relations at a more fundamental level. For Catholic Republicans, the ideology of a united Ireland is an ostensible objective that binds them together, particularly working-class Catholic supporters of Sinn Féin. For Protestant Unionists, it is the protection and promotion of an Ulster loyalism (Paul Nolan, interview, 9 May 2016). The power of myth in peoples' lives is strong, providing faith in a nobility of purpose, of destiny and heroism, of being on the side of history (Sorel, 1908). In Northern Ireland, the power of historic narratives results in an entrenchment of sectarian identities within politics (Paul Nolan, interview). Both sectarian blocs tend to tap into, and exaggerate, differences between the two communities in order to garner maximum political support, resulting in a 'mutually assured impasse' of policy gridlock (Gaffikin et al., 2016, p. 41). Concentration on winning at the narrative and symbolic level leaves little room for policy deliberations aimed at transforming society. Discussion of issues about shared future and equality consistently become tinged by, and subsumed within, the antagonistic symbolic politics of sectarianism.

*The multiplicity of departments that we thought satisfied the political equation fragments the very things – housing, planning, health, education – that we need to integrate at the urban level.*
Colin Knox, Professor of Comparative Public Policy, Ulster University, interview, 7 April 2016

An additional problematic feature of power-sharing government is its propensity to divide power rather than share it – the 'sharing out of power' across ministries and departments (James Anderson, Professor, Queen's University, interview, 22 March 2016). The distribution of ministry heads across the ten departments is required by the Good Friday Agreement in order to accommodate the various political parties. This institutional structure is seen as necessary so that all political interests feel they are included in public authority. Yet, this creates a vertically fragmented government structure tied to different, at times competing, political constituencies, a structure which restricts the ability of departments to coordinate their activities to seek joint gains. This institutional design of 'sharing out' political power intensifies the fragmentation of policymaking across different policy areas impacting the urban environment – such as planning, education, health, community regeneration, and housing. Such policy fragmentation divides and separates aspects of policymaking that should be integrated in a holistic way to address effectively the numerous multidimensional problems of Belfast's neighbourhoods. Fragmented and vertical policy channels result in uncoordinated urban policy less able to make significant and visible change to the city's social and spatial legacies of urban warfare. 'Contemporary Belfast remains as nobody's project', observes Liam O'Dowd (Professor, Queen's University, interview, 15 March 2016).

## The 'Closed Box' of Political Stability from 2007 to 2017

The macro-political restructuring of Northern Ireland's governing institutions, together with temporal disjunctions from 1998 to 2007, inhibited the capacity for public authorities to make significant changes in the structural inequalities and distortions of Belfast's segmented and sectarianized landscape. The achievement of political stability from 2007 to 2017 stands in marked contrast to the first 9 years after the Good Friday Agreement and is a major achievement of the Northern Ireland peace. Yet, the success of this institutional sustainability is only part of the story of peacebuilding. Since 2007, there has been a problematic tension between political stability and effective policymaking. The ruling coalition from 2007 to 2017 was composed of antagonistic parties – Sinn Féin and the Democratic Unionist Party – aligned with hard-core Republican and Unionist constituencies. This 'coalition of the unwilling' yielded a surprising degree of political stability but at the same time produced policy gridlock in terms of enacting constructive policies able to transform sectarianism in Belfast.

With the ascendance of the Democratic Unionist Party–Sinn Féin governing coalition from 2007 to 2017, there was political stability but at the cost of foreclosing on possibilities for progressive peacebuilding. Leadership became exerted through a 'straightjacket containment model operated by strict ethno-centrists' (Duncan Morrow, interview). The more moderate parties who formerly led government – the Ulster Unionist Party and the Social Democratic and Labour Party – were now increasingly outside of power. They still held ministerial positions according to power-sharing rules and sat in on meetings of the Executive,[2] but the DUP and Sinn Féin increasingly held power tightly to themselves. Political leadership by DUP and Sinn Féin started to resemble a closed box. So difficult for them to agree to co-govern in the first place and fragile in its holding together of opposing ideologies, the two parties in control 'can hardly bear to look around at the complexity around them' and have increasingly viewed engagement with other political parties and with the community sector as challenges to their rule rather than as necessary parts of democratic debate (Jacqueline Irwin, Community Relations Council, interview, 15 April 2016). In this 'wrestler's embrace', the two parties cannot step back to see outside the ring (Paul Nolan, interview).

Both parties have constructed a protective structure which each has an interest in maintaining. Political power has been locked in place to the detriment of transformative policymaking. To maintain political legitimacy and stability since 2007, government policymaking has been stalled in terms of addressing core issues that redress the systemic inequalities and the hardened spatial-territorial partitioning of Belfast. The community veto power of the Good Friday Agreement thwarts the development of progressive policymaking because forceful interventions seeking equality or shared space will tend to face opposition by one of the sectarian blocs. Indeed, the DUP and Sinn Féin remain hesitant even to bring their disagreements to the point of a formal vote, because a community veto would result in public damage. Republican dissidents would jump at the chance to use the loyalist veto of Sinn Féin to show that institutions are not working, while the DUP does not want to reveal to its hardened constituencies the ability of Sinn Féin to veto. Both sides step back from the possibility of a community veto to avoid wider conflict (Adrian Guelke, interview). Symptomatic of the closed box form of political leadership exhibited by the DUP and Sinn Féin is the growing detachment, described earlier, of the community sector from government, seen in the lack of civil society buy-in to documents such as *Cohesion, Sharing, and Integration* (2010) and *Together: Building a United Community* (*TBUC*) (2013). Also emblematic is that the *TBUC* initiative by Sinn Féin and the DUP was not signed by the other political parties. This has produced fundamental difficulties in implementing *TBUC* because several ministries in charge of the programmes are held by members of political parties who did not approve TBUC. This means the many urban programmes needing cross-sectoral interventions (integrating planning, housing, and community regeneration policies, for example) fall victim to uneven and partial implementation (Jacqueline Irwin, interview).

*If leadership does not address legacy issues, flags, marches, paramilitaries, and dissidents, then the 'new politics' will very quickly get stuck in the 'old politics'.*

Brian Rowan, Author and Journalist,
interview, 1 June 2016

An important distinction informs the realities of Northern Ireland – between 'input legitimacy' involving the acceptance by citizens of the design and machinery of institutions and 'output legitimacy' which involves the effectiveness of policy outcomes for people (Scharpf, 1999). The problem facing the Northern Ireland government is that while it achieved input legitimacy and public acceptance from 2007 to 2017 and thus some political stability, it has become difficult to achieve outcome legitimacy in terms of producing meaningful change in peoples' lives. Consociational governance arrangements are predicated on the building of input legitimacy, but it appears to come at the cost of outcome legitimacy (Colin Knox, interview). 'Devolution has produced a deal and trade-off arrangement rather than reconciliation' note Gaffikin et al. (2016, p. 22). The process of deals and trade-offs between empowered sectarian blocs has become the dominant force, rather than the peace process itself. The Northern Ireland Executive, in order to maintain legitimacy and stability, has had difficulty in meeting public expectations for improvements in their quality of life. Political stability, absolutely essential in a divided society, nevertheless has obstructed the ability of Northern Ireland institutions to address issues such as continued segregation and significant social deprivation (Knox, 2014). The shared city narrative stays at the level of rhetoric and discourse, while the strong 'reproductive dynamic' of sectarianism remains the force shaping policymaking (Liam O'Dowd, interview).

During the politically stable regime from 2007 to 2017, progressive policymaking that would address the objective needs of Catholics for more housing and poverty alleviation, or the social and psychological need of Protestant communities for neighbourhood viability, became hamstrung by potential criticism of sectarian bias that would threaten political stability. If government was seen as favouring one side over the other, extremists could use this as evidence that power-sharing is a failure for their side, setting up the conditions for possible re-engagement in de-stabilizing actions. This threat to political stability produces policy gridlock. Political stability through power sharing, although essential, appears not sufficient to advance peace; government policy becomes stalled in a *status quo* conflict management and avoidance approach rather than being able to move towards a more progressive conflict resolution approach that addresses the root issues of conflict in urban space.

The challenge facing power-shared government in Northern Ireland is how to transform sectarian forces which were incorporated into the institutional design of peace. 'Policies to build a shared society are overseen by institutions, whose own architecture fundamentally sustains division', state Gaffikin *et al.* (2016, p. 24). While there has been substantial rhetoric about new policies which would address and transform sectarianism, the institutional architecture of peace governance was based on accommodation and co-optation of these same forces (Duncan Morrow, interview). Whether constitutional principles and institutions can lead to transformation of the distortions and deep structural differences that exist in Belfast and whether the critical agents of political stability can buy into ideas of transformation remain fundamental stumbling blocks in Northern Ireland today.

*Instability is being created by the inability to create some post-conflict accommodation between groups.*
Brendan Murtagh, Town Planner and Reader, Queen's University, interview, 21 March 2016

The lack of significant transformative policies that effectively confront the sectarian and structural inequalities of Belfast calls into question the sustainability of the power-sharing system and of the governing coalition in place from 2007 to 2017. The preeminent goal of political stability may become endangered if it cannot produce results on the ground, as evident by the collapse of power sharing in 2017. Hard-line groups such as loyalist paramilitaries and dissident Republican groups are waiting to exploit opportunities to go backwards, and will use government ineffectiveness as an indicator of the futility of Protestants and Catholics sharing power. Citizens at large, who become despondent over the lack of meaningful progress on the ground, may create a populous alienated from governing institutions and more prone to radical messages. Young people, in particular, are experiencing greater detachment from, and locked out of, a political structure more absorbed with the legacy of the Troubles than engaging in the problems of contemporary life (BBC Northern Ireland, 20 April 2016).

The administration of power and influence through local rule may ring hollow to deprived Nationalist and Unionist communities if elected representatives fail to deliver on their promises for substantial improvement in community life (Murtagh and Shirlow, 2012). For working-class Republicans, to the extent the system is not delivering, Sinn Féin will find it increasingly difficult to explain why they are sharing power with Protestants (Paul Nolan, interview).[3] Lack of peace progress will also test the patience of those middle-class Catholics who voted for Sinn Féin; many of these are 'post-nationalist' and comfortable with their circumstance but voted for Sinn Féin because they viewed them as effective in opposing loyalism (Paul Nolan, interview). Indeed, Sinn Féin finds itself in an almost impossible position – moving from a protest party to a more normal party within government which needs to consistently make messy compromises with its opponents (John Brewer, interview). 'I think it's uncomfortable for them at times to be in power', observes Claire Hackett (interview), caught between nationalistic aspirations and the need to co-govern Northern Ireland in an effective way. Sinn Féin now has a stake in making Northern Ireland governable so they do not lose electoral strength. Yet, ironically, to the extent that power-sharing succeeds in bringing change and shows that Northern Ireland can be co-governed, Sinn Féin's larger project of a United Ireland may become less of a necessity and be endangered (Paul Nolan, interview). For Protestant Unionists, lack of significant improvements to their communities from power-shared government will intensify their deep-rooted feelings of being left behind in the peace process and will magnify the power and narratives of loyalist paramilitaries who control many working-class areas. The DUP is in a difficult dilemma in its need to protect the cultural elements of its constituencies (such as parades, flags, and bonfires) while seeking to engage in peacebuilding efforts that modify strict sectarianism. Too much attention to the former will obstruct agreements with its coalition partner, while too much focus on the latter will alienate and inflame its base.

Both the DUP and Sinn Féin need to find ways to move away from the conflict management/regulation model of institutional power sharing towards enactment of broader strategies of transformation and reconciliation. Yet parties, acting within a government structure which has successfully contained violence, are hesitant to risk stability for attempts at transformation. The need for transformative policies aimed at reconciliation is understood at the level of vision and rhetoric, but political parties commonly resort to narratives of threat and security. According to Duncan Morrow (interview), two possibilities for transformation exist. First, social and demographic changes and increased pressure from community initiatives may push transformative changes in policymaking. Second, due to risks to the stability of governing arrangements, elected political leaders may be forced to change their ways over time towards a more progressive, less sectarian strategy of urban intervention.

One source of hope for a less sectarian future is modest changes at the edges of the social structure of Northern Ireland which may lead to softening of sectarian identity over time. There is now more hybridity of identity than in the past, with 25 per cent of Census respondents in 2011 indicating their national identity as 'Northern Irish only' or as 'other' rather than the traditional identities of 'British only' or 'Irish only'. The percentage indicating 'Northern Irish only' has increased significantly over the past two decades. Although individuals who lived through the Troubles are likely to remain wedded to traditional identities, other people are relating to new identities rather than the traditional dyad. In addition, there is a sense that younger people are concerned with social issues such as gay rights which cut across traditional labels (John Brewer, interview). There is also greater foreign immigration into Northern Ireland than in the past, estimated at 10,000 between 2001 and 2011, and these immigrants are more likely to report their religious background as 'other' (Gaffikin *et al.*, 2016). These demographic tendencies give hope that over time society will be less bound to the traditional social and political divides and adds weight to the call for political engagement across the sectarian divide. An evolving social and identity structure may in this scenario influence a locked-in political system to engage more progressively in the urban landscape.

Yet, countering this increasing social fluidity is the possibility that sectarian tribal affiliations will reproduce themselves through the generations. This is especially true of the 35 per cent of Belfast population who reside in segregated and deprived sectarian communities flanked by interface barriers and safeguarded by community leaders aligned with the old fight. In addition, the fact that over 90 per cent of Belfast schoolchildren remain in segregated schools obstructs the ability of young people to learn of the 'other' in constructive settings. The hybridity and fluidity of part of society may create pressure for political change, but is faced with the countervailing force of Sinn Féin and DUP politicians who have an interest in maintaining and consolidating power through sectarian overtures.

## Paths through the Sectarian Labyrinth

The days of airbrushing the sectarian dimension out of policymaking appear to be over. It is clear to long-time observers of Belfast that policymaking that 'disregards the underlying social processes which shape space' in the city is meaningless and ineffective (Gaffikin *et al.*, 2016, p. 76). What is less clear is whether the government is capable of going forward with a set of policies which are both sensitive to sectarian realities while at the same time seeking their transformation. I now examine three policy programmes and strategies – neighbourhood anti-deprivation, city centre development, and local community planning – which attempt to intervene in the city amid its inequalities and the obstructions of its sectarian realities. There are limitations in each of these interventions and lessons to be learned in terms of future policy choices for government as it considers fuller engagement with transformative policymaking.

## *Neighbourhood Anti-Deprivation*

The Neighbourhood Renewal Strategy was a major effort, from 2003 to 2013, to directly confront the place-based social deprivation of communities. The programme expended considerable money (almost £200 million) over a 10-year period on improving conditions in thirty-six wards (fifteen in Belfast) that were among the 10 per cent most deprived wards in Northern Ireland. Its aim was economic, social, and physical renewal of Neighbourhood Renewal Areas (NRAs); more specifically, to increase employment and job training, educational performance and access to health services, resident engagement in community relations projects and use of community services, and improve building conditions and increase open space (RSM McClure Watters, 2014). Nearly half of all expenditure came from the Belfast Regeneration Office of the Northern Ireland Department of Social Development. The programme was coordinated at the local level by area partnerships which include stakeholders from throughout the area.

The Neighbourhood Renewal Strategy constituted a substantial place-based, targeted attack on social deprivation and appears as the type of programme needed in any future strategy seeking to redress inequalities and deprivation. However, the programme also exposes the difficulties in making substantial change. Evaluation of the programme is not positive. Although relative improvements took place in relation to a number of key social and economic indicators, on the whole, the gap between NRAs and non-NRAs did not narrow (RSM McClure Watters, 2014). After 10 years of concerted effort and expenditure, only eight wards overall (only one in Belfast) moved out of the list of the fifty most deprived wards in Northern Ireland. Factors found to limit success of the programme included a lack of buy-in by central government departments which lessened the programme's goal of delivering an integrated approach to neighbourhood renewal. The programme was also disrupted by the political instability of the period (especially the suspension of local rule 2002–2007) and by uncertainty caused by deliberations over local government reform and future devolution of responsibilities to local councils. Programme delivery was further hampered by sporadic periods of social unrest in many of the NRAs and neighbouring communities on issues such as parades and dissident paramilitary activities. Because many of the NRAs were single-identity, the process was found to be inward-looking, focusing on community development rather than community relations across the sectarian divide (RSM McClure Watters, 2014).

For the Shankill NRA (94 per cent Protestant) in Belfast, evaluation of the programme shows mixed impacts in stemming the social deprivation of this Protestant heartland area. During the 10 years, the Shankill experienced a 5 per cent decline in population and continued to be burdened by levels of economic activity and educational outcomes far below non-NRA averages. Only 48 per cent of the adult population is economically active and 18 per cent is on income support (compared to 68 and 5 per cent, respectively, for non-NRAs) (RSM McClure Watters 2014). Community input described the historic difficulties faced by the Shankill area – a 'perfect storm' of negative impacts on the area through the loss of primary sources of employment for people in the area, an economic collapse, massive redevelopment of areas causing significant societal change, as well as the lasting effects inflicted on the area during the Troubles (RSM McClure Watters, 2014, p. 175). Although the local partnership felt the Renewal programme helped focus work in the area, it believed the area 'was still not yet halfway to where it needed to be' and that there needed to be a recognition that turnaround within the area will take generations, observing that with 'three generations directly negatively impacted upon, the area needs to be given a fair chance to move forward once more' (RSM McClure Watters, 2014, p. 177).

The Neighbourhood Renewal programme also met with mixed outcomes in the Upper Springfield/Whiterock NRA (97 per cent Catholic). The local partnership there felt that the programme 'was simply not working within the area', that it was 'parachuted in' over existing community efforts and did not fit, and that it lacked integrated service delivery (RSM McClure Watters, 2014, p. 190). In a telling statement, the partnership observes that 'simply putting funding towards addressing the issue was not sufficient. People in the area are still asking the same questions they were 20 years ago' (p. 192). It was noted that the area had been under-resourced since it was built and that it was unrealistic to expect Neighbourhood Renewal to solve this. It was suggested that the government needed to ask itself what is the root cause of deprivation and then address all contributing causal factors in a properly integrated manner.

The Neighbourhood Renewal Strategy and the Shankill and Springfield cases reveal the hard and ingrained nature of social deprivation that appears highly resistant to a substantially funded neighbourhood-targeting programme. It shows the intractable persistence of urban deprivation together with social and religious segregation. Places remain mired in disadvantage, as if 'poverty was imprinted into their very DNA' (Gaffikin *et al.*, 2016, p. 54). One criticism of this programme is that it worked at too small a scale and engaged community leadership that was embedded and in some ways constituted a barrier to new ways of thinking (Mike Morrissey, interview). More effective approaches may be to assist households directly rather than structure programmes based on place, to increase access by communities to regional opportunities, to expand the geographic boundaries of recipient areas so they encompass both Protestant and Catholic populations, and to incorporate cross-sectarian community relations into government programming. Place-based programmes 'create further insularity and fixes community leadership in place' (Mike Morrissey, interview). Focus may be better placed on enhancing connectivity and mobility to the whole city so deprived residents can access a wider range of opportunities and services, rather than relocating resources out to the deprived communities (Duncan Morrow, interview). As one resident in the Ardoyne neighbourhood observed, 'regeneration in this area doesn't look like a factory, it looks like a bus'.

## *City Centre Redevelopment*

Another approach to policymaking in Belfast has been to focus on the city centre as a stimulus to wider regeneration. In 2016, the Belfast city centre was a different place compared to 30 years before. During the mid-1980s, at the height of the 'Troubles', the city centre was a high-security zone during the day and a 'no-go-zone' at night. No longer threatened by violence and subject to partitioning and checkpoints, the city centre is now an open and robust place of consumption. Urban interventions to enhance the city centre are a common approach in conflict cities as a means of revitalization (Bilbao, Spain and Beirut, Lebanon are other cases I have studied). Often, such interventions are seen as less difficult because they do not encounter sectarian issues directly. Over time they can change the public perception of a city and are able to bring in substantial amounts of foreign investment in the form of new buildings and employment centres. State agencies and private investment latch on to this strategy due to perceived stability and investment potential. And importantly for the discussion here, there is often the sense that city centre revitalization creates new cosmopolitan, non-sectarian spaces that can surpass entrenched dichotomies and create a new script for the city. The hope is that city centre revitalization will provide a spark that stimulates wider regeneration of the city.

In Belfast, during the 1990s, major investment in the revitalization of the downtown waterfront took place. Included in this 300 acre (121 ha) Laganside area is a major conference and cultural centre (Waterfront Hall), development of an office park and commercial area on a formerly contaminated city gasworks site, and a major new sports arena and entertainment complex. More recently, on the old docks of the city, there has been the building of the iconic and popular Titanic Museum, now one of the most popular tourist destinations in Europe which has helped spike the tourism industry in Belfast. The larger area where the museum is located – the 185 acre (75 ha) 'Titanic Quarter' – is being developed as a large mixed commercial, tourist, research, and residential area. A new shopping centre in the city, Victoria Square, has also been developed downtown, incorporating a material in its construction – glass – that no developer would use during the violent Troubles.

The impressive amount of revitalization in and around the city centre certainly constitutes an important foundation in Belfast's future. It represents a neoliberal approach to the problems of the contested city, premised on the stance that benefits of assisting major economic, commercial, and corporate interests will spread outwards into the rest of the city by providing economic and commercial opportunities for city residents. The Laganside waterfront development and Titanic Quarter are examples of policymakers tapping into universal processes that can help resuscitate a divided city. At the same time, the Titanic Museum represents an innovative use of pre-Troubles local history and heritage as a possible way forward in the city, and the use of iconic architecture seeks to imprint onto Belfast a new image as tourist destination.

Despite its economic and symbolic benefits, however, an over-emphasis on city centre revitalization and neoliberalism runs the risk of creating a 'twin-speed city' – one part hosting post-conflict revitalization whose benefits privilege middle-class consumers and particular sectors of the economy; the other part consisting of territorialized working-class community residents who do not feel part of the city centre and are more rooted to local community space (Brendan Murtagh, interview). Middle-class and more integrated communities are concentrated in a triangle extending south from the city centre and continuing to the suburbs. The social networks of people in these areas are spatially dispersed and residents have good access to city centre benefits through automobile accessibility. In contrast, working-class communities are highly territorialized and internalized within kinship, family, and community circles. These territorialized communities are physically disconnected from the city centre by 'shatter zones' – areas of disuse and abandonment and dominated by imposing highway and interchange infrastructures that enhance regional mobility but obstruct access to the city centre by working-class residents (Mark Hackett, interview). The physical legacy of compartmentalization and quartering off working-class neighbourhoods during the Troubles, for the purposes of security and stability, remains a major hindrance to any effort to connect the benefits of city centre revitalization to these deprived neighbourhoods. The neoliberal revitalization of the city centre is creating new non-sectarian cosmopolitan spaces, but in a city such as Belfast, 'you can't wave out history' (Brendan Murtagh, interview).

The key challenge facing revitalization strategies is to address the deprivation of working-class communities through place-based and individual-based programmes but at the same time to seek to restructure the wider city in ways that connect communities to each other and to the city centre. When walking to the city centre from middle-class and mixed South Belfast, one treks past a vibrant and diverse environment which propels the walker onwards to the centre. South Belfast is seamlessly connected to the city centre and is conducive to walking and biking. In contrast, in walking from the Falls or Shankill neighbourhoods towards the city centre, one experiences disconnected, unwelcoming, uninspiring, and unoccupied spaces that are dominated and fragmented by major highway arterials servicing regional businesses and middle-class drivers. With such a spatial structure of inequality in place, it is not realistic to assume that the gains from city centre revitalization will spread beyond its middle-class and corporate beneficiaries. Recognition of the dysfunctional spaces that separate working-class communities from the city centre is part of recent metropolitan and city plans (such as the Belfast Metropolitan Area Plan 2015 and the Belfast Masterplan Review 2012), yet there will need to be a concerted and coordinated effort by central and local governments and across Northern Ireland government departments, whose ministers represent different constituencies, in order for citywide connectivity and integration to take place. Without a successful effort at stitching back together this unshared Belfast, a city tormented by sectarian divisions in the past will become one increasingly characterized also by economic class divisions.[4]

## Local Community Planning

An empowered new actor in the Belfast policy environment is the local city council, now with devolved authority for community planning for the first time since 1971. With the transference of primary planning authority to the city level in 2014, local governments are now charged with engaging in a community planning process and producing a local development plan which will deliver the spatial aspects of the community vision. For Belfast, the public consultation period for the draft community plan (called the 'Belfast Agenda') was completed in April 2017, with the local development plan to be completed within 5 years after community plan adoption (Kim Walsh, Community Planning Project Officer, Belfast City Council, interview, 24 May 2016). This is a fundamental restructuring of the planning system, which heretofore was a unitary system where all planning powers rested with the Department of the Environment for Northern Ireland (DOENI), to a two-tier system where city councils have primary responsibility for local plan-making, development management, and planning enforcement while the DOENI retains responsibility for regional planning policy (DOENI, 2015).

In the future the City Council and planning staff of Belfast will be confronted with the hard and intractable issues of Belfast. Where they will allocate land for future development *vis-à-vis* traditional sectarian boundaries, how they address interface barriers in the planning process, and the extent to which they consider sectarian issues as germane to project review are among the issues where the peace process 'rubber will hit the road'. These will be critical decision points in the formulation of the local development plan which will reveal whether city government is willing to confront sectarianism constructively or bow down to its formidable and entrenched power.

*You can no longer pretend that urban planning does not have a central role in addressing the tough issues of a divided society.*

Frank Gaffikin, Professor, Queen's University,<br>interview, 15 March 2016

*When you devolve power here, you are likely devolving to recognized sectarian territories and the inefficiencies that come with such division.*

Mike Morrissey, Community Planner,<br>interview, 12 April 2016

Interviews with planners at local and central government levels reveal the challenges ahead for local planning and the different approaches they envision in confronting sectarianism. The Department of Planning and Place in the Belfast City Council is to be the lead agency in formulating the local development plan. Its head, Paul Williams, observes that in dealing with Belfast, 'it is almost like you are stepping back in time' in terms of its frozen physical structure. He sees planning as potentially enabling of change – 'almost like the release of a pressure valve' – and asks a fundamental question, 'in a post-conflict city, how do you make that next step beyond what history tells you that you should be doing?'. He envisions planning starting with the city centre and creating shared space there, with a 'rippling out' effect that will weaken the entrenched sectarian spaces over time. He admits, however, that 'there are a lot of people on a treadmill who are not going to be able to actively engage in what we are seeking to achieve'. He acknowledges the difficult balancing act planning must play in accommodating both communities' needs –meeting Catholic needs for new development while helping to sustain existing Protestant areas.

I probe Williams about the delicate issue of identifying land for future growth and the approval of projects in contested sectarian space. His responses indicate a willingness to confront sectarian territorial claims. 'If we altered our views of available land based on perceptions of who "owns" it, then I don't think we would be doing our job', he states, adding that the 'measure of accessibility to available land should not be determined by who "owns" it'. What this implies in practical terms is that if available land to meet Catholic housing needs is identified in areas traditionally thought of as Protestant that planning and project approvals would proceed.[5] 'Taking account of the perceptions of the two communities is not the role of the planning function', Williams adds. Building housing for Catholics in Protestant areas promises to shift the sectarian composition of electoral wards and is likely to face resistance, yet Williams states that, 'the skewing of an electoral constituency base due to a new social housing project is not a material planning consideration; on what possible planning basis could we not approve such a project? – we are fulfilling documented need'. Williams is acutely aware of the confrontation ahead as planning seeks to normalize the city amid sectarian territoriality; 'we are into new territory at this point and the genie will be out of the bottle'. When I observe that the designation of growth areas by the local development plan is 'when the rubber hits the road', Williams acknowledges, 'yes, and it is going to leave some marks'.

Keith Sutherland has 16 years experience in Belfast city government and is acutely aware during our interview of the elephant in the room – how to address contested territoriality through planning (interview, 14 April 2016). After decades when 'development tended to enshrine territoriality and obstruct fluidity, we are now basically tasked with turning around a supertanker'. He views planning's main role as 'raising peoples' gaze beyond the territoriality by providing a higher level spatial view and more expansive time scale'. 'If we are brutally honest, community background should not be a consideration in planning', he declares, while acknowledging that the practicality and viability of this strategy will be contentious. Sutherland points to the importance of buy-in by elected councillors: 'we need to get them to think about the bigger picture instead of within their own fiefdoms'. He describes the significance of public servants taking politicians through a process which will lead them to agree on general transformative principles from which more specific actions will follow. Sutherland wants to get elected councillors to the point where planners can say to them, 'you agreed to these general goals, then that means that these specific actions will logically follow'. 'If politicians support a process', he adds, the 'planners are empowered to take more risk'. He acknowledges hesitancy of planning at this time: 'to a certain extent now we are being evasive, at times tasking an officer to come up with a creative narrative to address the sectarian issue. At some stage, though, we will prompt decision-makers by presenting options to them'.

Callie Persic comes to her job as urban development officer with Belfast City Council after years of experience in the community sector (interview, 14 April 2016). She cites the main role of planning in Belfast as 'providing a challenge function to communities, to activate conversations about alternatives, and to provoke'. She describes the difficulties when planning seeks community input; typically there is a vocal minority in the community that is easier for planners to access, yet she observes that 'these gatekeepers may not really represent the community and the challenge is how to get beneath this level'.[6] After her experience in the community sector, she is struck by how tight the constraints are when working within government, but is resolute in asking: 'if we don't recognize contested space as a problem in planning, how do we work to change it?'.

The pulling together of community input into a vision for the city is the job of the 'Belfast Agenda' community plan. The community plan is to bring in community-based perspectives and at the same time incorporate local statutory agencies (dealing with health, economic investment, and education) which have the power and money to effect change directly. This visioning process is, in effect, an attempt to bring together around a strategic city vision both public partners who have spending power and communities who feel involved and listened to (Kim Walsh, interview). The goal is to get participants to engage their thinking more at the citywide level and then have this city vision translated to the neighbourhood level through coordinated policies and service delivery. Noticeably absent from required participation in this process, however, are central government statutory agencies (such as the Ministry of Infrastructure) which through their spending can help shape a new Belfast.[7] This is potentially problematic because in the past public programmes (such as the Neighbourhood Renewal Strategy) were hampered by lack of buy-in by central statutory agencies. The fact that central government departments did not want to be included in Belfast community planning 'speaks to the relationship hurdles, and lack of trust, we have here within the public sector' (Kim Walsh, interview).

Angus Kerr works for central government, as Director of the Planning Policy Division of the Department of the Environment (interview, 19 April 2016). His office has published two documents providing guidance for local development plans – *Living Places* (DOENI, 2014b) and the *Strategic Planning Policy Statement for Northern Ireland* (SPPS) (DOENI, 2015). The SPPS is a mixture of standard planning guidance that would be found in most such documents together with language more assertive of the need for local planning to create shared space. Shared space is defined as 'places where there is a sense of belonging for everyone, where relationships between people from different backgrounds are most likely to be positive, and where differences are valued and respected', and the 'planning system has an important role' in creating shared space in its 'influence on the type, location, siting, and design of development' (DOENI, 2015, pp. 17–18). Kerr expresses some pessimism in planning's ability to move society forward. 'Currently, I think politicians are not yet ready for a shared society', he admits, adding that 'when push comes to shove, which it does with planning, they are still wedded to their own community'. The value of pushing forward a more transformative vision is clear to him. Given the political situation, however, 'our approach is to come up with statements that allow local governments to do new things at the local level if they have the political cover that would allow it'. In a circumstance where there is resistance from both politicians and the wider general public to progressive planning, he views coercion through the planning system as not possible.

Observers from outside government view the current period as a critical point for planning. There is the need to move planning beyond its traditional land-use planning orientation to a strategic orientation that is more proactive, intervening, and coordinated across functions (Ken Sterrett, Senior Lecturer, Queen's University, interview, 23 March 2016). A wide-ranging and critical appraisal of planning is found in *Making Space for Each Other: Civic Place-Making in a Divided Society* (Gaffikin et al., 2016). Stating that 'orthodox technical and professional competencies of planning are insufficient to redress the delicate issue of contested space', it calls for a more integrated

Figure 7.1. Suffolk, Belfast (1995).

Figure 7.2. Suffolk, Belfast (2016).
A positive case – local cooperation between local community groups at an interface barrier (Lenadoon/Suffolk) has significantly improved the physical setting and social life of this area between neighbouring Catholic and Protestant neighbourhoods. This, unfortunately, is an atypical case in contested Belfast.

model of community and spatial planning that is holistic and lateral, coordinated across planning, community regeneration, housing, education, and cultural functions (p. 16). A 'new planning' must openly acknowledge the sectarian spatial divide and overcome the deficiencies of past policy approaches which separated a range of key planning functions such as land use, roads, housing, and regeneration (p. 103). Planning should be creative and proactive and move from a managerial to a transformational approach to conflict resolution, shifting from planning done to contain conflict to planning that seeks to transform the roots of spatial distortion and disadvantage in the city. In this strategy, the city would seek to catalyze greater transformation of sectarian territoriality, such as seen in the Lenadoon/Suffolk case (figures 7.1 and 7.2). Planning principles for divided Belfast include:

- All the city should be considered as shared space;

- Urban policy should create a pluralist city for a pluralist people – open, connected, and interdependent;

- Civic values should take precedence over ethnic or community values;

- Modification of peace walls and contested spaces should be considered within the regeneration of their wider environments;

- Development of disadvantaged areas should require cross-community local cooperation;

- Poor physical connectivity among neighbourhoods and to sites of employment, services, and education should be addressed as a priority;

- New housing should avoid replication of single identity religious communities and should create mixed neighbourhoods linked to wider city opportunities; and

- Public services should be located in areas that are securely accessible to all communities.

## Belfast and Northern Ireland Since 1994

To summarize chapters 5–7, findings highlight the disconnection between Northern Ireland peacemaking goals and their implementation in Belfast, how the peacebuilding process has been disrupted over time and subject to uneven advances on the ground, and how needed political stability in Northern Ireland has restricted urban peacebuilding.

The implementation of the political peacemaking goals of sharing, equality, and good relations has been a process awash with complexities and contradictions, which disrupt and restrict the effectiveness of the political mandates. Peace implementation has faced a rocky road when political agreements and compromises hit the ground of Belfast's spatial and territorial realities. In this contentious relationship between political aspirations and on-the-ground realities, Belfast remains an essential, yet highly problematic, component of peacemaking in Northern Ireland. Similar to Israel's hegemonic project, Northern Ireland's goals of a co-existent peace experience great difficulty when implemented in a contested urban area. Further, in the examination of the trajectories of national peace policies, it was found that national goals themselves have experienced disruptions over time in their formulation due to changes in governing regimes. The 'long peace' has been challenged by disruptive stops and starts in national governing arrangements, fragmentation of governing authority due to its power-sharing construction, interruptions and decay in central political concepts intended to guide urban peacebuilding, and by antagonistic and inflammatory phenomena on the ground which challenge cohesive and directive national policies. Finally, I identified a tension between the necessary requirement of political stability in a post-violence yet still contested society and the capacity of public authority to make meaningful adjustments in urban space associated with, and stimulating of, conflict and violence.

There is a compelling need for public policymakers to create an explicit strategic vision for Belfast that responds effectively to the differential needs of the two sectarian communities – the greater objective needs of Catholics for housing and poverty alleviation and the social-psychological needs of Protestants for revitalization of their neighbourhoods. In order to gain buy-in across the sectarian divide, both sides need to feel they will gain from a transformative policy approach. Without this strategic vision, communities will resist taking risks, as explained by Jacqueline Irwin (Community Relations Council, interview): 'if the city doesn't set out for itself a strategic vision for the city and explain this to citizens how it will meet their needs in a larger context, you can't be surprised when each community fights for its own needs and resists shared space. If you don't make it a win for each side, why should any citizen be ready to give up their immediate, fundamental needs for a higher aspiration that has not been clearly articulated?'

The central challenge facing policymakers of addressing and overcoming sectarian constraints at the local level has existed throughout the years of the peace process, but the costs of not more fully engaging with this challenge are mounting as the deep-rooted problems of the city persist and reproduce despite the peace. The failure to engage constructively with these hard issues jeopardizes the sustainability of a local rule political structure that remains a stunning and monumental achievement after decades of violent conflict. The Northern Ireland case exposes peacemaking as not solely a political process, but one that must be validated by spatial and social changes. Political reorganization enshrined by a peace agreement is of essential importance, yet peace implementation reveals itself as a long and difficult road. As asserted by Adlai Stevenson (American politician, 1900–1965), 'making peace is harder than making war'. A cold peace lacking in inter-group transformation and reconciliation – one not felt by Belfast's residents – will be a brittle and fragile one.

## Notes

1. The Good Friday Agreement states that Northern Ireland would remain part of the United Kingdom until a majority of the people of Northern Ireland and of the Republic of Ireland wished otherwise. Should that happen, the British and Irish governments are under 'a binding obligation' to implement that choice.
2. In 2016, for the first time in Good Friday local rule, there was a formal opposition bloc formed when these two political parties, who would otherwise have been part of the Northern Ireland Executive, chose not to participate in government.
3. Dissatisfaction with Sinn Féin was evident in the 2016 elections, when a non-Sinn Féin candidate representing the socialist People before Profits Alliance won the most votes in the Catholic heartland of West Belfast.
4. This would not be unusual in post-conflict societies. In contemporary South Africa, 'racial' apartheid has metamorphosed into a form of 'economic' apartheid.
5. About 80 per cent of easily accessible and developable land in Belfast is in traditionally Protestant/Unionist areas (Keith Sutherland, Development Policy and Plans Manager, Department of Planning and Place, Belfast City Council, interview, 14 April 2016).
6. Another planner observes that when he meets with political party representatives as part of community consultation, their meeting rooms resemble 'small embassies' with politically vivid posters on the wall (Dermot O'Kane, Local Development Plan Officer, Department of Planning and Place, Belfast City Council, focus group discussion, 6 March 2016).
7. Although not required to participate, the Northern Ireland Development of Social Development is participating voluntarily.

Chapter 8

# Conflict and Peace: Political and Spatial Trajectories

This book has investigated the complex interface between national political goals and their urban actualization in the everyday living environment of the city. For peace to take hold on the ground, peace accords need to be ultimately embedded in, and credible to, the most bereft communities in the conflict. Yet, tensions exist between the socio-spatial dynamics of a contested city and the goals and mandates of national peacemaking. I have examined the political, spatial, and personal dimensions of ethno-national conflict and have argued that spatial and social peacebuilding at the urban level must complement political peace processes because these conflicts are fundamentally concerned with not only political sovereignty, but also local territoriality and identity. As such, peace is not solely achieved by national politicians, but must be co-produced by both national politicians and urban stakeholders. The high politics of national compromises must be integrated with, and effectively translatable to, the grassroots level of local policymakers, civil society, and citizens.

The national-local relationship in these contested societies is characterized by non-linear, uneven, and sometimes contradictory relations between the aspirations of national policy goals and their outcomes in urban space. In addition, the longitudinal reach of this research has provided an understanding of the dynamic permutations and transformations of national political projects and reveals how the process of implementation can become temporally disrupted over time. In both post-Oslo Israel and post-Good Friday Northern Ireland, disconnection between the national and the urban, and disruptions in urban implementation over time, has meant that urban translation of national goals has lacked both stability and logicality. Further, we have seen how the hegemonic project of Israel, which has overshadowed and subordinated peacemaking, has, itself, faced similar difficulties when seeking to implement its goals in Jerusalem and the West Bank.

As the global increasingly urbanizes, so the urban sphere increasingly becomes a platform of larger concerns and a test-bed of how to deal with global challenges. With the emergence of Brexit and forms of nativist politics in Western Europe, and with Donald Trump's ascendance in America, we see a resurgence of nativism and nationalism in the contemporary world and the growth of populist politics that privileges localism and sovereign control over globalist forces. Such proliferation of chauvinism and xenophobia, particularly in an economic context of inequality, positions the 'other' – whether it is an immigrant or Muslim – as a threat to national solidarity and cohesion. With the politics of difference increasingly preeminent in world politics, this book reveals how these over-arching issues of the day are translated to specific consequences of daily urban living. The city is a container within which larger forces can be seen close-up and personal. At the same time, however, the city is not simply subsumable into the wider contest around difference in ethnicity, nationality, and sovereignty that dominates world politics, but rather is a distinctive location having its own grassroots ecology of on-the-ground socio-spatial legacies which can distort and resist the wholesale implantation of the national onto the local. For better or for worse, the city has a rationality that the state cannot understand.

Four major conclusions arise from my research. These are:

1. Disconnection between national political goals and their urban operationalization;
2. Peacebuilding as a process of disruptions and disjunctions;
3. The self-perpetuating dynamics and limits of hegemonic control; and
4. Competing demands of political stability and urban peacebuilding.

The first two conclusions apply to both the Jerusalem and Belfast cases, while the latter two are specific to Jerusalem and Belfast, respectively.

## Disconnection between National Political Goals and their Urban Operationalization

*The translation of national political goals onto the urban landscape – whether they are hegemonic in the case of Israel's strategy concerning Jerusalem or aimed at co-existent peace in the case of Northern Ireland's objectives toward Belfast – is a process replete with complexities and contradictions which can thwart and disrupt national goals.*

When national political ideology encounters the city, there is complex and erratic political-spatial enactment. National political goals such as 'united Jerusalem' in Israel and 'shared future' in Northern Ireland are problematized as they are operationalized and enacted in urban space. The political and institutional realm of goal setting and the urban realm where there is the attempted operationalization of these national goals exist in semi-autonomous spaces. National ideological goals characterized by abstraction stand in contrast to urban policies intended to actualize these commitments that require fine-tuned specificity. When abstract political concepts confront micro-scale, fine-grained urban systems consisting of established and resilient patterns of community power, their impacts become variant and contradictory. National mandates are not easily transferable onto urban space; implementation must be enacted through a political-spatial ecology consisting of a complex interaction between national political ideologies and on-the-ground implementation of these ideological goals. A national programme aimed at managing a city is not one of simply formulating national goals and implementing them in urban space in a straightforward and intuitive way, but rather is a political-spatial iterative process of engagement having unforeseen and erratic effects on the national programme.

The city and urban region comprise a semi-autonomous space with its own local dynamics and relationships, a space of urban interests and sectors. This space – full of local history, micro-geographies, and on-the-ground relationships – is not easily conceptualized by national politicians who endeavour, through ideological commitments, to embed either hegemony or peace in the urban space. In addition to the inadequacy of the state in understanding urbanism, the nature of the state institutional apparatus – distributed over numerous agents and agencies with differing missions – means that state policy intrusions into urban space can work at cross-purposes with overarching national goals. The impacts on the city of both national political hegemonic projects and national peacemaking programmes are not homogeneous and uniform, but rather substantively disaggregated and variant in outcomes as national goals encounter the multiple complexities of urban physical and social space. Whereas certain state policies support national political goals, other policies and interventions can have negative impacts on those goals. In both Israel/Palestine and Northern Ireland, such national-urban disconnections bring to the fore the importance of considering the city and its unique attributes in efforts to concretize national political goals in the everyday life of its residents. That national-urban disconnections were found in fundamentally different national programmes illuminates the resilient nature of urbanism in resisting and confounding national mandates.

## *Jerusalem*

Urban dynamics resulting from Israeli state intervention have unintentionally created cracks in Israel's hegemonic project and the city has complicated the operationalization of the larger Israeli national ideological programme. Amid the political impasse beginning with Oslo, Israel's hegemonic project has continued to imprint itself on the urban region, but since 1993 there also exist newer dynamics and impacts which add complexity and even contradictions to the Israeli project of control. The overall effect of these dynamics since 1994 is the creation of even more pronounced urban disequilibria and instability.

Israel's project of control in Jerusalem has continued unabated and has intensified over the past 20 years. In terms of the magnitude and location of Israel-promoted development for Jewish residents, the period from 1994 to 2017 has witnessed intensification and deepening of the Israeli hegemonic project and this has occurred irrespective of efforts at the diplomatic level to find a negotiated solution to the Israel-Palestine conflict. Whereas negotiations come and go, the Israeli project of strengthening Jewish control over Jerusalem and its wider region has a staying power undeterred by broader politics. Examination of the Municipality planning system across its full spectrum – from the citywide Master Plan to neighbourhood outline plans to detailed plans and the re-parcellation process – clearly reveals the existence of multiple layers of obstacles facing the Arab community that cumulatively result in the strong improbability, if not near impossibility, of Israeli-approved Arab development at a level anywhere near what is needed to meet natural demographic growth projections. Far from being a city where all residents – irrespective of ethnic and religious background – have equality of opportunity in terms of quality of life, instead Jerusalem is an asymmetric, divided city that reflects and reinforces larger power imbalances between Israel and Palestine.

One witnesses in 2017 a continuation and deepening of the hegemonic practices used by Israel since 1967. However, there are also new urban and spatial phenomena that are creating greater complexities and contradictions in the urban landscape that are not fully consistent with Israel's project of political control. The separation barrier, micro-penetration of Jewish settler activity in the core of the city, unlicensed Arab housing development, and the growing economic intrusion of Arabs into Jewish spaces of Jerusalem have produced a complex environment in contemporary Jerusalem: one that neither promotes Israel's hegemonic project nor supports a genuine sharing of the city, but rather increases the impossibility of managing the city as it is currently politically organized. At times, Israeli actions themselves cause consequences that work against their own political goals of strengthening their control of Jerusalem. There are important cracks in the hegemonic project as it is operationalized in a complex and dynamic urban system. Amid domination, there are aspects of urbanity and openness which run as cross-currents to the partisan project. There exist margins and soft spots in the hegemonic project where its implementation creates conditions of obstruction and resistance.

The implementation of Israel's hegemonic programme has produced impacts that are inconsistent with its goal, and in other cases have created complexities and uncertainties from an Israeli perspective. Despite Israel's consistent and intensifying structural efforts to strengthen its hold over Jerusalem, the Palestinian presence in and around the city (in terms of residential development) is greater today than in 1994. Israel is not winning the competition and the situation represents more of a stalemate. This brings into question the ability of the Israeli governing regime to 'control' a city through demographic-based partisan policy. Forty-eight years of such policies have not gained Israel true control over the city and inherent tensions in the Israeli project are exposed. Strict land-use planning controls have been so extensive in their ability to constrain sanctioned development that it has created Palestinian resistance and successful efforts to bypass the regulatory regime. The fact that Arab growth in the city has increased during a time of strict Israeli control over formal development exposes an important limitation to Israel's hegemonic project. Meanwhile, separation imposed through the barrier wall distorted the natural growth dynamics of the urban area, stimulating in-migration of Palestinians into the city to avoid loss of Jerusalem identity and the establishment of two major Palestinian development nodes outside the wall but inside the Municipality. Further, limitations on urban services, commercial developments, and employment opportunities for Palestinians in Arab East Jerusalem has created greater Arab presence in Jewish parts of the city which runs counter to Israel's ideological commitment to a Jewish Jerusalem.

In distinct contrast to Israel's rhetoric of 'united' Jerusalem, the city is divided in all but name. The reality is that there exists a *de facto* binational urban state regime, strongly partisan, asymmetric and unilateral. The urban region of Jerusalem appears to be an unsustainable situation that, lacking political resolve, may last a long time because the hegemonic dynamics seem locked in place. Political and material asymmetry is creating frustration and violence which creates further consolidation and tightening of control by Israel. There exists an unfortunate downward cycle, perpetuated by a focus on the symptoms generated by the disequilibrium rather than on the root issues of political sovereignty conflict. At the operational level, Israel's hegemonic project has inadvertently spawned local forms of Palestinian coping and resistance which have problematized its political-demographic aspirations. At the higher moral level, the Israeli hegemonic project is not achieving its goals of political and emotive unification.

## *Belfast*

National peacemaking goals have become distorted and obstructed as they are operationalized in the highly sectarian environment that is residual from 25 years of intense urban conflict and spatial rigidity. Northern Ireland has succeeded in creating a peace agreement that has included core political issues that spawned violent conflict and has effectively countered regression back to organized violence. However, manifested in the form of inflammatory murals, parades and marches, dividing walls, hardened territoriality, community deprivation, and sectarian-driven community dynamics, the identity dimension in Belfast remains robust and resistant to the change that is needed to transform a war-torn city into a post-war city of some normalcy.

Since the Good Friday Agreement, the Northern Ireland government has put forward meaningful and potentially impactful urban goals addressing the future of Belfast. The objectives of shared future, shared space, the ending of sectarian division, equality, and good relations show that public authorities in Northern Ireland have come a long way from the silence of Direct Rule period policymaking regarding sectarian realities. However, this advancement comes in the form primarily of policy language and rhetoric. With opposing sides coming to the negotiating table having ideologically opposed perspectives and narratives, language incorporated into political and policy agreements becomes necessarily abstract in order to accommodate these differences under one umbrella. Creative ambiguity in terms of how peace is to be translated socially and spatially have characterized the goals of both the Good Friday Agreement and subsequent policy documents intended to implement peace. Such abstraction of national peacebuilding goals creates significant embedded contradictions in their implementation and national goals become susceptible in their implementation to political appropriation and manipulation by sectarian interests.

It is a challenging trek when moving from shared future, equality, and good relations goals to their operationalization in Belfast. There is an inherent difficulty in connecting the political to the urban. In contrast to a political level that tends to remain at the high level of principles and goals, intervention in contentious places like Belfast requires a more detailed calibration of the myriad conflicting imperatives found in the city. Peace goals confront a sectarian divided city of structural inequality, major areas of community deprivation, and reinforced by numerous interface barriers. Supporting the sustainability of these spatial legacies are various local actors who feel they gain more by existing conditions than in changing them – paramilitaries and dissidents, local elected officials, residents, and single-identity community groups.

Peace implementation faces a rocky road when political agreements and compromises hit the ground of Belfast's contrasting spatial and territorial realities. The two communities – beset by territorial boundaries which preclude normal urban functionality – experience differential community needs: objective needs on the Catholic side, needs for community revitalization and viability on the Protestant side. The identification of land suitable for future development, where to build new and revitalize existing housing, the location of community recreation and health facilities, the intended removal of peace walls and other interface barriers, and development of sites for economic purposes each confront the sectarian physicality and distortions of the spatial landscape and challenge policymakers with deeply rooted antagonistic forces on the ground. Multiple dilemmas exist. The implementation of equality programmes faces problems because they are perceived as benefiting one community more than the other and because they also confront territorial obstructions. Land available to develop housing to accommodate greater Catholic need is primarily within traditional Protestant neighbourhoods, constituting a significant territorial obstruction to housing equality goals. 'Good relations' between antagonistic groups becomes jeopardized when policymaking seeks to change a social and spatial fabric that is viewed by many as assuring security and community identity. The objectives of sharing city space runs up against the obstructions of robust sectarianized territoriality, and are further bedevilled by one community's ability to capture politically the shared space ideology to support its desire for sustained segregation. And, building new integrated social housing estates is constrained by the use of objective need criteria which allocate housing significantly more to Catholics than to Protestants.

Due to the abstract, ambiguous goals used by political leaders, peacebuilding goals become susceptible to different interpretations and political manipulations as they are implemented in contested urban space. Efforts by policymakers to intervene in Belfast in ways to support peacebuilding reveal the difficulties of connecting often abstract political aspirations to tangible urban changes which seek to transcend spatial sectarianism. On-the-ground translation of laudable national political goals – equality, good relations, and shared space – aimed at creating co-existent peace is a process bedevilled by complexities and contradictions that obstruct and distort national goals. The basic challenge remains of how to intervene in a city with two sectarian and segregated communities having differing trajectories and needs. The formal peace process, composed of high-level political diplomacy and significant achievements in political restructuring, confronts during its implementation myriad local dynamics and obstructions created out of violent conflict. In the clash between political aspirations and on-the-the ground realities, a city such as Belfast constitutes an essential, yet highly problematic, component of peacemaking in Northern Ireland. With the advance of peace, the question becomes at what point, if ever, can there be a more natural progression of urban neighbourhoods that would transcend the strict territoriality created out of violent political conflict.

## Peacebuilding as a Process of Disruptions and Disjunctions

*National peace agreements encounter disrupted trajectories in their urban implementation. Peace accords – and also peace negotiation efforts – face complex and problematical challenges due to changing politics, urban spatial dynamics, and obstructive local incidents and influences.*

Peacebuilding is a spatial-social as well as political process – it takes place over an extended period and is jointly produced through the interaction of local, city-based, actors and national elites. Rather than solely a political agreement, the peacebuilding process is a phenomenon of multi-threaded complexity subject to uneven advances and problematic paradoxes. Restructuring a city takes a long time. Many aspects of cities are obdurate and not susceptible to quick change. In other cases, the urban dynamics of everyday life create resistance to political programmes which seek to order or rearrange basic components of the urban system. Due to the long duration in implementing urban change, national political programmes are susceptible to disruption owing to national and local dynamics, including but not limited to changes in national governing regimes and priorities, specific incidents such as violence that spawn short-term fixes not consistent with national programmes, the emergence of unintended or unforeseen urban outcomes which problematize achievement of national goals, and the pressures of real and perceived changes in demographic trajectories of competing populations. National political policies and programmes are clearly important to study in their design and formulation, but equally important to understand is how such mandates become disrupted or reinforced as they are implemented over long and belaboured periods of time.

## *Jerusalem*

Numerous Israeli-Palestinian national negotiations that have occurred since 1993 have impacted urban spatial dynamics and these on-the-ground changes have limited the possibilities for a genuine national peace. Urban outcomes and dynamics detrimental to urban tolerance and co-existence have imperilled prospects for sustaining national peacemaking.

National political settlements (in the case of Oslo) and national negotiation efforts (in the cases of Camp David, Clinton Parameters, and Geneva) have not been supported by on-the-ground changes in the Jerusalem urban region that would reinforce and embed such national peacemaking. There exists an intertwining or interlocking relationship between national political deliberations and socio-spatial dynamics and changes in the region. Jerusalem has not stayed in place amid national political activity; national peacemaking efforts have influenced changes in the social, spatial, and security aspects of Israeli control in the city. The pattern is one of antagonism between national peace efforts and Jerusalem dynamics. At the same time that national settlements or negotiation efforts open up possibilities for Israel-Palestinian mutual coexistence, the impact of Israeli interventions at the local level have run counter to these possibilities and increased consolidation of Israeli control in the urban region. This pattern of openings at the national level and consolidation of Israeli control at the local level is evident throughout the period since 1994 and can explain the dim prospects for peace that exist today.

Israeli interventions in the Jerusalem urban region have retarded, blocked, and resisted the possibilities for peace outlined in Oslo and deliberated in subsequent unsuccessful national negotiations. Jerusalem has existed as ideological quicksand – manipulated by state actors and right-wing groups in ways that retard possibilities for a truly shared city. Israeli actions on the ground in the Jerusalem urban region (and elsewhere) reveal the real story from 1994 to 2016, not the promises extended or discussed by Israel during the numerous peace negotiations.

The threat of negotiating Jerusalem in the future – together with the postponement in Oslo of actually negotiating the city – created an environment ripe for Israeli hegemonic actions in the city. A number of changes occurred after Oslo that effectively separated Jerusalem from the rest of the Palestinian West Bank and weakened Jerusalem as a centre of Palestinian life. With the emergence of Oslo and progress at the national political level, the paradoxical impact was the weakening of Jerusalem as a Palestinian centre and the detaching of it from the rest of the West Bank. The results of the Oslo 'peace' in effect fragmented Palestinian life, cordoning off the city from the rest of the West Bank. Israeli actions post-Oslo moved forward Israel's strategic objectives of separating and weakening Arab East Jerusalem. At the same time that Oslo at the national level was moving slowly towards greater Palestinian autonomy and self-governance in the West Bank outside of Jerusalem, the city as a centre for Palestinians was being restricted and eroded.

The practical effect of Jerusalem's removal from Oslo negotiations is that it enabled Israel to exploit fully its decidedly more powerful position and allowed it to use its superior power to tighten its control over the Holy City. This highlights how irresolution and indeterminacy in national diplomatic politics is not neutral but can provide the necessary time and void in institutional authority within which the stronger actor can continue to exercise unilateral actions. The spread out nature of the Oslo process did not put things on hold on the ground (as some envisioned and hoped) but rather gave Israel the time to consolidate its hold over Jerusalem and to separate it – socially, economically, politically, and psychologically – from the remainder of the West Bank. Israel has used temporality – the passing of time – as a leveraging mechanism.

Similar to Oslo, the 2000 Camp David negotiations and the subsequent Clinton Parameters spawned political and local spatial dynamics obstructive of urban peacemaking in Jerusalem. Feeling under threat prior to and during Camp David, right-wing opposition and leadership in Israel acted to block the advancement of peacemaking. Local inflammatory events and tactical actions occurred in response to the threat of negotiations and effectively obstructed progress. In the interplay between national diplomatic activity and on-the-ground reactions, local actions led to a downward spiral of violence and a reinforcement of the Israeli hegemonic approach to the city. Urban interventions by Israelis that occurred as reactions to the threat of negotiations have increased instability in the city, stimulated Palestinian violent responses, and hindered the possibility of effective negotiated outcomes. The power of local-spatial dynamics to thwart national peacemaking is revealed. By the time of Geneva (2003) and its aftermath, the intense and ongoing violence and loss of life in the second Intifada had by then constituted a debilitating momentum which overwhelmed possibilities for a negotiated peace and which led eventually to the building of the separation barrier. The interlocking and antagonistic relationship between national peacemaking and socio-spatial local dynamics is evident when examining the destructive spiral associated with violent conflict.

From Oslo to Geneva and beyond, national peacemaking was bedevilled by political-spatial dynamics in which on-the-ground and local dynamics were either insufficient to support political progress or acted as major retardants to peace prospects. Oslo's incremental process failed to deliver socio-spatial and material wellbeing to Palestinians in Jerusalem and in fact was associated with increased separation of Jerusalem from the rest of the West Bank. As Oslo opened up possibilities, changes on the ground were consolidating Israel's hegemonic power over the city. Camp David and the Clinton parameters provided opportunities for national peacemaking yet were associated with inflammatory local processes instigated by obstructive actors who felt under threat from political scenarios that would politically share the city. By the time of Geneva, local violence resulting in part from past negotiation failures were lethal impediments to national peace progress and in the end initiated the largest Israeli infrastructure project in its history to separate the two sides concretely and *de facto* expand Israeli control into major settlement zones in the West Bank.

The trajectories of national peacemaking and urban dynamics in Jerusalem have been interlocking. What happens at the national political level – whether actual agreements or prospective peace deals – has impacts on what goes on at spatial and social levels and these urban dynamics have commonly constituted obstructive influences on the success of negotiated peacemaking. The city has been a source of symbolic manipulation by hegemonic actors able to condemn national peace prospects to the dustbin of ineffectiveness and irrelevancy. Peacemaking is a complex emergent process that necessarily must engage elements at both national political and urban spatial levels and operates amid an unstable equilibrium always susceptible to disruption. Jerusalem, instead of providing a potentially moderating influence based on local agreements and accommodations, has instead become a battleground between exclusionary and rigid perspectives not conducive to political accommodation. The local spatial and social impacts of the continued failure of national peacemaking have hamstrung the capacity of the city to act as a place of local political accommodation potentially stimulating of a larger national peace.

## *Belfast*

Northern Ireland's 'long peace' has been characterized by disruptive stop-starts in national governing arrangements, fragmentation of governing authority due to its power-sharing construction, interruptions and decay in central political concepts intended to guide urban peacebuilding, and by antagonistic and inflammatory phenomena on the ground which challenge peace implementation. The path towards creating a sustainable devolved power-sharing government has been tortuous and subject to major disruptions and discontinuities. At the same time, the chequered evolution of political directives during transition from direct rule to local rule exposes the enigmatic nature of democratization and policy development in a complex political environment. Political goals and concepts pertaining to peacebuilding have been weakened with the emergence of democratic 'local rule' as different political actors with conflicting interests became preeminent in government leadership. As a result, political change has diluted the formation and acceptance of key policy directives aimed at guiding peacebuilding.

A key transitional disjunction occurred in the evolution of the important policy document *A Shared Future*. This was a Direct Rule document with strong community sector consultation but lacking participation by locally elected officials frozen out of the process by local rule suspension. Once power-sharing local rule was re-established, *A Shared Future* was viewed with suspicion by Northern Irish elected officials and this led to a weakening of peacebuilding goals pertaining to shared space and community relations. Subsequent local rule policy documents, in 2010 and 2013, have been more removed from, and are less meaningful to, the local community sector. Democratization and local rule have empowered politicians who tend to be more responsive to sectarian constituencies and thus constrained in their capacity to articulate in clear, specific terms the elements of a cross-community shared future. Consequently, Northern Ireland power sharing has devitalized institutional discourse regarding peacebuilding goals and directives.

The fragility of the political architecture for most of the 2000 to 2010 period resulted in a loss of momentum on the development of key urban and spatial directives and disrupted constructive movement on peacebuilding interventions needed to operationalize the Good Friday Agreement in ways that would begin to transcend sectarian constraints. In addition, the power-sharing model of governance has politically evolved in ways that counter expectations that such governing arrangements will over time spawn cross-cutting coalitions that moderate strict political sectarianism. Instead, power sharing in Northern Ireland has evolved from moderate to more extreme political leadership.

The shift from direct British rule to local democratic rule has problematized, not facilitated, the implementation of peace. With the emergence of formal peace and Northern Ireland local rule, elected representatives at national and local levels have increasingly bypassed community institutional infrastructure and this has led to lessened acceptance by the community sector to government initiatives such as the goal of removing all peace walls in the next decade. The institutionalization of sectarian political power within local rule governing institutions has produced differential impacts across the two traditions. Republicans are more effectively organized within government in terms of capacity and linkages to their community, while Loyalists/Unionists face internal divisions and are less effectively connected to new government structures. In the new Belfast, the two traditions are not operating from parity in terms of institutionalized political capacity.

Operating within this fragile and disrupted political environment, the nature of the peacebuilding process in Belfast has been unsteady, incremental, and uneven in outcomes. The peace process has churned along in erratic and jagged ways and appears not as a singular process, but one consisting of multiple threads moving at different trajectories, each one confronting distinctive dynamics and magnitudes of local resistance. There is a non-uniform granularity of the peace process in terms of local outcomes – substantively disaggregated across policy domains in terms of impact. Sectarian hate crimes are declining but remain at a high level, intimidation on housing estates remains a fact of life, domestic violence levels are the highest in the United Kingdom, paramilitaries and dissident republican activities remain embedded within certain communities, and interface barriers remain as reminders of the insecurity that community residents feel. Although there is an overall decline in segregation, it is an uneven one registering little change in the most segregated areas. In addition, decline in Protestant segregation appears not to be a product of genuine mixing between established Catholic and Protestant residents.

There remains an intractable persistence of urban poverty and social and religious segregation in Belfast's most troubled working-class neighbourhoods. Concentration of multiple types of disadvantage in these deeply sectarian neighbourhoods produces a debilitating environment corrosive of community and individual behaviours and attitudes, and creates a dynamic where poverty becomes self-perpetuating and intergenerational. Insular and cut off from larger opportunities in the urban area, these environments of disadvantage create feelings of extreme despair and alienation on the part of its residents. The persistence and durability of deprivation in working-class sectarian neighbourhoods reveals that the peace process has not made positive impacts where it matters most. The existence of this concentrated deprivation, in contrast to other areas of Belfast, which are more mixed and of higher incomes, presents the distinct possibility that there really are two cities in Belfast. Working-class neighbourhoods hit hard by the Troubles remain locked in traditional enclaves, prone to violence and a level of socioeconomic deprivation that has been relatively untouched by four decades of urban programmes designed to alleviate poverty.

There also exist challenging emotional and psychological adjustments that must be made in order to move towards a more constructive, less sectarian future. Without social and psychological adjustments on the part of citizens, a formal peace agreement runs the risk of producing a 'cold peace' lacking in reconciliation and ultimately unsuccessful in societal transformation. The insecurity produced by the peace process is apparent. During the early years of the peace transition (1996–2000), there emerged a considerable amount of community violence amid the insecurity and uncertainty of the peace process. The 'threat' of peace elicited physical changes in the city – partitioning of the city has increased, not decreased, since 'peace'. Peace has not been a smooth transition but has forced people to try to make sense of the violent conflict and to understand what it means to live in peace with the 'enemy'. Legacy issues, or dealing with the past, remain a fundamental stumbling block 18 years after formal peace. The essential dilemma in dealing with the perpetrators and victims of the Troubles is the choice between the demands of justice and the demands for truth recovery. Political progress has been made in Northern Ireland dealing with democratic institutions and power-sharing governance, but there has clearly been less progress on the social side of the peace process involving healing, reconciliation, and the restoration of broken relationships.

Outcomes spanning across measures of safety, equality, cohesion and sharing, and political progress reveal a quagmire of choppy and contradictory findings in terms of the impacts of peace on the larger society. Evidence can support both the portrayal of Northern Ireland as advancing towards a fuller peace and the darker view that it is at a precipice vulnerable to stagnation and regression. The temporalities of peacebuilding in Northern Ireland highlight it as a process that unfolds over time and is subject to disruptions and disaggregated outcomes. The 'long peace' has been challenged by disruptive stop-starts in the development of peacebuilding policies and by antagonistic local events and dynamics which operate amid the void of cohesive and directive national policymaking. In addition to being temporally interrupted, the peace process is also one with distinct spatial, social, and psychological threads moving at different trajectories of success, some advancing while others stagnate. The disruptive nature of the temporality of peacebuilding is revealed. This depiction of peacebuilding as temporally disjunctive and as substantively disaggregated in outcomes contrasts with views of peacebuilding that assume a singular process where state and society move through relatively well defined phases towards greater tolerance and normalization. Today, peace in Northern Ireland remains a problematic and unfinished achievement.

## The Self-Perpetuating Dynamics and Limits of Hegemonic Control

*Israel has been engaged in a self-perpetuating cycle of hegemonic territoriality in the Jerusalem region and beyond, characterized by a sequence of destabilizing partisan actions, which stimulate Palestinian resistance and violence, in turn leading to further destabilizing Israeli efforts at consolidation.*

Israel has been engaged in a decades-long project of hegemonic territorial expansion in Jerusalem, its urban region, and the larger West Bank. There is a clear pattern over time of Israeli territoriality engendering the need for further territorial intrusions as settlement activity expands outwards to try to achieve elusive goals of political control. Further, the hegemonic territorial project, far from stabilizing the political situation, has consistently and increasingly created inequalities and instabilities as its reach and depth increase in scope. Instead of achieving hegemonic control, territoriality has led instead to a reduction of Israeli control as Palestinian resistance and violence become embedded. Consequently, Israel's territorial project has required an expenditure of considerable financial resources by the State in efforts to maintain the semblance of stability and control amid a disrupted, destabilized and asymmetric human environment.

Israel's hegemonic territorial expansion in Jerusalem, its urban region, and the larger West Bank is characterized by a cycle of unilateral actions which stimulate Palestinian resistance and violence, in turn leading to further Israeli efforts of consolidation in pursuit of stability. Israel's focus on the threat of violence has led it to enact urban policies emphasizing security, group protection, spatial consolidation, and the uniting of Jerusalem governance under Israeli rule. Such programmes, however, have created disequilibria and asymmetries in the urban and regional environment, spawning inflammatory and violence-inciting feelings of hopelessness and exploitation, and objective conditions of socioeconomic deprivation and poverty, on the part of Palestinians. As Palestinians engage in episodes of violence and resistance in response, Israel counters with further efforts at controlling the urban area – militarily, politically, spatially, and demographically – thus introducing further destabilizing, dis-equalizing elements into territorial space. There exists a self-perpetuating and self-trapping cycle of hegemonic actions in response to the effects of previous territorial actions. Spatially, hegemonic projects have no stopping point, ever needing to expand control at broader geographic scales, therein further increasing spatial axes of conflict. In the end, actions meant to stabilize in the face of destabilization create further disequilibria in the impacted areas, recreating and extending conflict dynamics which argued for hegemonic policies in the first place. This self-perpetuating cycle is jeopardizing the sustainability of the Israeli national hegemonic programme itself, while simultaneously foreclosing on real opportunities for a viable peace between Israel and the Palestinians.

Israel's hegemonic project is countered by urban and regional demographic and spatial dynamics which militate against its ultimate success. Through demographic planning that promotes Jewish growth and obstructs Palestinian development, and by a separation barrier that cordons off Arab East Jerusalem from the rest of the West Bank, Israel has created a landscape conducive to Israeli sole political control of Jerusalem. Yet, at the same time, this landscape is an urban fabric of disequilibrium, nationalistic and increasingly religious conflict, vulnerable interfaces and inter-ethnic instability. Over time, the means towards achieving the political control goal – that of territorial penetration – creates spatial conditions of instability that militate against Israel's capacity to control the urban environment. The greater the territory that Israel has sought to control politically, the less capacity it has to fully control the urban and regional environment. Hegemonic territoriality pursues political control, but creates urban and regional instabilities that jeopardize and complicate its goal.

Due to the incompleteness of its territorial project within Jerusalem, the hegemonic project has an insatiable spatial appetite for further application at increasing geographic scale. This is because territorial control sought at the urban scale exposes Israel to vulnerability at the next more expansive scale – in this case, in the metropolitan area and the greater West Bank. Yet, penetration on the metropolitan fringes and in the rest of the West Bank exposes Israel even more to the same dynamics of penetration, resistance, and consolidation as found within Jerusalem proper. As the hegemonic project enlarges its geographic scale, it becomes increasingly entangled in the volatilities that it produces. The self-perpetuating process of Israel's partisan territoriality both exposes the limits of such an approach and provides the rationale for its continued destabilizing application. Seeking control through penetration and expansion has led Israel down a path of ever-increasing and ever-destabilizing incursions near Palestinian settlement areas in pursuit of political control.

In efforts to protect Israeli territorial settlement incursions into the West Bank, a substantial amount of territorial bordering and bounding by Israel is needed to demarcate functional safe zones for Jewish settlers. The establishment of the municipal border of Jerusalem by Israel in 1968 annexed vast amounts of land which was then used as development sites for subsequent Israeli growth nodes, while at the same time drawn in such a way to exclude existing Arab villages as much as possible from the new borders of Jerusalem. The demarcation in 1995 of the West Bank into three zones of differentiated sovereignty and control created a large expanse of territory (roughly 60 per cent of the West Bank) which to this day remains under full Israeli control and has become a repository for intensified building of Jewish settlements. Further, there are about 500 closure obstacles by Israel in the West Bank (full and partial checkpoints with observation towers, road gates, concrete roadblocks, earth mounds, earth walls, trenches, and road barriers of continuous fencing along roads) which facilitate Israeli mobility and obstruct Palestinian access. Finally, the construction of the separation barrier constitutes hard bordering that sets the conditions for future political annexations by Israel into the West Bank.

As it continually deepens and extends its reach, the limits of Israel's hegemonic territorial project are increasingly being revealed. As opposed to Israel proper, the West Bank constitutes a periphery or frontier for the Israeli state. With the geographic extension of territoriality into the volatile and shifting geographies of a peripheral West Bank, the contradictions and limits of the hegemonic project become more revealed. Consistent with Simone's (2010, p. 40) pronouncement that peripheral activities can be 'potentially destabilizing of the centre', the impacts of Israeli interventions in the contested periphery uncover the political limits of hegemonic territoriality as physical and demographic realities force new practical complexities upon Israeli policymakers – concerning the political future of the Israel/West Bank region and Jerusalem city and the tactics needed to protect settlements in the face of continuing instability and violence. First, the broad geographic reach of Israel's hegemonic project has produced a contemporary reality in which Israel is caught between a two-state solution increasingly problematic due to Jewish settlements in the West Bank and a binational, democratic one-state solution that would threaten Jewish majority control. Second, the construction of the separation barrier indicates a shift in Israeli thinking from sole reliance on settlement penetration of the West Bank to efforts to consolidate and protect settlements nearest to Jerusalem. Third, the territorial policies selected to operationalize the Israeli goal of group security in Jerusalem and the West Bank have created a landscape conducive to antithetical outcomes – heightened political contestation and violence that decrease Jewish personal security. The different individualistic type of Palestinian violence that has occurred since 2015 initiated a new thread in Israeli thinking about the sustainability of its hegemonic project in Jerusalem and the West Bank, and could reinforce a positional erosion, first seen in 2000 Camp David negotiations, of Israel's historic stance opposed to negotiating the sovereignty of the city. Individualistic and unorganized violence that is not connected to organizational networks is harder for Israel security agencies to control and combat because it is not traceable to group mobilization, and points to the pervasive effects of decades of Israeli hegemony and marginalization. In the violent environment that has characterized the West Bank through the decades, violence becomes accepted as a normal aspect of life, and youths, in particular, adopt violent proclivities as a learned behaviour. Spawned by widespread hopelessness and marginalization among young Palestinians in the West Bank and Jerusalem, the less trackable form of Palestinian violence since 2015 constitutes a further indicator of the limits of the sustainability of Israel's hegemonic project.

Whether the acknowledgement by the Israel government that its hegemonic project has produced an atmosphere of destabilizing hopelessness will lead to granting Palestinians greater political autonomy or sovereignty in the future is an important challenge faced by Israeli political negotiators. The 'interim' political geography of the West Bank that established three zones of differentiated control has remained in force for over 20 years, enabling Israel to continue to strengthen its territorial project in internationally disputed lands. Far from achieving its political objectives, however, such territorial aggrandizement has created a complex and destabilizing environment that both spawns Palestinian resistance and Israeli counter-actions in a self-perpetuating dynamic. Without progress on larger Israeli-Palestinian peace, the West Bank exists as a 'discriminatory binational regime' (Menachem Klein, interview, 21 October 2015) and is likely to continue to regress into a 'semi-permanent counterinsurgency frontier' for Israel (Ron, 2003, p. 201).

## Competing Demands of Political Stability and Urban Peacebuilding

*Northern Ireland illuminates the difficult balancing act between political stability through power sharing and the ability of government to institute changes in urban space to move national peace forward. There exists tension between the necessary requirement of political stability in a post-violence society and the capacity to make meaningful adjustments in urban space associated with, and stimulating of, conflict and violence.*

In order to stop the fighting, political compromises and restructuring are needed at the highest levels of society. It was necessary to replace the contested and unsettled nature of governance during the years of violent conflict with a functioning government that shares and apportions political power among the antagonistic sides. Because nationalistic conflict is primarily contested sovereignty, to begin the process of peace, sovereignty needed to be shared in a way that was at least minimally acceptable to each side. This is a necessary and essential first step on the ladder of peace. The Good Friday Agreement asserted high principles of a shared future and reconciliation, but at the same created a *realpolitik* set of power-sharing structures in order to get political buy-in by antagonistic communities. Yet, the political stability that has been painstakingly and fitfully established in Northern Ireland has created political conditions that make it difficult to take further steps up this ladder.

Macro-political restructuring has inhibited the capacity to make significant change in the lives of Belfast's residents living in segmented and sectarianized neighbourhoods. To maintain political legitimacy and stability in post-violent years, government policy has adhered to the middle ground and ultimately conservative stances so as not to incite community dissatisfaction and instability. Yet, such modest policy initiatives face difficulty in addressing the systemic inequalities and the hardened spatial-territorial partitioning of Belfast. Power sharing in Northern Ireland has also created an institutional structure within the governing machinery which constrains the ability to make meaningful urban change. Different political sectors in the society have been institutionally accommodated through the distribution of government department leadership positions across each of the main political parties. Although this institutional structure is perceived as necessary so that all political interests feel included in public authority, this 'sharing out' of distributed political power has fragmented policymaking across different policy areas impacting the urban environment – such as planning, education, health, community regeneration, and housing. Such policy fragmentation divides and separates into different, and at times competing, political compartments those aspects of urban policymaking that should be integrated in a holistic way to address effectively the numerous multidimensional problems of Belfast's neighbourhoods.

After the fits and starts of Northern Ireland governance from 1998 to 2007, the achievement of political stability from 2007 to 2017 stands in marked contrast and is a major achievement of the Northern Ireland peace. However, this surprisingly stable governing regime of the hardline Democratic Unionist Party and Sinn Féin parties also intensified policy gridlock in terms of enacting constructive policies that would transform sectarianism in Belfast. Policymaking seen as going too far either in addressing the objective needs of Catholics for more housing and poverty alleviation or the social and psychological needs of Protestant communities for neighbourhood viability are vulnerable to criticism of sectarian favouritism that could jeopardize political stability. This threat to political stability has resulted in power-sharing government stalled in a *status-quo* conflict management and avoidance approach rather than able to move towards a more progressive conflict resolution approach that can take on the root issues of conflict in urban space.

The two sides of the governing regime from 2007 to 2017 became stuck at the symbolic level, appealing to lingering political narratives, and seeking to maintain their own community's standing and its continuity with the past, rather than contemplating how to move forward and transform inter-group relations at a more fundamental level. Concentration on winning at the narrative and symbolic level leaves little discursive room for transforming society. Discussion of issues about shared future and equality consistently become tinged by, and subsumed within, the antagonistic symbolic politics of sectarianism. Both extremist parties constructed a 'closed box' protective structure which each has an interest in maintaining, yet this structure has both diminished the role of the community sector and stunted the development of transformative policymaking. The dilemma faced by Northern Ireland is that politically stable governance through power sharing is needed to move a contested society forward, yet the form this stability took from 2007 to 2017 obstructed the capacity of government to engage in transformative policymaking.

The problem facing Northern Ireland government from 2007 to 2017 was that while it produced input legitimacy, public acceptance, and political stability, it was not achieving outcome legitimacy in terms of it making meaningful change in peoples' lives. The process of deals and trade-offs between empowered sectarian blocs has become the dominant force, rather than the peace process itself. Both the Democratic Unionist Party and Sinn Féin, acting within a government structure which has successfully contained violence, are hesitant to risk stability for attempts at transformation. The need for transformative policies aimed at reconciliation is understood at the level of vision and rhetoric, but political parties commonly resort back to narratives of threat and security. At the same time, however, the limited advance of effective policymaking regarding the sectarian and structural inequalities of Belfast and Northern Ireland calls into question the sustainability of the power-sharing regime, a prospect realized with the collapse of the DUP-Sinn Féin government in January 2017.

Some demographic tendencies give hope that over time individuals will be less bound to the traditional social and political divides and that this may increase public pressure on political leaders to engage across the sectarian divide. An evolving social and identity structure may in this scenario influence a locked-in political system to engage more progressively in the urban landscape. Yet, a reality countering this social fluidity of some parts of society is that sectarian affiliations may reproduce themselves through the generations. The hybridity and fluidity of part of society may create pressure for political change, but is faced with the countervailing force of Sinn Féin and DUP politicians who have an interest in maintaining and consolidating power through sectarian overtures.

There is consensus that Northern Ireland government needs to find ways to move away from the conflict management/regulation model of institutional power sharing towards enactment of broader strategies of transformation and reconciliation. What is less clear is how to go forward with a set of policies which are both sensitive to sectarian realities while at the same time seeking transformation of them. A new actor in the Belfast policy environment is the local city council, now with devolved authority for community planning for the first time since 1971. The visioning process of the Belfast Agenda is an attempt to bring together, around a strategic city vision, both those public agencies which have spending power and communities who feel involved and listened to. The local council and planning staff of Belfast will now be confronted with the hard and intractable issues of Belfast. Where they will allocate land for future development *vis-à-vis* traditional sectarian boundaries, how they address interface barriers in the planning process, and the extent to which they consider sectarian issues germane to development project review are among the issues where the peace process 'rubber will hit the road'. Interviews with planners at local and central government levels reveal a willingness to confront sectarian geographic constraints but also an acknowledgement of the sensitive nature of their work. The devolved power of local government constitutes a potentially critical pivot point for planning. There is the need to move planning beyond its traditional land-use planning orientation to a strategic orientation that is more proactive, intervening, and coordinated across functions. There is a compelling need for public policymakers to create an explicit strategic vision for Belfast that responds effectively to the differential needs of the two sectarian communities – the greater objective needs of Catholics for housing and poverty alleviation and the social-psychological needs of Protestants for revitalization of their neighbourhoods. In order to gain buy-in across the sectarian divide, both sides need to feel they will gain from a transformative policy approach.

The central challenge facing policymakers of overcoming sectarian constraints at the local level has existed throughout the years of the peace process, but the costs of not more fully engaging with this challenge are mounting as the deep-rooted problems of the city persist and reproduce despite the peace. The failure to engage constructively with these hard issues jeopardizes the stability of a political structure that remains a stunning and monumental achievement after decades of violent conflict. The peacemaking of the Good Friday Agreement is not just a political process, but one that must be validated by spatial and social changes. The challenge facing power-shared government in Northern Ireland remains – how to transform sectarian forces which have been incorporated into the political-institutional design of its peace.

## Threats of Violence, Risks of Peace

The contrast between Northern Ireland and Israel is of fundamental and great magnitude and allows us to consider the role of urbanism in a 'post-peace' transitioning environment as well as one bedevilled by unresolved conflict. While Jerusalem reveals the dynamics of continued violent conflict and its self-reinforcing negative cycles, Belfast exposes the dynamics of a post-violent society and its conflicting institutional and policy imperatives.

My conclusions pertaining to national-urban disconnections and the problematic trajectories of peace processes can inform urban and policy practitioners at multiple levels – national, local, civil society, and international – about how to tackle the contentious issues of a polarized society more effectively. Findings argue for more specificity and translatability of national political goals for urban use, greater understanding of the urban system in negotiated agreements and as a distinct arena for policy intervention, and more durable attention over the long term to the dynamics of urban changes as they unfold in response to national goals and mandates. More awareness of national–local disconnections and the variable trajectories of peace processes by politicians, policymakers, diplomats, journalists, religious leaders, commentators, and academics will lead to a more informed and critical public less surprised by national policymaking futility and unexpected permutations of peace processes.

Peacebuilding is a political-spatial process that involves both political reorganization and urban spatial interventions that seek to operationalize peace in distinct places where antagonistic sides live, work, and cope in tight urban space. A national programme aimed at structuring a city – whether in pursuit of hegemony or peace – is not one of simple goal formulation and straightforward urban implementation, but rather is a difficult political-spatial process of engagement with urban realities having unforeseen and erratic effects on the national programme. The implementation of political aspirations confronts the realities of a political-spatial iterative process unfolding over time amid contested physical and social legacies. The national political programmes of Israel and Northern Ireland have been temporally disjunctive and dynamic and substantively disaggregated and multi-threaded in terms of outcomes. This complicated picture contrasts with perspectives that assume a singular process where 'state' and 'society' move through relatively well-defined phases towards either unilateral control or greater inter-group tolerance. The complex, at times contradictory, nature of the relationship between national politics and urban dynamics presents positive opportunities for anti-hegemonic actors in Jerusalem and difficult realities for peacebuilders in Belfast. Both Israel's hegemonic approach to Jerusalem and Northern Ireland's peace-promoting strategy concerning Belfast face significant obstacles in their urban implementation. In both cases, such national–urban disconnections bring to the fore the importance of considering the city and its unique attributes in efforts to concretize national political goals in the everyday life of its residents.

In considering the future of these conflicts in Israel/Palestine and Northern Ireland, the social-psychological foundations of nationalistic conflict are of core importance and point to possible perceptual shifts on the part of political leaders and the public at large that could change the direction of Israeli's hegemonic project and advance Northern Ireland's peace.

Walls on the ground are but physical manifestations of the walls in the minds of people trapped in conflict environments. In intractable conflicts, a 'conflict supporting narrative' or 'socio-psychological repertoire' develops within a society which legitimates and stimulates hegemony and its assertion of political power (Bar-Tal, 2013, pp. 130, 254). Such a narrative is functional in helping a group cope with, and explain, the conflict. It strengthens the justness of one group's goals and negates the goals of the rival group, singles out threats and suggests conditions that will ensure a society's security, and glorifies its own group's morality and humanity while viewing it as the sole victim of the conflict. The narrative, propagated by political leaders and the media, serves as a prism for perceiving the conflict's reality and for processing new information. It creates a specific angle of vision and generates a meaningful and unequivocal perception of the conflict. A key element in destabilizing or unfreezing a dominant conflict-supporting narrative within a society is the emergence of an 'instigating belief' that causes some tension or inconsistency with the dominant belief system (Bar-Tal, 2013, p. 328). One of the most influential beliefs leading to unfreezing of the dominant narrative, Bar-Tal suggests, is an acknowledgement that losses suffered if conflict continues will be greater than losses incurred from acceptance of a peace strategy. In Israel, two realities are instigating self-reflection about the dominant narrative in Israeli society. First, there is the emerging realization of the possible unsustainability of the Israeli hegemonic project owing to the mass hopelessness of Palestinians and patterns of individualistic violence that it has spawned. An Israeli society that needs to invest massively in civilian wellbeing and military protection in order to sustain a hegemonic project, which continues to incite violence and loss of Israeli life, may reach a level of collective self-reflection able to disrupt the hegemony-supporting narrative. Second, the hegemonic project is bumping up against political-geographic consequences of its own making. As geographic extension and deepening of the settlement project increasingly forecloses the political feasibility of a two-state sovereignty strategy, the alternative option of a one-state approach presents the prospect of a Jewish-minority state untenable to most Israelis.

Another powerful psychological element that operates in conflict-inflicted societies is 'delegitimization' of the other, a psychological process which denies humanity to the other and provides psychological license to carry out acts of cruel violence (Bar-Tal, 2013, p. 443). Delegitimization represents an extreme form of moral exclusion, moral disengagement, and moral entitlement. Of special importance in evoking delegitimization and violence is perception by a group of threat, insecurity, and trauma. Such perceptions freeze human reflective and moral thoughts and lead to violent behaviours as a way to defend against threat. There exists a path from group insecurity to delegitimization of the other to violence performed in the name of group defence. Based on this psychological causal path, it follows that as the sense of threat and insecurity lessens over time as a society normalizes and moves away from violent instability, the impetus toward delegitimizing the 'other' begins to attenuate. This is the optimism in Northern Ireland – that peacebuilding over time is able to transform and heal inter-group relationships to the point where the power of delegitimizing the other atrophies. For Israel and Palestine, such a bold and risky peacemaking experiment is hopefully in their future.

# Interviews

**JERUSALEM (70 interviews)**
**Onsite field research: 9 October 2015–20 February 2016**

*Nidal Sakr*, Activist/Educator, Al Aqsa Mosque Movement, 28 September 2015.
*Gillad Rosen*, Senior Lecturer in Geography, Hebrew University of Jerusalem, 11 October 2015.
*Eran Razin*, Director, Institute of Urban and Regional Studies, Hebrew University of Jerusalem, 11 October 2015.
*Yoni Dinur* and *Amitai Fain*, Israel Ministry of Tourism, Guides, Old City Jerusalem, 12 and 24 October 2015.
*Isaac Yerushalmi*, Center for Regional Engagement, East Jerusalem, 14 October 2015.
*Raed Hanania*, Center for Regional Engagement, East Jerusalem, 14 October 2015.
*Noam Shoval*, Professor, Department of Geography, Hebrew University of Jerusalem, 15 October 2015.
*Salah Khalaf*, Shop Owner, Al-Wad Street, Muslim Quarter, Jerusalem, 16 and 17 October 2015.
*Raphie Etgar*, Chief Curator, Museum on the Seam, Jerusalem, 17 October 2015.
*Omar Yousef*, Assistant Professor of Architecture, Al-Quds University, Jerusalem, 18 October 2015.
*Rami Nasrallah*, Director, International Peace and Cooperation Center, Jerusalem, 18 October 2015.
*Yehuda Greenfield-Gilat*, Architect and Director, SAYA Design, Jerusalem, 19 October 2015.
*Eldad Brin*, Ir-Amim (City of Nations), Jerusalem, 20 October 2015.
*Menachem Klein*, Senior Lecturer, Ban-Ilan University, Ramat Gan, 21 October 2015.
*Mahdi Abdul Hadi*, Chairman, Palestinian Academic Society for the Study of International Affairs (PASSIA), Jerusalem, 26 October 2015.
*Deniz Altayli*, Senior Researcher and Program Director, Palestinian Academic Society for the Study of International Affairs, Jerusalem, 26 October 2015.
*Adel Abu Zneid*, Member of FATAH Committee in Jerusalem, Secretary of Al-Quds Charitable Society for Disabled and Special Education, Shu'fat Refugee Camp, Jerusalem, 27 October 2015.
*Meir Margalit*, Center for Advancement of Peace Initiatives, Van Leer Institute (Jerusalem); Former two-term member of Jerusalem Municipality Council in charge of East Jerusalem portfolio, Meretz party, 27 October 2015.
*Ornat Post*, Former Head of Planning Department and City Engineer, Municipality of Jerusalem, 28 October 2015.
*Haim Yacobi*, Professor, Department of Politics, Ben Gurion University of the Negev; Formerly with BIMKOM (Planners for Planning Rights), 29 October 2015.
*Yehuda Doron*, Formerly Member of Shayetet 13 (S'13), 7 November 2015.
*Daniel Tirza*, Director of Separation Barrier Planning Team, Retired Army Colonel, 11 November 2015.
*Hillel Cohen*, Senior Lecturer, Department of Islamic and Middle Eastern Studies, Hebrew University of Jerusalem, 11 November 2015.
*Moshe Amirav*, Advisor to Prime Minister Ehud Barak, Camp David negotiations, 2000; Professor of Political Science, Hebrew University of Jerusalem, 12 November 2015.
*Muhannad Bannoura*, Alternative Tourism Group, Beit Sahour, West Bank, 16 November 2015.
*Amir Cheshin*, Arab Advisor to the Mayor 1984–1994, Municipality of Jerusalem, 17 November 2015.

*Albana Dwonch*, Researcher – Palestinian Activists, Doctoral Student, University of Washington, Seattle, 18 November 2015.
*Gillad Rosen* (II), Senior Lecturer in Geography, Hebrew University of Jerusalem, 19 November 2015.
*Riman Barakat*, CEO, Experience Palestine; Former Executive Director, Breaking the Impasse Initiative; Former Co-Director, Israel/Palestine Center for Research and Information (IPCRI), 22 November 2015.
*Eran Razin* (II), Director, Institute of Urban and Regional Studies, Hebrew University of Jerusalem, 23 November 2015.
*Galit Cohen-Blankshtain*, Senior Lecturer, School of Public Policy and Department of Geography, Hebrew University of Jerusalem, 24 November 2015.
*Eran Feitelson,* Professor, Department of Geography, Hebrew University of Jerusalem, 25 November 2015.
*Kareem Issa Jubran*, Field Research Director, B'Tselem (The Israeli Information Center for Human Rights in the Occupied Territories), 26 November 2015.
*Adam Aloni*, Researcher, B'Tselem (The Israeli Information Center for Human Rights in the Occupied Territories), 26 November 2015.
*Rassem Khamaisi*, Professor, Department of Geography, University of Haifa, 29 November 2015.
*Malka Greenberg Raanan*, Doctoral Candidate, Department of Geography, Hebrew University of Jerusalem, 30 November 2015.
*Shlomo Hasson*, Director, Shasha Center for Strategic Studies; Professor, Department of Geography; Leon Safdie Chair at Institute of Urban and Regional Studies, Hebrew University of Jerusalem, 30 November 2015.
*Abeer Al Saheb*, Manager, East Jerusalem Portfolio, United Nations Human Settlements Programme, Ramallah, 1 December 2015.
*Israel Kimhi*, Director of Jerusalem Studies, Jerusalem Institute for Israel Studies, Formerly Director of Policy Planning Department, Municipality of Jerusalem (1973–1985), 3 December 2015.
*Diana Dolev*, Lecturer, Faculty of Design, Holon Institute of Technology, 6 December 2015.
*Fouad Hallak*, Jerusalem Policy Advisor, Negotiations Support Unit, Palestine Liberation Organization, 7 December 2015.
*Muhannad Bannoura* (II), Alternative Tourism Group, Beit Sahour, West Bank, 15 December 2015.
*Avi Binyamin* (pseudonym), Planner, Municipality of Jerusalem, 16 December 2015.
*Nadav Shragai*, Author and Journalist, Senior Researcher, Jerusalem Center for Public Affairs, 17 December 2015.
*Jay Rothman*, Professor, Conflict Management, Resolution and Negotiation Program, Bar Ilan University, Ramat Gan, 13 January 2016.
*Oded Lowenheim*, Senior Lecturer, International Relations, Hebrew University of Jerusalem, 17 January 2016.
*Etay Levy* (pseudonym), Former Israeli Defense Forces Soldier, 2008–2009, 18 January 2016.
*Dan Miodownik*, Senior Lecturer, Political Science and International Relations, Hebrew University of Jerusalem, 19 January 2016.
*Avner de-Shalit*, Professor of Political Science, Hebrew University of Jerusalem, 20 January 2016.
*Efrat Cohen-Bar*, Planner/Architect, BIMKOM (Planners for Planning Rights), Jerusalem, 21 January 2016.
*Jonas Schaefer*, Research Officer and Team Facilitator, Ecumenical Accompaniment Programme in Palestine and Israel (EAPPI), Jerusalem, 18 and 22 January 2016.
*Adnan Husseini*, Governor of Jerusalem District and Minister of Jerusalem Affairs, A-Ram, 25 January 2016.
*Mohamad Aqel Halaseh*, General Manager, Office of the Governor of Jerusalem District, A-Ram, 25 January 2016.
*Yudith Oppenheimer*, Executive Director, Ir Amim, Jerusalem, 26 January 2016.
*Meir Kraus*, Director, Jerusalem Institute for Israel Studies, 27 January 2016.
*Marik Shtern*, Researcher, Jerusalem Institute for Israel Studies, 27 January 2016.

*James Dykstra*, United Nations Relief and Works Agency (UNRWA) for Palestine Refugees in the Near East, Department of External Relations, Jerusalem, 27 January 2016.

*Anna Veeder*, Emek Shaveh (Israeli NGO working to prevent the politicization of archaeology), Jerusalem, 31 January 2016.

*Daniel Seidemann*, Lawyer and Director, Terrestrial Jerusalem, 1 February 2016.

*Udi Dekel*, Managing Director and Senior Research Fellow, Institute for National Security Studies (INSS), Tel Aviv; Brigadier General (res) and Former Head of Strategic Planning Division, Planning Directorate, Israel Defense Forces (IDF), 3 February 2016.

*Husam Zomlot*, Ambassador at Large, State of Palestine Presidency, Ramallah, 4 February 2016.

*Nabeel Shaath*, Member of the Central Committee of FATAH (Palestinian National Liberation Movement); Commissioner of International Relations, and Member of Palestinian Legislative Council; Former Minister of Planning and International Cooperation, Ramallah, 4 February 2016.

*Mansour Nsasra*, Lecturer in Middle East Politics and International Relations, Department of Politics and Government, Ben Gurion University of the Negev, 4 February 2016.

*Timea Spitka*, Post-Doctorate Researcher, International Relations, Leonard Davis Institute of International Relations, Hebrew University of Jerusalem, 10 February 2016.

*Michael Dumper*, Professor in Middle East Politics, University of Exeter, 10 February 2016.

*Yosi Havilio*, Legal Advisor, Municipality of Jerusalem (2000–2010); Director, Tzahor Nongovernmental Organization, Jerusalem, 11 February 2016.

*Samih Al-Abid*, Deputy Minister, Ministry of Planning and International Cooperation, Palestinian Authority (1994–2003); Former Minister of Public Works and Housing, Palestinian Authority; Consultant, Palestine Investment Fund, Ramallah, 11 February 2016.

*Hubert Law-Yone*, Senior Lecturer, Department of Architecture and Town Planning, Technion-Israel Institute of Technology (retired), Kiryat Tiv'on, 14 February 2016.

*Yusuf Said Al-Natsheh*, Director of Tourism and Archaeology, Haram al-Sharif, 15 February 2016.

*Muhannad Bannoura* (III), Alternative Tourism Group, Beit Sahour, West Bank, 17 February 2016.

### *Jerusalem: Presentations Attended (5)*

*Jeff Halper*, 'War Against the People: Israel, Palestine, and Global Pacification', Presentation at Dar Isaaf Nashashibi, Sheikh Jarrah, Jerusalem, 17 November 2015.

*Meir Turgeman*, Deputy Mayor of Jerusalem and Chair of Local Planning and Building Committee, Public seminar: 'The Influence of the Political Situation on Planning and Construction in East Jerusalem', Van Leer Institute, Jerusalem, 11 January 2016.

*Midterm Orientation Program* (Group 59), Ecumenical Accompaniment Programme in Palestine and Israel (EAPPI), Jerusalem, 18 January 2016.

*Public presentation*, 'The "Non-Jew" in the Teachings of David Hartman', Closing Plenary of the David Hartman Memorial Conference for a Jewish-Democratic Israel, Shalom Hartman Institute, Jerusalem, 3 February 2016.

*Michael Dumper*, 'Rights, Rituals and Contestation: The Holy City of Jerusalem', Presentation at Dar Isaaf Nashashibi, Sheikh Jarrah, Jerusalem, 4 February 2016.

### *Jerusalem: Author's Presentations to Local Audiences (6)*

*Scott Bollens*, 'Palestinian Options Under Current Conditions 2015', Presentation at Palestinian Academic Society for the Study of International Affairs (PASSIA), East Jerusalem, 18 November 2015.

*Scott Bollens*, 'The Ungovernable City? Urban Transformations in Jerusalem over Two Decades', Jerusalem in Comparative Perspective Special Conference, Ben-Gurion University of the Negev, Department of Geography and Environmental Development and the Department of Politics and Government, Beer-Sheva, 2 December 2015.

*Scott Bollens*, 'City and Soul in Divided Societies: Jerusalem 1994–2016', Department Faculty Seminar, Department of Geography, Hebrew University of Jerusalem, Mt. Scopus, 10 January 2016.

*Scott Bollens*, 'Revisiting Jerusalem: Urban Spatial Changes during Political Uncertainty 1994–2016', Opening lecture, Public seminar: 'The Influence of the Political Situation on Planning and Construction in East Jerusalem', Van Leer Institute, Jerusalem, 11 January 2016.

*Scott Bollens*, 'What can be Learned from Politically Contested Cities', Presentation, sponsored by Ir Amim, Museum for Islamic Art, Jerusalem, 8 February 2016.

*Scott Bollens*, 'Jerusalem: Spatial Change and Political Stasis', Public seminar, Al-Quds University, Center for Jerusalem Studies, Old City Jerusalem, 11 February 2016.

**BELFAST (52 interviews)**
**Onsite field research: 10 March–8 June 2016**

*Seanna Walsh*, Coiste na Nalarchimi (Irish Republican ex-prisoners' support group), 20 May 2011.

*Padraig Adams* (pseudonym), Republican Ex-Combatant, 21 May 2011.

*David McKinley* (pseudonym), Loyalist Ex-Combatant, 21 May 2011.

*Paul Arthur*, Professor of Politics, Emeritus Director of the Graduate Programme in Peace and Conflict Studies, University of Ulster, 17 February 2015.

*Gerard McGlade*, Black Cab Tours, 14 March 2016.

*Frank Gaffikin*, Professor, School of Planning, Architecture, and Civil Engineering, Queen's University of Belfast, 15 March 2016.

*Liam O'Dowd*, Professor, School of Sociology, Social Policy and Social Work, Queen's University of Belfast, 15 March 2016.

*Adrian Guelke*, Professor of Comparative Politics, School of Politics, International Studies and Philosophy, Queen's University of Belfast, 16 March 2016.

*Brendan Murtagh*, Chartered Town Planner and Reader, School of Planning, Architecture, and Civil Engineering, Queen's University of Belfast, 21 March 2016.

*James Anderson*, Professor of Political Geography, School of Geography, Archaeology and Palaeoecology, Queen's University of Belfast, 22 March 2016.

*Ken Sterrett*, Senior Lecturer, School of Planning, Architecture, and Civil Engineering, Queen's University of Belfast, 23 March 2016.

*Ian Shuttleworth*, Senior Lecturer, School of Geography, Archaeology and Palaeoecology, Queen's University of Belfast, 23 March 2016.

*Milena Komarova*, Research Fellow, Institute for the Study of Conflict Transformation and Social Justice, Queen's University of Belfast, 24 March 2016.

*Gareth McAleese*, Community member, Belmont, East Belfast, 25 March 2016.

*Mark Hackett*, Hackett Architects, Forum for Alternative Belfast (2009–2014), 29 March 2016.

*Julia Murphy*, Doctoral Student, Conflict Transformation, Irish School of Ecumenics, Trinity College Dublin at Belfast, 31 March 2016.

*David Coyles*, Lecturer, Belfast School of Architecture, University of Ulster, Belfast Campus, 4 April 2016.

*Colin Knox*, Professor of Comparative Public Policy, School of Policy Studies, University of Ulster, Jordanstown, 7 April 2016.

*Karl O'Connor*, Lecturer in Public Policy and Management, School of Criminology, Politics and Social Policy, University of Ulster, Newtownabbey, 7 April 2016.

*Stanley McDowell*, Civil Servant, Northern Ireland Government; and Local Government Officer, Belfast City Council (retired), 10 April 2016.

*Mark Cousins*, Movie Producer and Director, *I Am Belfast*, Walking Tour, 10 April 2016.

*Claire Hackett*, Falls Community Council and Belfast Conflict Reconciliation Consortium, 11 April 2016.

*Mike Morrissey*, Community Economic Consultant, 12 April 2016.

*Dominic Bryan*, Director of Institute of Irish Studies, Department of History and Anthropology, Queen's University of Belfast, 12 April 2016.

*Keith Sutherland*, Development Policy and Plans Manager, Department of Planning and Place, Belfast City Council, 14 April 2016.

*Calllie Persic*, Urban Development Officer, Department of Planning and Place, Belfast City Council, 14 April 2016.

*Jennifer Hawthorne*, Head of Income and Communities, Northern Ireland Housing Executive, 14 April 2016.

*Jacqueline Irwin*, Chief Executive Officer, Northern Ireland Community Relations Council, 15 April 2016.

*Lisa Copeland*, Former Community Planner, Belfast; Lecturer, School of Planning, Architecture, and Civil Engineering, Queen's University of Belfast, 18 April 2016.

*Angus Kerr*, Director of Planning Policy Division, Department of the Environment for Northern Ireland, 19 April 2016.

*Paul Nolan*, Research Director and Author of *Northern Ireland Peace Monitoring Report 2012, 2013, and 2014*, 9 May 2016.

*Madeleine Leonard*, Professor of Sociology, School of Sociology, Social Policy, and Social Work, Queen's University of Belfast, 12 May 2016.

*Duncan Morrow*, Chief Executive Officer, Community Relations Council of Northern Ireland (2002–2011); Current Director of Community Engagement and Lecturer, School of Criminology, Policy and Social Policy, University of Ulster, 16 May 2016.

*Agustina Martire*, Lecturer in Architecture, School of Planning, Architecture, and Civil Engineering, Queen's University of Belfast, 16 May 2016.

*Brandon Hamber*, The John Hume and Thomas P. O'Neill Chair in Peace, and Director of the International Conflict Research Institute (INCORE), Ulster University, Working Group Discussion, 17 May 2016.

*Adrian Grant*, Research Associate, International Conflict Research Institute (INCORE), Ulster University, Working Group Discussion, 17 May 2016.

*Donovan Wylie*, Professional Photographer, Author of *The Maze* and *32 Counties*, among others, Working Group Discussion, 17 May 2016.

*Maggie Andrews*, Regeneration Manager, East Belfast (Eastside) Partnership, Working Group Discussion, 17 May 2016.

*Neil Galway*, Development Plan and Policy Officer, Belfast City Council (2015–2016); Planning Policy Officer, Department of the Environment (DoE) for Northern Ireland 2013–2015; Development Control Officer, DoE Planning Service, Belfast Planning Office (2007–2011); Currently Lecturer, School of Planning, Architecture and Civil Engineering, Queen's University of Belfast, 19 May 2016.

*John Brewer*, Professor of Post-Conflict Studies, George Mitchell Institute for Global Peace, Security, and Justice, Queen's University of Belfast, 19 May 2016.

*Neil Jarman*, Research Fellow, Institute for Conflict Transformation and Social Justice, Queen's University of Belfast; Director, Institute for Conflict Research, 23 May 2016.

*John McCorry*, Executive Director, North Belfast Partnership, 23 May 2016.

*Kim Walsh*, Community Planning Project Officer, Belfast City Council, 24 May 2016.

*Isaac May*, Project Coordinator Peace IV, Belfast City Council, 24 May 2016.

*Liam Dunlop*, Manager, Belfast Interface Project, 24 May 2016.

*Frederick Boal*, Professor Emeritus, School of Geography, Archaeology and Palaeoecology, Queen's University of Belfast, 25 May 2016.

*John McPeake*, Chief Executive, Northern Ireland Housing Executive (NIHE) (2011–2014), NIHE (1982–2014); Currently Interim Chief Executive, Helm Housing Association, 25 May 2016.

*Phil Williams*, Director of Planning and Place, Belfast City Council; President, Royal Town Planning Institute, 31 May 2016.

*Brian Rowan*, Journalist and Author, 1 June 2016.

*Michelle Hand*, Good Relations Unit, Belfast City Council, Focus group discussion, 3 June 2016.

*Arthur Acheson*, Chair, Ministerial Advisory Group for Architecture and the Built Environment for Northern Ireland, Focus Group Discussion, 3 June 2016.

*Dermot O'Kane*, Local Development Plan Officer, Department of Planning and Place, Belfast City Council, Focus Group Discussion, 3 June 2016.

***Belfast: Presentations Attended (10)***

*Kieran McEvoy*, Professor of Law and Transitional Justice, Queen's University of Belfast (Seminar), 14 March 2016.

*Daniel Holder*, Deputy Director, Committee on the Administration of Justice (Seminar), 14 March 2016.

*Cheryl Lawther*, Lecturer, Criminology, School of Sociology, Social Policy and Social Work, Queen's University of Belfast (Seminar), 14 March 2016.

*Martin McGuinness*, Deputy First Minister, Northern Ireland, Public Presentation: 'Reimagining Reconciliation', Queen's University of Belfast, 22 March 2016.

*Deaglan de Breadun*, Author, *Power Play: The Making of Modern Sinn Féin*, Presentation at Queen's University of Belfast, 6 May 2016.

*Susannah Tresilian*, Theatre Director and Journalist; Member of *Ariadne* (Politically Engaged Theatre in Conflict Settings), Discussion at Queen's University of Belfast, 12 May 2016.

*Ken Newell*, Minister of Fitzroy Presbyterian Church 1976–2008, Co-Initiator of Clonard-Fitzroy Fellowship, undertook secret discussions with Republican and Loyalist paramilitaries 1990–1993, leading up to 1994 ceasefires, Presentation, 22 May 2016.

*Arlene Foster*, First Minister of Northern Ireland and Member of Legislative Assembly (Fermanagh and Tyrone), Presentation, 23 May 2016.

*Bertie Ahern*, Taoiseach (Prime Minister), Republic of Ireland (1997–2008); Co-Signatory, Good Friday Agreement (1998), Presentation, 31 May 2016.

*Gladys Ganiel*, Author, *Transforming Post-Catholic Ireland*, Presentation, 5 June 2016.

***Belfast: Author's Presentations to Local Audiences (4)***

*Scott Bollens*, 'Planning in Contested Space', Presentation at Queen's University of Belfast, 19 April 2016.

*Scott Bollens*, Presentation before project working group: 'Communities as Constructs of People and Architecture', Ulster University, Belfast Campus, 17 May 2016.

*Scott Bollens*, 'Urban Interventions in Politically Contested and Transitioning Societies', Presentation to Community Planning Unit, Belfast City Council, 24 May 2016.

*Scott Bollens*, 'Civic Place-Making in a Divided Society', Presentation to 'Making Space for Each Other' focus group, Queen's University of Belfast, 3 June 2016.

# References

Abdelhamid, Ali (2006) Urban Development and Planning in the Occupied Palestinian Territories: Impacts on Urban Form. Paper presented at Nordic and International Urban Morphology Conference, Stockholm, Sweden.

Allport, G.W. (1954) *The Nature of Prejudice*. Cambridge, MA: Perseus Books.

Arafeh, Nur (2015) *In Jerusalem, 'Religious War' is used to Cloak Colonialism*. Policy Brief. Washington DC: Al-Shabaka, The Palestinian Policy Network. Available at: https://al-shabaka.org/briefs/in-jerusalem-religious-war-is-used-to-cloak-colonialism/.

Aydinli, Ersel and Rosenau, James N. (2004) Courage versus caution: a dialogue on entering and prospering in IR. *International Studies Review*, **6**(3), pp. 511–526.

Bar-Tal, Daniel (2013) *Intractable Conflicts: Socio-Psychological Foundations and Dynamics*. Cambridge: Cambridge University Press.

Bassok, Moti (2003) The cost of the settlements, the extra non-military price tag: at least NIS 2.5 billion per year. *Haaretz*, 23 September.

BBC Northern Ireland (2016) Report on Brexit and Young People. Television.

Belfast City Council (2004) *Belfast Masterplan 2004*. Belfast: Belfast City Council.

Belfast City Council (2012) *Belfast Masterplan Review 2012*. Belfast: Development Department, Belfast City Council.

Belfast City Partnership Board (1999) *The Belfast Vision*. Belfast: Department of the Environment.

Belfast Interface Project (2012) *Belfast Interfaces: Security Barriers and Defensive Use of Space*. Belfast: BIP.

Belfast Interface Project (2015) *Strategic Plan 2015–2020*. Belfast: BIP and Community Relations Council.

Benvenisti, Meron S. (1995) *Intimate Enemies: Jews and Arabs in a Shared Land*. Berkeley, CA: University of California Press.

Benvenisti, Meron S. (2007) *Son of the Cypresses: Memories, Reflections, and Regrets from a Political Life*. Berkeley, CA: University of California Press.

Bhavnani, Ravi, Donnay, Karsten, Miodownik, Dan, Mor, Maayan and Helbing, Dirk (2013) Group segregation and urban violence. *American Journal of Political Science*, **58**(1), pp. 226–245.

Bilski, Raphaella and Galnoor, Itzhak (1980) Ideologies and values in national planning, in Bilski, Raphaella, Galnoor, Itzhak, Inbar, Dan, Manor, Yohanan and Sheffer, Gabriel (eds.) *Can Planning Replace Politics? The Israeli Experience*. The Hague: Martinus Nijhoff, pp. 77–98.

Bimkom (2013) *Survey of Palestinian Neighborhoods in East Jerusalem: Planning Problems and Opportunities*. Jerusalem: Bimkom.

Bimkom (2014) *Trapped by Planning: Israeli Policy, Planning and Development in the Palestinian Neighborhoods of East Jerusalem*. Jerusalem: Bimkom.

Boal, Frederick W. (1995) *Shaping a City: Belfast in the Late Twentieth Century*. Belfast: Queen's University, Institute of Irish Studies.

Boal, Frederick (2006) Big processes and little people: the population of metropolitan Belfast 1901–2001, in Boal, Frederick and Royle, Stephen (eds.) *Enduring City: Belfast in the Twentieth Century*. Belfast: Blackstaff Press, pp. 57–83.

Bollens, Scott A. (1999) *Urban Peace-Building in Divided Societies: Belfast and Johannesburg*. Boulder, CO: Westview Press.

Bollens, Scott A. (2000) *On Narrow Ground: Urban Policy and Ethnic Conflict in Jerusalem and Belfast*. Albany, NY: State University of New York Press.

Bollens, Scott A. (2007) *Cities, Nationalism, and Democratization*. London: Routledge.

Bollens, Scott A. (2009) Comparative research on urban political conflict: policy amidst polarization. *The Open Urban Studies Journal*, **2**, pp. 1–17.

Bollens, Scott A. (2012) *City and Soul in Divided Societies*. London: Routledge.

Bollens, Scott A. (2013) Urban planning and policy, in Mac Ginty, Roger (ed.) *Routledge Handbook of Peacebuilding*. London: Routledge, pp. 375–386.

Braier, Michal (2013) Zones of transformation? Informal construction and independent zoning plans in East Jerusalem. *Environment and Planning A*, **45**(11), pp, 2700–2716.

Brand, Ralf and Fregonese, Sara (2013) *The Radicals' City: Urban Environment, Polarisation, Cohesion*. Farnham: Ashgate.

Brewer, John (2010) *Peace Processes: A Sociological Approach*. Cambridge: Polity.

Brooks, Robert D., Khamaisi, Rassem, Hanafi, Sari *et al*. (2007) An IPCC survey of Jerusalemite perceptions of the impact of the wall on everyday life, in International Peace and Cooperation Center (ed.) *The Wall – Fragmenting the Palestinian Fabric in Jerusalem*. Jerusalem: IPCC, pp. 139–150.

B'Tselem (The Israeli Information Centre for Human Rights in the Occupied Territories) (2008) Restrictions on Movement: Information on Checkpoints and Roadblocks. Available at: http://www.btselem.org/freedom_of_movement/statistics.asp.

Byrne, Jonny, Heenan, Cathy and Robinson, Gillian (2012) *Attitudes to Peace Walls*. Research report to the Office of the First Minister and Deputy First Minister. Belfast: University of Ulster.

Calame, Jon and Charlesworth, Esther (2009) *Divided Cities: Belfast, Beirut, Jerusalem, Mostar, and Nicosia*. Philadelphia, PA: University of Pennsylvania Press.

Charlesworth, Esther (2006) *Architects Without Borders: War, Reconstruction and Design Responsibility*. Oxford: Elsevier.

Chartered Institute of Housing (2010) *Shared Housing: The Building Block for Cohesion, Sharing, and Integration*. Belfast: Chartered Institute of Housing.

Chesterman, Simon (2004) *You, The People: The United Nations, Transitional Administration and State-Building*. Oxford: Oxford University Press.

Cochrane, Feargal (2013) *Northern Ireland: The Reluctant Peace*. New Haven, CT: Yale University Press.

Cohen-Bar, Efrat and Ronel, Ayala (2013) *Resident Initiated Dynamic Planning: Implementable Plans in East Jerusalem*. Jerusalem: Bimkom.

Community Relations Council (Northern Ireland) (2009a) *Towards Sustainable Security: Interface Barriers and the Legacy of Segregation in Belfast*. Belfast: CRC.

Community Relations Council (Northern Ireland) (2009b) Available at: http://www.community-relations.org.uk.

Cunningham, Tim (2014) Changing direction: defensive planning in a post-conflict city. *City*, **18**(4/5), pp. 455–462.

Cunningham, Tim (2016) Cutting with the grain: human rights, conflict transformation and the urban planning system – lessons from Northern Ireland. *Human Rights Review*, **17**(3), pp. 329–347.

Darby, John and Mac Ginty, Roger (2000) Conclusion: the management of peace, in Darby, John and Mac Ginty, Roger (eds.) *The Management of Peace Processes*. Basingstoke: Macmillan, pp. 228–261.

DOENI (Department of the Environment (Northern Ireland)) (1988) Pre-Inquiry response to CTA's objections to the draft BUAP, in Blackman, Tim (1991) *Planning Belfast: A Case Study of Public Policy and Community Action*. Aldershot: Avebury, pp. 187–221.

DOENI (1989) *Belfast Urban Area Plan 2001: Adoption Statement*. Belfast: HMSO.

DOENI (1990) *Belfast Urban Area Plan 2001*. Belfast: HMSO.

DOENI (2014a) *Belfast Metropolitan Area Plan (BMAP) 2015*. Belfast: Department of the Environment (Northern Ireland).

DOENI (2014b) *Living Places: An Urban Stewardship and Design Guide for Northern Ireland*. Belfast: Department of the Environment (Northern Ireland).

DOENI (2015) *Strategic Planning Policy Statement for Northern Ireland (SPSS): Planning for Sustainable Development*. Belfast: Department of the Environment (Northern Ireland).

Doty, Roxanne Lynn (2004) Maladies of our souls: identity and voice in the writing of academic international relations. *Cambridge Review of International Affairs*, **17**(2), pp. 377–392.

DRD (Department of Regional Development (Northern Ireland)) (2001) *Shaping Our Future: Regional Development Strategy 2025*. Belfast: Department of Regional Development.

DRD (2010) *Regional Development Strategy 2035*. Belfast: Department of Regional Development.

Dumper, Michael (2014) *Jerusalem Unbound: Geography, History, and the Future of the Holy City*. New York: Columbia University Press.

Dumper, Michael and Pullan, Wendy (2010) Jerusalem: The Cost of Failure. *Briefing Paper*. London: Chatham House/ Royal Institute of International Affairs.

DuRant, R.H. et al. (1994) Exposure to violence and victimization and fighting behavior by urban black adolescents. *Journal of Adolescent Health*, **15**(4), pp. 311–318.

Emek Shaveh (2015) *Archaeological Activity in the Old City: Political and Religious Consequences*. Jerusalem: Emek Shaveh.

Environmental Design Consultants (1991) *Belfast Peacelines Study*. Prepared for the Belfast Development Office, in conjunction with the Northern Ireland Housing Executive. Belfast: NIHE.

Fainstein, Susan (2011) *The Just City*. Cornell, NY: Cornell University Press.

Forester, John (2009) *Dealing with Differences: Dramas of Mediating Public Disputes*. Oxford: Oxford University Press.

Friedmann, John (1987) *Planning and the Public Domain: From Knowledge to Action*. Princeton, NJ: Princeton University Press.

Gaffikin, Frank and Sweeney, Paul (1995) 'Listening to People'. *Making Belfast Work*. Belfast: Northern Ireland Office.

Gaffikin, Frank, McEldowney, Malachy and Sterrett, Ken (2000) *Shaping Our Future: Public Consultation on a Regional Strategic Framework for Northern Ireland*. London: The Stationery Office.

Gaffikin, Frank, Sterrett, Ken, McEldowney, Malachy, Morrissey, Mike and Hardy, Maeliosa (2008) *Planning Shared Space for a Shared Future*. Belfast: Queen's University and Community Relations Council.

Gaffikin, Frank and Morrissey, Mike (2011) *Planning in Divided Cities: Collaborative Shaping of Contested Space*. Oxford: Wiley-Blackwell.

Gaffikin, Frank, Karelse, Chris, Morrissey, Mike, Mulholland, Clare and Sterrett, Ken (2016) *Making Space for Each Other: Civic Place-Making in a Divided Society*. Belfast: Queen's University, School of Planning, Architecture and Civil Engineering.

Galtung, Johan (1969) Violence, peace, and peace research. *Journal of Peace Research*, **6**(3), pp. 167–191.

G-Gagnon, Alain and Tully, James (eds.) (2001) *Multinational Democracies*. Cambridge: Cambridge University Press.

Graham, Stephen (2010) *Cities Under Siege: The New Military Urbanism*. London: Verso.

Greenberg, Raphael and Mizrachi, Yonathan (2010) *From Shiloah to Silwan: Visitor's Guide to Ancient Jerusalem and the Village of Silwan*. Jerusalem: Emek Shaveh.

Guelke, Adrian (2012) *Politics in Deeply Divided Societies*. Cambridge: Polity.

Harbom, Lotta, Hogbladh, Stina and Wallensteen, Peter (2006) Armed conflict and peace agreement. *Journal of Peace Research*, **43**, pp. 617–631.

Harvey, David (1973) *Social Justice and the City*. London: Edward Arnold.

Hatuka, Tali (2011) *Violent Acts and Urban Space in Contemporary Tel Aviv: Revisioning Moments*. Austin, TX: University of Texas Press.

Hay, Colin (2002) *Political Analysis: A Critical Introduction*. Basingstoke: Palgrave.

Hepburn, A.C. (2004) *Contested Cities in the Modern West*. New York: Palgrave Macmillan.

Hever, Shir (2013) Economic cost of the occupation to Israel, in Bar-Tal, Daniel and Schnell, Izhak (eds.) *The Impacts of Lasting Occupation: Lessons from Israeli Society*. Oxford: Oxford University Press, pp. 326–358.

Iadicola, Peter and Shupe, Anson (2003) *Violence, Inequality, and Human Freedom*, 2nd ed. Lanham, MD: Rowman and Littlefield.

Institute for National Security Studies (2015) The Strategic Situation in Jerusalem Demands a Change of Policy. INSS Insight No. 756 (Udi Dekel author). Available at: http://www.inss.org.il/he/wp-content/uploads/sites/2/systemfiles/No.%20756%20-%20Udi%20for%20web684229504.pdf.

International Crisis Group (2010) Tipping point? Palestinians and the search for a new strategy. *ICG Middle East Report*, No. 95, 26 April.

IPCC (International Peace and Cooperation Center) (2007) *The Wall – Fragmenting the Palestinian Fabric in Jerusalem*. Jerusalem: IPCC.

IPCC (2008) *Jerusalem and its Hinterland*. Jerusalem: IPCC.

IPCC (2013) *East Jerusalem – Housing Review*. Jerusalem: IPCC.

Ir Amim (2013) *Dangerous Liaison: The Dynamics of the Rise of the Temple Movements and their Implications*. Jerusalem: Ir Amim.

Ir Amim (2015) *Displaced in their Own City: The Impact of Israeli Policy in East Jerusalem on the Palestinian Neighborhoods of the City Beyond the Separation Barrier*. Jerusalem: Ir Amim.

Israel Ministry of Foreign Affairs (2011) Suicide and other Bombing Attacks in Israel since the Declaration of Principles (September 1993). Available at: http://www.mfa.gov.il/MFA/Terrorism.

Israel Ministry of Foreign Affairs (2016) Wave of Terror 2015/16. Available at: http://mfa.gov.il/MFA/ForeignPolicy/Terrorism/Palestinian/Pages/Wave-of-terror-October-2015.aspx.

Jabareen, Yosef (2015) The right to space production and the right to necessity: insurgent versus legal rights of Palestinians in Jerusalem. *Planning Theory*. Published online before print.

Jerusalem Institute for Israel Studies (1996) *Statistical Yearbook of Jerusalem*. Jerusalem: JIIS.

Jerusalem Institute for Israel Studies (2012) *Statistical Yearbook of Jerusalem*. Jerusalem: JIIS.

Jerusalem Institute for Israel Studies (2014) *Statistical Yearbook of Jerusalem*. Jerusalem: JIIS.

Jerusalem Institute for Israel Studies (2016) *Statistical Yearbook of Jerusalem*. Jerusalem: JIIS.

Kalyvas, Stathis (2006) *The Logic of Violence in Civil War*. Cambridge: Cambridge University Press.

Kashti, Or and Hasson, Nir (2016) Israel's Education Ministry to pay East Jerusalem schools to 'Israelize' curriculum. *Haaretz*, 29 January.

Kelly, S. (2010) The psychological consequences to adolescents of exposure to gang violence in the community: an integrated review of the literature. *Journal of Child and Adolescent Psychiatric Nursing*, **23**(2), pp. 61–73.

Kershner, Isabel (2016) Israel quietly legalizes pirate outposts in the West Bank. *New York Times*, 30 August.

Khamaisi, Rassem (2006) Planning and Developing a New Palestinian Urban Core under Conditional Israeli Occupation: Ramallah City. Paper presented at ISoCaRP Congress. Available at http://www.isocarp.net/Data/case_studies/710.pdf.

Kilcullen, David (2013) *Out of the Mountains: The Coming Age of the Urban Guerrilla*. Oxford: Oxford University Press.

Klein, Menachem (2003) *The Jerusalem Problem: The Struggle for Permanent Status*. Gainesville, FL: University Press of Florida.

Klein, Menachem (2007) *A Possible Peace Between Israel and Palestine: An Insider's Account of the Geneva Initiative*. New York: Columbia University Press.

Klein, Menachem (2010) *The Shift: Israel-Palestine from Border Struggle to Ethnic Conflict*. New York: Columbia University Press.

Knox, Colin (2010) Peace building in Northern Ireland: a role for civil society. *Social Policy and Society*, **10**(1), pp. 13–28.

Knox, Colin (2011) Cohesion, sharing, and integration in Northern Ireland.' *Environment and Planning C*, **29**, pp. 548–566.

Knox, Colin (2014) Northern Ireland: where is the peace dividend? *Policy and Politics*, **44**(3), pp. 485–503.

Kriesberg, Louis (1993) Intractable conflicts. *Peace Review*, **5**(4), pp. 417–421.

Kriesberg, Louis (1998) Intractable conflicts, in Weiner, Eugene (ed.) *The Handbook of Interethnic Coexistence*. New York: Continuum, pp. 332–342.

Legrand, Olivier (2014) Urban Regimes and Ethnic Relations: Globalization and Sovereignty in Three Polarized Cities. PhD dissertation, Ben-Gurion University of the Negev.

Lehrs, Lior (2013) *Peace Talks on Jerusalem: A Review of the Israeli-Palestinian Negotiations Concerning Jerusalem 1993–2013*. Jerusalem: Jerusalem Institute for Israel Studies.

Levi, Margaret (1997) A model, a method and a map: rational choice in comparative and historical analysis, in Lichbach, Mark and Zuckerman, Alan (eds.) *Comparative Politics: Rationality, Culture and Structure*. Cambridge: Cambridge University Press, pp. 19–41.

LeVine, Mark and Mossberg, Mathias (eds.) (2014) *One Land, Two States: Israel and Palestine as Parallel States*. Berkeley, CA: University of California Press.

Levinson, Chaim (2010) Settlements have cost Israel $17 billion, study finds. *Haaretz*, 23 March.

Lijphart, Arend (1968) *The Politics of Accommodation: Pluralism and Democracy in the Netherlands*. Berkeley, CA: University of California Press.

Lijphart, Arend (1977) *Democracy in Plural Societies: A Comparative Exploration*. New Haven, CT: Yale University Press.

Lis, Jonathan (2016) Flaws in IDF checkpoints still unfixed, six years after State Comptroller Report. *Haaretz*, 16 August.

Lowenheim, Oded (2010) The 'I' in IR: an autoethnographic account. *Review of International Studies*, **36**, pp. 1023–1045.

McEvoy, Joanne and O'Leary, Brendan (eds.) (2013) *Power Sharing in Deeply Divided Places*. Philadelphia, PA: University of Pennsylvania Press.

Mac Ginty, Roger (2010) Hybrid peace: the interaction between top-down and bottom-up peace. *Security Dialogue*, **41**(4), pp. 391–412.

Mac Ginty, Roger (2013) Introduction, in Mac Ginty, Roger (ed.) *Routledge Handbook of Peacebuilding*. London: Routledge, pp. 1–8.

Magnusson, Warren (2011) *Politics of Urbanism: Seeing Like a City*. London: Routledge.

Malpass, Peter (2011) Path dependence and the measurement of change in housing policy. *Housing, Theory and Society*, **28**(4), pp. 305–319.

Marcus, Ann Dockser (2007) *Jerusalem 1913: The Origins of the Arab-Israeli Conflict*. New York: Penguin.

Margalit, Meir (2014) *Demolishing Peace: House Demolitions in East Jerusalem*. Jerusalem: International Peace and Cooperation Center.

Massey, Douglas and Nancy Denton (1993) *American Apartheid: Segregation and the Making of the Underclass*. Cambridge, MA: Harvard University Press.

Melander, Erik, Pettersson, Therése and Themnér, Lotta (2016) Organized violence, 1989–2015. *Journal of Peace Research*, **53**(5), pp. 727–742.

Merton, Robert K. (1948) The self fulfilling prophecy. *Antioch Review*, **8**(2), pp. 193–210.

Middle East Quartet (2016) Statement of the Quartet Principals on the Release of the Quartet Report. July.

Ministry of Planning and Administrative Development (2014) *Palestinian National Development Plan 2014–2016: State Building to Sovereignty*. Ramallah: MOPAD.

Ministry of Planning and International Cooperation (1998a) *National Policies for Physical Development in the West Bank and Gaza*. Ramallah: MOPIC.

Ministry of Planning and International Cooperation (1998b) *The Regional Plan for the West Bank Governorate*. Ramallah: MOPIC.

Mitnick, Joshua (2016) Palestinians ask whether 1 state is better than 2. *Los Angeles Times*, 30 December, pp. A1, A4.

Mitnick, Joshua (2017) Israel backs West Bank settlers. *Los Angeles Times*, 7 February, p. A3.

Moser, Caroline (2004) Urban violence and insecurity: an introductory roadmap. *Environment and Urbanization*, **16**(2), pp. 3–16.

Municipality of Jerusalem (2004) *Local Outline Plan Jerusalem 2000*. Jerusalem: Municipality.

Murtagh, Brendan (1994) *Ethnic Space and the Challenge to Urban Planning: A Study of Belfast's Peacelines*. Belfast: Centre for Policy Research, University of Ulster.

Murtagh, Brendan and Shirlow, Peter (2012) Devolution and the politics of development in Northern Ireland. *Environment and Planning C*, **30**, pp. 46–61.

Niksic, Orhan, Eddin, Nur Nasser and Cali, Massimiliano (2014) *Area C and the Future of the Palestinian Economy*. Washington DC: World Bank.

Nolan, Paul (2012) *Northern Ireland Peace Monitoring Report*. Belfast: Community Relations Council.

Nolan, Paul (2013) *Northern Ireland Peace Monitoring Report*. Belfast: Community Relations Council.

Nolan, Paul (2014) *Northern Ireland Peace Monitoring Report*. Belfast: Community Relations Council.

Nolan, Paul and Bryan, Dominic (2016) *Flags: Towards a New Understanding*. Belfast: Institute of Irish Studies, Queen's University.

Northern Ireland Executive (2016) *Draft Programme for Government 2016–2021*. Belfast: Northern Ireland Executive.

Northern Ireland Statistics and Research Agency (2011) *Census 2011*. Belfast: NISRA.

Oberschall, Anthony (2007) *Conflict and Peace Building in Divided Societies: Responses to Ethnic Violence*. London: Routledge.

OCHAOPT (United Nations Office for the Coordination of Humanitarian Affairs in the Occupied Palestinian Territory (2011) *Barrier Update*. East Jerusalem: OCHAOPT.

OCHAOPT (2012) *The Humanitarian Impact of Israeli Settlement Policies: Update December 2012*. East Jerusalem: OCHAOPT.

OCHAOPT (2013) *The Humanitarian Impact of the Barrier*. East Jerusalem: OCHAOPT.

OCHAOPT (2016) *Fragmented Lives: Humanitarian Overview 2015*. East Jerusalem: OCHAOPT.

Ochs, Juliana (2011) *Security and Suspicion: An Ethnography of Everyday Life in Israel*. Philadelphia, PA: University of Pennsylvania Press.

Office of the President (Palestine) (2010) *Palestinian Strategic Multi-Sector Development Plan (SMDP) for East Jerusalem*. Ramallah.

OFMDFMNI (Office of the First Minister and Deputy First Minister (Northern Ireland)) (2005) *A Shared Future: Policy and Strategy Framework for Good Relations in Northern Ireland*. Belfast: OFMDFMNI.

OFMDFMNI (2010) *Programme for Cohesion, Sharing and Integration*. Belfast: OFMDFMNI.

OFMDFMNI (2013) *Together: Building a United Community*. Belfast: OFMDFMNI.

O'Leary, Brendan (2013) Power sharing in deeply divided places: an advocate's introduction, in McEvoy, Joanne and O'Leary, Brendan (eds.) *Power Sharing in Deeply Divided Places*. Philadelphia, PA: University of Pennsylvania Press, pp. 1–64.

O'Leary, Brendan and McGarry, John (1995) Regulating nations and ethnic communities, in Breton, A., Galeotti, G., Salmon, P. and Wintrobe, R. (eds.) *Nationalism and Rationality*. Cambridge: Cambridge University Press, pp. 245–289.

OECD (Organization for Economic Co-operation and Development) (2016) *States of Fragility 2016: Understanding Violence*. Paris: OECD.

Palestinian Academic Society for the Study of International Affairs (2013) *Arab East Jerusalem: A Reader*. Jerusalem: PASSIA.

Palestinian Central Bureau of Statistics (2014) *Food Security Sector 2014, Clusters, Vulnerability Profile Project*. Ramallah: PCBS.

Palestinian National Authority (2011) *Palestinian National Development Plan 2011–2013: Establishing the State, Building Our Future*. Ramallah: PNA.

Paris, Roland (2004) *At War's End: Building Peace after Civil Conflict*. Cambridge: Cambridge University Press.

Pierson, Paul (2000) Increasing returns, path dependence and the study of politics. *American Political Science Review*, 94(2), pp. 251–267.

Pollack, David (2011) *Poll Shows 40 Percent of Jerusalem Arabs Prefer Israel to a Palestinian State*. Washington, DC: Washington Institute for Near East Policy.

Poole, Michael (1990) The geographical location of political violence in Northern Ireland, in Darby, John, Dodge, Nicholas and Hepburn, A.C. (eds.) *Political Violence: Ireland in Comparative Perspective*. Ottawa: University of Ottawa Press, pp. 64–82.

Powell, Jonathan (2012) *Security is Not Enough: Ten Lessons for Conflict Resolution in Northern Ireland*. London: London School of Economics and Political Science.

Pullan, Wendy and Baillie, Britt (eds.) (2013) *Locating Urban Conflicts: Ethnicity, Nationalism and the Everyday*. Basingstoke: Palgrave Macmillan.

Pullan, Wendy, Sternberg, Maximilian, Kyriacou, Lefkos, Larkin, Craig and Dumper, Michael (2013) *The Struggle for Jerusalem's Holy Places*. London: Routledge.

Raanan, Malka Greenberg and Shoval, Noam (2014) Mental maps compared to actual spatial behavior using GPS data: a new method for investigating segregation in cities. *Cities*, **36**, pp. 28–40.

Richmond, Oliver (2005) *The Transformation of Peace*. Basingstoke: Palgrave.

Roberts, David (2011) *Liberal Peacemaking and Global Governance: Beyond the Metropolis*. London: Routledge.

Roeder, Philip G. (2005) Power dividing as an alternative to ethnic power sharing, in Roeder, Philip G. and Rothchild, Donald (eds.) *Sustainable Peace: Power and Democracy After Civil Wars*. Ithaca, NY: Cornell University Press, pp. 51–82.

Roeder, Philip G. and Rothchild, Donald (eds.) (2005) *Sustainable Peace: Power and Democracy After Civil Wars*. Ithaca, NY: Cornell University Press.

Ron, James (2003) *Frontiers and Ghettos: State Violence in Serbia and Israel*. Berkeley, CA: University of California Press.

Rotbard, Sharon (2015) *White City, Black City: Architecture and War in Tel Aviv and Jaffa*. Cambridge, MA: MIT Press.

Rowan, Brian (2015) *Unfinished Peace: Thoughts on Northern Ireland's Unanswered Past*. Newtownards, NI: Colourpoint Books.

RSM McClure Watters Consulting (2014) *Evaluation of the Neighbourhood Renewal Strategy*. Report Commissioned by the Department of Social Development (Northern Ireland.) Belfast: RSM McClure Watters.

Sack, Robert (1983) Human territoriality: a theory. *Annals of the Association of American Geographers*, **73**(1), pp. 55–74.

Sack, Robert (1986) *Human Territoriality: Its Theory and History*. Cambridge: Cambridge University Press.

Sandercock, Leonie (1998) *Towards Cosmopolis: Planning for Multicultural Cities*. Chichester: Wiley.

Savitch, H.V. and Garb, Yaakov (2006) Terror, barriers, and the changing topography of Jerusalem. *Journal of Planning Education and Research*, **26**, pp. 152–173.

Scharpf, Fritz (1999) *Governing in Europe: Effective and Democratic?* Oxford: Oxford University Press.

Scott, James C. (1999) *Seeing Like a State: How Certain Schemes to Improve the Human Condition Have Failed*. New Haven, CT: Yale University Press.

Segal, Rafi and Weizman, Eyal (eds.) (2003) *A Civilian Occupation: The Politics of Israeli Architecture*. Tel Aviv: Babel and London: Verso.

Seidemann, Daniel (2015) *A Geopolitical Atlas of Contemporary Jerusalem*. Jerusalem: Terrestrial Jerusalem.

Seliger, M. (1970) Fundamental and operative ideology: the two principal dimensions of political argumentation. *Policy Sciences*, **1**, pp. 325–338.

Shavit, Ari (2013) *My Promised Land: The Triumph and Tragedy of Israel*. New York: Spiegel and Grau.

Shragai, Nadav (2015) *Jerusalem: Delusions of Division*. Jerusalem: Jerusalem Center for Public Affairs.

Shtern, Marik (2016) Urban neoliberalism vs. ethno-national division: the case of west Jerusalem's shopping malls. *Cities*, **52**, pp. 132–139.

Shtern, M. (2017) *Polarized Labor Integration: East Jerusalem Palestinians in the City's Employment Market*. Publication No. 469. Jerusalem: Jerusalem Institute for Policy Research.

Shuttleworth, Ian and Lloyd, Christopher (2007) *Mapping Segregation in Belfast*. Belfast: Northern Ireland Housing Executive.

Shuttleworth, Ian and Lloyd, Christopher (2009) *Mapping Segregation in Northern Ireland*. Belfast: Northern Ireland Housing Executive.

Simone, AbdouMaliq (2010) *City Life from Dakar to Jakarta*. London: Routledge.

Sorel, Georges (1908) *Reflections on Violence*. New York: B.W. Huebsch.

Spano, R., Rivera, C. and Bolland, J.M. (2010) Are chronic exposure to violence and chronic violent behavior closely related developmental processes during adolescence? *Criminal Justice and Behavior*, **37**(10), pp. 1160–1179.

Stern, Marik (2017) *Polarized Labor Integration: East Jerusalem Palestinians in the City's Employment Market*. Publication No. 469. Jerusalem: Jerusalem Institute for Policy Research.

Sufian, Sandy and LeVine, Mark (eds.) (2007) *Reapproaching Borders: New Perspectives on the Study of Israel-Palestine*. Lanham, MD: Rowman Littlefield Publishers.

Tarazi, Michael (2004) Two peoples, one state. *New York Times*, 4 October.

Taylor, Rupert (2006) The Belfast agreement and the politics of consociationalism: a critique. *The Political Quarterly*, **77**(2), pp. 217–226.

*The Gatekeepers* (2012) Documentary. Directed by Dror Moreh. A Production of Dror Moreh Productions, Les Films du Poisson, Cinephil. 101 minutes.

Todd, Jennifer and Ruane, Joseph (2010) From 'A Shared Future' to 'Cohesion, Sharing, and Integration': an analysis of Northern Ireland's policy framework documents.' York: Joseph Rowntree Charitable Trust.

Trounson, Rebecca (1996) 3 years after Rabin-Arafat handshake, process endures. *Los Angeles Times*, 13 September, p. 4.

Tunenbom, Tuvia (2015) *Catch the Jew!* Jerusalem: Gefen Publishing House.

UN-Habitat (United Nations Human Settlements Programme) (2007) *Enhancing Urban Safety and Security: Global Report on Human Settlements 2007*. London: Earthscan.

UN-Habitat (2015) *Right to Develop: Planning Palestinian Communities in East Jerusalem*. Palestine: UN-Habitat.

United Nations Development Programme (1994) *Human Development Report 1994*. Oxford: Oxford University Press.

United Nations Development Programme (2004) Urban Trialogues: Visions, Projects, Co-Productions. Brussels: Local Agenda 21 Programme.

Varshney, Ashutosh (2002) *Ethnic Conflict and Civic Life: Hindus and Muslims in India*. New Haven, CT: Yale University Press.

Wallace, Alison (2015) *Housing and Communities' Inequalities in Northern Ireland* (Commissioned by Northern Ireland Equality Commission). York: Centre for Housing Policy, University of York.

Wallace Consulting (2016) Building Peace through the Arts: Re-Imaging Communities Program. Final Executive Summary. Belfast: Arts Council for Northern Ireland.

Weizman, Eyal (2007) *Hollow Land: Israel's Architecture of Occupation*. London: Verso.

Wiener, Ron (1976) *The Rape and Plunder of the Shankill in Belfast: People and Planning*. Belfast: Nothems Press.

Zandberg, Esther (2015) Why a renowned Palestinian architect quit Jerusalem. *Haaretz*, 15 September.

# Index

*Note*: illustration figures are indicated by italic page numbers (e.g. Figure 1.3, on page 22), notes denoted by suffix 'n' (e.g. '28n[14]' means note 14 on page 28)

A-Ram [village], reason for growth 72, 73, 105
Abbas, Mahmoud 54, 101n[7]
   summit [2005] with Sharon 101n[12]
Abdelqader, Senan 46
Abdul Hadi, Mahdi 46, 119
Abu Tor [in Jerusalem Municipality], Arab and Jewish neighbourhoods *84*
Abu Zneid, Adel 59
Ahern, Bertie 167
Aida refugee camp 31
Al-Abid, Samih 74, 76, 97–98
Al-Aqsa Mosque [Haram/Temple Mount] 94, 99
Al Quds Committee [of Organization of the Islamic Conferences] 76
Al Saheb, Abeer 71, 78
Amirav, Moshe 55, 91, 92, 93, 100n[2], 110
amnesty for security-related crimes 180
Anderson, James 133, 148
Annapolis Conference [2007] 32, 88, 101n[10], 108
Antebi, Albert 29
Arab–Israeli War [1948] 32, 84n[1]
Arab Peace Initiative [2002] 88
Arafat, Yasser 54, 93
Arafeh, N. 73
Ateret Cohanim [Jewish settler NGO] 63
auto-ethnography, use in case studies 22–23
Ayalon, Ami 106

Bar-Tal, D. 15, 173, 178, 224
Barak, Ehud [Israeli prime minister] 93, 94
Barakat, Riman 97, 110
Beilin, Yossi 101n[7]
Belfast
   changes since 1994 201–203
   child poverty rates 177
   city centre development 194–196
   community plan [Belfast Agenda] 145–146, 196, 198–199, 222
   community/voluntary sector 170–171, 181n[3]
   compared with Jerusalem 6
   Cupar Way 'peace wall' 131
   demographic [Protestant/Catholic] ratio 137–138, 164n[8]
   depopulation of inner neighbourhoods 142
   early years of peace 137–140
   housing need 149–150
   immigrants 176
   integrated/shared housing developments 151–153
   Laganside waterfront development 194, 195
   land allocation for future development 144
   Lenadoon/Suffolk interface groups *200*
   local development plan (LDP) 146
   loyalist parades 131–132, 139, 156
   loyalist paramilitary groups 130, 131, 152, 172
   murals 23, 130, 131, 157
      Re-Imaging Communities programme 131, 157
   national–urban disconnections 208–210
   Neighbourhood Renewal Strategy 192–193, 199
   population 138, 164n[10]
   as post-violent society 6, 10, 16, 129
   sectarian territoriality 138–140, 175
      Catholic segregation levels 175
      decline in Protestant segregation levels 175–176
      planning principles to transform 201
   segregated schools 191
   shared space approach 153–162
   'shatter zones' of separation 141, 143, 161–162, 195
   social deprivation 139, 215
      targeted strategy 192–194
   social housing 141–142
      de-densification 142
      segregation in 139, 151, 175
      waiting list 149, 164n[19]
   suburbanization 138
   super output area (SOA) analysis 139, 164n[11], 175
   Titanic Quarter and Museum 194, 195
   'two cities in one' model 144, 149, 150, 177, 195, 215
   Victoria Square shopping centre 194
   violence [1969–1983] 16
   Wellbeing and Treatment Centres 155
   working-class access to city centre 161–162, 196
   Workman Avenue gate 131, *132*
   *see also* East Belfast; North Belfast; West Belfast
Belfast Agenda [community plan] 145–146
Belfast City Council
   balance of power 137
   City Vision process 142, 169
   Department of Planning and Place 197
   flying of Union Jack flag 156, 157, 179
   local community planning 144, 196–201, 222
Belfast City Partnership Board, 'Mutual City' plan 142, 169
Belfast Interface Project (BIP) 134, 139, 159, 175, 182n[11]
*Belfast Masterplan 2004* [and Review, 2012] 143, 196
*Belfast Metropolitan Area Plan* (BMAP) [2015] 143, 144, 196
   Equality Impact Assessment 164n[16]
*Belfast Urban Area Plan* [2001] 141
Benvenisti, Meron S. 10, 34
Betar Illit settlement 38
Bethlehem
   checkpoint in Separation Barrier 30, *54*
   separated from Jerusalem 53, 90
Bimkom [Israeli non-profit organization] 47–48
   resident-initiated planning for East Jerusalem 78–79
binational democratic one-state solution 121
Binyamin, Ari 44
Boal, Frederick 159
Bollens, Scott A. [author]
   encounter with IDF soldiers 68
   encounter with ultra-orthodox Jew 30
   journal notes, on Jerusalem 88, 102
   picture(s) [in Jerusalem and Belfast] *22, 23*
   research methodology used 19–24
Bosnia-Herzegovina, power sharing in 164n[7], 181n[5], 183
Braier, M. 48
Brewer, John 10–11, 12, 178, 179–180, 184, 190, 191
Bryan, Dominic 133, 157, 179

Calame, J. 19
Camp David Summit [2000] 32, 88, 89, 93–94, 96, 108
   failure 94
   local actions to thwart peacemaking 94–95, 212, 213
'Center of Life' policy [Jerusalem residency test] 91
Charlesworth, E. 19
Cheshin, Amir 55, 59, 71, 92, 110
citizenship aspirations, poll of Arab East Jerusalemites 82

city
    relationship with state 4–5
    role in national peacemaking 3
'City of David' archaeological park [Jerusalem Old City] 62, 64
civil society [Northern Ireland], resistance to government programmes 171–172, 188
Clinton parameters [Camp David, 2000] 88, 93–94, 96, 108, 125, 212, 213
    statistical assessment of violence under 109
Cohen, Hillel 90, 119
Cohen, Leonard, quoted 123
Cohen-Bar, Efrat 43, 60, 70
Cohen-Blankshtain, Galit 47, 48, 79–80
*Cohesion, Sharing, and Integration* [Northern Ireland, 2010] 8, 9, 136, 168, 169, 171, 188
'cold peace' 178, 203, 215
community planning, Arab Jerusalem neighbourhoods 79
Community Relations Council [Northern Ireland] 134
conciliatory strategy [Northern Ireland] 9, 10, 137
'Conflict in Cities and the Contested State' research project 13
conflict studies 13
consociationalism 164n[7]
    Northern Ireland governance arrangements 134, 185, 188
continued violent conflict, in Jerusalem 6, 10
Council of the Isles 129
counter-insurgency policy, in urban areas 2, 141
Coyles, David 142
'creative ambiguity' in terminology
    Northern Ireland documents 146, 209
    US Housing Act [1949] 164n[18]

Darby, John 16–17, 166–167
*de facto* planning, East Jerusalem 78, 79
de Shalit, Avner 119
defensive planning, Belfast 141
Dekel, Udi 31–32, 83, 106, 111, 119, 120
delegitimization [of the 'other'] 225
Democratic Unionist Party (DUP)
    arrangement with Conservative Party 164n[4]
    coalition with Sinn Féin 135, 167, 170, 187–191, 221
    dilemma 190
demographic [Jewish/Arab] ratio
    factors affecting 55, 124
    Israel and Palestinian territories 127n[16]
    Jerusalem metropolitan region 72, 127n[10]
    Jerusalem Municipality 29, 32–33, 34, 40, 49, 68, 70, 100
demographic [Protestant/Catholic] ratio
    Belfast 137–138, 164n[8]
    Northern Ireland 164n[8], 164n[9]
demographically-based planning, Israel 35, 40, 104, 217
demolition of 'unlicensed' Arab housing 70
detailed [re-parcellation] plans 39, 42–43
    Arab-initiated 48
    privately initiated 48
'disorganized-opportunistic' violence, in Northern Ireland 16
Dome of the Rock [Haram/Temple Mount] 94
Doran, Yehuda 108
Dumper, Michael 68, 92
Dwonch, Albana 119

East Belfast
    loyalist paramilitary murals 130
    Shankill neighbourhood 131, 176–177
    deprivation 177, 193
    Renewal programme 193
East Jerusalem
    compared with West Jerusalem 42, 43, 44
    Damascus Gate area 67, 105
    elections [2006] 99
    financial support for housing 76
    Israeli occupation of 32, 38
    Jewish settlers in 37, 96
    lack of employment opportunities 80
    lack of strategy by PNA 73
    planning for Arab communities 44–46
    reshaping after Israeli annexation 35, 38–39
    resident-initiated planning 78–79
    restriction of Arab community development in 38, 41–42, 43, 49
    restriction on Palestinian institutions 91
    separation of Arab areas from rest of West Bank 91, 92
    spatial planning framework 77
    Strategic Multi-Sector Development Plan (SMDP) 75–76
    'unlicensed' Arab housing development 47, 68–79
    urban infrastructure in Arab areas 43–44, 79
economic development organizations, post-conflict urban interventions 2
Elad Ir David [Jewish settler NGO] 62
    'City of David' tours 62–63
'equality' goal [in Northern Ireland] 9, 136–137
    implementation of 147, 149, 162–163
Etgar, Raphie 119
ethnography, use in case studies 22
ethno-national disagreements, Northern Ireland 128

Fatah political party, emphasis on national issues 97, 99
Feitelson, Eran 34
field observations, methodology 21–22
First Intifada [1987–1993] 90
'freedom from fear' 2
'freedom from want' 2
Gaffikin, Frank 129, 142, 148, 151, 154, 155, 159, 165n[26], 169, 175, 176, 177, 188, 189, 193, 197, 199
Galtung, Johan 3, 182n[8]
Galway, Neil 135
The Gatekeepers [Israeli documentary film, 2012] 32, 106
Geneva Accord [2003] 95
    Jerusalem Annex 111
Geneva Initiative [2003] 32, 88, 89, 95, 96, 101n[12], 212, 213
Gillon, Carmi 32
Golani, Yehonathan 104
Good Friday Agreement [Northern Ireland, 1998] 8, 9, 17, 129, 208
    community veto 187–188
    'creative ambiguity' in terminology 146, 209
    'equality goal' 9, 136–137, 147
    'good relations goal' 9, 137, 147
    implementation of 134, 214
    Nationalists' objectives 185, 186
    political parties in negotiations 135, 170
    political reorganization of 171
    power-sharing arrangements 146–147
    reduction of violence since 16
    Unionists' objectives 185, 186
'good relations' goal [in Northern Ireland] 9, 137
    implementation of 147, 162–163, 209–210
'green line' [in Jerusalem] 32
    and Israeli separation barrier 52, 53
Greenberg-Raanan, Malka 47, 81
Greenfield-Gilat, Yehuda 39, 111
group security, Israel 117, 124, 219

Guelke, Adrian 147, 185, 188

Haass–O'Sullivan talks 157
Hackett, Claire 160, 171, 172, 190
Hackett, Mark 142, 154, 159, 161–162, 195
Hallak, Fouad 57, 73, 75
Hamas 59, 99
Har Homa [Jewish] settlement 35, 36, 90, 116
Haram al Sharif/Temple Mount complex [Jerusalem Old City] 65, 67–68
   Arafat's view 93
   Ariel Sharon's visit [2000] 68, 94
   *see also* Al-Aqsa Mosque; Dome of the Rock
Hasson, Shlomo 46, 110
Havilio, Yosi 85n[16]
Hawthorne, Jennifer 149, 151–152, 153, 164n[19]
Hebron 85n[23]
Hebron Protocol [1997] 88
hegemonic project
   accomplishments 123–124
   basis 8, 107
   characteristics 49
   complexities and contradictions 49–82, 83, 106, 122, 124–125, 207
   counter-argument 108
   effect on Palestinians 11, 119
   field research 34–35
   limits 118–123, 218
   methods of countering 85n[16]
   outcomes inconsistent with goals 116, 124, 125, 207–208
   Palestinian reactions 97–100, 126
   and planning system 39–44, 207
   self-perpetuating cycle 26–27, 83–84, 102–127, 216–219
   and two-state proposal 121
   unintended effects 124–125
   and 'unlicensed' Arab housing development 70–71, 124
   and West Bank 114–115
hopelessness and despair [among Palestinians] 11, 72
   violence influenced by 26, 104, 118, 119, 120, 125, 217, 219
Housing Act [U.S., 1949] 164n[18]
'human security' 2–3
   contrasted with 'national security' 2
humanitarian organizations, post-conflict urban interventions 2
Husseini, Adnan 40, 76, 97, 118
Husseini, Faisal 74, 90–91, 110
'hybrid peace' 18, 28n[15]
Hyman, Benjamin 40
hyper-segregation, Belfast 138–139

ideology
   meaning of term 7
   and urban policy 9
'input legitimacy', Northern Ireland 188, 221
interface areas
   Israeli–Palestinian 106, 109
   Northern Ireland 133, 140, *200*
interface barriers [Northern Ireland] 131, 133, 134, 139–140, 182n[11]
   increase in numbers 133, 134, 164n[13], 174–175
   intention to remove 136, 157, 159, 160–161, 171
   negative effects 140
   *see also* 'peace walls'; Separation Barrier [Jerusalem/West Bank]
International Court of Justice (ICJ), on Israel's Separation Barrier 53–54
International Peace and Cooperation Center (IPCC)

Arab community plans created by 47
'open city' discussions 110
on 'unlicensed' Arab housing development 70
inter-state conflicts, contrasted to intra-state conflicts 2
interview methods [used in research] 20
Intifada *see* First Intifada; Second Intifada
intractable conflicts 14–15, 29
   and conflict-supporting narrative 15, 224
   Northern Ireland 128
Irish Republican Army (IRA)
   ceasefire [1994] 134
   political party 135, 167–168, 170
Irwin, Jacqueline 135, 166, 168, 173, 187, 188, 202
Islamic Development Bank 76
Islamic Movement 99–100, 101n[14]
Israel
   compared with Northern Ireland 129
   map *4*
   self-perpetuating cycle of hegemonic territoriality 26–27, 83–84, 102–127, 216–219
Israel Palestine Center for Regional Initiatives (IPCRI), 'Two States in One Space' report [2014] 110
Israeli Defense Forces
   author's encounter with IDF soldiers 68
   awareness of causes of violence 120
Israeli government
   Ministry of Construction and Housing 35, 42
   Oslo Accords/agreements signed by 33
   on status of Jerusalem 7–8, 26
   *see also* hegemonic project
Israeli Land Authority 35
Israeli nongovernmental organizations, involvement in Arab community plans 47–48
Israeli–Palestinian negotiations [1994–2016] 32, 88–96
   [listed] 32, 88
   see also Annapolis Conference; Camp David Summit; Clinton parameters; Geneva Initiative; Kerry-led talks; Mitchell-led talks; Oslo Accords; Taba Summit; Wye River Memorandum
Israeli planning system 34, 39–49
   detailed [re-parcellation] plans 39, 42–43
   Master Plan for Jerusalem 39–40
   neighbourhood outline plans 39, 41–42
   political power of 44–46
   restriction of Arab developments by 38, 40, 41–43
   working with 46–49
Israelization of Arab population 81–82
Issawiya
   Bimkom-assisted plan for 47–48
   lack of services 79
   'unlicensed' development in *69*

Jabareen, Yousef 35, 73, 77
Jabran, Kareem 116
Jarman, Neil 132, 140, 156, 163, 173, 178
Jerusalem
   annexed land 32
      Arabs as residents of city 86n[30]
      Jewish settlements 35, *36*, 96, 104
      restriction on Arab developments 38, 40, 41–43
   Arab workforce 80
   as background 100
   border checkpoints 91
   compared with Belfast 6
   as divided city 83, 106, 121, 208
   'green line' in 32, 52, 53, *84*, 104, 105
   Hebrew University 30, *69*
   Israeli policy on status 7–8, 93, 101n[7]
   lack of Palestinian collective strategy for 73, 75

Mamilla district
　David's Village apartments 96
　shopping mall 80, 81
national–urban disconnections 206–208
'open city' [peace] proposals 108–112
　Israeli security concerns 111
Palestinian development of 'unlicensed' housing 47, 68–79, 124
political division proposals 107–108, 125
residency status 91, 101n[5]
road networks 31, 35, 37, 41
security measures 11, 26, 52–53, 54
　*see also* Separation Barrier
separated from Bethlehem 53, 90
separated from Ramallah 53, 86n[27]
shared-sovereignty [peace] proposals 94, 101n[7], 107, 108, 122
　continuing [but reduced] violence 109
'two cities/two capitals' proposal 91, 93–94, 110
'two states in one space' proposal 110
weakened as centre of Palestinian life 90, 212
　*see also* East Jerusalem; West Jerusalem
Jerusalem/Al Quds Metropolitan Authority (JAMA) 110
Jerusalem identity cards 11, 58
Jerusalem Institute of Israel Studies 110
Jerusalem Law [1980] 7
Jerusalem Master Plan [2000] 39–40
　on Silwan area 63
Jerusalem metropolitan region 72
　Palestinian plan for 74
Jerusalem Municipality 32
　Arab development outside 72
　Jewish/Arab demographic ratio 29, 32–33, 34, 40, 68, 70, 100, 124
　Palestinian development within 58, 75, 124
　population 29, 32–33, 34, 70
　separation barrier within 31, 57–59
　suburban development outside 72
Jerusalem Old City 78
　Damascus Gate *60*, 67
　Haram al Sharif/Temple Mount complex 65, 67–68, 94
　Jewish settler penetration of Arab neighbourhoods 49, 61–68, 94, 95
　Muslim Quarter, Jewish settler activity in 65, *66*, 94
　tourism developments 63–65
Jewish commercial areas, Arab use of 80–81
Jewish settlers
　in East Jerusalem 37, 61
　in Jerusalem Old City 49, 61–68
Jubran, Kareem 55

Kafr Aqab area 31, 57–58, 59, *59*
　housing development 58, 68, 105
　social-spatial integration strategy 75
Kedem Center [Jerusalem Old City] 63–65
Kerr, Angus 181n[4], 199
Kerry, John, Israeli–Palestinian talks led by 84n[2], 88, 108
Khamaisi, Rassem 46–47, 79
Kimhi, Israel 40, 44, 60, 72, 83, 91, 100, 110, 118, 127n[10]
Klein, Menachem 94, 99, 121, 219s
Knox, Colin 146, 147, 149, 161, 171, 177, 188
Komarova, Milena 141, 154, 163, 173
Kraus, Meir 55

land ownership, Arab patterns 85n[13]
land registration, and building permits [Jerusalem] 42
land-use planning
　Belfast 141, 143, 199, 222

Jerusalem 34, 83, 208
Law-Yone, Hubert 77
Lebanon, power sharing in 164n[7], 181n[5], 183
legacy issues [in peacebuilding] 179–180, 216
　approaches to deal with past 180
Leonard, Madeleine 140, 177
Levy, Etay [pseudonym of IDF soldier] 87
Lijphart, Arend 164n[7], 183
Lipshitz, Lea [Elad Ir David tour guide] 62–63
local development plan (LDP), Belfast 146
'lone wolf' attacks 15, 103–104, 118
Lowenheim, Oded 55–56

Maale Adumim settlement 37, *38*, 116
McAleese, Gareth 164n[14]
McBride, Alan 134
McCorry, John 171, 172, 183
Mac Ginty, R. 16–17, 28n[15]
McGlade, Gerard [Black Cab Tours] 129, 130, 131, 133, 157
McGuiness, Martin 179, 181n[2]
Mack, Eitay 53
McPeake, John 149, 153, 164n[19], 165n[22], 170
Magnusson, W. 4, 5
Making Belfast Work initiative 142
Making Space for Each Other [Gaffikin *et al*., 2016] 199, 201
Margalit, Meir 34, 71, 83, 91
marriage counselling advice 96–97
master plan(s), Jerusalem region 39–40, 74
Mazin, Abu *see* Abbas, Mahmoud
Meir, Golda [Israeli prime minister], on demographic ratio of Jerusalem 40
methodology [used in case studies] 14, 19–24
Middle East Quartet, quoted 49, 121
military security, Israel 8, 117
Miodownik, Dan 82, 108, 119
Mitchell, George, Israeli–Palestinian talks led by 84n[2], 88, 108
Morrissey, Mike 151, 174, 193, 194, 197
Morrow, Duncan 146, 150, 172, 185, 187, 189, 190, 194
Multi Deprivation Measure 164n[12]
　Northern Ireland 139
Murray, Sean 180
Murtagh, Brendan 146, 149, 176, 177, 189, 195

Nasrallah, Rami 47
national governing ideology 7
national peacemaking
　effect of local dynamics 89, 96
　results of stalling 88
　studies 13
　and urban peacebuilding 12, 13, 14, 16, 24–25, 205–210
　　factors affecting 17
　research on relations 20–21
'national security', contrasted with 'human security' 2
national–urban disconnections 24–25, 205–210, 224
　Belfast 208–210
　Jerusalem 206–208
national–urban relationships 1, 3, 19, 24–25, 204
'negative peace' 174, 182n[8]
neighbourhood outline plans, Jerusalem Municipality 39, 41–42
Neighbourhood Renewal Strategy, Northern Ireland 192–194
Netanyahu, Benjamin [Israeli prime minister] 8, 90
'new planning' [to transform sectarian territoriality] 201
Newell, Ken 131
Nolan, Paul 135, 167, 172, 173, 174, 180, 182n[9], 187, 190

North Belfast
  Alliance Avenue peace wall *158*
  Girdwood project 150–151, 154, 165n[25]
  loyalist parade *156*
  Manor Street peace wall *159*
  Tiger's Bay
    graffiti *152*
    peace wall *160*
North–South Council [island of Ireland] 129
Northern Ireland
  'Brexit' decision 163n[4]
  civil society 171–172
  'closed box' political stability [2007–2017] 187–191
  community/voluntary sector 170–171, 181n[3]
  compared with Israel 129
  crime rates 174
  demographic [Protestant/Catholic] ratio 164n[8], 164n[9]
  Department of the Environment (DOENI)
    *Belfast Metropolitan Area Plan (BMAP) 2015* 143, 144
    *Living Places...* guide [2014] 145, 199
    *Strategic Planning Policy Statement* 144, 199
  Department of Regional Development (DRD), regional development plans 143
  Department of Social Development 203n[7]
    Belfast Regeneration Office 192
  direct rule by Britain 128, 134, 135, 167
  disruption in peacebuilding 167–173
  dissident Republican groups 132, 152, 165n[21], 182n[6], 188, 189
  domestic violence 174, 215
  DUP–Sinn Féin coalition [2007–2017] 135, 167, 170, 187–191
  First Minister 134
  flying of flags 156, 157, 179
  immigrants 176, 191
  local government plans, community plan(s) 145–146
  local rule democracy, effect on peacebuilding goals 169–170
  local rule governance 185
  'long peace' 26, 181, 202, 213, 216
  loyalist paramilitary groups 130, 131, 152, 172, 189
  map 5
  Neighbourhood Renewal Strategy 192–194
  Orange Order 156
  Parades Commission 156
  'peace dividend' 177
  political stability [2007–2017] 184, 187–191, 221
  poverty rates 175
  power sharing in 129, 134, 135, 146–147, 170, 185–186, 214, 221
  sectarian hate crimes 174, 215
  sectarian parades 131–132, 139, 156, 179
  'shared future' objective 136
    implementation of 147
  'shared space' objective 136
    implementation of 147, 150–151, 154
  softening of sectarian identity 191
  suspension of devolution 135, 167, 181n[2]
  transformative policies 190
  'Troubles' [1969–1998] 128
    deaths and injuries 133, 174
    physical legacies 133, 148
  violence 16, 129, 133–134
  *see also* Good Friday Agreement
Northern Ireland Act [1998]
  'equality' mandate 9, 136–137, 164n[20]
  'good relations' goal 9, 137, 164n[20]
Northern Ireland Arts Council, Re-Imaging Communities programme 131, 157
Northern Ireland Assembly 129, 134
Northern Ireland Equality Commission, on housing quotas 152, 164n[20]
Northern Ireland Executive 129, 134, 135, 188
  *Draft Programme for Government* [2016] 145
  political control of 135, 167–168, 170, 185
Northern Ireland Housing Executive (NIHE) 149, 151–153, 165n[22]
*Northern Ireland Peace Monitoring Report* 173, 174, 175
Nsara, Mansour 87, 92

Ochs, J. 8, 11, 117
O'Dowd, Liam 180, 189
O'Kane, Dermot 203n[6]
Oppenheimer, Yudith 35, 65, 72, 83, 90, 103
'organized-strategic political violence 129
Orient House [PLO headquarters, East Jerusalem] 95, 99
Oslo Accords [1993/1995] 17, 32, 33, 88, 90–93, 211–212, 213
  criticisms 92, 96, 107
  and Israel's hegemonic project 92
  on status of Jerusalem 7, 33, 90, 92, 211–212
  territorial division of West Bank 33, 100n[1], 101n[6], 112, 114
'output legitimacy', Northern Ireland 188, 221

Paisley, Ian 135, 167
Palestine Liberation Organization (PLO)
  negotiations support unit office 73
  Oslo Accords/agreements signed by 33
Palestinian Academic Society for the Study of International Affairs (PASSIA) 73
Palestinian Housing Council 76
Palestinian leadership, void in local 99
Palestinian National Authority (PNA)
  administrative offices 72, 73
  disallowed from operating in Jerusalem Municipality 59
  emphasis on national issues 99
  financial support for 'unlicensed' housing 76
  focus on West Bank 73
  lack of collective strategy for Jerusalem 73, 75, 97
  Ministry of Local Government (MOLG) 74–75
  Ministry of Planning and Development 74, 75
  Ministry of Planning and International Cooperation (MOPIC) 74
  National Development Plan [2014–2016] 75
  and Oslo Accords 33
  Strategic Multi-Sector Development Plan (SMDP) for East Jerusalem 75–76
Paris, R. 28n[14]
partisan ideology, Israel's project for Jerusalem 8, 26, 80, 83
'path dependence' concept 17
'peace dividend', Northern Ireland 177
Peace Now movement, Jerusalem settlements data 35, 85n[7]
peace process
  disruption of 167–173
  outcomes 173–178
peace studies 13
'peace walls' [in Northern Ireland] 11, *131*, 131, 133, *158*, *159*, *160*
  *Attitudes to Peace Walls* survey 160–161
  intention to remove 136, 157, 159, 160–161
peacebuilding
  characteristics 19
  criticism 18, 28n[14]

dominant form 18
'duality' of 173
emotional costs 178–181
and peacemaking 28n[5], 88
as political-spatial process 18, 136, 161, 223
as process of disruptions 25–26, 210–216
Belfast 213–216
Jerusalem 211–213
social dimensions 18
and urban realities, in Northern Ireland 135–146
*see also* urban peacebuilding
peacemaking
effects on urban environment 10–11, 14
impacts on urban dynamics 14
and peacebuilding 28n[5], 88
political-institutional aspects 18, 147, 223
as political-spatial process 1, 3, 19, 25, 87–88, 163, 181
*see also* national peacemaking
peace-promotive strategy [in Northern Ireland] 9, 137
Persic, Callie 155, 198
personal security, Israel 117
photo-documentation methods 21
planning
Palestinian view 47
as political instrument 44–45, 47
Planning and Building Law [Israel, 1995], Amendment [43] 46
polarized cities
literature on 14
political control contestation in 14–15
'polarized integration' [of Arab workforce] 80
political security
Israel 8, 117
see also group security; personal security
political-spatial iterative process, peacemaking as 1, 3, 19, 25, 87–88
politically contested cities, literature on 13, 14
*The Politics of the Trail* [Lowenheim, 2014] 56
Pollack, D. 82
'positive peace' 174, 182n[8]
Post, Osnat 45, 71
post-violent society, Belfast as 6, 10, 16, 129
Powell, Jonathan 183
power sharing 183
in Bosnia-Herzegovina and Lebanon 164n[7], 181n[5], 183
conflict management through 185–186
criticisms 183–184
in Northern Ireland 129, 134, 135, 146–147, 170, 185–191, 214, 221
political stability through 187–191
Pullan, W. 62, 65

Qalandia checkpoint [in Israeli Separation Barrier] 31, 56

Rabin, Yitzhak [Israeli prime minister] 7–8, 92, 101n[7]
Rachel's Tomb area [near Bethlehem] 30
Ramallah 31, 72
growth 72
separated from Jerusalem by the Barrier 53, 86n[27]
*The Rape and Plunder of the Shankill in Belfast* [Weiner, 1976] 142
Razin, Eran 65, 107
'resolution planning' 77
'right to plan and develop', Palestinian view 74, 77
Road Map for Peace [Middle East, 2003] 88, 101n[12]
road networks
Belfast 141
Jerusalem 31, 35, 37, 41

Roeder, P.G. 184
Romann, Michael 116
Rosen, Gillad 38, 59, 87, 116
Rotbard, Sharon 103
Rothman, Jay 77, 92
Rowan, Brian 133, 161, 180, 188

Sack, R. 102
Sands, Bobby 132
Schlomo, Oren 81
Second Intifada [2000–2005]
casualties during 15, 52–53, 68, 85n[18], 96
catalyst for 68, 94
effect on peace talks 95
end 101n[12]
sectarian political power [in Northern Ireland], institutionalization of 172–173
sectarianism [in Northern Ireland] 163n[2]
policy making affected by 189
public-sector consideration of 140–146, 172
security goals
Israel 8, 52–53, 54, 117
*see also* military security; political security
Seidemann, Daniel 35, 60, 82, 83, 111, 120, 121
self-perpetuating cycle of Israeli hegemonic territoriality 26–27, 83–84, 102–127, 216–219
Seliger, M. 9
Separation Barrier [Jerusalem/West Bank] 11, 22, 49–61, *50–52*, 95
characteristics 5
checkpoints 30, 31, *54*, 56
effect on Arab mobility 54–55
effect on Palestinians 11, 52, 56
and 'green line' 52, 53
guided tour 30–31
impact on security 54
Jerusalem areas behind 57–59
political attitudes hardened by 56
purpose 52–53, 55, 60, 103, 122, 217
route 31, 46, *50*, 52, *57*
size 52
[unintended] consequences 56–60, 105
*see also* 'peace walls' [Northern Ireland]
Shaath, Nabeel 93
Shalom, Avraham 32
Shankill neighbourhood [East Belfast] 131, 176–177
deprivation 177
*A Shared Future* [Northern Ireland, 2005] 8, 136, 147, 168, 169, 181n[4], 214s
'shared space'
definition 144–145, 165n[26], 199
Northern Ireland 8, 24, 136, 140, 144–145, 146, 147, 153–162
implementation of concept 155, 162, 209–210
Sharm el-Sheikh Memorandum [1999] 88
Sharon, Ariel [Israeli prime minister]
criticism of Geneva Accord 95
and Separation Barrier 53, 95
on status of Jerusalem 8
summit [2005] with Abbas 101n[12]
visit to Haram al Sharif complex 68, 94
Shas Party 94
Shavit, Ari 49
Shlomo, Oren 81
shopping malls [Jerusalem], Arab use of 80–81
Shoval, Noam 55, 81, 86n[29]
Shragai, Nadav 33, 52, 106–107
Shtern, Marik 80
Shuafat refugee camp area 57, 59

housing development 68, 105
  social-spatial integration strategy 75
Shuttleworth, Ian 176
Silwan [Palestinian village in Jerusalem] 62
  Al-Bustan neighbourhood 63, *64*
Simone, AbdouMaliq 122, 218
Sinn Féin
  coalition with DUP 135, 167, 170, 187–191, 221
  dissatisfaction by electorate 190, 203n[3]
  objectives 185, 186
  organizational coherence 172
  'United Ireland' ideology 185, 186, 190
Six-Day War [1967] 32
'Slope of Mount of Olives' National Park 48
Social and Democratic Labour Party (SDLP) 135, 167, 170, 187
South Africa
  Israel compared with 107
  Northern Ireland compared with 185
Standing Committee on Security Implications of Housing Problems in Belfast (SCH) 141
state–city interactions 5, 20–21
Sterrett, Ken 199
Stevenson, Adlai 203
Stone, Michael 130
Strategic Multi-Sector Development Plan (SMDP), East Jerusalem 75–76
'structural violence' 3
*sumud* [steadfast perseverance] 71
Super Output Area (SOA) analysis, Belfast City 139, 164n[11], 175
Sutherland, Keith 154–155, 164n[16], 198, 203n[5]

Taba Summit [2001] 32, 88, 101n[10]
Temple Movement 67
temporality 14, 26, 169, 212, 216
territoriality
  in Jerusalem 103–106
  meaning of term 102
Tirza, Daniel [Director of Separation Barrier Planning Team] 46, 49, 53
*Together: Building a United Community* [Northern Ireland, 2013] 8, 136, 152, 157, 161, 169, 171, 188
trajectories, conflict and peace 5, 12, 14, 96, 211–216
truth and reconciliation commission 180
truth recovery process 180
Turgeman, Meir 45
'two cities in one'
  Belfast 144, 149, 150, 177, 215
  Jerusalem 110
two-state proposals
  Clinton's ideas 93–94
  effect of Jewish settlements in West Bank 121
  Geneva Accord 95

Ulster Defence Association (UDA) 130, 131, 152
Ulster Freedom Fighters (UFF) 130, *152*
Ulster Unionist Party (UUP) 135, 167, 170, 187
Ulster Volunteer Force (UVF) 130, 131, 152
ultra-orthodox Jews, proportion of population 34, 37
UN Office for the Coordination of Humanitarian Affairs in the Occupied Palestinian Territory 115
UNESCO, on Haram/Mount area 86n[24]
UN-Habitat, report on Palestinian communities in East Jerusalem 43–44, 71, 77–78
United Kingdom, map 5
United Nations Partition Plan [Israel/Palestine, 1947] 84n[1]
'unlicensed' Arab housing development 49, 68–79, 124

lack of supporting infrastructure 59, 72
Uppsala Conflict Data Program, on armed conflicts 28n[1]
urban peacebuilding
  and national peacemaking 12, 13, 14, 16, 24–25, 205–210
  factors affecting 17
  research on relations 20–21
  as political-spatial process 18
urban redevelopment, Belfast 194–196

Varshney, A. 101n[13]
violence
  author's experience 29–30
  as indicator of urban conflict/peace 16
  individualistic [non-group based] 15, 103–104, 118–119
  Israelis killed or injured 15, 115, 117
  Northern Ireland 16, 129, 133–134
  Palestinians killed or injured 15–16, 115, 118

Walsh, Kim 161, 171, 196, 199
Waqf Administration 76
Weizman, E. 122
Welfare Organization [Palestinian NGO] 76
West Bank
  area 'A' 12, 33, 100n[1], 101n[6], 112
  area 'B' 30, 33, 100n[1], 101n[6], 112
    development of planning capacity 75
  area 'C' 33, 100n[1], 101n[6], 112
    Israeli settlements 114
    Palestinian development in 113–114
  as binational regime 121, 219
  humanitarian need 115
  Israeli occupation of 32
  Jewish settlements 37–38, *38*, 96, 112–113, 114, 115, 218
    costs of maintaining 116
    retroactive legalization of 116–117
  maps *4*, *113*
  PNA focus on 73
  security measures 115–116, 218
    see also Separation Barrier
  separation from East Jerusalem 91, 92
  territorial division under Oslo Accords 33, 100n[1], 101n[6], 112, 114
  territoriality in 112–118
  violence in 115, 117–118
West Belfast
  Ballymurphy neighbourhood 132
  Falls neighbourhood 132, 176
    deprivation 176
  Milltown Cemetery 130, 132–133
  Springfield area 132
    Neighbourhood Renewal programme 193
  Springmartin Road police station 132
West Jerusalem
  Arab workforce in 80
  compared with East Jerusalem 42, 43, 44
  economic intrusion of Arabs into 49, 79–82, 124
  Malha [shopping] Mall 81
Williams, Paul 197–198
written source material 20
Wye River Memorandum [1998] 88, 100n[1]

Yacobi, Haim 61, 106, 121
Yerushalmi, Isaac 60

Zomlot, Husam 74, 75, 79